From Pews
to Polling Places

Bonds of Affection: Civic Charity and the Making of America—Winthrop, Jefferson, and Lincoln, Matthew S. Holland, Editor

The Catholic Church and the Nation-State: Comparative Perspectives, Paul Christopher Manuel, Lawrence C. Reardon, and Clyde Wilcox, Editors

The Christian Right in American Politics: Marching to the Millennium, John C. Green, Mark J. Rozell, and Clyde Wilcox, Editors

Faith, Hope, and Jobs: Welfare-to-Work in Los Angeles, Stephen V. Monsma and J. Christopher Soper

From Pews to Polling Places: Faith and Politics in the American Religious Mosaic, J. Matthew Wilson, Editor

Of Little Faith: The Politics of George W. Bush's Faith-Based Initiatives, Amy E. Black, Douglas L. Koopman, and David K. Ryden

The Origins of Christian Anti-Internationalism: Conservative Evangelicals and the League of Nations, Markku Ruotsila

Reaping the Whirlwind: Liberal Democracy and the Religious Axis, John R. Pottenger

School Board Battles: The Christian Right in Local Politics, Melissa M. Deckman

Uncompromising Positions: God, Sex, and the U.S. House of Representatives, Elizabeth Anne Oldmixon

The Values Campaign? The Christian Right and the 2004 Elections, John C. Green, Mark J. Rozell, and Clyde Wilcox, Editors

From Pews to Polling Places

Faith and Politics in the
American Religious Mosaic

Editor
J. MATTHEW WILSON

Georgetown University Press
Washington, D.C.

As of January 1, 2007, 13-digit ISBN numbers have replaced the 10-digit system.

13-digit	10-digit
Paperback: 978-1-58901-172-4	Paperback: 1-58901-172-4
Cloth: 978-1-58901-173-1	Cloth: 1-58901-173-2

Georgetown University Press, Washington, D.C. www.press.georgetown.edu

Library of Congress Cataloging-in-Publication Data

From pews to polling places : faith and politics in the American religious mosaic / edited by J. Matthew Wilson.
    p. cm. — (Religion and politics series)
  Includes bibliographical references and index.
  ISBN 978-1-58901-173-1 (hardcover : alk. paper) — ISBN 978-1-58901-172-4 (pbk. : alk. paper)
  1. Religion and politics—United States. 2. Christianity and politics—United States. I. Wilson, J. Matthew.
  BL2525.F76 2007
  322'.10973—dc22   2007007014

14 13 12 11 10 09 08 07   9 8 7 6 5 4 3 2
First printing

Printed in the United States of America

Contents

List of Figures and Tables   vii
Preface   xi

ONE
Prayers, Parties, and Preachers: The Evolving Nature of Political
    and Religious Mobilization   1
Clyde Wilcox and Carin Robinson

TWO
Evangelical and Mainline Protestants at the Turn of the
    Millennium: Taking Stock and Looking Forward   29
Corwin E. Smidt

THREE
Whither the Religious Left? Religiopolitical Progressivism in
    Twenty-First-Century America   53
Laura R. Olson

FOUR
The Political Behavior of American Catholics: Change
    and Continuity   81
Stephen T. Mockabee

FIVE
Dry Kindling: A Political Profile of American Mormons   105
David E. Campbell and J. Quin Monson

SIX
From Liberation to Mutual Fund: Political Consequences
    of Differing Conceptions of Christ in the African
    American Church   131
Melissa Harris-Lacewell

SEVEN
Power in the Pews? Religious Diversity and Latino Political
    Attitudes and Behaviors   161
    Louis DeSipio

EIGHT
The Evolution of Jewish Pluralism: The Public Opinion and
    Political Preferences of American Jews   185
    Paul A. Djupe

NINE
The Politics of American Muslims   213
    Paul A. Djupe and John C. Green

TEN
Secularists, Antifundamentalists, and the New Religious Divide
    in the American Electorate   251
    Louis Bolce and Gerald De Maio

ELEVEN
Religion and American Political Life: A Look Forward   277
    J. Matthew Wilson

References   287
Contributors   309
Index   315

Figures and Tables

Figures

4.1	Content of Important Party Differences, 1960 and 2000	92
5.1	Partisanship over Time	108
5.2	Presidential Vote over Time	109
5.3	The Impact of Religious Participation on Political Activity	121
8.1	The Ideological Identification of American Jews, 1972–2004	188
8.2	Should Unpopular Groups Be Able to Speak in Public? 1972–2004	192
8.3	Jewish Party Identification, 1972–2004	196
8.4	The Jewish Vote for President, 1968–2000	197
10.1	The Religious Divide in Party Identification, 1988–2004	265
10.2	The Religious Divide in Presidential Elections, 1988–2004	266

Tables

2.1	The Theological Characteristics of Members of Different Religious Traditions	36
2.2	Distribution of Religious Traditions in America over Time	38
2.3	The Social Characteristics of Members of Different Religious Traditions over Time	40
2.4	The Salience of Different Issues by Religious Tradition	43
2.5	Politicization by Religious Tradition	45
2.6	Partisanship by Religious Tradition	46

3.1	Traditions with Sizable Numbers of Self-Described Religious Liberals	62
3.2	Demographic Characteristics of Self-Described Religious Liberals	64
3.3	Theological Characteristics and Religious Practices of Self-Described Religious Liberals	66
3.4	Issue Positions of Self-Described Religious Liberals	68
3.5	Cues Heard in Congregation by Self-Described Religious Liberals	69
3.6	Political Participation by Self-Described Religious Liberals	72
3.7	Congregation Size and Views on Denominational Relevance among Self-Described Religious Liberals	74
3.8	Approval of Clergy and Congregational Political Activism by Religious Liberals	76
4.1	Partisan Alignment of White Catholics, 1952–2004	84
4.2	Sociopolitical Profile of White Catholics, 1952–2004	88
4.3	Predictors of White, Non-Hispanic Catholics' Party Identification, 1972–2004	94
4.4	2004 Profile of White, Non-Hispanic Catholics by Generation	97
4.5	Model of 2004 Major-Party Presidential Vote Choice (Only White, Non-Hispanic Catholics)	100
5.1	Attitudes toward Abortion	113
5.2	Levels of Religious and Political Participation	117
5.3	Religious Participation and Political Activity	120
6.1	Models of Differing Notions of Christ	152
6.2	Model of Political Action	156
7.1	Latino Religious Preference, 1989–2002	163
7.2	Nativity and Latino Religious Preference, 2001 and 2002	170
7.3	Voter Participation among U.S.-Citizen Latinos	173
7.4	Influence of Latino Religious Beliefs on Political Practice, by Religious Tradition	175
7.5	Latino Attitudes toward Policy Issues with Moral and Religious Dimensions, by Religious Tradition	177
7.6	Partisanship in Latino Communities	180
8.1	The Correlation of Spending Opinions and Time for Jewish and Non-Jewish Respondents, 1972–2004	190

8.2	Demographic, Geographic, and Media Use Differences between Jewish Democrats and Non-Democrats	203
8.3	Contributing Factors to Party Identification and Political Ideology among American Jews	204
8.4	The Issue Positions of American Jews and the Differences between Jewish Democrats and Non-Democrats, 1996	207
8.5	The Agendas of American Jews and the Differences between Jewish Democrats and Non-Democrats, 2000	210
9.1	American Muslim Demography and Religiosity, 2004	219
9.2	American Muslims' Favorable Stances on Social Welfare and Cultural Issues, 2004	223
9.3	American Muslims and Foreign Affairs, 2004	226
9.4	American Muslim Party Identifications and Political Ideologies, 2004	227
9.5	American Muslim Views about Democracy and the United States and Religion and Political Participation, 2004	229
9.6	American Muslim Political Participation, 2001 and 2004	231
9.7	American Muslims and Voting Behavior, 2001 and 2004	233
9.8	American Muslim Experience with Discrimination, 2001 and 2004	235
9.9	American Muslim Summary Views of American Society and Discrimination, 2001 and 2004	236
9.10	Correlations between Religious Commitment, Public Policy Support, and Political Attachments for the Major Ethnic Groups, 2004	238
9.11	Determinants of American Muslim Public Policy Stances: Support for Debt Relief for Poor Nations, Abortion Restrictions, Government Aid to Poor People, and Ideology	241
9.12	Determinants of the Muslim Presidential Vote, 2000 and 2004 Elections	243
9.13	Determinants of Muslim Political Participation, 2001 and 2004	245
10.1	Religious Worldview, Moral Outlook, and Attitudes toward the Social Issues	260

10.2   The Impact of Intensely Disliking the Religious
       Right on Respondents' Perceptions of Christian
       Fundamentalists   263
10.3   The Impact of Anti–Christian Fundamentalism
       in Recent Presidential Elections   268
10.4   Predictors of Anti–Christian Fundamentalism   271

Preface

The relationship between religious faith and political action is an increasingly important and popular area of inquiry, both for scholars in the social sciences and for pundits in the popular press. Domestically, the presidential contest of 2004 was widely seen as a "moral values" election, and prominent politicians in both parties are making increasingly public overtures to people of faith. Internationally, the interaction of Judaism, Christianity, Islam, and secularism will be a central focus of American foreign policy for years to come, undoubtedly with important political consequences for religious groups here at home. Yet even as we acknowledge the importance of these phenomena, we all too often approach them with a very limited understanding of how religious and political life intersect in America. The temptation is either to resort to reductionist oversimplifications (e.g., "religious people support party x and favor policies y and z, whereas nonreligious people do the opposite") or to throw up one's hands at the diversity of American religious life and despair of ever speaking about religion and politics in a sufficiently nuanced way.

The chapters in this volume seek to avoid both these traps. They reveal the rich diversity of the American religious fabric, especially highlighting the growing religious traditions outside conventional Christianity and the growing importance of racial and ethnic minority perspectives within it. They remind us that different theologies, histories, and social situations drive very different conceptualizations of the relationship between religious and political life in America's varied faith traditions. They also, in different ways, remind us that the set of "moral issues" is potentially very broad and may differ from one religious tradition to the next. Yet the chapters also point to important commonalities across traditions that can inform discussions of religion and politics. The challenges of mobilization, dilemmas about the appropriate level of politicization, and the intersections of religion and ethnicity are recurring themes. If the book illustrates the highly nuanced and contextual nature of religious–political interaction across America's varied faith traditions while not "losing the forest for the trees," I will count it a success.

This comprehensive survey of faith and political action in America has been evolving as a project for some time. The book had its origins in a conference on Religion and American Political Behavior held at Southern Methodist University in the fall of 2002 under the auspices of the John Goodwin Tower Center for Political Studies. Most of the chapters in this volume were originally presented in some form at that conference, though all have been updated to account for developments since that time. The idea underlying the conference, and in turn this book, was to take a comprehensive, multifaceted look at the relationship between religious faith and political action in America. In doing so, two considerations were especially important: to consider religious groups that play important roles in American political life but are often overlooked in the literature on religion and politics (e.g., Mormons, Jews, Latino Christians, Muslims, and secularists); and to bring together some of the most prominent, established figures in research on religion and politics with some of the most promising emerging scholars in the field. I am pleased that both the conference and the book have succeeded in meeting these objectives.

I am deeply indebted to the Tower Center and to its former and current directors, Calvin Jillson and James Hollifield, for supporting the conference and the book project. This volume would not have been possible without their support. I am also grateful to Georgetown University Press director Richard Brown, both for his patience as this book was revised and took final form and for his excellent suggestion that the volume would benefit from a chapter on the politics of American Muslims. In that vein, I owe a special debt of gratitude to John Green and Paul Djupe for stepping into the breach and providing that chapter relatively quickly. Finally, thanks are due to my wife, Carole, for her personal and scholarly support in this as in all my research endeavors.

ONE

Prayers, Parties, and Preachers: The Evolving Nature of Political and Religious Mobilization

Clyde Wilcox and Carin Robinson

IN JANUARY 2004, GEORGE W. BUSH launched his reelection campaign in his State of the Union Address. He condemned steroid use, called for expanded spending on abstinence education, seemed to endorse a constitutional amendment to bar same-sex marriage, and announced an executive order opening up many federal grants for faith-based institutions. Republican Party strategists hoped that each of these policies would appeal to various religious constituencies, and especially to the president's base of white evangelical Christians. During the ensuing campaign, Bush often spoke openly of his faith (Robinson and Wilcox 2007).

Republicans are not alone in seeking to mobilize religious sentiments and values. Speaking to the Metropolitan Baptist Church in December 1997, President Bill Clinton declared that "Ephesians says we should speak the truth with our neighbors for we are members one of another. I believe that. I think that is the single most important political insight, or social insight, in the Bible. And I think it is what should drive us as we behave together. . . . Is my destiny caught up in yours? Are we part of the same family of God? It's not enough to say we are all equal in the eyes of God. We are all also connected in the eyes of God" (Dionne 2003). Clinton's words at this predominantly black Washington church linked religion to healing national divisions on race and ethnicity, and also served to increase his appeal to African American voters. After some hesitation, the Democratic presidential candidate, John Kerry, also spoke of his faith during the 2004 campaign, but his pro-choice position on abortion put him at odds with the Catholic Church's leadership and made it difficult for him to reach out to observant Catholics.

Even more secular candidates now feel the need to talk about religion. During the Democratic presidential nomination contest in 2004, Vermont governor Howard Dean, after professing to know a good deal about the Bible, named the Book of Job as his favorite in the New Testament (Wilgoren 2004). His gaffe helped to reinforce the stereotype that the Democrats are the party of nonreligious Americans. It also provided undergraduates with an important lesson: Before speaking about a book, you should at least study the table of contents.

The intersection of religion and politics involves both religious leaders mobilizing political pressure on policymakers and political parties, and political leaders trying to use religious issues to mobilize electoral support. Early in 2004, religious conservatives pressured George W. Bush to formally endorse a constitutional amendment defining marriage as the union of one man and one woman. Meanwhile, Bush's chief political adviser, Karl Rove, planned ways to use same-sex marriage as a wedge issue to win support from Catholics, Latinos, and African Americans, and to discourage Democratic partisans from voting in the 2004 election.

Early in the new millennium, conventional wisdom holds that religious conservatives are ascendant and that the political influence of religious liberals is waning. Some observers predict an escalation of a "culture war" that pits religious Americans from a variety of traditions against their more secular counterparts (Green et al. 1996). This narrative suggests that the vast diversity of hundreds of Christian denominations and non-Christian faiths is coalescing into a "two party" religious system. In 2004, religiosity was a better predictor of voting behavior than religious affiliation, and Bush won among churchgoing Catholics against the first Roman Catholic presidential nominee since John F. Kennedy. In 1960, Kennedy had sought to convince voters that he was not "too Catholic"; in 2004, Kerry sought to convince voters that he was "Catholic enough." Geoffrey Layman (2001, 415) concludes his thoughtful study of "the great divide" in American politics by predicting that "the religious and cultural polarization of the political parties quite likely will be an outstanding feature of American politics well into the new millennium."

Others, however, argue that America's religious scene is a more complex tapestry, where religious traditions and doctrines are interwoven with race and class. African American evangelicals are surely no less religious than whites, yet they take very different lessons from the Bible (Emerson and Smith 2000; Harris 1999; chapter 6 by Harris-Lacewell in this volume). American Catholics are conflicted participants in any culture war, with highly observant Catholics drawn to both sides (Bendyna 2000). Latinos are a growing segment of both Catholic and evangelical America, with distinctive attitudes about many issues (see chapter 7 by DeSipio in this volume).

The future of the intersection between religion and politics in the United States depends on many factors—including the changing contours of American religion, the strategies of political elites, and the changing set of political issues touching on religious values. Although political scientists have learned a great deal about the impact of religious characteristics on individual political attitudes and behavior, they know less about the impact of politics on religion or the impact of the changing issue agenda on how religious groups mobilize into politics.

In this chapter, we begin with a discussion of religious mobilization into politics and then focus on the political mobilization of religion. Religious mobilization into politics occurs when religious citizens or bodies try to influence public policies. The political mobilization of religion involves parties or political elites appealing to religious constituencies for electoral and other political support. We then examine the three factors that will decide the nature of religious-political interactions over the next few decades: the changing nature of American religion, the changing nature of politics, and the changing matrix of issues where the two intersect.

Voices Crying in the Wilderness: Religious Mobilization into Politics

Religious organizations and religious citizens seek to influence politics for a variety of reasons. Most religious Americans merely seek to make policies more consistent with the values of their faith. Catholic leaders and activists seek to limit abortion and at the same time to promote health care for the poor. White evangelical activists seek to ban gay marriage and also urge the government to protect Christians in Sudan (Bummiller 2003). African American evangelicals seek to expand government programs to feed the poor and also to fight illegal drugs in their communities. Mainline Protestants advocate increased foreign aid to poor countries and stronger environmental protections in the United States. Jews seek greater protections for civil rights and continued American support for Israel. The agendas of religious activists are diverse, both across and within traditions, with many members opposing one or both of the policies listed above.

Others seek to intervene in politics because they believe that God will punish the nation if it violates his rules. Abraham Lincoln articulated this theme movingly in his Second Inaugural Address, noting that the Civil War might drag on as God's judgment against the sin of slavery: "Yet, if God wills that it continue until all the wealth piled by the bondsman's two hundred and fifty years of unrequited toil shall be sunk, and until every drop of blood drawn with the lash shall be paid by another drawn with the sword, as was said three thousand years ago, so still it must be said that 'the judgments of the Lord are true and righteous altogether.'" Jerry Falwell made a similar, if less majestic, claim after the September 11, 2001, terrorist attacks, suggesting that they were God's punishment on a sinful nation. He said, "I really believe that the pagans, and the abortionists and the feminists, and the gays and the lesbians who are actively trying to make that an alternative lifestyle, the ACLU, People for the American Way—all of them who have tried to secularize America—I point the finger in their face and say, 'You helped this happen'" (Harris 2001).

Still others do not focus on God's judgment but see politics as a battle between divine and satanic forces. In several surveys, significant numbers of Christian conservatives have stated that they believe God is active in elections and parties and that Satan is an active force opposing Christian policies. This kind of apocalyptic vision naturally leads to intense political mobilization, even among those whose theology previously inclined them to avoid politics (Wilcox 2003).

For the purposes of this volume, it is important that in these instances, the mobilization is by religious groups, not political elites. These are examples of religious organizations and citizens pushing their agenda into the political realm, not political elites pulling religious groups into politics.

How Religion Matters in Religious Mobilization

Whatever political scientists may have thought two decades ago about the influence of religion on politics, a consensus has since emerged that religion plays a major role in political life, in both America (Wald 2003; Layman 2001) and elsewhere (Jelen and Wilcox 2002). Many scholars who do not specialize in religion have come to recognize its power (e.g., Verba, Schlozman, and Brady 1995), but others remain reluctant to use religious variables in their explanations of American politics (Wald and Wilcox 2006).

The source of this reluctance probably has much to do with the myriad ways that religion influences individuals and campaigns. Religion is a complex phenomenon, and fully tracing the tributaries of its influence is a difficult task. For largely secular social scientists, this complexity seems forbidding. These scholars know that political attitudes vary by theological tradition, by denomination, by congregation, by doctrine, by religious identity, by religiosity, and even by styles of religiosity. Each of these variables has been shown to play a role in shaping political attitudes and behaviors, yet they overlap in many complicated ways (Leege and Kellstedt 1993).

Denomination

Religious denominations are one important locus of political mobilization. The leaders of various denominations and faith traditions make statements about the relationship between church teaching and politics, with varying frequency and authoritativeness. They often then seek to influence policymaking, both by quietly using their lobbyists to alter legislation and by mobilizing the faithful to support or oppose it (Hertzke 1988).

Denominations matter because religious elites promote theological positions that have implications for politics and often take positions on political issues. Over time, many American Christian denominations have taken official positions on abortion, hunger, homosexuality, war, taxes, and other key issues. These teachings can collide in highly visible ways, as when some churches condemned and some supported America's invasion of Iraq in 2003. Denominations can change over time; the leadership of the Southern Baptist Convention has been known for taking fundamentalist and Republican positions since the 1980s, but it recently elected a moderate as president, which may signal a softening of the group's conservative agenda (Guth 1996; Dionne

2006). In chapter 4 of this volume, Stephen Mockabee notes how Catholics' affiliation with the Democratic Party has waned over time. He notes that among older Catholics, the most devout are more likely to identify as Democrats, but among younger Catholics the most devout are more likely to be Republicans. Younger conservative Catholics are more likely to choose their partisanship based on policy views rather than social group identity. As the Church has come to emphasize its opposition to abortion and homosexuality over its teachings on poverty or the death penalty, many of its most devout members have altered their voting accordingly.

Denominational leaders frequently take strong positions on issues and seek to throw the entire weight of their church behind those policies. During the debate over the Clinton health care plan, Catholic officials worked behind the scenes to strike abortion coverage from the plan, and they announced opposition to any proposal that would include abortion as a covered benefit. The Mormon Church has channeled significant resources into the fight against same-sex marriage, as noted in David Campbell and Quin Monson's discussion in chapter 5 of this volume.

Yet there are significant limits to the effectiveness of denominational mobilization. First, although denominations are communities of faith, not all members share the same views on political issues. Consider, for example, the Catholic Church, which has a hierarchical structure and makes authoritative moral claims. After decades of active mobilization against abortion and contraception in the United States, recent General Social Surveys shows that three in four Catholics favor allowing abortion in cases of rape, that more than a third favor allowing abortion for families too poor to afford additional children, and a majority favor allowing birth control to teenagers who are sexually active. Nearly half of those who attend mass at least two to three times a month would allow contraception to teenage girls. When the Catholic Church lobbied in New York for exemptions for Catholic-run businesses (e.g., hospitals and schools) from state requirements that employers cover contraceptive costs in 2003, surveys showed that a majority of New York Catholics opposed such exemptions and favored mandated coverage.

A second barrier to denominational mobilization is the sheer diversity of American denominations, leaving none with close to majority status in the United States. The combined American National Election

Studies from 1990 through 2000, which include more than 120 denominations or traditions with at least one respondent, reveal that the handful of largest denominations together account for only about 60 percent of all Americans. Thus, no single religious tradition can prevail on matters of faith and morals without entering into compromises on the issues.

Even the smallest denominations have their own distinctive theology, often with political implications. Guth and others (1997), in their study of Protestant clergy, note that there are two competing blocs of liberal and conservative clergy. Yet there are subtle differences in theology between the denominations within each bloc that lead to equally subtle political differences.

Finally, denominational mobilization is limited by the rapid growth of nondenominational churches—especially the megachurches in suburban areas. These huge churches can exert political influence, and they draw young, well-educated members—the very ones most likely to be effective in politics—away from established denominations.

Congregations

Although denominations may promote specific theological views and take political positions on issues, individual congregations within those denominations may promote a different doctrine and advocate different policies. For instance, the Walnut Grove United Methodist Church in Fairmont, West Virginia, is an evangelical congregation that blends elements of charismatic worship with fundamentalist theology in a manner that is characteristic of Appalachian Methodist churches but very different from mainline, liberal Methodist churches in Fairfax County, Virginia.

Congregations form political communities that provide their members with many political cues (Wald, Owen, and Hill 1988). Their leaders can preach politics overtly or subtly, helping to shape their congregations' politics. In many congregations, members form friendships that can lead to political discussions and deliberations and thus help to reinforce or resist pastoral messages. For example, the members of a women's Bible study group in Wausau, Wisconsin, used their weekly meeting time to greet then–vice presidential candidate Dick Cheney at a fly-in during the 2000 presidential campaign. Bible studies, fellowship circles, and mentoring relationships are just a few ways in which political socialization can take place in a religious setting.

Congregations are also politically important because they are a place where likeminded citizens meet on a regular basis. They can therefore provide important political infrastructure, from voter registration drives in African American churches to the distribution of Christian Coalition voter guides in white evangelical churches. Small wonder that both political parties seek to enlist congregation leaders and active members in their political networks.

Yet there are limits on the ability of individual churches, mosques, and synagogues to mobilize politically. Congregations can constrain their leaders in the exercise of their prophetic function by making it clear that members will leave or withdraw their support if sermons become too political (Jelen 1991, 1993; Djupe and Gilbert 2003). If key members of a congregation oppose a political agenda, their leader may refrain from advocacy because his or her job might be at stake, he or she does not want to split the faithful, or he or she perceives that political advocacy would hamper their religious mission. During the formative years of the Ohio Moral Majority, several congregations splintered when their pastors became active in the organization.

Doctrine

One reason that denominations matter is that they attempt to teach their members a consistent doctrine. Yet not all congregations within a denomination will adhere to that doctrine, and not all members of each congregation will agree with its prevailing doctrine. Over the past two decades, scholars have shown that religious doctrine has an enormous impact on political attitudes, on party preference, and on vote choice, and that doctrine has an impact that is independent of, and sometimes quite different from, that of denomination.

Although there are important doctrinal differences among Catholics, Jews, Muslims, and other faith traditions, most of the research has focused on attitudes toward the Bible among Protestants. Most evangelical, fundamentalist, and Pentecostal Christians believe that the Bible is at least the inerrant word of God, and some further believe that it is literally true, word for word. Belief in an inerrant Bible is associated among white Protestants with opposition to a range of policies, including abortion, egalitarian gender roles, social welfare programs, environmental protection, and expanded gay rights, as well as support for defense spending, the death penalty, and aid to Israel. Black evangelicals come to different conclusions about gender roles, social welfare programs, and other issues, however, reasoning from the same Bible.

We know much less about the way that the Bible's meaning is socially constructed. A Bible study guide used by various members of the Walnut Grove United Methodist Church in the 1980s interpreted a passage in Exodus as calling for the death penalty for abortion providers, and over time this interpretation spread throughout the church. This view became widespread in the church not because it was an obvious interpretation of the passage, but because it fit the political discussion within the church and was adopted by those with influence in the congregation.

The social construction of doctrine is evident in the connection between evangelicalism and opposition to environmental programs. Research has shown that those who hold to premillennialist doctrine are more likely than other Christians to oppose environmental protection (Guth et al. 1995). This opposition has been tied to the belief that Christ will soon come again, and that God gave Adam and Eve dominion over animals. Yet surely this is only one construction of premillennialist doctrine, for if God knows of the falling of a single sparrow, and made the Dusky Seaside Sparrow different from the Cape Sable Seaside Sparrow, then he might not be terribly happy that it was driven to extinction because of human desires to develop the Florida coastline. The National Association of Evangelicals has launched an initiative called Creation Care, and the Evangelical Environmental Network sparked discussion in evangelical circles with their What Would Jesus Drive? campaign in 2002, calling attention to transportation pollution. In sum, the political meaning of the Bible with regard to environmental policy is contested within evangelicalism (Fowler 1995).

The social construction of biblical meaning varies with race, ethnicity, and social class. Evangelical doctrine translates into very different gender politics in white and African American churches. Many observant white evangelicals embrace very traditional gender roles that circumscribe women's active participation in public life. In 1993, a group of white evangelical women attended the Virginia Republican convention, but they chose not to be voting delegates because this was not a proper role for women. They did, however, run a day care center for other delegates with a different theology. In contrast, evangelicalism is a source of support for gender equality in many African American churches (Wilcox and Thomas 1992). Clearly, the social construction of biblical meaning is linked to race, ethnicity, and even social class.

In chapter 6 of this volume, Melissa Harris-Lacewell recounts important theological distinctions among African American Protestants. Churches that preach Black Liberation Theology help to mobilize their congregations into electoral politics. Yet the new strand of prosperity gospel theology emphasizes individualistic values and lifestyles that can lead to material rewards. The prosperity gospel, therefore, has a depoliticizing effect on African American churchgoers.

Similarly, theology likely plays a role in explaining political behavior for Muslims. One study examines the relationship between doctrine and mobilization for a number of mosques in Northern Virginia (Mian 2006). However, social scientists know very little about how doctrine shapes political behavior for religious minorities in the United States such as Buddhists, Hindus, and Muslims.

Religiosity

We know that religiosity matters, across traditions. Religious attendance is linked to particular political attitudes. Sometimes the effects are uniform, regardless of the teachings of the denomination. Among Jews and in all Christian denominations, those who attend religious services regularly are more conservative on abortion than infrequent attendees. This is true despite the explicitly pro-choice position of some theological traditions.

In other matters, frequent attendees echo the political teachings of their denominations. Committed mainline Protestants support more environmental programs than nominal mainline Protestants—precisely the opposite pattern from white evangelicals. Committed African American Protestants support a wider range of government programs to help the poor than do the less committed—again the opposite of white evangelicals (Kohut et al. 2000).

Among African Americans, frequent church attendance is associated with increased political participation, but high levels of private religiosity (prayer, Bible reading, etc.) are often associated with lower levels of participation. Recent research reminds us that some black churches are politicized and others are not. Politicized churches help to mobilize their members politically, but other churches focus on serving individual spiritual needs.

Attendance is critically important for political mobilization. Most Protestant churches appear to help their members build the kinds of personal skills needed for political participation (Verba, Schlozman, and Brady 1995). One reason why evangelical churches (both white and black) are increasingly involved in political mobilization is that they constitute a place where large numbers of citizens who share a common worldview meet together regularly. The lower rate of church attendance among religious liberals coupled with declining congregational size constitutes more than a religious liability; it is also a political liability.

It is not just the level of religiosity that matters, but also the type. The political scientist David Leege argues that "it is not merely how religious you are that matters, it is also how you are religious" (personal communication with Clyde Wilcox, February 1998). Leege and Welch (1989) show that Catholics with an evangelical worship style hold distinctive political values, especially on issues where the Church has no official position.

Religious Mobilization in the Twentieth and Twenty-First Centuries

There have been waves of religious mobilization throughout American history, against institutions such as slavery and segregation, seeking to prohibit vices like alcohol and gambling, attempting to ameliorate social problems such as poverty and inequality, and focusing on issues such as war and abortion. These mobilizations have come from denominations, individual congregations, parachurch organizations, and coalitions of religious activists.

The most impressive religious mobilization in the past century took place in African American churches over civil rights. Churches provided the leadership, space, and infrastructure, and perhaps most important the courage that allowed African Americans to confront hostility and violence—courage that perhaps could only come from a belief in divine support. White churches were deeply divided by the civil rights movement, but liberal white pastors marched with Martin Luther King and northern white churches provided funds and other resources.

The mobilization over civil rights came from denominations and churches, and also from organizations like the Southern Christian

Leadership Conference. Its success was due in no small part to the blending of racial consciousness with religion. The Bible became a document of liberation, with the freeing of the Jews from Egyptian slavery serving as a metaphor for civil rights. Today many African American churches still conduct voter registration drives, encourage their members to vote and be politically active, and allow candidates to speak from the pulpit. Some even pass around collection plates on behalf of candidates.

By the end of the 1960s, networks of religious opposition to the Vietnam War had developed within and across denominations. Priests poured blood on draft records and pastors joined protestors in blocking Washington streets to protest the war. After the war ended, the Christian left mobilized again to a far lesser extent to provide sanctuary for refugees from brutal Central American regimes. But after the mid-1980s, the Christian left was an almost invisible force in American politics. During the next two decades, the pro-life movement and the Christian Right became predominant. In chapter 3, Laura Olson argues that there remain large numbers of religious liberals who care about socioeconomic justice, programs to support minorities, liberal internationalism, and other issues. Yet today religious liberals are handicapped by their membership in declining denominations, by their belief in the separation of church and state, and by their general satisfaction with the status quo.

The *Roe v. Wade* decision in 1973 prompted a massive, if thus far unsuccessful, religious mobilization. Within a few years, Catholic activists were pushing hard for a constitutional amendment to ban abortions, and evangelicals soon joined the crusade. Some mainline Protestant churches took an explicitly pro-choice position, as did Jewish leaders, but the religious energy on this issue was heavily concentrated in the pro-life forces.

In the late 1970s and again in the late 1980s, two different waves of Christian Right mobilization took place. The initial sparks involved local controversies (Wald 2003), but the formation and mobilization of the Christian Right nationally was primarily a political mobilization of religious sentiment, not a religious mobilization into politics.

In 2004, the Massachusetts Supreme Court ruled that the state's constitution required that the state allow same-sex marriage. This resulted in a significant mobilization among religious conservatives and a much smaller one among religious liberals (Campbell and Robinson 2007;

Wilcox, Merolla, and Beer 2007). Coalitions of unlikely partners had been working against gay marriage for several years—Mormons, fundamentalists, Catholics, and even some Muslim groups. Many evangelicals saw the gay marriage battle as a last stand against encroaching secular forces. Yet different religious constituencies supported different versions of the amendment, with Christian Right activists seeking to ban civil unions and perhaps even antidiscrimination laws, Catholics favoring antidiscrimination laws but no civil unions, and the Mormon Church and some African American leaders favoring allowing civil unions. Political elites began focusing considerable attention on how to harness or derail the religious mobilization against gay marriage. Polls show that support for same-sex marriage is highest among liberals and secular Americans, many of whom organize their political beliefs around their opposition to Christian fundamentalists and the Christian Right. In chapter 10, Louis Bolce and Gerald De Maio offer a fascinating analysis of this antifundamentalism as a force in American politics.

From Pews to Precincts? The Political Mobilization of Religion

Not all religious mobilization arises spontaneously in response to issues and conditions. Political elites use issues to appeal to religious constituencies, and they seek the political support of religious leaders. In this way the politics of religion is similar to the politics of ethnicity, class, and other cultural differences (Leege et al. 2002).

Candidates and parties appeal to religious groups for votes. For instance, Ronald Reagan's appeal to religious Catholics greatly aided his campaigns in key midwestern states, and the Bush campaign in 2004 mounted an appeal to orthodox Catholics on the abortion issue. In chapter 7, Louis DeSipio describes Bush's efforts to court the Latino vote through his socially conservative policy positions. DeSipio finds, however, that this strategy holds its greatest potential with non-Catholic Latinos, who currently make up a clear minority of the Latino population.

Parachurch organizations can aid in the political mobilization of religious belief. In the 1990s, the Christian Coalition distributed tens of millions of voter guides in conservative Protestant churches, seeking to win Republican votes. Pastors can also welcome candidates into churches, allowing them to speak from the pulpit while stopping short of an endorsement (Harris 1999; Rozell and Wilcox 1996). In 2004, the Christian Coalition was revived in several states, and other organizations were formed to help mobilize voting for Bush among evangelicals. Let Freedom Ring distributed a video focusing on Bush's personal faith to pastors in Ohio and Pennsylvania, along with promises of legal support for any church whose tax-exempt status was challenged as a result of the action.

Candidates seek to organize religious groups to mobilize votes. In 2004, the Bush campaign gathered church membership lists that would enable it to mobilize supportive voters. This tactic provoked opposition even among some who strongly supported the president's reelection. Democratic candidates frequently seek to build networks in black churches.

Candidates also seek to mobilize religion for political contributions. George W. Bush appealed with some success to Jewish donors (Hallow 2003b), who have provided until now a major source of funding for Democratic candidates. Bush's father mobilized a network of Hindu doctors to give to his campaign (Brown, Powell, and Wilcox 1995). Muslim donors constitute networks for both parties. To date, evangelical Christians are underrepresented among political donors, although they do give during presidential primaries.

To win votes and contributions, candidates emphasize their positions on issues of concern to faith communities, and they also stress their own religious faith. Before his 2000 presidential bid, George W. Bush gave private testimony to his born-again experience to evangelical leaders. This helped him win enough political support so he did not need to take clear public positions on many key social issues (Rozell 2002). Bush seldom talks about religious doctrine, which can divide Americans, but instead has focused on how religion has changed his life and on how it makes him feel. During the 2004 presidential debates, he claimed to feel the prayers of Americans (Robinson and Wilcox 2007).

Political leaders often can cultivate religious mobilization. Indeed, much of the mobilization of the Christian Right, and a significant amount of pro-life activity in the 1990s, were stimulated and coordinated by Republican Party officials. This does not mean that there is no genuine religious enthusiasm for these movements, for no mobilization can succeed without a pool of voters and activists who care about issues.

A political mobilization of religion differs, however, from a religious mobilization into politics, and these differences have consequences.

It was conservative Republican activists, most of whom were not evangelical Christians, who coordinated the formation of the Moral Majority and other groups in the late 1970s. Alert to the success of small, scattered, spontaneous religious movements and to the increased turnout of white evangelicals in response to Jimmy Carter's presidential bid in 1976, they recruited leaders, helped organize fund-raising, and sought to tie the movement directly to the Republican Party.

In 1989, after Pat Robertson's failed presidential bid, the National Republican Senatorial Committee made the largest contribution to the fledgling Christian Coalition, and the coalition's head, Ralph Reed, worked closely with the committee in support of Jesse Helms and other Republican senators. In the beginning, Robertson announced that the Christian Coalition's goals were a Republican Congress by the mid-1990s and a Republican president by 2000. Reed worked behind the scenes to negotiate Christian Right support for moderate Republican candidates such as Kay Bailey Hutchinson in Texas, and to head off the presidential candidacy of Pat Buchanan in 1996.

The partisan leanings of the Christian Coalition were perhaps most evident in the 1992 presidential campaign. Coalition leaders worked closely with the George H. W. Bush campaign, insinuating their local leaders into official positions in the campaign and sending them as delegates to the Republican convention. The coalition's massive voter mobilization effort in 1992 was funded in part by fund-raising events hosted by Republican Party officials (including Bush), and its voter guides were almost always structured to make Republicans appear more favorably than Democrats. Republicans also gave the National Right to Life Committee money to help coordinate voter mobilization efforts, and George W. Bush sought their aid in his primary victory in South Carolina in 2000.

On the Democratic side, the regular voter mobilization efforts in black churches are often carefully negotiated with Democratic Party officials. Moreover, many observers believe that Democratic money went into the creation of the Interfaith Alliance, which also distributed voter guides favoring Democratic candidates, modeled on the Christian Coalition's guides.

After the 2004 election, many Democratic activists began to ponder their party's inability to appeal to religious voters, and they formed several organizations to study the religious beliefs of swing voters. Underlying these efforts is a hope that the party might begin to mobilize a new religious left among liberal Catholics, black Protestants, and white mainline churches.

As churches have become more deeply involved with electoral politics, Republican officials have pushed for legislation that would exempt churches from Internal Revenue Service (IRS) regulations about partisan activity by tax-exempt institutions. Although only one church has ever lost its tax-exempt status for partisan activity (for accepting contributions for a newspaper advertisement asserting that Clinton's policies were "in rebellion to God's Laws"), the IRS has investigated other churches and advised them to "cease and desist" from their activity. Moreover, an IRS investigation into the tax-exempt status of the Christian Coalition helped accelerate changes in that organization that made its voter guide distribution less effective.

Although many religious conservatives welcomed this proposed legislation, others were less sanguine about the prospect of turning pews into precincts. With no limitation on what churches could do in campaigns, political activists and candidates might seek to insert partisan politics more thoroughly into churches. Already churches can mount voter mobilization campaigns and even bus their members to the polls. They cannot, however, use their tax-exempt contributions to endorse or work for candidates and parties. Many religious conservatives and liberals alike fear the intrusion of partisanship into buildings consecrated to a very different type of task.

Those who favor the political mobilization of religion argue that politicians and political parties are best suited to articulate policy choices and make the consequences of these choices clear to voters. Indeed, when political leaders mobilize religious groups, they are more likely to listen to their preferences and to take their moral concerns seriously.

Those who worry about the political mobilization of religion cite three specific concerns. First, when religious groups become too closely connected with politicians, they may lose their prophetic voice. African American pastors who oppose abortion have found it difficult to preach that message while working closely with Democratic elected officials. When Republican leaders in the late 1990s pushed welfare reform that would, among other things, force single mothers with young children who receive government aid to enter the labor force,

Concerned Women for America withheld criticism, perhaps in part because of its close ties to the Republican Party. Even more worrisome is that political agendas may trump religions ones. In 1993, the Christian Coalition's top agenda item was opposition to an increase in the gasoline tax—a position that Republican strategists believed could help them win control of Congress in 1994 but is notably absent from the religious texts of any major faith tradition.

Second, many fear that the divisive partisanship prevalent among political elites might come to divide congregations, drowning out religious messages. Political advertising in the last decade has been especially negative, and political activists have found that demonizing the opposition leaves a lasting impression in voters' minds. This has infiltrated the rhetoric of quasi-religious groups with strong partisan ties. Christian Right direct mail materials have demonized Democratic politicians, many of whom have a deep and sincere faith. Indeed, it has become common in many evangelical circles to deny that a Christian can be a Democrat (see Hertzke 1993). The moral scorecards of the Christian Voice in 1980 gave perfect 100 scores to members who had moral failings in the past term, including one member who had an affair with a teenage page, and it gave scores of 0 to religious leaders such as Robert Drinan, SJ, a Catholic priest who then was serving in Congress. The purpose of these communications is political, not religious, and the religious message of love and forgiveness gives way to one of fear (for an elaboration, see Thomas and Dobson 1999).

Third, if pews turn into precincts, genuine religious work can be hampered. Evangelical churches believe in the importance of winning souls for Christ, but if a Democrat wanders into a church that is heavily involved in Republican Party politics, she might leave again without being exposed to the church's message of salvation. Politics can divide congregations, drive members from their pews, and otherwise hamper church activity.

Religious Mobilization in the Twenty-First Century: Sources of Change

In 1958 religious leaders in Fairfax County, Virginia, met in an integrated setting to plan their response to court-ordered school desegregation. These leaders and their congregations formed the core of opposition to Virginia's Massive Resistance strategy, which would have shut down public schools rather than allow blacks to attend. The 1990s saw more religious mobilization in the county over education, but in this case it involved school board candidates rallying Christians behind the teaching of creationism and to limit sex education classes.

What accounts for the changing relationship between religion and politics in America, and what might this tell us about the future? This changing relationship is due in part to changing religion and in part to changing politics. Moreover, the policy space where religion and politics intersect has changed as new issues have emerged.

Changing Religion in America

If religious membership and attendance rates had remained constant over the past forty years, it is possible that the Christian Right would face an equally strong Christian left. But over time, mainline Protestant denominations have lost members, and evangelical churches and the Mormon Church have gained members. This process has produced a gradual but significant change in the composition of America's religions. As Corwin Smidt notes in chapter 2, the proportion of American citizens belonging to mainline Protestant denominations has fallen by 50 percent since 1964, while that belonging to white evangelical churches has grown. Wuthnow (2000) notes that the six largest mainline Protestant denominations lost a combined total of 5.6 million members between 1965 and 1990, and the trend has continued since then.

Mainline Protestant churches used to dominate American politics, and their members still retain important resources. Yet the mainline denominations are in decline for several reasons. First, the more educated members of these denominations have children later and have smaller families. Their children also have children later and have smaller families, and this difference in fertility rates becomes cumulatively significant over time. Moreover, there is some evidence (though contested) that the mainline churches are less likely to hold onto their young, who often drift into secularism or join conservative evangelical churches.

The decline of mainline Protestantism is unlikely to reverse itself anytime soon. A young couple that moves to a new community might first visit a Methodist church where most members collect Social Security and then an Assembly of God church packed with young people, which has activities throughout the week specially geared for young couples with children. They will most likely join the Assembly of God congregation.

During the 1990s, the fastest-growing churches in the United States were the Catholic Church (which grew primarily through immigration), the Mormons, and the Assemblies of God. The local churches of these denominations are full, and there are many members with youth, energy, and the willingness to engage in politics if it seems important to the mission of the church. The important infrastructure of these conservative churches was used by the Christian Coalition in the 1990s to distribute its voter guides; one volunteer from the coalition could distribute hundreds of guides in a church to potential voters who were not members of the coalition but who were likely to be influenced by the information.

In urban areas, denominational and theological boundaries are undermined not only by nondenominational megachurches but also by the tendency to use churches for multiple congregations. For instance, a small Presbyterian church building in Wheaton, Maryland, is home to four congregations. The elderly Presbyterian congregation worships quietly first, followed by an affluent congregation of Taiwanese Presbyterians who worship in Chinese. Next up is the New Baptist Creation Church, an African American congregation headed by a lively woman pastor. Finally, in the late afternoon, the Iglesia Pentecostal Christo Rey holds a Spanish service that attracts Central American immigrants and stretches on for as much as four hours (Ruane 1999).

Two other types of religious change over the past decades are worth tracing, because they may portend even more rapid change in the future. First, the portion of Americans who do not fall into the Judeo-Christian category is growing. Surveys typically do not identify sufficient numbers of Hindus, Muslims, Sikhs, or other groups to provide useful data, but there is evidence that these groups can play a key role in elections. Moreover, the slow increase in their numbers nationally is concentrated in major cities on the east and west coasts. In the Washington area, for example, it is not unusual to see a Sikh, a Muslim, and a Hindu in line at a store, all in distinctive attire. One ten-mile stretch of road just outside Washington contains a synagogue, a mosque, a Cambodian Buddhist temple, a Hindu temple, two Jehovah's Witness kingdom halls, and one Unitarian, three Catholic, one Ukrainian Orthodox, two Seventh-Day Adventist, and twenty-one Protestant churches, including several that serve immigrant populations (Levine 1997).

Second, the number of Americans with no attachment to religion is growing, albeit far more slowly than predicted by those who argued that the United States would undergo the same secularization as Europe. By 2000, the number of secularist Americans had surpassed the number who belonged to mainline Protestant denominations. It is possible that the developing political cleavage based on religiosity may increase the secularity of liberals and Democrats, who may come to see religion as closely tied to conservative Republican politics.

Early in the twenty-first century, several key religious traditions face significant challenges. The Catholic Church has endured a series of costly and embarrassing lawsuits from members and former members who claim to have been sexually molested by priests. This scandal cost the Church significant sums in legal costs and payouts to victims. It has also clearly weakened the Church's ability to articulate its issue agenda, as lobbyists across the country have discovered. Whether this will remain an impediment to the Church in the long run remains to be seen.

Among Protestants, the United Methodist, Presbyterian, and (especially) Episcopal churches are deeply divided over homosexuality. The ordination of an openly gay Episcopal priest as bishop in 2003 and the election of a gay-friendly woman to head the denomination in 2006 led to an exit by some conservative priests and congregations. Once again, the long-term impact of this issue on these denominations remained unclear, but it clearly has distracted church officials and weakened their ability to speak authoritatively for members.

Changes in Politics

Many scholars have written about the interaction between religion and politics as though the former has always influenced the latter. In fact, changes in politics over the past several decades have had a profound impact on American religion, and they promise to do so even more in the future. This impact is a function both of political issues that religious institutions and individuals must face and of conscious actions by political elites to mobilize religious sentiments.

During the past two decades, the political attitudes of partisan elites have become polarized. There are fewer liberal Republicans and conservative Democrats in Congress, so the victory of one party seems to have greater ideological consequence. Among political activists, dislike of the other party has grown along with this polarization. The technology of fund-raising contributes to growing interparty hostility by increasing fear and distrust. One Christian conservative fund-raising letter in 2003 declared that Hillary Clinton was seeking to have the Bible banned as "hate speech." Another claimed that liberals were solely focused on destroying the American family. Conservative religious groups hosted "Justice Sunday" events across the country to protest Democrats in the Senate filibustering the president's court nominees who were "people of faith." Liberal direct mail materials frequently associate Christian conservatives with Nazis, the Taliban, and other extremist, antidemocratic movements. Small wonder, then, that electoral politics in the past decade has taken on the air of desperate combat, and that campaigns of both parties use tactics and strategies that exceed the bounds of good taste and good ethics as well.

As Christian conservatives and pro-life forces have surged into the Republican Party and influenced nominations, the party has moved to the right on social issues. As secularists have surged into the Democratic Party, its candidates have become increasingly reluctant to use religious language and rhetoric, and its positions on social issues have shifted to the left. Republican operatives increasingly seek to portray the party divide as one between religious and secular America. If American religion is in fact moving toward a two-party system, it would clearly be in part due to the actions of the two major political parties.

Politically polarized parties, narrow party majorities in Congress, and extremely close presidential elections have led both parties to concentrate on mobilizing their own voters and demobilizing those of the opposition. Republicans now send narrowly targeted messages to religious conservatives in the mail and by telephone while staking out more moderate positions in public. Democrats target narrow messages to secularist voters, whose support is critical. Yet they also depend on a large turnout among African American Christians to win elections.

Changing Political Issues

In all societies, political issues sometimes intrude on religious bodies. Religious elites feel compelled to speak on behalf of their community of faith and their theological beliefs. Political issues provide the context for the intersection of religion and politics—the source of religious mobilization and the tools of political mobilization. Some issues thrust themselves onto the public scene, and religious and political leaders must respond. In other cases, religious and/or political events create issues in the interstitial zone between religion and politics.

But the nature of issues can change over time, altering the prospects for religious mobilization. In the 1960s, for example, the civil rights movement polarized America's religious institutions. As civil rights leaders marched in the streets facing dogs and fire hoses, religious liberals were joined by some religious conservatives in condemning segregation and discrimination. Some churches were hostile to deseg-regation, expelling black activists who sought to speak to their con-gregation and condemning pastors who marched. In 1997, the Southern Baptist Convention officially apologized for its previous sup-port for segregation.

Similarly, the Vietnam War mobilized Christian liberals to oppose U.S. involvement and to protest the use of napalm, the drafting of young men, and the support of the South Vietnamese government. Yet many churches supported the war, and debates arose over whether Americans owed their government obedience with regard to the draft. Conservatives argued that young men should "render unto Caesar," but religious liberals argued that humans are made in the image of God, in marked contrast to the coin that Jesus discussed.

Racism and war remain issues today, but for many reasons they arouse less passion among religious liberals. Racism in 1962 meant all-white schools, segregated restaurants and drinking fountains, black cit-izens denied the vote, and white police with dogs and fire hoses. Today, race politics is about affirmative action and more subtle types of dis-crimination. Mainline Protestant churches have a harder time con-vincing white middle-class members that racism requires a coordinated religious response. Unlike the Vietnam War, the war in Iraq has been fought by volunteers, and it involves a complex religious subtext. Although prominent religious leaders, including Pope John Paul II, have opposed the war, there has been far less rumbling in the pews. Moreover, the terrorist attacks of 2001 allowed the president to frame the war as a defensive effort.

Today, issue-based religious mobilization centers on questions related to sexuality and reproduction. Abortion continues to mobilize religious conservatives, although public opinion remains essentially unchanged after years of mobilization on both sides. New issues have begun to insinuate themselves into these debates—notably stem cell research and cloning. Stem cell research divides some in the pro-life community, and mobilizes others.

By the spring of 2004, the issue of same-sex marriage was moving to center stage in the culture wars. The Massachusetts Supreme Court ruled that the state must allow gays and lesbians to marry, and soon after the mayor of San Francisco allowed gays and lesbians to marry in his city, in violation of state law. For many evangelicals, conservative Catholics, Mormons, and others, same-sex marriage is the ground for a last stand in the culture wars. The issue has brought previously hostile religious groups together in concerted action.

The Bush administration has proposed two policies that Republican activists hope will have special appeal to Catholic, Latino, and African American voters. In education policy, Bush seeks to withdraw federal funding from failing schools and to give it to parents to help subsidize a private education, including one provided by a religious school. The administration has also interpreted a number of laws in ways that allow public funds to go to faith-based charities, a policy with some appeal to Catholic churches, and to black and Hispanic churches that offer such services. These policies fit with Bush's personal religious views, and also with Karl Rove's political plans to demobilize Democratic electoral strength. Many Republican strategists hope that African American churches that receive federal funds for schools and social programs might be more favorable toward the party that supplied these funds, or at least less aggressive in their political mobilization on behalf of the opposition.

Perhaps the most unpredictable issue for religion and politics over the next few years is the relationship between Islam and Christianity. After the September 11 attacks, some Americans took out their anger on mosques and on Muslims or anyone who looked like a Muslim. On a flight soon after September 11, a Sikh sat on an airplane wearing a large button that said, in bold letters, "A Proud Sikh American." Many Christians responded with sympathy and concern for Muslims, and there were scattered instances of churches reaching out to help repair mosques or to join Muslims in prayer.

Many evangelicals, however, issued vehemently anti-Muslim comments. In June 2002 at the Southern Baptist Convention, the Reverend Jerry Vines called Muhammad a "demon-possessed pedophile." Other evangelicals echoed the sentiment. Lieutenant General William Boykin, a three-star general who led American forces in Afghanistan, made headlines by stating that "America's battle is not against one or another terrorist leader or group, but against Satan himself. I knew my God was bigger than his. I knew that my God was a real God, and his was an idol."

President Bush eventually responded, carefully and quietly in a press conference in Britain, that Muslims and Christians worship the same God. Sayyid M. Syeed, secretary general of the Islamic Society of North America, praised Bush's statement, saying "Alhamdullah" (thanks be to God). But Richard Land, the president of the Ethics and Religious Liberty Commission of the Southern Baptist Convention, said that Bush was "simply mistaken" (Cooperman 2003).

The Missing Agenda

What has been missing from the latest wave of religious mobilizations has been a concern for economic policy—for poverty and social justice. At a conference at the Ethics and Public Policy Center in 1993, Clarke Cochran commented on the Christian Coalition's view of the Christian agenda. "A lot of issues that Christians should be supporting, such as gun control, justice in health care, protecting the vulnerable widows and orphans (to use biblical language), dignified work for people, and property for the common good (from the Catholic natural-law tradition) never appear because the religious groups, in this case the Christian Coalition, have been captured by the conservative ideological position" (Cromartie 1994, 36).

Liberal Christians, Jews, and Muslims often oppose cuts in social welfare programs and in taxes on wealthy Americans on religious grounds. They point to numerous biblical passages that call for greater policies to help the poor, or at the very least oppose policies that benefit the rich. One liberal pastor in Northern Virginia reminds his congregation that Jesus told the rich young ruler to sell all he had and give it to the poor, not to lobby for tax breaks and cuts in antipoverty programs. The Industrial Areas Foundation is busy in some American cities building a multidenominational liberal coalition that crosses class and racial lines. Yet in the early years of the new century, there is no broad-based religious mobilization on behalf of social justice.

In part, the economic agenda may be a casualty of the culture wars. Because the political debate has centered on abortion, gay rights, and other issues, some religious groups that care about economic justice have been drawn to the Republican Party. The Catholic Church has a long history of advocacy for policies that help the poor, for example, but if abortion and gay marriage are more salient, then the Church is drawn to supporting Republican candidates whose economic policies are at odds with its teaching. The Catholic Church's opposition to the death penalty, to nuclear weapons, and to certain wars has also been muted somewhat by a religious mobilization that centers on issues of sexuality and reproduction.

Some religious writers have raised these issues. Writing in the *Washington Post*, E. J. Dionne (2003) asked, "Does Bush's budget, tilted toward those big tax cuts for the most well-off, match his godly talk?" Yet it may be that religious opposition to regressive tax policies and cuts in social programs is inherently difficult to mobilize (see Wuthnow 1994 and chapter 3 by Olson in this volume). Many evangelical churches have developed a theology that embraces the accumulation of wealth and opposes progressive taxation and government programs to help the poor.

The Plan of the Book

The chapters that follow explore the theme of religious mobilization across religious traditions and racial and ethnic identities. In chapter 2, Corwin Smidt traces the decline in political influence of mainline Protestant churches and the rising power of evangelicals. He notes that mainline Protestants have steadily declined as a portion of the population but retain important resources, including wealth and education. Yet these resources are more important individually than collectively, for mainline Protestants are not frequent churchgoers and are typically not inclined to activism. In contrast, evangelicals constitute a growing and active portion of the electorate. They are a relatively cohesive voting bloc that can be reliably contacted at church on Sundays. Evangelicals do, however, face challenges in the next decade.

In chapter 3, Laura Olson ponders the fate of the Christian left. She identifies a significant number of Americans who are religious liberals—numerically enough to challenge the Christian Right. They participate in politics as often as the Christian Right, and they have a cohesive and distinctive policy agenda. Yet the Christian left suffers from several disadvantages—it is disproportionately concentrated in declining denominations where pastors may not want to risk political activism, its supporters believe in strict separation of church and state and therefore may resist religious mobilization, and its adherents are, generally speaking, relatively content with current political arrangements.

In many presidential elections, Catholics are the swing voters who decide the outcome. In chapter 4, Stephen Mockabee traces the gradual realignment of Catholics from strong Democratic partisans to a group that is up for grabs. He notes a generation gap in which churchgoing older Catholics tend to identify as Democrat, but their observant younger counterparts are strongly Republican. He tests four explanations for the gradual partisan realignment of American Catholics: increasing socioeconomic status, social and cultural issues, superior mobilization by the Republican Party, and general ideological conservatism. He concludes that over time the power of group identity as a voting cue has subsided, allowing younger conservative Catholics to align their partisanship and vote with their ideological leanings.

Studies of American denominations often lump Mormons into a miscellaneous "other" category. Yet there are more than 4 million Mormons in America, and that number is growing rapidly. In chapter 5, David Campbell and Quin Monson explain that Mormons can be readily mobilized on those relatively infrequent occasions when church leaders call them to action. They note that Mormons constitute a cohesive voting bloc with a partisan loyalty that rivals African Americans. And they demonstrate that Mormon religious observance helps build political skills and social capital, which can then be translated into effective political action when Church leaders urge a response to policy issues.

In chapter 6, Melissa Harris-Lacewell argues that earlier debates over whether the black church is an opiate or a mobilizer made little headway because there are important theological differences within African American religion. Some churches teach Black Liberation Theology, which holds that Christians must struggle together to overcome racism and economic inequality. In contrast, the more recent prosperity gospel theology prevalent in many black megachurches teaches that prayer, faith, and right living can lead to prosperity. This theology demobilizes African Americans by casting racism and income inequality as individual rather than collective moral problems.

The rapidly growing Latino population will play a very important role in the religion and politics of the new century. In chapter 7, Louis DeSipio traces the political fault lines in this increasingly important electoral constituency. Latinos already constitute almost 40 percent of American Catholics, and that proportion is growing steadily. Yet nearly a third of Latinos are Protestant, and there are growing numbers of Latino Pentecostal churches in major cities and in the Southwest. The Catholic Church has not typically been a source of mobilization for Latinos, in part because most attend parishes with European American priests. Both Catholic and Protestant Latinos generally hold conservative positions on social issues like abortion and homosexuality, but it is primarily among Protestants that this translates into greater levels of Republican identification and mobilization.

There have been few studies of the political behavior of American Jews, because most national surveys contain too few for analysis. In chapter 8, Paul Djupe traces changes in Jewish political attitudes, partisanship, and voting behavior over time, combining data from the General Social Surveys. He argues that American Jews have political views that are more diverse than is commonly believed. Yet skepticism about the Republican Party's close association with the Christian Right limits the ability of Republicans to make gains among Jewish voters. The more recent efforts by the Christian Right to support Israel, along with President Bush's strong support for the Jewish state, suggest the possibility that this may change in the future.

One of the fastest-growing but least-understood religious groups in America is the Muslim community. In chapter 9, Paul Djupe and John Green interpret surveys of American Muslims done in 2001 and 2004 to provide one of the first broad profiles of this group's political attitudes and behavior. Djupe and Green argue that despite significant ethnic diversity, American Muslims are largely unified in their liberalism on social welfare questions, their conservatism on moral issues, and their opposition to America's Middle East policy. Since 2001, these foreign policy attitudes, combined with perceived hostility and discrimination from their government and fellow citizens, have come to the fore politically, transforming what was a politically heterogeneous community into a solid Democratic voting block. Whether this partisan uniformity will outlast the Bush presidency and the Iraq war, however, remains unclear.

It is not surprising that most books on religion and politics focus primarily on the politics of the religious, but secularist Americans constitute a growing portion of the public, and their opposition to the Christian Right has provided Democrats with leverage to mobilize their votes. In chapter 10, Louis Bolce and Gerald De Maio explore the politics of secularist Americans. They argue that secularists are united in their antipathy toward Christian fundamentalists, have a coherent political worldview, and constitute a substantial bloc of Democratic elites and voters. Their work has important implications for studies of the culture wars, and it explains the reluctance of Democratic politicians to use religious rhetoric to mobilize political support.

Finally, in chapter 11, Matthew Wilson concludes with an examination of the challenges and prospects for faith-based political action in the years to come. He discusses the increasing diversity of religious belief in America, particularly the emergence in significant numbers of avowedly secularist Americans and the growth of religions outside the Judeo-Christian tradition. He examines the difficult choices confronting religious groups that have traditionally been highly circumscribed in their political activity (like Catholics and Mormons) but that wonder if their quiescence is still tenable in the face of what they see as assaults on traditional values. At the same time, he argues, highly politicized religious groups (like evangelicals and black Protestants) are in some ways growing disenchanted and disillusioned with the sordid compromises of politics. The chapter and the book then conclude with several alternative scenarios for the future role of religion in American political life.

TWO

Evangelical and Mainline Protestants at the Turn of the Millennium: Taking Stock and Looking Forward

Corwin E. Smidt

AMERICAN SOCIETY IS DISTINCTIVELY religious in nature, and religion has played an important role in American politics since the beginning of the republic. This is due in part to the fact that, compared with those in many other Western industrial states, Americans continue to exhibit a high level of religiosity. But even the presence of such religious life and vitality does not, in and of itself, guarantee that religion would play an important role in American politics; it is a necessary but not sufficient condition for it to do so. Rather, the presence of certain distinctive features within the American political system, coupled with unique developments in American society, have enabled religion to play such a central role in American politics (Smidt et al. 2003).

This chapter seeks to analyze the religious life and political significance of two major religious traditions within American politics today: evangelical and mainline Protestants. The chapter begins with a discussion of the concept of religious tradition. It then outlines the characteristic patterns that serve to differentiate the evangelical and mainline Protestant religious traditions. After discussing the data employed to assess the political significance of evangelical and mainline Protestantism, the chapter seeks first to validate the measurement approach employed. It then assesses the political significance of evangelical and mainline Protestants in terms of those factors that serve to contribute to the political significance of any social group—size, issue consensus, politicization, ease of mobilization, and voting cohesion. The chapter concludes by assessing some recent developments within evangelical and mainline Protestantism and how such developments may affect the nature of both religious traditions as well as their relative political significance.

The Analytical Framework of Religious Tradition

As understood here, a religious tradition reflects a characteristic way of interpreting and responding to the world that is evident among people who are affiliated with religious bodies that are interrelated in some historical and organizational fashion. Several implications are embedded in such a definition. First, because the concept of religious tradition denotes some characteristic way of interpreting and responding, not all those within a religious tradition necessarily think alike. Nevertheless, as a whole, members of a particular religious tradition tend to exhibit characteristics that differentiate them from those associated with other religious traditions.

Second, such characteristic patterns are viewed as being linked to people who are affiliated with particular religious bodies that exhibit some historical and organizational linkages. In other words, the concept of religious tradition, as defined here, is understood to be both a religious and a sociological category. Members of a religious tradition are linked together socially, whether through patterns of social interaction, networks of social memberships, weak forms of social ties, or the institutions of which they may be a part. At the core, members are tied together through relatively regular and frequent patterns of social interaction. At the outer limits, members of a religious tradition are linked only weakly through relatively infrequent patterns of social interaction, where characteristic ways of interpreting and responding to the world reflect cultural residues of earlier periods in which greater integration was evident.

Third, membership in a religious tradition is distinct from being a religious traditionalist. Each religious tradition has its traditionalists, but not all members are traditionalists. For example, among Roman Catholics, on one hand, there are traditionalists who subscribe to papal infallibility, to the restoration of the Latin mass, and/or to restricting the priesthood to celibate, male clergy; on the other hand, there are

Catholics who do not subscribe to papal infallibility, who embrace the liturgical changes rooted in Vatican II, and who favor permitting priests to marry and/or allowing women to become priests. Obviously, not all who are part of a religious tradition think and act alike, and some may be part of a tradition without necessarily responding in a traditional manner.

Fourth, religious traditions have a historical legacy. The characteristic way of thinking and responding associated with a tradition develops over time. Religious traditions are not born overnight; they develop and become rooted. Nor do religious traditions bloom and wither within a short span of time. Religious traditions, by definition, have some historical standing.

Fifth, religious traditions are different from religious movements. Traditions can change, albeit slowly. At any point in time, the beliefs that define a tradition, while rooted in a common past, can be modified by present-day factors. In contrast, a social or religious movement seeks change—either to recapture the past or to transform the future. Some religious movements span different religious traditions (e.g., the charismatic movement), whereas others arise within religious traditions (e.g., the movement to restore the Latin mass within the Roman Catholic Church). There may arise, for example, evangelical movement(s) that are tied to, or evident within, the evangelical tradition, but the two are not the same thing. In short, a religious movement is only a segment of the tradition (or a segment that spans several traditions). A religious movement cannot encapsulate a tradition, but it can seek to steer it in a particular direction. Thus, for example, the evangelical tradition is much more diverse and less cohesive than any particular evangelical movement seeking to guide and shape the tradition.

Sixth and finally, although a religious tradition as a framework of analysis is primarily sociological (patterns of social interaction) in its measurement strategy, the use of religious identities reflects a more psychological approach. Members of a religious tradition may not even perceive themselves to be part of that tradition, and thus not self-consciously identify as members. For example, there may be many who by virtue of their denominational affiliation (or even religious beliefs) are evangelical Protestants but who, when asked, do not perceive themselves to be evangelical Protestants; the same may be true for mainline Protestants. Moreover, individuals may adopt particular religious identities which, by virtue of their denominational affiliations, stand outside the religious tradition linked to their specific denominations. When survey respondents are given a list of religious labels from which to choose, there may be those who label themselves as evangelicals even though they are part of mainline Protestantism by virtue of denominational affiliation. Conversely, there may be evangelical Protestants who see their religious life as being typically reflective of American life and may choose, as a result, to label themselves "mainline." Thus, religious traditions and religious identities reflect different conceptual and measurement strategies even when they seek to tap the same general phenomena—namely, identifying which respondents should be labeled evangelical and mainline Protestants. The former, rather than the latter, is the approach adopted here.

Evangelical and Mainline Protestantism

Evangelical and mainline Protestantism are two major, deeply rooted traditions within American religious life. Broadly speaking, each tradition is composed of particular congregations and denominations that are socially and organizationally linked together and whose members share beliefs that constitute a distinct worldview (Kellstedt et al. 1996). However, because each religious tradition is composed of diverse elements and because social and organizational ties within each tradition vary from religious body to religious body, these categories capture general characteristics.

In certain ways, evangelical Protestantism can be viewed both to have preceded mainline Protestantism as well as to have arisen out of it. At its core, evangelicalism is the school of Protestant Christianity that emphasizes personal salvation through Jesus Christ and regards the Bible as the final authority on all matters of faith and practice (Quebedeaux 1974). During the nineteenth century, evangelicalism constituted the dominant form of religious expression in America (Coleman 1980). Indeed, evangelicalism's ethical and interpretive system permeated American culture to such an extent that "the story of American evangelicalism is the story of America itself in the years 1800 to 1900" (McLoughlin 1968, 1). Thus, an evangelical tradition has existed within American religious life for several centuries and continues to exist today.

The division of American Protestantism into the evangelical and mainline traditions began after the Civil War and finally led to major institutional changes that transpired during the 1920s.[1] These institutional changes were the result of the fundamentalist/modernist debate that culminated in the Scopes "monkey trial" of 1925. Following the trial, when many denominations split in the wake of various theological divisions linked to that debate, many evangelical Protestants left their historic denominations and formed what they deemed to be more orthodox churches and denominations. In so doing, evangelical Protestants became, at least in the short term, located largely outside the mainstream of American society, while mainline Protestants remained at the center of American culture, holding positions of influence and power.[2]

Even today, evangelical and mainline Protestants continue to differ in terms of certain characteristic ways of interpreting and responding to the world they inhabit (Coleman 1980; Fowler and Hertzke 1995; Wald 2003). First, biblical beliefs and practices differentiate the two traditions. Evangelical Protestants emphasize that the Bible *is* the Word of God, whereas mainline Protestants have been more willing to hold that the Bible either *contains* the Word of God or *becomes* the Word of God to the believer. Second, evangelical Protestants tend to be exclusivist theologically, whereas mainline Protestants tend to be more universalistic in their religious perspective, noting that there may be "many roads unto salvation." Third, evangelicals tend to emphasize religious conversion, a "born again" experience, as necessary for salvation; mainline Protestants are less likely to view conversion as specific in time and place, typically describing personal belief in terms of being nurtured in the faith, religious commitment, or simply church membership. Fourth, evangelical Protestants are more oriented toward sharing their faith than mainline Protestants, whereas the latter are more likely to espouse the "Social Gospel" of reform.

Evangelical and mainline Protestants differ not only in terms of their theology but also in terms of their worship style. In mainline Protestant churches, one is less likely to hear fiery sermons on sin and damnation and more likely to hear scholarly discussions related to the meaning of divine incarnation or the ethical insights of Jesus' teaching. Within mainline Protestant churches, services are likely to be rather orderly, with well-prepared choral and organ music. Within evangelical Protestant churches, one is more likely to encounter contemporary praise services, informal worship styles, and more "free-flowing" services.

Evangelical and mainline Protestants also differ in terms of their social response as Christians. It has long been noted that American evangelicalism has primarily preached an "individual gospel," emphasizing personal salvation and focusing largely on converting sinners (Marty 1970). For this perspective, true social reform comes through the transformation of individual lives by means of conversion. For many mainline Protestants, however, the ills of society are not simply a function of human depravity; they also reflect structural injustice. Thus, members of the mainline Protestant tradition are much more sympathetic to the idea of the Social Gospel, whereby Christians must address the world's injustices not just with individual charity but also with collective efforts to change social structures (Thuesen 2002). Accordingly, mainline Protestants have been more prone to abandon the historic revivalist emphasis on spiritual conversion in favor of efforts to promote structural reforms. This broader adoption of a Social Gospel theology shapes the more liberal politics linked to mainline Protestantism.[3]

Finally, evangelical and mainline Protestants differ in terms of the organizational affiliations of the denominations of which they are a part. The Social Gospel was also, in part, a bureaucratic and ecumenical phenomenon, and "the bureaucratic, establishment mentality of mainline Protestants . . . was clearly evident" in the establishment of the Federal Council of Churches and later in the founding of the National Council of Churches (Thuesen 2002, 44). Consequently, mainline denominations are linked to the National Council of Churches, whereas evangelical denominations often belong to the more loosely associated National Association of Evangelicals (Kellstedt, Smidt, and Kellstedt 1991).

Data and Methods

This assessment of the relative political significance of evangelical and mainline Protestants at the turn of the millennium draws on data from several different sources. The primary data source employed in this chapter is the Religion and Politics 2000 survey conducted in the early months of that year. This national, random-sample telephone survey was conducted as part of a major Pew-funded study of mainline Protestantism.[4] The data from this survey not only have a rich variety of variables related to religious affiliations, beliefs, identities, and practices, but the number of respondents in the survey (5,603) ensured large samples of both evangelical and mainline Protestants. In addition to these primary data, data from several other sources are utilized to address certain specific questions about change over time.

In the analysis presented here, members of different religious traditions are identified through their patterns of religious affiliation. Within the United States, six religious traditions have historically dominated in terms of membership. These include evangelical Protestants, mainline Protestants, black Protestants,[5] Roman Catholics, Jews, and secularists.[6] Obviously, there are other groups in American society whose members fall outside of these categories, but their numbers are relatively small as a proportion of the American electorate. In fact, on the basis of the Religion and Politics 2000 survey, more than 85 percent of all Americans fall within the five dominant categories—namely, the three Protestant, the Roman Catholic, and the secularist categories.[7] Throughout the remainder of this chapter, the members of the evangelical and mainline Protestant categories are primarily compared with each other, but the remaining three large religious traditions are also presented so that patterns evident among these two Protestant traditions can be compared with those who fall outside their ranks as well.

Respondents are assigned to specific religious traditions based on precise measures of denominational affiliation. This approach emphasizes sociological patterns of religious affiliation or belonging rather than, for example, adherence to particular theological beliefs, the expression of specific religious identifications, or the manifestation of certain religious behaviors. In so doing, respondents are assigned to religious traditions in terms of the religious networks within which they tend to be enmeshed. Note, in this regard, the use of the black Protestant tradition as a religious category, not a racial one per se.

Primarily on the basis of these denominational measures, respondents were assigned to their appropriate religious tradition category. As a step toward validating these particular assignments, the theological stances of members of the various religious traditions are analyzed in table 2.1.[8] It will be recalled that, theologically, evangelical Protestants are more likely than mainline Protestants to emphasize that the Bible is the Word of God. Second, given the greater authority that evangelical Protestants ascribe to scripture, they are more prone than their mainline counterparts to advance literalism in biblical interpretation as well. Finally, evangelical Protestants tend to be more exclusivist theologically than mainline Protestants, because the latter generally view the Christian faith as one of various paths that might lead to salvation.

These theological differences are evident in table 2.1. First, each of the four Christian traditions analyzed views the Bible as divinely inspired, because nearly 90 percent or more of the respondents in each tradition report agreement with the statement that the Bible is the

TABLE 2.1   The Theological Characteristics of Members of
Different Religious Traditions (percent)

Characteristic	Evangelical Protestants	Mainline Protestants	Black Protestants	Roman Catholics
Agree that Bible is inspired word of God	95	88	96	87
Agree that everything in Bible should be taken literally, word for word	48	22	65	26
Agree that all religions contain some truth about God	66	83	79	87
Agree that Christianity is the best way to understand God	82	72	79	66
Agree that God has been fully revealed to humans in Jesus Christ	91	85	89	83

Source: Religion and Politics 2000 survey, Princeton University; Robert Wuthnow, principal investigator. Data made available on the American Religion Data Archive.
Note: Total N = 5,603 (weighted using weight3, N = 5,262); 2000 data.

inspired Word of God. Nevertheless, evangelical Protestants (95 percent) are more likely than mainline Protestants (88 percent) to agree with the inspired nature of the biblical text. More important, when one turns to the question of whether everything in the Bible should be taken literally, word for word, evangelical Protestants (48 percent) are more than twice as likely as mainline Protestants (22 percent) to agree with the assertion.

When one moves to the relationship of the Christian faith to other major religions, most evangelical Protestants acknowledge, as does Paul in his letter to the Romans, that all people have some knowledge of God and that all religious faiths thus contain some truth about God. Still, evangelical Protestants are much more likely than the other three traditions being examined to express exclusivist views of the Christian faith. For example, though two-thirds of evangelical Protestants (66 percent) hold that all religions contain some truth about God, four-fifths or more of those in the other traditions agree with the statement. In addition, though one-half of evangelical Protestants agree that "all religions are equally good ways of knowing about God," two-thirds or more of the other Christian traditions do so. Finally, evangelical Protestants are the most likely of the four traditions to hold that Christianity is the "best way to understand God" and that "God has been fully revealed to humans in Jesus Christ."

Given the data presented in table 2.1, it appears that the denominational assignments employed to classify respondents into the evangelical and mainline Protestant traditions are validated in terms of the characteristic theological outlooks associated with the two groups. Those classified as evangelical Protestants are more prone than those classified as mainline Protestant to hold higher views of biblical authority and to express exclusivist views of the Christian faith. Having shown that the measurement strategy and assignments employed reveal the expected theological differences between the two traditions in the directions anticipated, we can now move on to analysis of the relative political importance of the two traditions.

Demographic Analysis

Obviously, everything else being equal, social groups that are larger tend to be more important politically than those that are smaller. Consequently, analysis of the political importance of evangelical and mainline Protestants begins with assessing their size within the American electorate. To place this matter within a larger historical context, the distribution of religious traditions within the American electorate in 2000 is compared, as shown in table 2.2, with the distribution of such traditions found in 1964.[9]

Clearly, at the turn of the millennium, evangelical Protestantism and Roman Catholicism are the largest religious traditions in America. Evangelical Protestants (25.8 percent) and Roman Catholics (25.4 percent) each constitute a quarter of the electorate, whereas mainline Protestants (13.9 percent), secularists (14.3 percent), black Protestants (6.2 percent), and those expressing other religious affiliations (14.4 percent) make up the other half. Thus, the ranks of evangelical Protestants are nearly double those of mainline Protestants today.

Many analysts (e.g., Roof and McKinney 1987) have noted that, over the past several decades, mainline Protestants have experienced a significant decline in membership and support, that there has been a growth in religious diversity with American society, and that there have been increasing numbers of those who claim no religious ties. These

TABLE 2.2   Distribution of Religious Traditions
in America over Time (percent)

Tradition	1964	2000
Evangelical Protestants	22.7	25.8
Mainline Protestants	25.5	13.9
Black Protestants	9.9	6.2
Roman Catholics	24.7	25.4
Seculars	10.7	14.3
Others	6.5	14.4
N	1,975	5,262

Sources: For 1964 data, Anti-Semitism in the United States project, Charles Glock, Getrude Selznick, Rodney Stark, and Stephen Steinberg, principal investigators; data made available on the American Religion Data Archive. For 2000 data, Religion and Politics 2000 survey, Princeton University; Robert Wuthnow, principal investigator; data made available on the American Religion Data Archive.

Note: For 1964 data, total N = 1,975. For 2000 data, total N = 5,603 (weighted using weight3, N = 5,262).

changes are clearly evident in table 2.2. First, mainline Protestants made up more than a quarter of the electorate in 1964 and constituted a plurality of Americans at the time (though Roman Catholics trailed close behind). Four decades later, the ranks of mainline Protestants have been cut nearly in half, but Catholics have basically maintained their share of the American electorate and the ranks of evangelical Protestants appear to have grown slightly. Second, increasing religious diversity in America is reflected in the growth of the "other" religious category in table 2.2; in 1964, 6.5 percent of the American electorate was so classified, compared with 14.4 percent in 2000. Third, the size of the secularist component of the American electorate has also increased during the past four decades, having grown from 10.7 percent in 1964 to 14.3 percent in 2000.

Thus, at the turn of the millennium, evangelical Protestants have replaced mainline Protestants as the primary reflection of Protestantism within American religious life (at least in terms of numbers). Despite the significant social and political changes within American society during the past half century, evangelical Protestants have been able to maintain, if not extend, their numbers within the American electorate. Thus, in terms of one key ingredient of the political significance of any social group—its size—evangelical Protestants clearly rank ahead of mainline Protestants.

But sheer numbers are not all that matters; the social characteristics of a group's members also affect its political significance. For example, social groups need generational replacement to survive; as the ranks of a social group are being depleted by the death of older members, they need to be replaced by younger members coming to maturity. Thus, at least in the long term, the relative distribution of age within a social group is important and also affects its political significance.

In addition, the relative level of political resources possessed by a social group and the relative level of political skills within the group are also important. For example, previous research has shown that education is a valuable resource that provides skills important for political participation; those with higher levels of education tend to exhibit greater skills that can be employed in efforts to advance their political goals (Conway 1991). Consequently, the relative level of education within a social group also shapes its political significance, because resources and skills can, to some extent, compensate for smaller numbers in shaping its political significance (Wuthnow and Evans 2002).

Table 2.3 examines the patterns of educational attainment and age distribution among members of different religious traditions in 1964 and in 2000. In 1964, mainline Protestants and secularists were clearly the two religious traditions exhibiting the highest levels of educational attainment, for more than a quarter of the members of both groups reported having had at least some college education. In contrast, fewer than one in five evangelical Protestants and Roman Catholics (19 percent) and just a little more than one in ten (12 percent) black Protestants exhibited such educational attainment at the time. Thus, not only were mainline Protestants more numerous than evangelical Protestants in 1964; they also possessed greater resources and skills derived from their higher levels of educational attainment.

Conversely, black Protestants, Roman Catholics, and evangelical Protestants had the highest percentage of young members within their ranks (30 percent or more), whereas secularists tended to be middle aged or older. In addition, the forthcoming decline in the relative number of mainline Protestants is suggested by the age distribution evident within their ranks in the early 1960s. In 1964, nearly two out of every

TABLE 2.3   The Social Characteristics of Members of Different
Religious Traditions over Time (percent)

Social Characteristic	Evangelical Protestants	Mainline Protestants	Black Protestants	Roman Catholics	Secularists
1964					
Education					
Some college	11	14	7	10	15
College graduate	8	13	5	9	14
Age					
Under 35	30	23	33	33	27
35–55	36	38	38	46	42
56 and above	34	39	29	33	32
2000					
Education					
Some college	26	24	25	24	28
College graduate	19	33	17	25	30
Age					
Under 35	27	21	37	35	48
35–55	43	41	42	41	41
56 and above	30	37	20	24	11

Sources: For 1964 data, Anti-Semitism in the United States project, Charles Glock, Getrude Selznick, Rodney Stark, and Stephen Steinberg, principal investigators; data made available on the American Religion Data Archive. For 2000 data, Religion and Politics 2000 survey, Princeton University; Robert Wuthnow, principal investigator; data made available on the American Religion Data Archive.
Note: For 1964 data, total *N* = 1,975. For 2000 data, total *N* = 5,603 (weighted using weight3, *N* = 5,262).

five mainline Protestants (39 percent) were fifty-six years of age or older, while less than a quarter (23 percent) were under the age of thirty-five. Thus, given the age differences within the ranks of evangelical and mainline Protestants in 1964, time appeared to be more on the side of the former than the latter.

Did the passage of time change these particular patterns and expectations? To a certain extent, yes; in other ways, no. Clearly, educational attainment has risen within American society since World War II, and this increase is evident when one examines the level of education exhibited by members of different religious traditions in 2000. Members of those religious traditions that, in 1964, exhibited the lowest levels of educational attainment now report much higher levels. Today, nearly half of all Roman Catholics (49 percent), evangelical Protestants (45 percent), and black Protestants (42 percent) report having had some college education.

However, despite such educational strides among members of these three religious traditions, mainline Protestants and secularists continue to hold the educational advantage. Though educational attainment among evangelical Protestants, black Protestants, and Roman Catholics has grown, it has also increased among mainline Protestants and secularists, for nearly three out of every five mainline Protestant (57 percent) and secularists (58 percent) today report some college education. Thus, given their higher levels of educational attainment, it may well be that mainline Protestants continue to possess greater political resources and skills than evangelical Protestants. Nevertheless, these particular resources and skills are probably more than offset by the much greater number of adherents currently found within the ranks of evangelical Protestantism.

Moreover, in 2000, black Protestants and Roman Catholics continued to be relatively young, as more than a third reported being thirty-five years of age or younger, though it is the secularists who exhibit the greatest youth, as nearly half (48 percent) of all secularists in 2000 were under the age of thirty-five. Evangelical Protestants continue to be younger than mainline Protestants, but there was also a slight shift in the age distribution among evangelical Protestants between 1964 and 2000, so that today evangelical Protestants are somewhat older than they were in 1964.

Consensus, Cohesion, and Mobilization

Size, resources, and skills are important but not sufficient for political clout. If the members of a large social group are divided politically, holding no distinctive political opinions, then getting the members of that group to the polls does not work to the advantage of any party in building a winning coalition. But the more the members of a particular social group are distinctive and cohesive in their attitudes and opinions, the more likely parties and candidates will be to appeal to their distinctive perspectives in an effort to secure their electoral support.

Previous studies have shown that evangelical Protestants tend to express somewhat different positions than mainline Protestants on major issues of the day (Kellstedt et al. 1994). However, the Religion and Politics 2000 survey does not contain any questions that assess the particular policy positions of the respondents, and, as a result, the relative level of issue consensus exhibited by evangelical and mainline Protestants cannot be directly assessed here. However, the survey does include a variety of questions that assess the extent to which respondents express interest in particular policy matters. Table 2.4, then, examines the relative salience of certain public policy issues among members of different religious traditions, reported at the beginning of 2000. All eleven policy issues included in the survey are analyzed and divided according to whether they fall primarily within the domestic or international arena.

Not surprisingly, members of some religious traditions were more likely than others to indicate that they were quite interested in particular public policies. For example, members of the black Protestant tradition were by far the most likely to indicate that they were interested in issues related to racial equality and aid to the poor. In addition, secularists were distinctive in their relatively high level of interest in issues related to gay rights. However, on certain policy issues, relatively little difference was evident across religious traditions in terms of the level of interest expressed (e.g., campaign finance reform). On other matters, despite some differences across religious traditions, a majority of each of the traditions expressed high levels of interest—on environmental protection, gender equality, aid to the poor, and international peace.

Nevertheless, overall, mainline Protestants were much more likely than evangelical Protestants to indicate that they were "quite interested" in the various policy issues examined. On seven of the eleven issues, mainline Protestants expressed higher levels of interest than evangelical Protestants, with members of the two traditions expressing identical levels of interest on an eighth topic (international human rights).[10] To a certain extent, such differences are likely a function of the educational differences between the two groups, because higher levels of education among mainline Protestants likely contribute to their higher levels of interest in policy matters. Only on issues related to aid to the poor, church-state separation, and relief for the developing world did a higher percentage of evangelical Protestants express interest than mainline Protestants.

A second means of assessing the level of political consensus within a religious tradition is to examine the reported ideological and partisan orientations of its members. Ideologically, evangelical Protestants tend to be the reverse image of secularists, for evangelicals tilt in a con-

TABLE 2.4   The Salience of Different Issues by Religious Tradition (percent quite interested)

Issue	Evangelical Protestants	Mainline Protestants	Black Protestants	Roman Catholics	Secularists
Domestic					
Environmental protection	55	61	60	62	62
Gender equality	52	60	77	59	61
Gay rights	20	26	29	27	37
Racial equality	45	51	83	55	57
Aid to the poor	58	56	82	62	54
Campaign finance reform	28	34	28	28	28
Church-state separation	41	37	43	34	43
Corporate responsibility	39	42	50	41	40
International					
International peace	54	59	70	60	51
Developing world relief	25	23	41	29	23
International human rights	41	41	64	45	39

Source: Religion and Politics 2000 survey, Princeton University; Robert Wuthnow, principal investigator. Data made available on the American Religion Data Archive.

servative direction and secularists in a liberal direction. Among secularists, a plurality (45 percent) are moderates, but self-classified liberals more than double conservatives (38 to 17 percent). Conversely, a plurality of evangelical Protestants (45 percent) are moderates, but self-classified conservatives nearly double liberals (36 to 19 percent). Mainline Protestants, by contrast, are more moderate ideologically. Not only are half mainline Protestants self-classified moderates, but the percentage of self-classified conservatives within their ranks only slightly exceeds the percentage of liberals (27 to 23 percent).

In terms of reported partisan identifications, evangelical and mainline Protestants are the only two religious traditions where a plurality of the members are Republicans. And though mainline Protestants were historically the core of the Republican coalition (Kellstedt and Noll 1990), evangelical Protestants have become more Republican in their partisan identifications than mainline Protestants. Since 1980, there has been a pronounced shift toward increased Republican identifications among evangelicals (Smidt 1993; Kellstedt 1989). As a result, by the turn of the millennium, a higher percentage of evangelical than mainline Protestants expressed identification with the Republican Party (40 vs. 37 percent).

Although political consensus is important in contributing to the electoral significance of a group, it is still not sufficient in itself. Even if the members of a large group are united in their issue positions and partisan orientations, this consensus is of little importance politically if the members choose to abstain from the political process. Obviously, the more the group's members choose to make the effort to go to the polls and cast their ballots, the more important the group is politically.

Historically, evangelical Protestants were less likely than their nonevangelical counterparts to be politically involved (Liebman and Wuthnow 1983). In the late 1970s and early 1980s, however, considerable efforts were made to register evangelical Protestant voters and to get them to the polls. Is there any evidence, then, to suggest that these efforts at politicization have succeeded? Table 2.5 analyzes the level of politicization among members of different religious traditions. It does so in terms of psychological engagement (whether or not one follows politics most of the time), voter registration, voter turnout, and four additional, frequently asked questions related to specific acts of political participation.

Mainline Protestants tend to be the most engaged politically, whereas secularists, despite their relatively high level of education, tend to be the least engaged.[11] This is true whether one assesses psychological engagement in politics, reports of whether or not one voted in the previous election, or some combined measure of participation. Obviously, mainline Protestants make up, in part, for their smaller numbers by their higher levels of political engagement.

Evangelical Protestants trail mainline Protestants in their level of political engagement. Of the five traditions examined in table 2.5, however, evangelical Protestants generally rank second in their level of political participation. Given these patterns, it would seem that evangelical Protestants have discarded much of their earlier abstention from the political process. Though mainline Protestants continue to be more politicized than evangelical Protestants, it would appear that evangelical Protestants have closed the gap during the past several decades.

TABLE 2.5   Politicization by Religious Tradition (percent)

Measure of Politicization	Evangelical Protestants	Mainline Protestants	Black Protestants	Roman Catholics	Secularists
Follow politics most of the time	42	49	39	38	35
Registered to vote	84	88	87	80	76
Voted previous presidential election	76	78	80	69	62
Attended rally/meeting	11	15	11	11	11
Worked for campaign	7	6	11	6	5
Gave money	13	18	9	12	10
Contacted public official	29	30	22	25	27
High score (3 or more activities) on a cumulative index of the six acts of political participation listed above	36	43	34	33	30

Source: Religion and Politics 2000 survey, Princeton University; Robert Wuthnow, principal investigator. Data made available on the American Religion Data Archive.

Even if a group is relatively large, holds distinctive political attitudes, and turns out at the polls in relatively large numbers, such a group could still be relatively unimportant politically if its members choose to vote on the basis of different issues that move them to cast their ballots in different partisan directions. To serve as an important component of an electoral coalition, a group must vote in a relatively cohesive fashion.

Table 2.6 examines the partisanship of members of different religious traditions in the 1996, 2000, and 2004 elections. Because the Religion and Politics 2000 survey employed in this chapter was conducted in the early months of that year, it was of course unable to ascertain how respondents would vote in either the 2000 or 2004 elections. Consequently, to assess the voting behavior of evangelical and mainline Protestants in the two most recent elections, different surveys are employed for table 2.6.[12]

It is clear that evangelical and mainline Protestants are the two religious traditions most closely aligned with Republican Party. Black Protestants are clearly the most Democratic of the five groups. Though they trail black Protestants, secularists are clearly solidly Democratic

TABLE 2.6   Partisanship by Religious Tradition (percent)

Vote	Evangelical Protestants	Mainline Protestants	Black Protestants	Roman Catholics	Secularists
1996 election					
Presidential vote					
Dole	39	36	6	25	17
Clinton	38	47	88	57	62
Other	23	17	6	18	22
Congressional vote					
Republican	55	54	10	37	26
Democrat	38	40	86	54	59
Other	7	6	4	9	15
2000 election					
Presidential vote					
Bush	70	55	7	42	33
Gore	28	39	92	53	54
Other	2	7	1	5	13
Congressional vote					
Republican	69	59	14	44	28
Democrat	29	38	85	52	68
Other	2	3	1	4	3
2004 election					
Presidential vote					
Bush	78	50	17	52	28
Kerry	22	50	83	47	70
Other	*	*	*	1	2
Congressional vote					
Republican	74	52	19	51	29
Democrat	25	45	77	46	68
Other	1	3	5	3	3

Sources: For all three elections, postelection survey, University of Akron. For 1996 election: Second National Survey of Religion and Politics. For 2000 election: Third National Survey of Religion and Politics. For 2004 election: Fourth National Survey of Religion and Politics. *Note:* * = less than 1 percent.

as well. Roman Catholics have generally remained more Democratic than white Protestants when one examines the last three presidential elections, though such support slipped consistently with each election so that by 2004 Catholics, as a whole, voted more Republican than Democratic in both the presidential and congressional contests.

Although evangelical and mainline Protestants are clearly the most Republican of the five traditions, evangelicals are more heavily Republican than are the mainline Protestants. In 1996, evangelical Protestants were only marginally more Republican than mainline Protestants in their voting patterns, with the latter trailing the former in their Republican voting by a few percentage points. In 2000, both evangelical and mainline Protestants were more Republican than they had been in the previous election. Still, evangelical Protestants were clearly more supportive of Bush and Republican candidates for Congress than were mainline Protestants. Though a majority of mainline Protestants reported voting for Bush and for the Republican candidate for Congress in the 2000 election, more than two-thirds of evangelical Protestants reported doing so. By 2004, evangelical Protestants clearly eclipsed mainline Protestants in their support both for Bush and for Republican candidates running for Congress.

Conclusion

During the past forty years, important changes occurring within American society have affected the relative political significance of evangelical and mainline Protestants. Evangelical Protestants have maintained, if not increased, their share of the American electorate, while the proportion of mainline Protestants has diminished dramatically. Moreover, evangelical Protestants enjoy certain political advantages over mainline Protestants in several other important factors—their greater level of voting cohesion and, because of their more regular attendance at worship services, the relative ease of contacting them as a means of mobilizing them to political engagement.

Conversely, mainline Protestants enjoy particular political advantages over evangelical Protestants. First, by virtue of their higher levels of educational attainment, mainline Protestants, as a whole, tend to possess greater political resources and skills. In addition, mainline Protestants tend to be more interested in political matters generally and find a broader array of political issues to be of interest than do evangelical Protestants. As a result, mainline Protestants exhibit a higher level of political engagement than evangelical Protestants.

Despite their decline in numbers, mainline Protestants remain politically significant. Evangelical and mainline Protestants are the two religious traditions comprising the core of the Republican electoral coalition. Though evangelical Protestants have become the largest component of the Republican base, mainline Protestants still make up a substantial share of the Republican vote and are, therefore, a crucial component of the Republican coalition. At the same time, a substantial and increasing number of mainline Protestants vote Democratic. Thus, mainline Protestants are becoming more important to Democratic success, and, with the breakdown of the old New Deal coalition, it would be unwise for Democratic candidates to ignore their interests.

Although evangelical Protestants remain politically important for Republican success, important social changes occurring within evangelical Protestantism will likely reshape its future political importance. In fact, some of these changes seemingly mirror changes that occurred within mainline Protestantism several decades ago. As a result, it is unclear whether the unity that historically held evangelicalism together is dissolving (Penning and Smidt 2002), for four main reasons.

First, the ongoing decline of denominationalism that affected mainline Protestantism early is likely to be more strongly encountered within evangelical Protestant denominations in the near future. In other words, the decline in denominational loyalties that mainline Protestantism experienced over the past forty years will become a greater challenge for evangelical Protestantism as congregational loyalties and resources will stand increasingly in tension with denominational loyalties and financial obligations.

Second, there will be growing diversity within evangelical Protestantism due to growing immigration. For example, the growing number of Hispanic and Asian immigrants in this country is coloring evangelical Protestantism in new, and different, ways. Many Hispanic Protestants attend Pentecostal churches, which are rooted in the evangelical Protestant tradition. Likewise, many Asian Christians (particularly Koreans) have aligned their congregations with evangelical Protestantism. Though such changes can lead to a revitalization of the tradition religiously, such growing diversity will likely make it more difficult for the tradition to maintain its relatively high levels of issue and voting cohesion politically.

Third, the relationship between evangelical Protestantism and the Christian Right organizations appears to be in an important period of transition, given the important organizational changes transpiring within the Christian Right. Though the political positions of evangelical Protestants, as a whole, are much broader and more politically diverse than those espoused by the Christian Right, it is also true that the core of the Christian Right is composed of evangelical Protestants. In fact, Christian Right organizations, such as the Moral Majority and the Christian Coalition, appear to have played an important role, over the past several decades, in mobilizing many evangelical Protestants into political life. However, the rapid demise of the Christian Coalition, the "premier" organization of the Christian Right, raises questions about the extent to which evangelical Protestants will remain politicized and mobilized electorally. In other words, the demise of such organizational capacities coupled with the call of some Christian Right leaders (e.g., Thomas and Dobson 1999) to make political life less of a priority makes a continuation of the current level of evangelical political engagement less than certain.

Fourth and finally, important changes have been occurring within and across religious traditions generally. For example, evangelical Protestants have historically been among the most anti-Catholic of the Protestant groups, but over the past decades there has been growing acceptance of, and cooperation with, Roman Catholics within the tradition. This growing accommodation, if not outright embrace, of Roman Catholics is likely the result of various changes that have been taking place within American society—including a growing relativism in social morality, higher levels of education among evangelical Protestants, and efforts by elites within both religious traditions to find common ground.[13]

Such efforts to find common ground across religious traditions have not been confined to evangelical Protestants and Roman Catholics. By the end of the twentieth century, theological divisions within religious traditions (between traditionalist and modernist elements) had begun to rival old ethnocultural boundaries in political importance (Wuthnow 1988; Kellstedt et al. 1999). Accordingly, it is "now easier in some cases for Catholics and conservative Protestants to find common moral ground than for warring Protestants within the same denomination to achieve consensus" (Thuesen 2002, 47). As a result, traditionalists in each religious group are now much more likely to be aligned with the Republican Party, whereas nontraditionalists are more prone to Democratic attachments; in some cases, the political differences *within* religious traditions exceed the gaps *between* traditions (Kellstedt et al. 1999).

Thus, membership within religious traditions continues to remain important politically, but it is less clear whether it will continue to be so several decades from now. On the one hand, despite many social and cultural changes, religious traditions have long endured within

American society and even now continue to shape the political responses of those associated with each tradition. On the other hand, a new religious order in American politics may be emerging, one in which theological divisions within and across religious traditions move to create new political cleavages that transcend, though perhaps not fully replace, the old political cleavages associated with membership in different religious traditions.

Notes

1. For a brief discussion of this history, see Guth et al. (1997, 8–12).

2. At the same time, narrower evangelical movements have waxed and waned over time, and some continue to exist today.

3. E.g., Sweet (1989) identifies three "modernist" sources of meaning: ecumenism, "actionism," and pluralism.

4. Robert Wuthnow of Princeton University served as the principal investigator of the study. The data were made available through the American Religion Data Archive.

5. Separation of black Protestantism from the evangelical and mainline traditions has been a common practice. E.g., see Kellstedt et al. (1996) and Guth et al. (1998). In addition, Wald (2003, 171–72) argues that "by virtue of its historical situation, social role, and organizational independence, black Protestantism requires separate treatment."

6. In the future, Muslims may need to be added to this list. There has been considerable debate over the size of the Muslim community in the United States, with estimates varying greatly. In any case, the percentage of Muslims in this country has clearly grown over the past thirty years, largely through immigration. See chapter 9 of this volume for a more thorough discussion.

7. This is evident from the data presented in table 2.2 found later in the chapter.

8. Given that these questions related primarily to the Christian faith, only those respondents who are members of the four Christian religious traditions are analyzed.

9. This particular date was chosen due to the availability of a national survey that contained relatively precise denominational measures that enabled the construction of a comparable religious tradition measure approximately four decades earlier. The study employed was the Anti-Semitism Study of October 1964. The study involved 1,975 respondents.

10. In fact, on six of the eight domestic issues examined, evangelical Protestants, of all the religious traditions examined, expressed the lowest levels of interest.

11. Seculars tend to be the least engaged politically, in part because of their relative youth and because, in comparison with the other religious traditions, they tend to be social "isolates."

12. Here I use the third quadrennial Survey of Religion and Politics, conducted by the University of Akron Survey Research Center for the Ethics and Public Policy Center, and sponsored by the Pew Charitable Trusts. For additional information on this survey, see Guth et al. (2001). I wish to thank the other investigators for the use of these data here.

13. An example of this latter point is the "Evangelicals and Catholics Together" statement, signed in 1994 (with a follow-up in 2005) by a number of prominent Catholic and evangelical intellectuals, that affirmed a common conservative stance on abortion and other issues.

THREE

Whither the Religious Left?
Religiopolitical Progressivism
in Twenty-First-Century America

Laura R. Olson

After the 2004 presidential election, much was made of conservative Christian voters' role in the reelection of George W. Bush to a second term in the White House. The much-touted exit poll finding that moral values were the most important election day concern of 22 percent of voters highlights the fact that a sizable number of Americans expect political leaders to offer a prophetic vision. Many observers might assume that such a prophetic vision can and does come only from the Religious Right. Yet this expectation of moral leadership by politicians is neither new nor the sole historical province of the Republican Party.

Through much of the twentieth century, politically influential religious voices envisioned Jesus Christ as a champion for the poor and disadvantaged. During the civil rights movement, thousands of liberal white clergy and laity linked arms with African Americans. The 1970s saw clergy-led protests against the Vietnam War and inequality in urban housing policy, and in the 1980s religious progressives worked for nuclear disarmament and illegally sheltered refugees from war-torn Latin America. Things changed, however, when the "new Christian right" (as it was then called) emerged and began reshaping the meaning of morality politics by emphasizing abortion and homosexuality more than economic justice and racism. Religious progressives remained complacent as the political zeitgeist slowly shifted to favor religious conservatives. In this sense, the religious left may have been victimized by its own success—perhaps it assumed that a progressive witness would forever remain the leading political voice of religious Americans.

Over the past several decades, American academics and journalists have paid substantial attention to the "Religious Right." This movement of politically engaged evangelical Protestants, which came into being in the late 1970s, has had its voting behavior, issue agendas, participation patterns, and interest-group activism studied in great detail (among others, see Green et al. 1996; Liebman and Wuthnow 1983; Moen 1992; Oldfield 1996; Wilcox 1992). Is there also some semblance of a "religious left" in the United States, attempting to do battle with the Religious Right? Or are the Religious Right's main opponents secular? Virtually no attention has been paid to a "religious left" in the past few decades. As Martin Marty (1999) observed, "[Perhaps] the religious left flies stealthily low and gets unnoticed. Or [maybe] there is not much of a religious left about which to speak." This chapter identifies the forces that might constitute an American religious left, and it explores why it has been so little discussed in recent times.

The religious left today is difficult to describe because it is anything but a unified political movement. Instead, to the extent that it exists at all, it is a loosely knit coalition of religious people who approach politics from a liberal/progressive vantage point. "There is no one entity called 'the religious left.'. . . [Instead], many different groups . . . advocate a range of issues with common themes of peace, justice, and support for the disenfranchised" (Alpert 2000, 2). Intertwining themes of liberalism—theological and political—tend to define the religious left. These twin liberalisms by their very nature increase the diversity and lack of cohesion that characterize the religious left. Theological liberalism in particular means that differences in religious viewpoints are not just tolerated but also celebrated. And whereas political liberalism has seemed to attach to religious liberalism over the years, it is incorrect to assume that all politically liberal believers are theological liberals. To wit, the *evangelical* left is a growing component of the broader religious left, yet almost no evangelicals would be considered theological liberals.

It is therefore a tricky business to determine who is, and who is not, a part of the religious left. Even arriving at a clear, descriptive, and inoffensive label for people who hold some combination of liberal religious and political views is a difficult task. Many people who advocate a leftist religiopolitical voice prefer to avoid the label "religious left" altogether. Some have attempted to adopt the label "mainstream," with little success. I shall use the label "religiopolitical progressive," and occasionally, "the religiopolitical left."

In this chapter, I explore the possible components of religiopolitical progressivism in the United States today. After a brief exploration of the history of the religiopolitical left, I launch a search for religiopolitical progressives at both the elite and mass levels. At the elite level, sympathetic homes for religiopolitical progressivism exist in several easily identifiable locations. At the mass level, however, it is harder to identify people who might identify comfortably with any sort of religiopolitically progressive movement. Using data from a recent survey of over 5,600 Americans, I seek out potential religiopolitical progressives, characterize their political attitudes and behaviors, and assess their potential for political mobilization.

A Brief History of Religiopolitical Progressivism in the United States

The roots of the religiopolitically progressive worldview lie in the fundamentalist/modernist split that reached its peak in the 1920s (Marty 1970; Wuthnow 1988). With the dawn of industrialism and Darwinism came a divergence in American Protestantism over the extent to which religious beliefs ought to be reconciled with expanding scientific knowledge and modernity in general. Most of the major Protestant denominations in the United States ultimately chose to accommodate themselves to modernity, driving away many who wished to preserve more traditional, fundamentalist worldviews. Those on the modernist side of this split were the antecedents of today's religiopolitical progressives. They favored adapting their faith to the modern world and eschewed strict adherence to traditional scriptural interpretation. Many modernists also embraced a sociopolitical agenda known as the Social Gospel, which encouraged Christians to be active in *this* world by challenging the injustices of industrial capitalism and viewing Jesus

Christ as a champion of the disadvantaged (Niebuhr 1951). Involvement by the faithful in the broader society was not just tolerated; it came to be encouraged and expected.

Fundamentalists separated themselves from mainline Protestantism because of the theological errors they perceived in accommodation to modernity. Nevertheless, the Social Gospel tradition, as it came to be known, took root in many American religious circles, and the political orientations of some Protestant denominations were quite transformed. The Social Gospel imperative to assist the downtrodden was given new life in the 1950s and 1960s, when thousands of white clergy and laity linked arms with African Americans to demand justice and equality in the South (Campbell and Pettigrew 1959; Chappell 2004; Findlay 1993; Friedland 1998). Civil rights activism gave way to antiwar protests in the 1970s (Hall 1990; Quinley 1974), which were in turn replaced by activism against the policies of President Ronald Reagan in the 1980s. Religiopolitical progressives fought Reagan through the nuclear freeze movement and the sanctuary movement, which was designed to give shelter to refugees of war-torn Latin America, where the Central Intelligence Agency and other covert forces were trying to overthrow socialist governments (Smith 1996). Indeed, Allen Hertzke (1988), among others, has argued—correctly—that most religiopolitical activism in the United States originated from the left until at least the late 1970s. This fact makes the absence of the religious left from discussions of contemporary religion all the more curious.

Since the late 1970s, the Religious Right has become a "lead story" for scholars and journalists alike because since its inception the movement has actively sought notice. Meanwhile, religiopolitical progressives seem to have become rather complacent. For decades they may have taken for granted that a Social Gospel–style witness was the dominant religious force in American politics—and because of this complacency, the Religious Right successfully swept it off the stage. In this sense, the religiopolitical left may have been victimized by its own success. Equally important is political context: In the 1980s political conservatism became more accepted and prominent in the United States. The ascendancy of conservatism understandably disadvantaged the religiopolitical left, because for the first time in decades, it could no longer count on lobbying a government that would for the most part be sympathetic to its policy goals.

Religiopolitical Progressivism as an Agenda

What does it mean, in terms of specific policy goals, to be a religiopolitical progressive? Several issue sets create a broad-based consensus among religiopolitical progressives (Wuthnow and Evans 2002). For decades they have displayed great unity in the struggle for socioeconomic justice. True to their roots in the Social Gospel tradition of the 1920s, religiopolitical progressives have long concerned themselves with what Jesus called "the least of these"—the poor and disadvantaged. Religiopolitical progressives tend to favor a national health care plan and "economic empowerment" for people who are socioeconomically challenged. They have opposed welfare reform quite vehemently, and they continue to fight for a "fair living wage." They favor government-sponsored job training programs for the unemployed, and they have long stood in solidarity with organized labor.

To a lesser extent, religiopolitical progressives also share a commitment to equal rights for disadvantaged minority groups in the United States (Wuthnow and Evans 2002). They tend to support affirmative action and have long supported African Americans' fight for equal rights. The civil rights movement might not have succeeded so dramatically without the support and involvement of religiopolitical progressives. In recent years this commitment to equality has extended to advocacy for gay and lesbian rights, though this is less universally accepted.

Several other issue areas round out the political agenda of the religiopolitically progressive movement. As advocates for a high wall separating church and state, many religiopolitical progressives have opposed voucher programs that would assist poor families wishing to send their children to religious schools. They have expressed concern about corporate responsibility and compassionate investing (Robinson 2002). Internationally, they have advocated debt relief for developing nations, nuclear disarmament, open immigration laws, and environmental protection. Most recently, they have been concerned with civil liberties during the "war on terror" that the United States has been waging since September 11, 2001.

This agenda, of course, looks suspiciously similar to that of the secular left. To be sure, religiopolitical progressives have for decades worked side-by-side with secular groups that share their agenda. Yet the religiopolitical left is primarily motivated by their belief that to be faithful to God's teachings, individuals in this world must devote themselves to the care and protection of all of God's creation, in particular people who cannot take care of themselves adequately and who are often left behind by the twin engines of democracy and capitalism.

The Religiopolitically Progressive Movement at the Elite Level

When considering who should bear the label "religiopolitical progressive," it is essential to distinguish between the elite and mass levels. It is relatively easy to identify religiopolitical progressives at the elite level, because there are several obvious institutional settings where they may be found. The interest group universe is one such institutional setting. Many interest groups exist today that undertake conventional political activism (primarily in the form of lobbying) informed by theological and political liberalism. A few of these are broad-based groups that pursue a diverse progressive agenda but face criticism for trying to be "all things to all people." The best known of these broad-based groups is the Interfaith Alliance, which presents itself as a direct opponent of the Religious Right, as well as the Progressive Religious Partnership, founded in 2001. Sojourners, a liberal group headed by the evangelical pastor and activist writer Jim Wallis, gained substantial visibility during the 2004 election campaign when it sponsored a series of advertisements proclaiming that "God is not a Republican . . . or a Democrat." Call to Renewal and Evangelicals for Social Action, both of which are anchored in evangelical Protestantism, also focus on a wide range of issues. Other groups—such as the anti-hunger lobby Bread for the World, the National Religious Partnership for the Environment, the National Interfaith Committee for Worker Justice, and the Religious Coalition for Reproductive Choice—key on single issues and thus sometimes meet with more success than wide-ranging groups. Also important to consider is the interfaith National Council of Churches of Christ in the USA (NCC) and its state-level equivalents. The NCC, founded in 1950, claims thirty-six member religious bodies that endorse its ecumenical work. It pursues broad, ambitious, liberal political agendas, including the amelioration of poverty and racism, the protection of the environment, and the promotion of peaceful conflict resolution.[1]

Organized religious bodies themselves engage in elite-level progressive politics. In the United States, religiopolitical progressivism has found adherents in many mainline, Anabaptist, and African American Protestant denominations, as well as in the Roman Catholic Church and the Reform, Reconstructionist, and Conservative movements of Judaism. These religious traditions contribute resources to many of the aforementioned interest groups and have also maintained their own lobbying offices in Washington for decades (Adams 1970; Ebersole 1951; Hertzke 1988; Hofrenning 1995; Olson 2002). At times they play important roles in policy debates, particularly over international economic and human rights issues, but they rarely exercise a great deal of political power.

Although there has not been a great deal of unconventional, social-movement-style activism on the part of the religiopolitical left in recent years, a rich history of such involvement exists. The best-known social movement activism by religiopolitical progressives, of course, came during the civil rights movement, but there are many other examples ranging from the struggle against racial apartheid in South Africa to the movement to halt the Vietnam War. In recent years, there has been a social movement–style flavor to local-level organizing in large cities (and now less urban areas as well) by offshoots of the Industrial Areas Foundation (IAF), a network of community organizations that count religious congregations among their key partners. IAF-style organizing is confrontational and unconventional and focuses specifically on addressing economic and other injustices in American neighborhoods. In recent years, other IAF-like organizing networks have also emerged, such as the Gamaliel Foundation, the Pacific Institute for Community Organizing, and Direct Action Research and Training (Alinsky 1946; Hart 2001; Olson 2000; Rooney 1995; Warren 2001; Wood 2002).

It is reasonable to expect that religiopolitically progressive interest groups, religious traditions, and social movements would be adept at mobilizing supporters for their causes at the mass level. After all, activism—or at least support—on the ground fuels most political success. Yet it is not at all a straightforward matter for these organizations and networks to mobilize support at the mass level, primarily because it is not clear that there is such a thing as a coherent (much less cohesive) set of religiopolitically progressive Americans on the ground.

Identifying Religiopolitical Progressives at the Mass Level

To identify religiopolitical progressives at the mass level, I begin by finding *religious* liberals and then proceed to examine their politics. My reasoning here is that many political liberals do not come at politics primarily from a religious point of departure, whereas religious liberals frequently do apply their theological orientation to their political orientation. Moreover, the religiopolitically progressive movement is most identifiably *religious*—it has been a collection of religious liberals bearing witness to their faith through political advocacy, not vice versa. Religious liberalism must therefore be the starting point.

The most straightforward, but not most preferable, method of identifying people who might classify themselves as religiopolitical liberals at the mass level would be to categorize them solely on the basis of their religious affiliation. Historically in the United States, several religious traditions, most of them quite small, have articulated a highly unified and constrained leftist political agenda. Among these traditions are the Unitarian Universalist Association (UUA), the United Church of Christ (UCC), and the historic "Peace Protestant" Anabaptist denominations, including the Quakers (Friends), Mennonites, and Church of the Brethren. These traditions have long given voice to a social justice agenda in policy debates in Washington and at the state and local levels (Hertzke 1988; Reichley 1985). Yet these traditions are very small, and their numbers may be declining (Finke and Stark 1992; Kelley 1972). In fact, in a recent survey of 5,603 Americans conducted by scholars at Princeton University, only 70 people (1.3 percent) belonged to these five religious traditions combined.[2]

The problem with approaching the religiopolitical left from a purely ecclesiastical perspective is that we ought not assume that all people belonging to these select few religious traditions (the UUA, the UCC, and Peace Protestants) are religiopolitical progressives, or that a leftist witness has not also come from other corners of the religious universe. Indeed, Americans from nearly every religious tradition have at one time or another voiced left-leaning policy preferences informed by their religious beliefs. Most notable are Catholics and Jews, who have long joined with liberal Protestants to fight for social justice (Hertzke 1988), as well as the thriving evangelical left, headed by nationally known figures including Jim Wallis and Tony Campolo. It is wrong to assume that members of a religiopolitical left would come exclusively from certain religious traditions and not from others.

A better way to categorize religiopolitical progressives is to ask survey respondents whether they *self-identify* with the label "religious liberal." The Princeton research team's survey, undertaken between January 6 and March 30, 2000, as one component of a major study of mainline Protestantism, includes several questions that effectively ask respondents whether they consider themselves to be religious liberals. Among those who said their religious affiliation was Protestant or "other," 581 individuals (21.4 percent) said that the term "liberal" best described their religious outlook, as compared with "fundamentalist" (11.1 percent); "evangelical" (13.7 percent); "mainline" (9.6 percent); "none" (35.6 percent); or "other" (1.3 percent).[3] Of the seventy respondents who belong to the five aforementioned religious traditions that have been historically progressive (the UUA, the UCC, and Peace Protestants), only 32 (46.4 percent) identify themselves as liberal, underscoring the importance of finding a better measure of religious liberalism than the proxy of religious tradition.

Another question in the survey asked respondents to characterize their religious views on a six-point scale ranging from "very conservative" (1) to "very liberal" (6). The mean score for respondents of all religious backgrounds was 3.8 (median = 4; standard deviation = 1.7). Fully 966 respondents (17.2 percent) classified themselves as "very liberal," compared with only 696 (12.4 percent) claiming to be "very conservative" in their religious beliefs. It is striking that so many respondents claim the mantle of religious liberalism in light of the fact that so little has been heard in recent decades about any organized activity on the part of the religiopolitical left. At the mass level, at least, it may just be a convenient label for individuals of low religious commitment. Nevertheless, these individuals could claim a secular affiliation or none at all, but do not, suggesting that they have some affinity toward religion of a left-leaning variety.

There are also interesting patterns among these respondents in terms of their religious affiliations. Table 3.1 presents a list of the Protestant and "other Christian" traditions in which at least 20 percent claimed to be "liberal" (as opposed to fundamentalist, evangelical, mainline, none, or other). In this list are some of the usual suspects—and some who are more surprising. Table 3.1 also shows the average scores for various religious traditions—including Catholics, Jews, Mormons, Muslims, Orthodox Christians, and adherents of other religions—on the six-point religious views scale. Table 3.1 again underscores the fact that it is exceedingly difficult to identify potential religiopolitical progressives on the basis of religious tradition alone. Some denominations, such as the Disciples of Christ and the Presbyterian Church (USA), contain a fair number of liberals—but conservatives, either beside them

TABLE 3.1 Traditions with Sizable Numbers of Self-Described Religious Liberals

Tradition (number in sample)	Percent Self-Described Liberals[a]	Mean Score on Religious Views Scale[b]
Peace Protestants		
Church of the Brethren (11)	27	*3.4*
Society of Friends (Quakers) (7)	33	3.9
Mainline Protestants		
American Baptist Churches, USA (30)	23	*3.6*
Christian Church (Disciples of Christ) (7)	43	*2.7*
Episcopal Church (86)	28	3.9
Evangelical Lutheran Church in America (111)	26	3.8
Presbyterian Church (USA) (55)	36	*3.3*
United Church of Christ/Congregationalist (49)	35	3.8
United Methodist Church (311)	28	3.7
African American Protestants		
African Methodist Episcopal Church (25)	20	*4.1*
African Methodist Episcopal Zion Church (3)	33	*3.3*
National Baptist Convention, USA (26)	31	*4.1*
Evangelical Protestants		
Christian and Missionary Alliance (13)	23	*4.0*
Church of God (35)	23	*3.3*
Church of the Nazarene (20)	32	*3.6*
Free Will Baptists (11)	27	*3.1*
Lutheran Church-Missouri Synod (72)	28	3.6
Other		
Unitarian Universalist Association (19)	79	*4.8*
Roman Catholic Church (1,414)	29[c]	3.7
Jews (104)	—	*4.4*
LDS Church (Mormons) (38)	—	3.8
Muslims (41)	—	3.9
Orthodox Christians (17)	—	3.8
Other non-Christian religions (301)	—	*4.1*

Source: Data come from the Religion and Politics 2000 survey, Princeton University; Robert Wuthnow, principal investigator (made available on the American Religion Data Archive). Total N = 5,603.

[a]Respondents who indicated that their religious affiliation was Protestant or "other" were asked which of the following terms best describes them: fundamentalist, evangelical, mainline, liberal, none, or other. Data presented here are percentages of respondents who indicated that "liberal" best described them, for religious traditions in which at least 20 percent claimed that label. (Of the entire sample, 21 percent claimed to be "liberal.")

Continued on next page.

in the pews or in their denominational hierarchy, might be overshadowing their ability to exercise political clout (see Wuthnow and Evans 2002). Moreover, traditionally liberal denominations, such as the Quakers, are not uniformly liberal at the mass level.

For purposes of clarity, from here on I employ only the categorical measure of religious liberalism, with the categories collapsed from six to four (I combine "fundamentalist" and "evangelical" into one category and "none" and "other" into another). By deciding to use the categorical measure, I am forced to code out Catholic and Jewish respondents because the question was asked only of Protestants and people of "other" faiths. Although both Catholics and Jews have been important members of religiopolitically progressive alliances, they differ in important theological ways from Protestants. Also, the Catholic Church is liberal on some issues but conservative on others. Moreover, because the Religious Right is overwhelmingly Protestant, it will be instructive to see whether there is an identifiably liberal alternative to that movement within the Protestant world. Finally, the survey was administered to such a large sample of individuals that it is still meaningful to use the Protestant subsample alone (N = 2,521).

Demographic Characteristics

What are the demographic characteristics of those who claim to be religiously liberal? As table 3.2 reveals, liberals distinguish themselves vis-à-vis people in the other categories as slightly more educated, slightly more likely to be African American, less likely to be married, more likely to be retired, and substantially more likely to be female.

Religious Attitudes

The Princeton survey includes items that tap respondents' views of Holy Scripture as well as their attitudes toward ecumenism, or willingness to

TABLE 3.1   (continued)

[b]All respondents were asked to self-classify their religious beliefs on a 6-point scale ranging from "very conservative" (coded 1) to "very liberal" (coded 6). Data presented here are average scores for respondents in each tradition. The overall sample mean score on the scale is 3.8. Figures in bold italics fall at least 0.2 below this mean and represent particularly conservative religious traditions, whereas figures in regular boldface fall at least 0.2 above the mean and represent particularly liberal religious traditions.

[c]Catholic respondents were asked which of the following terms best describes them: traditional, moderate, liberal, none, or other. The figure presented here is the percentage of Catholics in the sample who indicated that "liberal" best describes them.

TABLE 3.2   Demographic Characteristics of Self-Described
Religious Liberals (percent)

Characteristic	Liberal	Mainline	Fundamentalist or Evangelical	None or Other
*Education**				
Less than high school	5.3	3.4	5.2	11.5
High school graduate	22.5	13.0	26.9	30.7
Some college	22.0	27.2	28.4	25.8
Trade/technical/vocational	4.1	4.2	4.4	4.5
College graduate	26.5	29.5	21.4	16.5
Postgraduate work	16.5	21.1	12.6	9.9
*Race**				
White	83.0	85.1	82.5	75.2
African American	12.7	10.3	10.9	17.8
Asian or Pacific Islander	0.3	0.4	1.0	0.5
Native American	0.5	1.1	1.0	1.4
Other	1.5	2.3	3.0	2.8
*Marital status**				
Single, never married	21.3	13.8	14.8	24.3
Married	53.7	63.6	63.2	50.6
Separated	2.1	0.8	1.5	2.3
Divorced	12.7	11.9	10.8	11.4
Widowed	8.8	8.8	7.8	9.4
*Gender**				
Male	37.5	51.3	42.8	42.6
Female	62.6	48.7	57.2	57.4
*Age** ($F = 12.2$; $p < 0.001$)				
In years	50	50	49	47

Source: Data come from the Religion and Politics 2000 survey, Princeton University; Robert Wuthnow, principal investigator (made available on the American Religion Data Archive). *Note:* *$p < .001$ for chi-square, except as otherwise noted (analysis of variance for age). Total $N = 5,603$; subsample $N = 2,521$ (those whose religious affiliation is Protestant or "other").

work cooperatively with other religious traditions. Using these items, I created two additive indices to measure attitudes toward scripture and ecumenism. The scripture index consists of three items that were posed to respondents as true-false questions and coded as follows:

1. The Bible is the inspired word of God (true = 2, false = 1).
2. Everything in the Bible should be taken literally (true = 2, false = 1).

3. The Bible may contain historical or scientific errors (false = 2, true = 1).

The higher the respondent's score on this index, the higher view he or she has of scripture. Religious liberals should score low, given their openness to alternative interpretations of scripture. Similarly, the ecumenism index consists of four items posed as statements with four-point response sets ranging from "strongly agree" (1) to "strongly disagree" (4). The items are:

1. All religions contain some truth about God (reverse coded).
2. All religions are equally good ways of knowing about God (reverse coded).
3. Christianity is the best way to understand God.
4. Religious doctrines get in the way of truly relating to God (reverse coded).

The higher the respondent's score on this index, the more highly he or she values ecumenism—and thus the more accurately may be described as a religious liberal. Religiopolitical progressives hold favorable attitudes about the notion of interfaith dialogue and cooperation. Table 3.3 displays the relationship between religious self-categorization and the two indices and their components. Self-identifying religious liberals, not surprisingly, take the loosest view of scripture and the most welcoming view of ecumenism. The data presented for the components of the two indices bear these findings out quite clearly. The categorical self-identification measure thus seems to be a valid measure of religious liberalism.

Religious Behavior

Table 3.3 also shows that self-identifying liberals are vastly less observant than people who classify themselves in the other three categories. They attend services far less often; they are least likely to be members of religious congregations; and they read the Bible and pray least frequently. This is not to say that religious liberals are irreligious. The data indicate otherwise. It is just that in comparison with people who do not claim the liberal mantle, liberals appear to be less observant. And it is incorrect to think that their relative lack of religious observance is simply a reflection of declining numbers within mainline

TABLE 3.3   Theological Characteristics and Religious Practices of
Self-Described Religious Liberals (percent)

Characteristic or Practice	Liberal	Mainline	Fundamentalist or Evangelical	None or Other
Scriptural views[a]	4.4	4.6	5.2	4.8
Bible is inspired word*	83.8	88.1	97.8	91.5
Biblical literalism*	25.0	25.3	50.0	39.5
Bible has factual errors*	66.8	60.9	26.8	48.7
Ecumenical views[b]	11.4	10.1	8.7	10.5
All religions have truth*	87.9	77.0	55.9	76.9
All religions lead to God*	78.0	57.1	33.3	61.4
Christianity is best way*	67.3	81.6	90.3	76.8
Doctrines get in the way*	61.7	57.5	54.8	54.7
Religious practices				
Attend services weekly*	29.3	50.2	70.7	40.1
Congregation member*	65.3	76.9	81.3	70.5
Read Bible weekly or more*	31.0	45.6	74.5	41.6
Pray daily*	63.5	72.0	88.0	68.8

Source: Data come from the Religion and Politics 2000 survey, Princeton University; Robert Wuthnow, principal investigator (made available on the American Religion Data Archive).
Note: *$p < .001$ for chi-square. Total $N = 5,603$; subsample $N = 2,521$ (those whose religious affiliation is Protestant or "other").
[a]Values for the "scriptural views" row are average scriptural scale scores. Analysis of variance: $F = 92.4$; $p < .001$. Values for each of the scale components are percentages of each group who said the statement was true.
[b]Values for the "ecumenical views" row are average ecumenical scale scores. Analysis of variance: $F = 132.9$; $p < .001$. Values for each of the scale components are percentages of each group who agreed or strongly agreed with the statement.

Protestantism, because as I have already emphasized, religious liberals fall into many different denominational homes.

Political Attitudes

The Princeton survey included a wealth of questions measuring issue positions, approval of various political practices, and participatory acts. First, does the religiopolitically progressive movement's agenda, as discussed above, trickle down to religious liberals on the ground? In which issues do religious liberals express the greatest interest? The Princeton survey asked respondents to indicate whether they were quite, fairly, or not very interested in eleven domestic and international policy issues. The questions were phrased to capture the respondent's own *position* on the issue more than whether they were interested in the policy area in general. Left-leaning religious traditions, as well as religiopolitically progressive interest groups, have emphasized each of these eleven issues in recent years:

1. legislation to protect the environment,
2. overcoming discrimination against women in our society,
3. reducing intolerance toward homosexuals,
4. achieving greater equality for racial and ethnic minorities in our society,
5. social policies that would help the poor,
6. campaign finance reform,
7. maintaining strict separation between church and state,
8. government policies to promote international peace,
9. relief and development programs for people in countries of the developing world,
10. international human rights issues, and
11. the social responsibilities of corporations.

Table 3.4 shows the percentages of each of the four self-identified groups who say they are "quite interested" in each of these issues. On most of the domestic issues, religious liberals indeed support the long-standing peace-and-justice agenda of the religiopolitically progressive movement. There is much less differentiation, however, when it comes to international issues. Also shown in table 3.4 are average index scores for each of the groups on domestic issues and international issues. In both cases, I created an additive index of respondents' level of support for the religiopolitically progressive agenda in each of the two areas. Self-identified liberals score highest on both indices, and the differences among the groups are significant in both cases.

The next question is whether people who identify themselves as religious liberals are being *socialized* into the agenda of religiopolitical progressivism when they attend religious services. The Princeton survey asked respondents who attended religious services at least a few times a year and who are members of a place of worship whether they had heard a sermon, lecture, or group discussion in their congregation about six different topics. These topics again reflect the long-standing peace-and-justice agenda of religiopolitical progressivism, including:

TABLE 3.4   Issue Positions of Self-Described Religious Liberals (percent)

Issue	Liberal	Mainline	Fundamentalist or Evangelical	None or Other
Domestic[a]	16.6	15.6	15.3	15.6
Environmental protection***	64.5	55.9	48.5	59.9
Gender equality***	66.3	59.0	50.3	58.2
Gay rights***	33.0	22.2	16.7	24.7
Racial equality***	63.0	45.6	50.9	52.0
Aid to the poor**	64.5	54.0	57.8	60.3
Campaign finance reform***	33.0	37.5	34.2	24.8
Church-state separation*	41.5	38.3	42.0	35.9
International[b]	9.2	8.9	9.0	8.7
International peace***	60.6	57.9	53.3	55.6
Developing world relief***	28.1	21.1	31.5	22.7
International human rights***	47.8	40.6	47.5	40.8
Corporate responsibility***	46.0	46.4	41.7	38.2

Source: Data come from the Religion and Politics 2000 survey, Princeton University; Robert Wuthnow, principal investigator (made available on the American Religion Data Archive).
Note: $*p < .05$, $**p < .01$, $***p < .001$ for chi-square. Total $N = 5,603$; subsample $N = 2,521$ (those whose religious affiliation is Protestant or "other").
[a]Values for the "domestic issues" row are average domestic agenda scale scores. Analysis of variance: $F = 18.9$; $p < .001$. Values for each of the scale components are percentages of each group who said they were "quite interested" in each policy goal.
[b]Values for the "international issues" row are average international agenda scale scores. Analysis of variance: $F = 6.4$; $p < .001$. Values for each of the scale components are percentages of each group who said they were "quite interested" in each policy goal.

1. the government's policies toward the poor,
2. protecting the environment,
3. being more supportive of homosexuals,
4. the widening gap between rich people and poor people,
5. improving relations between blacks and whites, and
6. the social responsibilities of corporations.

Table 3.5 lists the percentages of respondents in each of the four groups (liberal, mainline, fundamentalist/evangelical, and none/other) who reported hearing cues about these six policy goals in their congregations during the past year. In each case, self-identified religious liber-

TABLE 3.5   Cues Heard in Congregation by Self-Described
Religious Liberals (percent)

Cue	Liberal	Mainline	Fundamentalist or Evangelical	None or Other
Aid to the poor**	42.0	40.3	31.3	35.6
Environmental protection**	48.6	37.2	32.3	41.9
Support for gays**	22.9	18.9	11.4	13.2
Gap between rich and poor**	42.9	31.1	30.8	31.1
Race relations*	68.0	59.7	58.0	57.0
Corporate responsibility*	26.6	18.9	20.5	19.3

Source: Data come from the Religion and Politics 2000 survey, Princeton University; Robert Wuthnow, principal investigator (made available on the American Religion Data Archive). *Note:* $*p < .01$, $**p < .001$ for chi-square. Total $N = 5,603$; subsample $N = 2,521$ (those whose religious affiliation is Protestant or "other"). Values are percentages of each group who heard each cue in their congregation in the past year.

als were exposed in their congregations to cues emphasizing the political agenda of the religiopolitically progressive movement. This finding reinforces scores of previous studies that emphasize the powerful political-socialization effect of involvement in a religious congregation (Djupe and Gilbert 2003; Gilbert 1993; Wald, Owen, and Hill 1988, 1990).

In light of the socialization that self-identified religious liberals encounter in their religious congregations, is it reasonable to assume that they are more interested in politics in general than people who claim other religious labels? We might expect others, especially fundamentalists and evangelicals, to be more interested in politics than liberals, even though it is evident that liberals do both hear and reflect a relatively consistent peace-and-justice agenda. As it turns out, *mainline* Protestants report the highest levels of interest in government and politics, with 62.0 percent of them saying they "follow what's going on in government and public affairs most of the time." Religious liberals and those in the fundamentalist/evangelical category are both less interested (53.0 and 51.8 percent, respectively). A similar pattern applies to these individuals' levels of voter registration, a plausible proxy measure for political awareness. Mainline identifiers lead the pack with 93.9 percent registered to vote, compared with 89.5 percent of fundamentalists and evangelicals, 87.8 percent of religious liberals, and 84.3 percent of those in the none/other category. The principal explanation for these findings is socioeconomic: It is a thoroughly documented fact that people with high levels of education and income are best attuned to politics (Verba, Schlozman, and Brady 1995). Table 3.2 establishes the high educational attainment of mainline Protestants, and although the Princeton survey did not ask questions about income, previous studies have demonstrated that mainline Protestants tend to be wealthier than people in other religious groupings (Wuthnow 1988). Education and income are highly correlated, and ranking high on both measures explains high levels of political participation (Verba and Nie 1972; Wolfinger and Rosenstone 1980).

And what of the more direct measures of political ideology and partisanship? Results from the survey show that religious liberals are significantly more liberal in their political outlook than people in the other three groups. Political ideology is measured using a six-point scale ranging from "very conservative" (1) to "very liberal" (6), similar to the ordinal measure of religious liberalism discussed above. In fact, these two measures are closely correlated, as we might expect ($r = 0.5$; $p < 0.01$). Religious liberals' average score on this political ideology scale is 4.0, whereas mainline Protestants rank one full point lower at 3.0. Fundamentalists and evangelicals average 2.8. Those in the none/other category come closest to the liberals in their political ideology, with an average of 3.5. These differences are highly significant ($F = 70.3$; $p < 0.01$). More than anything else, this finding reveals a striking disparity between religious liberals and self-identified mainline Protestants, who clearly do not approach politics from a progressive vantage point. Similar results appear for party identification. Religious liberals are the least likely of the groups to identify with the Republican Party (20.3 percent) and are far more likely to prefer the Democrats (42.0 percent). Again they differentiate themselves from mainline Protestants (44.1 percent Republican; 27.6 percent Democrat). Clearly, religious liberals approach politics from a more leftist vantage point than do people with other religious orientations.

Political Participation

The question that might matter most in a practical sense for the religiopolitically progressive movement is whether religious liberals on the ground are likely to take political action. The mere existence of Americans who hold religiopolitically progressive views would by no means constitute a *movement*. Do religious liberals actually get involved in politics? The Princeton survey included questions about whether respondents have taken various political actions in the past year, including

1. contacting a political official,
2. giving money to a political candidate or party,
3. attending a political rally or meeting,
4. attending a class or lecture about social or political issues,
5. working for a political campaign or voter registration drive,
6. reading about social or political issues on the Internet, and
7. voting in the 1996 presidential election.

Table 3.6 displays the percentages of people in each of the four religious categories who said they had engaged in each of these seven activities in the past year. It also displays average scores for each group on an additive participation index, in which respondents scored one point for each of the seven participatory acts. Following the pattern established in the results for political interest, religious liberals trail mainline Protestants on most measures of participation. Liberals' levels of political engagement are roughly equivalent to those of fundamentalists and evangelicals, with those in the none/other category far behind. The primary hypothesis for mainline Protestants' increased level of participation is again demographic, because mainline Protestants are wealthier and better educated.

When it comes to voting behavior, religious liberals stand out as far stronger supporters of former president Bill Clinton than any of the other three groups. Respondents were also asked for whom they would vote "if the 2000 presidential election were held today." Religious liberals were twice as likely as any other group to say they planned to vote for Vice President Al Gore, and they were also most likely to say they favored Senator Bill Bradley. Again, mainline identifiers appear quite Republican with their strong support for then-governor George W. Bush—note that they do not trail fundamentalists and evangelicals by a very wide margin.

Is a Religiopolitically Progressive Movement Conceivable?

The results presented above strongly imply that the real challenge facing religiopolitical progressives is not a lack of Americans who share their policy views—clearly, there are people in the mass public who do seem to embrace a religiopolitically progressive agenda. So what, then, are the main challenges facing a liberal religious movement?

TABLE 3.6   Political Participation by Self-Described Religious
Liberals (percent)

Measure of Participation	Liberal	Mainline	Fundamentalist or Evangelical	None or Other
Cumulative participation[a]	2.3	2.5	2.2	1.7
Contacted official**	32.9	41.0	37.7	23.9
Gave money**	18.4	24.9	17.3	11.8
Attended rally/meeting*	16.0	18.8	17.8	12.0
Attended class/lecture**	28.9	27.2	23.1	19.5
Worked for campaign**	8.6	13.0	9.5	6.0
Read on Internet**	38.2	41.0	34.9	28.6
Voted in 1996**	87.4	93.9	88.3	79.7

Source: Data come from the Religion and Politics 2000 survey, Princeton University; Robert Wuthnow, principal investigator (made available on the American Religion Data Archive). *Note:* *$p < .01$, **$p < .001$ for chi-square. Total $N = 5,603$; subsample $N = 2,521$ (those whose religious affiliation is Protestant or "other").
[a]Values for the "cumulative participation" row are average participation scale scores. Analysis of variance: $F = 30.3$; $p < .001$. Values for each of the scale components are percentages of each group who said they had undertaken each activity in the past year.

Some have argued that the religious traditions in which religiopolitical progressivism historically has thrived have been in numerical decline (Finke and Stark 1992; Kelley 1972), though there is mixed evidence on this point (see Wuthnow and Evans 2002). Moreover, the results presented above suggest that it might not matter much if traditionally liberal denominations are shrinking in size, because those who identify with the religiopolitically progressive movement are not located exclusively within these religious traditions, nor can we assume that historically liberal religious traditions consist of uniformly liberal laity. Yet congregational size ought not to be ignored entirely. If religiopolitical progressives tend to belong to declining congregations, there might be a structural challenge hampering left-leaning Christians politically. Congregations facing survival issues are likely to curtail their participation in political action; they are more likely to turn inward in an attempt to survive. They are also likely to avoid any activities that might be perceived as controversial and that might accelerate the congregation's numerical decline.

The Princeton survey asked respondents who attend religious services at least a few times a year and hold formal membership in a congregation to indicate, first, the size of their congregation, and second, whether the congregation's size had been "increasing, staying about the same, or decreasing in the past few years." Table 3.7 reveals that religious liberals are not at a huge disadvantage when it comes to congregation size, but they do report membership decline in their congregations more than their counterparts in the other three categories. Moreover, liberals' congregations are least likely to be growing. The picture looks less bleak for those who self-identify as mainline Protestants, which suggests that there are many nuances to the story of mainline and liberal Protestant decline (as documented in Wuthnow and Evans 2002). Still, it must be difficult for religiopolitical progressives to mobilize for political action when many of their congregations seem to be facing membership challenges.

Another significant challenge is posed if religious liberals do not *desire* religiopolitical activism on the part of their congregations and clergy. These are, after all, typically strong church-state separationists. If there is little push for activism from the grass roots, those at the elite level face challenges in finding fellow workers for their cause and in legitimately claiming legions of passionate backers on the ground. Both deficiencies are bound to result in political setbacks. The Princeton survey asked respondents whether they desired various forms of political activism by (1) their denomination at large, (2) clergy, and (3) congregations. What follows is an examination of whether self-identified religious liberals favor religiopolitical activism by these three entities.

Respondents were asked whether the "public influence" of their denomination today is stronger, the same, or weaker than it was in the 1960s; whether they would like to see their denomination "doing more to influence public policy in Washington"; and whether they would like the denomination to do "more to influence public policy in your state." Table 3.7 displays the results for all three of these questions. Religious liberals and mainline Protestants are *more* likely than fundamentalists and evangelicals to believe that their denominations are *more* influential now than they were in the 1960s, which would seem to counter the conventional wisdom that these traditions have actually been marginalized in the past few decades. Yet it is also apparent that both religious liberals and mainline Protestants are *less* likely to approve of denominational activism at both the federal and state levels than are fundamentalists and evangelicals—a finding that undoubtedly would have been reversed in the 1960s. One problem plaguing denominational lobbying offices in recent years has been the perception

TABLE 3.7   Congregation Size and Views on Denominational
Relevance among Self-Described Religious Liberals (percent)

Characteristics	Liberal	Mainline	Fundamentalist or Evangelical	None or Other
Congregation size[a]	3.7	4.2	3.6	3.4
Growth/decline*				
Growing	50.3	57.7	64.7	57.9
Staying about the same	32.3	29.6	23.6	32.3
Declining	15.1	10.2	8.8	7.8
Don't know	2.3	2.6	2.8	2.0
Views on denomination's political impact[b]	2.8	3.0	2.6	2.7
Approve Washington lobbying*	33.2	30.3	48.1	36.1
Approve state lobbying*	40.6	38.3	55.6	47.1

Source: Data come from the Religion and Politics 2000 survey, Princeton University; Robert Wuthnow, principal investigator (made available on the American Religion Data Archive).
Note: $*p < .001$ for chi-square. Total $N = 5,603$; subsample $N = 2,521$ (those whose religious affiliation is Protestant or "other").
[a] Analysis of variance: $F = 9.5$; $p < .001$. Values for the "congregation size" row are average scores for a variable coded as follows: 1 = fewer than 100 members; 2 = 100–199; 3 = 200–299; 4 = 300–499; 5 = 500–999; 6 = 1,000–1,999; 7 = 2,000 or more.
[b] Analysis of variance: $F = 6.7$; $p < .001$. Values for the "political impact" row are average scores for a variable coded as follows: "Compared with the 1960s, do you think your denomination is . . ." 1 = a lot stronger now; 2 = a little stronger now; 3 = about the same now; 4 = a little weaker now; 5 = a lot weaker now.

that many laity disapprove of such work, which undercuts the effectiveness of the Washington offices (Olson 2002). The importance of this factor for the religiopolitically progressive movement should not be understated, because all the mainline Protestant denominations—not just predictably liberal traditions like the UUA and Peace Protestants—have long been integral elements of the religiopolitically progressive coalition.

Clergy have long been some of the most influential leaders of the religiopolitically progressive movement (Campbell and Pettigrew 1959; Guth et al. 1997; Hadden 1969; Quinley 1974; Stark et al. 1971). If their congregants felt that they ought not to be involved in political activism, however, their political legitimacy would be threatened. Clergy must maintain the respect and approval of their congregations to protect their job security and effectiveness as religious leaders (Crawford 1995; Crawford, Olson, and Deckman 2001). When clergy get involved in politics, sometimes their congregations do not approve, in which case they often have to scale back their activism. The Princeton survey asked respondents several questions about whether clergy should be involved in politics. First, "Should the leaders of religious organizations keep silent on social and political issues, or should they express their views on these issues?" Second, "Do you think it is ever right for clergy to discuss political issues from the pulpit?" Third, "In the next few years, would you like to see more or less of religious leaders (1) appearing on television talk shows; (2) criticizing elected officials; (3) running for public office; and (4) forming political movements?" Table 3.8 presents results for people in the four self-identified groups on these measures of approval of political activism by clergy. I also created an index that measures approval of all four activities. On all measures, fundamentalists and evangelicals appear to feel more favorably toward clergy activism than do people in the other groups, including religious liberals. Particularly telling is the fact that so few religious liberals approve of clergy criticizing elected officials and forming political movements, both of which were integral parts of the religiopolitically progressive movement's influential past.

And what about activism by congregations? Sometimes laity will feel that they do not want to be led either by denominational officials or by clergy. Perhaps liberal laity approve of *congregational* activism more than *denominational* activism.

The Princeton survey included five items in which respondents were asked whether they favor or oppose religious congregations in their community doing each of the following:

- working with government agencies to provide better services for low-income families,
- receiving government funds to help provide services to the poor,
- making statements to public officials on topics of concern to the community,
- sponsoring meetings to which public officials are invited, and
- forming alliances among different religions, such as Christians, Jews, and Muslims.

Table 3.8 presents the four groups' levels of approval of all five activities independently as well as cumulatively via an additive index

TABLE 3.8   Approval of Clergy and Congregational Political
Activism by Religious Liberals (percent)

Mode or Degree of Activism	Liberal	Mainline	Fundamentalist or Evangelical	None or Other
Clergy should keep quiet**	16.9	19.2	10.9	15.6
Clergy can speak from pulpit**	36.2	39.8	48.2	34.5
Approve clergy activism[a]	5.3	5.5	6.0	5.6
On TV talk shows**	32.0	39.8	51.9	40.1
Criticizing elected officials	24.1	27.0	28.4	22.0
Running for office***	32.7	36.0	58.1	44.8
Forming political movements**	25.0	28.4	41.7	34.8
Approve congregational activism[b]	3.2	3.1	2.7	2.7
Partnering with government*	88.3	88.9	82.4	85.7
Receiving government funds**	70.2	62.8	58.7	73.0
Making statements to officials**	81.2	78.9	84.2	74.8
Sponsoring meetings**	73.3	75.5	79.7	69.9
Forming interfaith alliances**	78.7	78.9	62.6	65.2

Source: Data come from the Religion and Politics 2000 survey, Princeton University; Robert Wuthnow, principal investigator (made available on the American Religion Data Archive).
Note: $*p < 0.05$, $**p < 0.001$, for chi-square. Total $N = 5,603$; subsample $N = 2,521$ (those whose religious affiliation is Protestant or "other"). Values in the first two rows are percentages of those who agree with the statement.
[a]Values for the "approve clergy activism" row are average activism approval scale scores. Analysis of variance: $F = 23.8$; $p < 0.001$. Values for each of the scale components are percentages of each group who said they would like to see *more* clergy engaging in each activity.
[b]Values for the "approve congregational activism" row are average activism approval scale scores. Analysis of variance: $F = 9.5$; $p < 0.001$. Values for each of the scale components are percentages of each group who said they favor congregations engaging in each activity.

that combines them. This time, religious liberals and mainline Protestants appear to *favor* activism more than their counterparts, except when it comes to making statements to public officials and sponsoring meetings to which such officials are invited (although one might argue that these are the only truly *political* activities on the list). In both cases, fundamentalists and evangelicals are most likely to approve. Notice, too, that liberals are more approving of receiving government funds than either mainline Protestants or fundamentalists and evangelicals. As is the case for mainline Protestants, religious liberals' tradition of ecumenism leads them to favor interfaith alliances, now a dominant paradigm of local-level activism on behalf of the poor. When it comes to local-level antipoverty activism, then, religious liberals appear to be leading the way.

Finally, how satisfied are religious liberals with today's status quo? It might be that today's religiopolitical progressives do not share the previous generation's conviction that there are things about American society that *need* to change. In the heyday of the religiopolitically progressive movement, there were many social problems that religious liberals felt deeply compelled to solve politically. Is that still the case, or are religious liberals now complacent about changing the status quo? To assess this, I use a question from the Princeton survey that asks respondents "How satisfied are you with the way things are going in our society today?" The survey data show that religious liberals are substantially *more* satisfied with the social status quo than are people in other groups. Fully 61.5 percent of religious liberals are at least fairly satisfied with the status quo, as compared with 55.6 percent of mainline Protestants and only 36.7 percent of fundamentalists and evangelicals. It often takes a certain "fire in the belly" that stems from deep dissatisfaction with the status quo to move people to political action (Marx and McAdam 1994; Miller et al. 1981). That most religious liberals believe things in America today are going fairly well may explain, at least in part, why the religiopolitically progressive movement has had so little recent visibility.[4] Perhaps the movement is a victim of its own success, lulled into complacency as a result of its previous policy victories.

Conclusion

Religiopolitical progressivism was born of twentieth-century America and came to shape the history and culture of that era in profound and lasting ways. Whether this impulse in American religious and political life is still viable in the twenty-first century, however, is an open question. This chapter has shown that it is premature to begin a deathwatch for religiopolitical progressivism. But at the same time, we must acknowledge that the movement faces significant challenges if it hopes to recapture its past political, social, and moral influence in the United States. These challenges revolve primarily around two thorny themes: a lack of mobilization and an inhospitable political context.

The foregoing analysis shows that there are identifiable nuclei of religiopolitical progressivism in American society today. Yet there are practical reasons to believe that religiopolitical progressives on the ground are not well connected either with each other or with the elite-level organizations that share their policy agenda. In part, this lack of connection is due to the strong possibility that religious liberals' congregations are in numerical decline, which makes it challenging for them to organize for any kind of sociopolitical action. The lack of connection may also be due in part to the astonishing lack of belief among mass-level religious liberals that the status quo needs to change. If there is no impetus for change coming from the mass level, then elite-level organizations are bound to find mobilization (and even fund-raising) difficult. The religiopolitical left may also be stymied by the fact that many of its clergy and other elites endorse what might be termed "scriptural relativism." Because there is no one authoritative interpretation of scripture, clergy and other religious leaders are not widely viewed as authoritative speakers on most subjects, and it is therefore hard for them to have much success in attempts to mobilize others for political action. Finally, some might argue that the religiopolitical left is hindered by its long-standing support for a high wall between church and state. Many religiopolitical progressives would argue that their work is designed to address *social*, as opposed to political, problems. But this does not negate the very real mobilizational problem that results when religious elites vehemently argue that church and state should not be excessively entangled yet ask the people in the pews to take political action to address injustice.

An additional challenge is that the dominant macro-level political story of the end of the twentieth century (and the beginning of the twenty-first) has been the ascendancy of conservatism after the New Deal and Great Society eras. The trending away from visible movements for equality has by definition moved religiopolitical progressivism out of the national spotlight, and it has foundered as a result. The religiopolitical left has tried since the 1980s to continue articulating its 1960s-style peace-and-justice agenda, but these attempts have gone largely unnoticed. The Religious Right has captured most of the media's attention in recent decades not just because it was new but also because it fit the tenor of the times. The religious left, to the extent that it has remained visible at all, seems largely to have been perceived as a dinosaur by most observers since the 1980s.

Yet religiopolitical activism is not extinct, and to some extent it has managed to reinvent itself in the form of local-level movements.

Industrial Areas Foundation community organizations (and similar networks) have distinguished themselves in many American cities for their work to ameliorate poverty and racism. Indeed, much of the sociopolitical work of left-leaning congregations is now done at the local level, making it much less visible, but not necessarily less effective, than nationally visible manifestations of religiopolitical progressivism in the 1960s and 1970s (Hart 2001; Olson 2000, 2002). Whether the religiopolitical left will again rise to national prominence remains to be seen. Unless elements of the movement are able to resolve mobilizational issues, and until the American political context becomes more hospitable to broad-based challenges to the socioeconomic status quo, religiopolitical progressives should be expected to remain as they are now—working behind the scenes.

Notes

1. For more information on the NCC, see www.ncccusa.org. See also Findlay (1993), Hertzke (1988), and Pratt (1972) for discussions of the NCC's political influence.

2. These data are available via the American Religion Data Archive (ARDA) and were originally collected by a research team at Princeton University, Robert Wuthnow, principal investigator. Neither ARDA nor the collectors of the data bear responsibility for the analyses contained herein.

3. Notice that "liberal" and "mainline" constitute separate categories in this survey. This is illustrative of the fact that the two terms should not be equated, even though they are not necessarily mutually exclusive. Some Protestants who are anything but liberal identify as "mainline." By the same token, some Protestants who identify themselves first as "liberal" may also affiliate with mainline traditions. I am principally concerned here with those who choose the "liberal" label above all others.

4. It is important to note that the Princeton survey was conducted in the early months of 2000. The American economy was still strong. The 2000 presidential election and all its attendant controversy had not yet come to pass. Most significant of all, the terrorist attacks of September 11, 2001, were still well in the future.

FOUR

The Political Behavior of American Catholics: Change and Continuity

Stephen T. Mockabee

Dᴜʀɪɴɢ ᴛʜᴇ ʟᴀsᴛ sᴇᴠᴇʀᴀʟ American presidential campaigns, even a casual observer would have encountered a considerable amount of news coverage devoted to candidates' efforts to attract the "Catholic vote." The size of the Roman Catholic tradition—comprising about 25 percent of the electorate—combined with the geographic concentration of Catholics in competitive states with large numbers of electoral votes (Ohio, Michigan, Pennsylvania, etc.) makes the Catholic voter an appealing target for presidential aspirants. In 2000, both major party candidates made efforts obviously designed to appeal to Catholics. In a typical exchange during May 2000, George W. Bush spoke in support of continued recognition of the Vatican as a permanent observer state in the United Nations and emphasized his pro-life positions, and Al Gore's campaign staff countered by pointing to Bush's controversial appearance at Bob Jones University during the primary season and by accusing Bush of trying to obscure his right-wing record (Meserve 2000).[1]

The focus on the Catholic vote further intensified in 2004 when John Kerry became the first Roman Catholic to win his party's presidential nomination since John Kennedy in 1960. Kerry did not face the same scrutiny that Kennedy's Catholicism had brought four decades earlier, but the Democratic nominee's disagreements with the

Church on the abortion issue led to controversy when some bishops declared that they would withhold Holy Communion from a Catholic politician who supported abortion rights. The Kerry candidacy inspired interest groups such as Catholics for Kerry and Catholics Against Kerry to join the fray, and strategists on both sides plotted mobilization efforts designed to reach Catholics.

In spite of all the talk in the popular press about efforts to secure "the Catholic vote," some scholars and political observers have argued that no single, monolithic Catholic voting bloc exists (Leege 1996a, 2000; Dionne 2000; Leege and Mueller 2000). First, socioeconomic differences between Catholics and non-Catholics have diminished over time, making it less likely that Catholics will behave in ways diverging from the political patterns of non-Catholics (Corbett and Corbett 1999; Kenski and Lockwood 1991; Wald 2003). In addition, there are important differences *within* the Catholic tradition. Sociologists of religion have identified differences along lines of ethnicity, gender, generational cohort, and religious commitment as reasons to discount the notion of Catholics as a cohesive bloc (D'Antonio et al. 2001).

In this chapter, I examine patterns of political behavior and attitudes among American Catholics over the past five decades. Analyses of data from the American National Election Studies (ANES) reveal two related trends. First, the distinctiveness of Catholics as a bloc of voters has greatly diminished. In socioeconomic status, issue attitudes, and voting behavior, Catholics look increasingly similar to non-Catholics. A second clear trend is diminishing Democratic dominance. For both party identification and vote choice, 2004 stands out as the election in which the Democratic advantage among Catholics finally disappeared after a long period of decay. My analyses suggest that the decline in Democratic alignment among Catholics has as much to do with changes in the parties' ideological positions as with changes in the public's attitudes on issues. I argue that partisan polarization in Washington has created a political environment with clearer ideological differences between the parties, enabling individuals to more easily base their partisanship and voting decisions on policy preferences rather than group identifications. Conservatives have largely deserted the Democratic Party, and the evidence presented here suggests that white Catholics are part of this broader ideological realignment.

I begin by examining trends in Catholic political behavior and offering an assessment of the likely causes of long-term shifts in Catholics' political alignment. I then examine issue attitudes, partisanship, and the presidential vote in 2004. The chapter concludes with a discussion of the findings, and of expectations for the future political behavior of Catholics.

Trends in Catholic Political Behavior

Unlike those in Protestant subtraditions, Catholic respondents can be easily identified in a long series of national surveys, making it feasible to do analyses over time. Treating a religious tradition as monolithic can be misleading, however, because variations within each tradition shape political behavior. A key division within the Catholic tradition is Hispanic ethnicity. Hispanic Catholics are much more Democratic than other Catholics, and more liberal on many policy questions. Thus, previous researchers examining the voting behavior of Catholics have controlled for race and ethnicity (e.g., Kenski and Lockwood 1991; Leege and Mueller 2000; Wald 2003). Given the differences along lines of ethnicity, and the small numbers of Hispanic Catholics included in national surveys (e.g., less than one hundred in the 2000 and 2004 ANES), the remainder of the analyses in this chapter will be limited to white, non-Hispanic Catholics.[2]

Partisanship and Voting Behavior

A logical starting point for any analysis of changes in political behavior is an examination of party identification in the mass public.[3] Party identification can be thought of as providing the terrain on which election battles are waged (Weisberg and Kimball 1995). For many years, Republicans faced an uphill struggle to win votes among Catholics, because the Democrats held a large advantage in party identification. In the past two decades, however, the Democratic advantage among Catholics has severely eroded (Stanley and Niemi 2004). Table 4.1 shows the percentage of white Catholic respondents identifying themselves as Democrats, Republicans, and independents in each ANES survey.[4] The Democrats maintained a sizable advantage in party identification among Catholics for four decades, with the gap reaching a high of 45 percentage points during the victorious Kennedy campaign of 1960. From the high-water mark of 63 percent in 1960, Democratic identification among white Catholics declined steadily, dropping to 35 percent in 1988. After climbing above 40 percent in the 1990s, Democratic

TABLE 4.1 Partisan Alignment of White Catholics, 1952–2004

Measure of Alignment	1952	1956	1960	1964	1968	1972	1976	1980	1984	1988	1992	1996	2000	2004
Party identification and affect (percent)														
Democratic	55	52	63	58	51	49	47	41	41	35	38	41	32	30
Independent	26	27	21	25	32	36	36	39	35	36	40	34	40	39
Republican	18	21	17	17	16	15	17	19	23	29	22	25	27	32
Democratic advantage	37	31	46	41	35	34	31	22	18	5	17	17	5	-2
Democratic plus "leaners"	68	61	73	69	64	63	61	55	51	45	53	53	46	47
"Pure" Independent	7	11	9	9	11	12	13	15	11	10	11	8	10	12
Republican plus "leaners"	25	28	19	22	25	25	27	31	37	45	36	39	44	40
Democratic advantage	42	33	54	47	39	37	34	24	14	0	18	14	2	7
Democratic Party thermometer mean	—	—	—	73	66	69	62	61	62	61	59	57	59	58
Republican Party thermometer mean	—	—	—	57	62	64	57	57	58	61	51	55	56	53
Democratic advantage	—	—	—	16	3	5	6	4	5	0	8	2	2	5
Major party vote choice (percent)														
Voted Democratic for president	51	45	83	78	60	37	55	44	43	47	60	55	46	50
Voted Democratic for House	55	60	81	72	60	65	61	57	57	62	59	45	51	52
Voted Democratic for Senate	55	61	85	71	61	55	67	49	52	59	51	55	55	50

Source: Weighted ANES data.

Note: Entries are column percentages except where noted. A dash indicates that the relevant question was not asked in the ANES survey that year. Percentages may not add to 100 due to rounding.

partisanship among Catholics again declined, reaching its low point in the 2004 survey. In 2004, only 30 percent of white Catholics chose the Democratic label.

While Democratic ties were breaking down, Republicans made inroads. The proportion of white Catholics identifying with the Republican Party increased from a low of 15 percent in 1972 to 29 percent in 1988, dipped to 22 percent in 1992, and rebounded to a high of 32 percent by 2004. This marked the first time in the ANES presidential election series that more white Catholics chose the Republican label than the Democratic label on the party identification question. Not all the Democratic losses among Catholics translated into Republican gains, however. Independents increased significantly over this time period. The proportion of white Catholics calling themselves independents rose from just 21 percent in 1960 to 39 percent in 1980. Among white Catholics, identification as an independent reached a high of 40 percent in 1992 and again in 2000, and it is now the plurality identification.

Catholics were long considered a pillar of the Democratic presidential electorate, making up about a third of the party's coalition despite comprising about a quarter of the population (Axelrod 1986). As with party identification, however, Democratic voting has waned among Catholics (Leege and Mueller 2000; Miller and Shanks 1996; Prendergast 1999). Table 4.1 displays the Democratic share of the two-party vote among Catholic and non-Catholic whites in presidential elections from 1952 to 2004. The Catholic Democratic vote ranges from a high of 83 percent in the Kennedy victory of 1960 to a low of 37 percent in the Nixon landslide of 1972. A majority of white Catholics supported Jimmy Carter in 1976 but voted for Ronald Reagan and George H. W. Bush in the 1980s. In the 1990s, Bill Clinton won a majority of white Catholics' votes, but neither Gore in 2000 nor Kerry in 2004 could duplicate this feat.

Of course, white Catholics have not been the only group undergoing partisan change during the past few decades. Among whites in general, there has been a drift away from the Democrats and toward the Republicans. But at the beginning of this period, non-Catholic whites were far less Democratic than their Catholic counterparts. For example, in 1960 just 42 percent of non-Catholic whites identified themselves as Democrats, compared with 63 percent of white Catholics. The spread of 21 percentage points in 1960 was the largest in the

ANES time series, although the party identification gap between Catholics and non-Catholics remained above 10 percentage points until 1980. The 2000 study marked the first time in the ANES series that a greater percentage of white Catholics than non-Catholics were Republicans. In the 2000 election, the partisan landscape among Catholics looked very much like the terrain among non-Catholics.

The gap in Democratic voting during the preceding decades was even more pronounced than the disparity in party identification. Again, the largest difference occurred in 1960, when an overwhelming 82.5 percent of white Catholics voted for their coreligionist. Just 37 percent of non-Catholic whites backed Kennedy, resulting in a chasm of 45 points between the two groups. This difference declined in subsequent elections, but it remained at or above 9 percentage points until dipping to 6 points in 1996, before disappearing altogether in 2000. A gap of 11 points between Catholics and non-Catholics emerged in 2004, due mostly to the stronger support George W. Bush received among Protestants in his second election bid. The difference between Catholics and non-Catholics in their support for Democratic House candidates has also declined, but not yet vanished; this gap was 5 percentage points or more until dropping to 3 points in 2004.

Explaining the Democratic Decline

The fact that many Catholics have deserted the Democratic coalition is clear; the reasons for this exodus, however, are not as well understood. A standard explanation for the decline in Democratic identification among Catholics is the decrease in the gap between the socioeconomic status of Catholics and non-Catholics during the same period (e.g., Corbett and Corbett 1999; Kenski and Lockwood 1991; Prendergast 1999). The argument is that as Catholics became more affluent and increasingly held white-collar jobs, they became more attracted to the probusiness, antitax policies espoused by the Republican Party.

Another potential explanation for the changing political alignment of Catholics centers on social and cultural issues. Since the 1980s, the two parties have taken increasingly divergent positions on controversial issues such as abortion and gay rights, and this clarity can lead to polarization of attitudes among party activists and identifiers (Adams 1997; Layman 2001). Changes in political alignments among white Catholics might also simply parallel the changes among all whites—

shifts in party loyalties thought by some scholars to be driven by differences over issues of race (Carmines and Stimson 1989), and found by others to be caused primarily by divisions over government spending on social welfare programs (Abramowitz 1994), or by a more general ideological polarization (Abramowitz and Saunders 1998). Finally, the movement of many Catholics away from the Democratic Party could be due in part to changes in mobilization efforts by the major parties. If Republicans bolstered their efforts to target Catholics, this could account for the decline in Democratic affiliation and concomitant increase in Republican identification. Previous research leaves unanswered the question of which of these factors—socioeconomic status, cultural issues, racial issues, social welfare issues, or party mobilization—can best explain changes in Catholics' party support. One of the tasks of this chapter, then, is to assay the relative influence of each of these variables in reshaping the political allegiances of Catholics.

A first step in this analysis is to look at change in these prospective determinants over time. Table 4.2 offers a sociopolitical profile of white Catholics based on ANES data from 1952 through 2004. The first section of the table shows an upward trend in Catholics' socioeconomic status during this period, as the proportion attending college, holding a white-collar job, and considering themselves middle class increased. The trend in the proportion of white Catholics attending college is particularly striking, growing from 10 percent in 1952 to over 50 percent in the 1990s. This increase in educational attainment brought white Catholics even with non-Catholics by the mid-1980s. Given these data, there is good reason to hypothesize that increased social status contributed to Catholics' move toward the Republican Party.

The trends are less clear with respect to the other potential explanations for declining Democratic alignment. On the question of women's role in society, white Catholics' attitudes have moved primarily in a liberal direction. Abortion attitudes have moved in the prochoice direction since the 1970s, but with a fair amount of volatility from one election to the next. If there is a trend on cultural issues, it appears to be in the liberal direction. Conversely, a clear conservative trend is found on the question of the federal government helping blacks. Support for aid to blacks declined from 30 percent in 1972 to 12 percent in 2000, with a majority of white Catholics preferring that blacks and other minority groups "help themselves" rather than receive help from the government.

TABLE 4.2 Sociopolitical Profile of White Catholics, 1952–2004 (percent)

Characteristic	1952	1956	1960	1964	1968	1972	1976	1980	1984	1988	1992	1996	2000	2004
Socioeconomic status														
Some college education	10	16	16	23	27	27	30	36	45	48	54	58	54	54
Middle class (self-identification)	—	31	—	—	51	47	48	52	51	56	56	—	62	62
White-collar job	29	24	25	33	41	38	41	48	50	55	61	62	60	65
Union member in household	41	39	38	32	32	36	30	34	28	28	18	24	23	26
Religiosity														
Attend church regularly	64	71	76	65	63	54	48	53	47	43	49	46	42	39
Great deal of guidance from religion	—	—	—	—	—	—	—	32	27	25	29	28	27	32
Warmth toward Catholics (mean)	—	—	—	86	82	80	74	—	74	79	77	—	76	77
Issue attitudes and ideology														
Abortion always permitted	—	—	—	—	—	19	19	29	35	33	43	39	37	37
Women should have equal role	—	—	—	—	—	31	31	29	35	41	57	48	55	59
Favor government help for blacks	—	—	—	—	—	30	26	16	26	19	19	14	12	16
Favor government guaranteeing jobs	—	—	—	—	—	27	25	21	25	23	25	20	21	31
Conservative (self-identification)	—	—	—	—	—	26	25	26	27	33	31	35	32	30
Liberal (self-identification)	—	—	—	—	—	18	16	18	21	16	22	22	14	22
Conservatism index (0–100)	—	—	—	50	52	54	52	54	50	53	51	52	51	52
Turnout and mobilization														
Voted (self-reported turnout)	86	81	89	86	81	81	75	76	83	77	86	78	84	100
Contacted by Democratic Party	—	13	10	16	19	25	19	16	18	19	16	22	29	42
Contacted by Republican Party	—	11	8	19	21	17	15	15	18	15	12	24	32	33

Source: Weighted ANES data.

Note: Entries are column percentages except where noted. A dash indicates that the relevant question was not asked in the ANES survey that year.

There is a less pronounced trend to the right on the question of government involvement in providing jobs and a good standard of living. Increasingly, white Catholics have preferred that the government "let each person get ahead on his or her own" rather than guaranteeing people jobs, although 2004 saw a reversal of this trend—perhaps because of the heavy emphasis on jobs as a presidential campaign issue. There are no striking trends to be found with respect to ideology, whether measured with self-identification or a conservatism index built from "feeling thermometer" ratings of liberals and conservatives (which range from 0 to 100 degrees). For both ideological labels, there has been an increase in self-identification of about 4 percentage points since 1972, when the ANES began asking the liberal/conservative ideology question. Affect toward liberals and conservatives shows no trend whatsoever, with scores in the late 1960s virtually identical to those in the late 1990s. Finally, with respect to mobilization, both Democrats and Republicans made gains in contacting white Catholics. Republican mobilization increased at a slightly higher rate, so that by 2000 the Republican Party had a 3-percentage-point edge (32 vs. 29 percent). However, the Democrats held an edge in mobilization during the 2004 campaign (42 to 33 percent), as both parties reached unprecedented levels of voter contacts. Thus, increased Republican mobilization may account for some movement toward the Republican Party in the 1990s, but this effect may be partially offset because Democratic contacts have also increased in recent years.

In sum, when assessing the possible reasons for the decline in Democratic support among Catholics, it appears that a broad conservative shift in attitudes is not a likely explanation. Though white Catholics' attitudes on racial issues and the role of government have moved to the right, their views on cultural issues have moved slightly leftward and their overall ideological orientation has changed relatively little over the past four decades.

What has clearly changed, however, is the ideological positioning of the political parties. There is considerable evidence that the two parties have become polarized along ideological lines, particularly with respect to voting patterns in Congress (Poole and Rosenthal 1997; Taylor 1996). This elite polarization has made it easier for individuals in the mass public to perceive policy differences between the parties (Hetherington 2001; Mockabee 2001). Over the past five decades, the ANES has periodically asked respondents if they think there are "any important differences in what the Republicans and Democrats stand for." In the 1960s slightly more than half the respondents saw important differences between the parties, but in the 1970s this figure dipped below 50 percent. The 1980s and 1990s saw a durable increase in perceived differences, as the proportion of "yes" responses among Catholics remained at or above 60 percent in each presidential election year. In 2004 the perception of party differences rose to 77 percent among white Catholics and 80 percent among non-Catholic whites.

This increased awareness of party differences has made it easier for voters to select party affiliations and make candidate choices based on ideological criteria. As Abramowitz and Saunders (1998, 643) put it, "Voters are more likely to choose a party identification based on their policy preferences because they are more likely to recognize the differences between the parties' positions." As a result, the link between ideology and partisanship grew stronger from the 1970s to the 1990s (Knight and Erikson 1997), and this relationship holds even after controlling for group memberships, including religion (Levine, Carmines, and Huckfeldt 1997). A simple illustration of this trend is found by examining the percentages of self-identified conservatives who called themselves Republicans, Democrats, and independents in the ANES surveys. In 1972, conservative white Catholics split three ways, with about a third choosing each partisan label and a third identifying as independent. In the Reagan election of 1980, the proportion of independents shot up to 47 percent and Democratic identification dropped to 20 percent, suggesting a dealigning of the Democratic coalition. Republican identification among white Catholic conservatives rose to 55 percent in 1988, dropped to 36 percent in the midst of the Bush-Clinton-Perot race of 1992, then rebounded to around 50 percent in the two subsequent presidential elections. In 2004, 69 percent of white conservatives (both Catholic and non-Catholic) identified as Republicans.

This stronger link between ideology and partisanship resulting from the partisan polarization of the 1980s and 1990s helps to explain why white Catholics deserted the Democratic Party despite the absence of a major change in their ideological outlook. Although not writing specifically about Catholics, Carmines and Stanley (1992, 236) provide a good summary of changes in partisanship during this period: "It is not that the proportion of conservatives has sharply increased; the increase has been quite modest. But what has changed is the connection between ideology and partisanship. Once loosely connected, ideology and partisanship are now much more tightly bound together, and this close connection has rebounded to the benefit of Republicans."

Additional insight into Catholics' changing partisan preferences can be gained by examining the content of respondents' answers to a follow-up question asking them to specify the content of the "important differences" between the parties. In 2000, both Catholic and non-Catholic whites overwhelmingly gave responses dealing with broad political philosophy or specific public policy issues (77.3 percent of Catholics, 78.5 percent of non-Catholics). In an era of ideological polarization by the parties in government, the public has come to more clearly recognize policy differences between the parties. This is true for Catholics as well as non-Catholics. However, it is instructive to compare these results with those from earlier periods. Figure 4.1 shows one such comparison: between 1960 and 2000.[5] Just 28 percent of respondents in 2000 mentioned party differences related to social groups (e.g., the parties' treatment of or policies toward religious, ethnic, or racial groups). In sharp contrast, when these questions were first asked in the 1960 ANES, 47 percent of respondents mentioned a group-related party difference.

Of particular note is the change in the difference between Catholics and non-Catholics on these measures. In 1960, white Catholics and non-Catholics were about equally likely to believe that there were important differences between the two parties, but they gave different responses when asked to identify the nature of those differences. Catholics were significantly more likely to mention group-related differences (69 vs. 41 percent) and less likely to mention domestic policies or political philosophy (51 vs. 70 percent). By 2000, however, these statistically significant differences between Catholics and non-Catholics had vanished. Both Catholics and non-Catholics in 2000 were less likely than their 1960 counterparts to mention group-related differences, and they were more likely to mention ideological or policy differences between the parties. This is further evidence of the breakdown of the old ethnocultural alignments of Catholics. Group politics has faded, but ideological politics has emerged.

To tie together the preceding discussion, it is useful to move to a multivariate model of Catholics' partisanship. Such a model allows the analyst to determine the impact of each independent variable while holding the other variables constant. This helps to sort out the relative impact of each of the variables discussed above, and to directly test

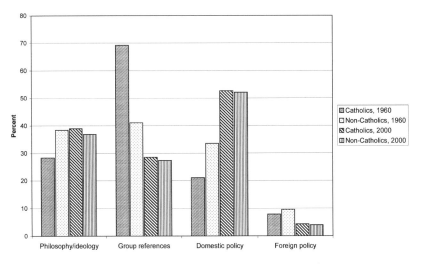

Figure 4.1   Content of Important Party Differences, 1960 and 2000

the hypothesis that increased awareness of the parties' policy positions has enhanced the effect of ideology on party identification. I estimated a regression model of party identification among white, non-Hispanic Catholics with data pooled from the ANES cumulative file.[6] The dependent variable is the standard seven-point party identification scale, with higher values indicating a stronger Republican identification. The independent variables include controls for gender, age, and the factors discussed above as potential explanations of shifts in Catholic political behavior. Socioeconomic status is captured through measures of educational attainment, occupational status, and union membership. Two variables are included as indicators of attitudes on cultural and moral issues: a seven-point scale asking about women's role in politics and society, and a four-point scale asking about abortion. The abortion measure is coded so that higher values indicate a more pro-choice position, and the women's role scale has "women's place is in the home" at the far-right endpoint. Attitudes toward social welfare spending are measured using a seven-point scale asking what the government's role should be in seeing to jobs and a good standard of living. An item asking respondents how much the government should help blacks is included as a measure of attitudes on racial issues. On each of these seven-point scales, higher values correspond to conservative views. Two dummy variables are included to represent mobilization by each of the two major parties. If a respondent reported being contacted by the respective parties, the variables are coded 1; if the respondent was not contacted, they are coded 0.

Of particular interest in this analysis is the "important-differences" variable. To test the hypothesis that the perception of party differences will lead to a greater impact for ideology on partisanship, I included multiplicative terms that interact the important-differences measure (a dichotomous variable coded 1 if the respondent sees important differences and 0 otherwise) with each issue variable. If perceiving differences between the parties leads to a greater impact for issue positions, then the interaction terms should be statistically significant. The results of the model are shown in table 4.3.[7]

As expected, those who have attended college and those who hold white-collar jobs lean in the Republican direction, all else being equal, whereas the opposite is true of union members. Younger Catholics are more likely to be Republican than older Catholics; interestingly, this effect persists even when issue attitudes are controlled. Of particular concern for the analysis here are the important-differences variable and the interaction terms with the issue variables. The results in table 4.3 show that, as hypothesized, recognizing important differences between the parties enhances the effect of policy attitudes on party identification. The interaction terms for the abortion and social welfare variables are statistically significant, indicating that the perception of party differences enabled these issues to have a greater impact on vote choice. For example, when an individual does not see any difference between the parties, the effect of abortion attitudes on partisanship is insignificant. However, when the individual perceives important party differences, the abortion variable has an impact on partisanship, with those who are more pro-choice being less likely to identify as Republicans. Similar effects are found for the "government guarantee jobs" variable and the "aid to blacks" variable. Previous analyses have focused on the role of racial conservatism as a driving force behind white Catholics' movement away from the Democratic Party (Leege 1996a, 2000; Leege and Mueller 2000; Leege et al. 2002). The results from this model offer additional support for that view.

In sum, it appears that the partisan polarization of the 1980s and 1990s has affected white Catholics in much the same way it has affected non-Catholics: The ideological positions of the two parties

TABLE 4.3   Predictors of White, Non-Hispanic Catholics' Party
Identification, 1972–2004

Variable	Coefficient	Standard Error	Beta
Constant	0.968	0.389**	
Age < 40	0.477	0.109**	0.113
Age 40–60	0.174	0.109	
Female	−0.164	0.083**	−0.040
College education	0.624	0.093**	0.151
White-collar job	0.166	0.090*	0.040
Union member	−0.434	0.094**	−0.092
Church attendance	0.042	0.037	
Abortion (pro-choice)	0.066	0.067	
Government not help blacks	0.016	0.045	
Women's role in society	−0.013	0.041	
Government not guarantee jobs	0.157	0.043**	0.126
Contacted by Democrats	−0.555	0.105**	−0.111
Contacted by Republicans	0.630	0.110**	0.121
Important party differences	−0.814	0.407**	−0.189
Abortion* imp. diff.	−0.313	0.081**	−0.239
Government not help blacks* imp. diff.	0.187	0.056**	0.230
Women's role* imp. diff.	0.071	0.050	
Government not guarantee jobs* imp. diff.	0.128	0.054**	0.155

Source: ANES data.
Note: $*p < .10$, $**p < .05$; $n = 2,219$, $R^2 = .18$; * imp. diff. = important party differences.
The model was estimated with ordinary least squares regression. The dependent variable is
a seven-point party identification scale.

are more clearly recognized, making it easier for voters to make their
political choices based on policy preferences rather than group affiliations. Yet white Catholics are still slightly more Democratic than are
non-Catholic whites, and Catholics' movement away from the Democratic Party has been a slower drift than has been the case among white
Protestants. This slower realignment results in part from the hesitancy
of older Catholics, who were socialized in an era of group-centered
New Deal politics, to leave the Democratic coalition. In contrast,
younger Catholics who grew up in an era of greater ideological polarization are far less likely to identify or vote with the Democrats. In the
next section, I examine some of the generational differences in the attitudes and behavior of Catholics, with a focus on voting behavior in the
2004 election.

The Catholic Electorate in the New Millennium

Scholars have identified the Second Vatican Council (known as "Vatican II" or the "Ecumenical Council") as a pivotal event in the recent history of American Catholicism (D'Antonio et al. 2001; Ebaugh 1991; Hanna 1979; Wald 2003). A meeting of the world's bishops called by Pope John XXIII, the council took place from 1962 to 1965. Although Vatican II reaffirmed many core doctrines of the Catholic Church, such as the Incarnation and Resurrection, it also brought many significant changes in Church norms and values. D'Antonio and colleagues (2001, 8) describe these changes as follows:

> Although it has not abandoned the teaching authority of the magisterium, the Church has placed more emphasis on individual responsibility for one's own faith. . . . The number of priests has declined and the number of lay leaders, including women, has increased. . . . The Church has transformed the uniform liturgy of the early twentieth century into the more culturally grounded liturgy of the late twentieth century. Finally, it has promulgated a more open attitude toward the world and other faiths.

Perhaps the most important development with respect to politics was the Church's call to individual Catholics to apply the principles of their faith to address political problems such as poverty, injustice, and war (Wald 2003).

Given the importance of Vatican II, sociologists of religion have classified Catholics into three generational cohorts: pre–Vatican II, Vatican II, and post–Vatican II (D'Antonio et al. 2001; Davidson et al. 1997). Pre–Vatican II Catholics were born before 1941. They grew up in the "old Church" and tend to hold traditional views on social and moral issues. The pre–Vatican II generation experienced political socialization during the Roosevelt and Truman years of Democratic dominance. This generation made up about 23 percent of white Catholics in 2004.

Vatican II Catholics were born between 1941 and 1960. Their early years of socialization were marked by stability both inside and outside the Church. The relative tranquillity of the Dwight Eisenhower years coincided with the "old Church" of the 1950s. During their teens and early twenties, however, this generation experienced both sweeping changes within the Church and the social and political upheaval of the 1960s. In 2004, this generation made up about 41 percent of white Catholic voters.

Post–Vatican II Catholics were born after 1960 and grew up entirely in the postconciliar era. They are more likely than older Catholics to rely on conscience (rather than church teaching) as a guide in making moral decisions. Many of these younger Catholics were politically socialized during the Reagan years, when taxes were cut, the role of the federal government was reduced, the economy grew, and the Cold War was won. This generation made up about 36 percent of white Catholic voters in 2004.

Table 4.4 gives a profile of these three generations of Catholics. Differences are present with respect to educational attainment, religiosity, issue attitudes, partisanship, and voting behavior. As discussed above, younger Catholics have enjoyed greater educational opportunities than previous generations, and the resulting difference in social status partly explains the intergenerational differences in partisan alignment. The differences across generations on the religiosity items are particularly striking. On each of the indicators of commitment—mass attendance, prayer, and salience of religion—pre–Vatican II Catholics score much higher than younger Catholics. For example, just 8 percent of post–Vatican II Catholics attend church weekly, compared with 26 percent of Vatican II Catholics and 55 percent of pre–Vatican II Catholics. Younger Catholics also show a lower sense of closeness to the Church, as measured by their average rating on feeling thermometer scales.

In both partisanship and voting behavior, pre–Vatican II Catholics are much more Democratic than are younger Catholics. Nearly three-fifths of pre–Vatican II Catholics identified with the Democratic Party and voted for Kerry in 2004. The Democratic advantage was slimmer among Vatican II Catholics, with 52 percent identifying with the Democratic Party and 51 percent voting for Kerry. In contrast, 51 percent of post–Vatican II Catholics identified as Republicans, and 57 percent of major-party voters supported Bush.

The intergenerational differences in voting behavior and partisanship are driven by a complex combination of religiosity and political attitudes. At times, these combinations of attitudes result in cross-pressures and surprising loyalties. For example, both Vatican II Catholics and post–Vatican II Catholics are more pro-choice on abortion than are pre–Vatican II Catholics, yet older Catholics are more loyal to the pro-choice Democratic Party. Similarly, post–Vatican II Catholics are the

TABLE 4.4   2004 Profile of White, Non-Hispanic Catholics by Generation (percent)

Characteristic	Pre–Vatican II	Vatican II	Post–Vatican II
Education			
Some college	31	57	64
Religiosity			
Attend mass weekly or more	57	26	8
Pray several times a day	37	25	12
Great deal of guidance from religion	58	29	17
Warmth toward Catholics (mean)	79	76	76
Warmth toward Catholic Church (mean)	77	65	68
Issue attitudes			
Abortion always permitted	21	46	37
Abortion never permitted	30	11	7
Favor legalizing gay marriage	9	45	45
Favor laws protecting gays	67	86	89
Favor death penalty	48	69	77
Increase spending on aid to poor	57	45	45
Increase spending on welfare	14	14	18
Favor government help for blacks	30	11	13
Increase spending on war on terrorism	55	49	34
Increase spending on border security	90	61	57
Favor increasing defense spending	60	52	58
Iraq war was worth the cost	29	37	48
Favor Bush tax cuts	47	64	71
Self-identification			
Conservative	18	37	40
Liberal	14	33	23
Democratic	46	34	16
Independent	36	35	44
Republican	18	31	40
Democratic plus "leaners"	57	52	37
"Pure" independent	16	10	12
Republican plus "leaners"	27	38	51
Major party vote choice			
Voted for John Kerry	60	51	43
Voted for Democratic House candidate	61	60	36
Voted for Democratic Senate candidate	71	53	36
Warmth toward parties			
Democratic Party thermometer mean	67	57	51
Republican Party thermometer mean	48	51	58

Source: Weighted ANES data.

Note: Entries are column percentages except where noted.

least likely to favor increased spending to fight terrorism and secure borders against illegal immigration, yet they are the most likely to vote Republican. What issues might account for younger Catholics' support for Bush in 2004? The data in table 4.4 suggest that tax cuts and the war in Iraq may have been important factors.

In sum, the portrait of the Catholic electorate that emerges from this analysis is a complicated mixture of change and continuity. A majority of pre–Vatican II Catholics have remained loyal to the Democrats, whereas the younger generations of Catholics have become highly independent and now frequently lean Republican. Clearly, the 2004 vote decision hinged on a complex assortment of policy attitudes and social characteristics. Sorting out which of these variables had the greatest impact on the vote is the task of the next section.

The 2004 Vote Decision

In this section, I present a multivariate logit model of the 2004 major-party presidential vote that brings together many of the variables discussed above. The modeling strategy is based on the vote choice models developed by Weisberg and Mockabee (1999). The dependent variable is two-party presidential vote choice, with vote for John Kerry coded 1 and vote for George Bush coded 0. The model includes variables for demographic characteristics and religiosity, as well as party identification and issue attitudes. The explanatory variables are described below.

Demographic controls include gender (coded 1 if female), generational cohort, education, and occupational status. For party identification, the standard seven-point scale is used. To measure religious commitment, I use an additive scale similar to the indices constructed by Guth and Green (1993) and Mockabee, Monson, and Grant (2001). This index is constructed using the following items: frequency of attendance at religious services, frequency of prayer, and the amount of guidance religion provides in one's life.[8] Each item was rescaled to range from 0 to 1, and then the three items were summed to create a religious commitment scale. The scale is highly reliable, with an alpha coefficient of .83. This scale taps three of the elements of commitment identified by religion and politics scholars (Kellstedt et al. 1996; Leege and Kellstedt 1993): ritualistic behavior (attendance at religious services), private devotionalism (prayer), and psychological commitment (salience, "provides guidance"). In addition to controlling for religious commitment, I also control for feelings of closeness to other Catholics using a feeling thermometer rating. If a sense of Catholic identity attracted voters to their coreligionists, this variable should be positively related to voting for Kerry.

Several controls for issue attitudes are found in the model. First, I include the respondent's retrospective sociotropic evaluation of the economy (whether the national economy has improved or gotten worse over the past year as a five-point scale). These sorts of economic assessments have been held to have a strong impact on voters' evaluations of the incumbent (Fiorina 1981; Kinder and Kiewiet 1981), and this variable has been found to be a significant predictor of vote choice in previous presidential contests (Weisberg and Mockabee 1999).

In addition to economic evaluations, I include several variables that measure attitudes toward some major lines of conflict in American politics. On some of these issues, the Catholic Church has clearly stated positions: opposition to abortion, capital punishment, and the war in Iraq. On other issues, such as government assistance to the poor and environmental protection, Kerry argued that Church teachings support the "liberal" position. Controls are also included for the respondent's attitudes toward the Bush-sponsored tax cut, as well as the issues of gun control and affirmative action in hiring.

The results of this logit model are shown in table 4.5. All the independent variables in the model have been rescaled to range from zero to one, to facilitate comparison of the coefficients. This vote choice model correctly predicts 97 percent of the cases, and has a pseudo-R^2 value of .89.

As expected, party identification is a statistically significant predictor of the vote. The effects of gender, age cohort, religious commitment, and educational attainment on vote choice do not reach statistical significance in the multivariate setting. Apparently, the effects of these social characteristics are being captured through the attitudinal variables in the model. However, statistically significant effects do remain for white-collar job status and union membership. The persistence of these social status variables as significant predictors suggests that class divisions remain important political fault lines.

Four issue variables emerge as significant predictors of the vote at the conventional .05 level: the Iraq war, tax cuts, gay marriage, and capital punishment. On the first two issues, white Catholics were to the

TABLE 4.5   Model of 2004 Major-Party Presidential Vote Choice (Only White, Non-Hispanic Catholics)

Variable	Coefficient	Standard Error
Vatican II generation	–1.104	1.382
Post–Vatican II	0.743	1.675
Female	–1.145	1.159
Education	1.719	2.134
White-collar job	–3.657	1.720**
Union household	2.040	1.256*
Religious commitment	3.259	2.651
Warmth toward Catholics	0.006	0.022
Party identification	–9.462	2.902**
Evaluation of economy	1.774	1.215
Abortion (+ pro-choice)	1.881	1.866
Gay marriage (+ oppose)	–5.099	1.993**
Death penalty (+ favor)	–3.920	1.790**
Environment vs. jobs	2.005	2.050
Government aid to poor	1.996	1.685
Affirmative action in hiring	2.279	1.618
Gun control (+ oppose)	–1.931	2.665
Iraq war worth cost	–2.734	1.135**
Favor tax cuts	–3.073	1.358**
Constant	9.481	4.382**

Source: ANES data.

Note: $*p \leq .10$, $**p \leq .05$. Correctly predicted: 97 percent. Nagelkerke $R^2 = 0.89$. Number of cases: 142. The model was estimated with logistic regression. The dependent variable was coded 1 = vote for Kerry, 0 = vote for Bush.

left of center; on the second two, they were on the conservative side. Both the tax cuts and Iraq war variables had means of approximately .40, indicating a potential Democratic advantage. In contrast, the gay marriage and capital punishment variables had means of .60 and .67, respectively, indicating a potential Republican advantage. Thus, the issue effects partly cancelled each other out, resulting in a tight race between the candidates.

It is interesting to note the issues that are *not* significant, as these results go against some of the conventional wisdom among election pundits. First, evaluations of the economy did not have a significant impact on vote choice, all else being equal. This finding contrasts sharply with the "It's the economy, stupid" results of 1992 and 1996. Second, the abortion issue did not have an impact on the vote decision once other factors were controlled. Though abortion is often referred to as a "Catholic issue," its effects on the vote paled in comparison with other issues such as tax cuts, the Iraq war, and gay marriage. Some Republican strategists have hoped to forge a coalition of culturally conservative Catholics and conservative Protestants based largely on the abortion issue, but this finding suggests that abortion was not a powerful determinant of vote choice in 2004, once other factors were controlled.[9]

More generally, the evidence that white Catholics were part of a "culture war" in 2004 is mixed. On the one hand, some cultural issues emerged as statistically significant predictors of political alignment: gay marriage and capital punishment. On the other hand, some expectations of the culture war view failed to be supported by the analysis. First, no effects of religiosity on vote choice emerged once other variables were controlled for. Second, though the gay marriage issue was a significant predictor of vote choice, it is important to note that Catholics are to the left of center on many issues related to homosexual rights. For example, more than three-quarters of Catholic voters supported granting gays legal protection from discrimination and favored allowing gays to serve in the military.

Other data from the ANES also call into question the importance of "cultural" issues to Catholic voters. The 2000 ANES survey posed an open-ended question asking respondents to name the single "most important problem" facing the country. The responses to this open-ended item were coded into eight issue areas: social welfare, natural resources/environment, racial issues, public order/crime, cultural/moral issues, economic issues, foreign affairs/national defense, and the functioning of government.[10] One might expect more mentions of "cultural" issues among the more religious, with mentions of economy and social welfare spending issues more prevalent among less religious Catholics. An analysis of the 2000 most important problem data does not support these expectations, however. Catholics who attend mass frequently are no more likely than infrequent attendees to mention cultural and moral issues as the most important problem facing the country. Interestingly, white non-Hispanic Catholics are *less* likely than non-Hispanic, non-Catholic whites to mention a cultural and moral issue as the nation's most important problem. This result runs counter to the conventional wisdom that Catholic voters are disproportionately concerned with issues like abortion and gay rights.

Conclusion

This chapter has attempted to shed light on trends in political attitudes and behaviors among Catholics. The picture that emerges is a complex mosaic involving generational differences, religiosity, the ideological polarization of the political parties, and various policy attitudes. Much of the evidence reviewed here suggests that changes in Catholics' political behavior are as much a function of changes in the American political party system as in the views of Catholics themselves. Partisan polarization has resulted in conservatives lining up with the Republicans, and liberals with the Democrats. This phenomenon has affected both Catholics and non-Catholics, but the ideological realignment among white Catholics has followed a somewhat different trajectory than it has among white Protestants. In part, this is to be expected. Catholic doctrine does not map neatly onto the agenda of either political party, often leaving Catholics cross-pressured between human life issues on the one hand and social justice concerns on the other. The analysis in this chapter suggests that parties' efforts to win the Catholic vote will not succeed on so-called Catholic issues alone. Rather, issues with broad appeal, such as national security or tax cuts, may attract Catholics and non-Catholics alike.

The group-centered politics of the mid–twentieth century has largely given way to an ideologically driven politics. As time passes and generational replacement continues, it seems likely that Catholics will be characterized by their independence rather than their loyalty to one party. Yet it is also likely that, because of the sheer size of the Catholic electorate and its concentration in politically important states, the parties and their presidential candidates will continue to pursue the so-called Catholic vote relentlessly. As the commentator E. J. Dionne (2000) put it, "There is no 'Catholic vote.' And yet it matters."

However, despite the considerable interest shown by media and party elites in the political alignment of Catholics, the attention of religion and politics scholars in recent years has often been focused elsewhere. Though social scientists have rediscovered religion as an important explanatory variable in the study of social and political behavior and attitudes, much of this increased interest has been attracted by the high-profile activities of the Christian Coalition and other conservative Protestant groups. The research agenda spawned by the politicization of evangelicals in the 1970s and 1980s has produced fascinating work on a range of topics, including grassroots activism, political mobilization, partisanship, voting behavior, and political tolerance (for a review, see Jelen 1998). But the predominant focus on conservative Protestants in the literature on religion and politics may have resulted in the exclusion of important research questions dealing with other religious groups. For example, scholars have developed theories about how religiosity has an impact on partisanship and voting behavior, but these explanations are based largely on studies of Protestants. The data examined in this chapter suggest that the effect of religious commitment among Catholics is complex and seems to be conditioned by generational differences. Thus, the conclusion that religious people vote Republican does not apply equally across religious traditions. Similarly, proclamations by clergy and church officials will likely have differing effects across various traditions. Continuing to investigate the political behavior of Catholics, then, should reap theoretical benefits for scholars of religion and politics.

This chapter takes a step toward developing a better understanding of the political patterns of American Catholics, but there is more work to be done. During the past few years, the Catholic Church has confronted sex abuse scandals involving criminal misconduct by priests and, in some cases, inaction by Church leaders. These scandals have shaken confidence in the Church among some Catholics, but it is too soon to determine what (if any) lasting political consequences will result. Even before the priest sex abuse cases surfaced, younger Catholics placed less confidence in the Church hierarchy than did previous generations, and they relied more on individual conscience than on doctrinal pronouncements as the basis for making decisions on moral issues. Scholars should monitor future generations of Catholics to determine whether religious commitment and an accompanying sense of Catholic identity will further decline, and to gauge the impact of these changes on Catholics' political behavior.

Notes

1. For a discussion of the Bob Jones controversy and the role of anti-Catholic prejudice in the 2000 campaign, see Segers (2003).

2. In the 2004 ANES, 64 percent of Hispanic Catholics voted for Kerry, compared with 50 percent of white non-Hispanic Catholics. For more on the political behavior of Hispanics, see chapter 7 in this volume.

3. A detailed history of Catholic involvement in the American party system falls outside the scope of this chapter. My focus here will be confined to the time period for which reliable national survey data are available. For more on the history of Catholic alignment with the political parties, see Hanna 1979; Petrocik 1981; Prendergast 1999; Wald 2003.

4. The analyses in this chapter draw on data from the ANES cumulative file, the 2000 ANES survey, and the 2004 ANES survey. The data may be downloaded from www.electionstudies.org. Wording for all questions can be found in codebooks available for download at the ANES website (www.electionstudies.org). Details of variable coding are available from the author upon request.

5. The open-ended follow-up question was not asked in the 2004 ANES survey.

6. The data from the ANES provide a long time series that often facilitates such comparisons over time. However, the analyst is constrained by the fact that many of the issue questions did not appear until 1972 and may not appear on the survey in each study year. Thus the analysis does not include data collected before 1972 or in 1974, 1978, 1982, 1986, and 2002.

7. In this regression there is cause to be concerned about correlation in the errors because the data are pooled from across multiple study years. To account for this possibility, dummy variables representing the year of the ANES survey are included in the model (Stimson 1985). To simplify presentation of the results, the coefficients for these dummy variables are not shown in table 4.3.

8. The other religiosity item on the ANES—frequency of Bible reading—is a less effective measure of commitment among Catholics because reading the Bible daily is not considered normative in the Roman Catholic tradition, e.g., as it is in the evangelical Protestant tradition (Leege 1996b). The three items included in the religious commitment scale used here have been shown to provide reasonably good indicators of commitment for Catholics as well as for members of other religious traditions (Mockabee, Monson, and Grant 2001).

9. It is possible that abortion's impact is partially captured through the party identification variables in the model. If the abortion issue has contributed to a partisan realignment, as some scholars argue (Adams 1997; Layman 2001), then abortion's impact on voting may operate via partisanship rather than as a direct effect.

10. For the most part, I followed the existing ANES codes, with the following exceptions. I combined "agriculture" with the natural resources, foreign affairs with defense, and labor with economic issues. Also, the ANES classifies mentions of abortion, gay rights, euthanasia, etc., in the public order category. I extracted these cultural/moral issues into a separate category.

FIVE

Dry Kindling: A Political Profile of American Mormons

David E. Campbell and J. Quin Monson

THIS CHAPTER IS PREMISED on the simple assertion that, in seeking to understand the impact religion has on American politics, Mormons matter.[1] Sheer demographics alone would suggest this to be the case: Since its founding in 1830, the Church of Jesus Christ of Latter-day Saints (the LDS Church) has grown to have over 4 million American members. Mormons are now the sixth largest religious body in the United States. This means that there are twice as many Mormons as Episcopalians and nearly equal numbers of Mormons and Jews. And Mormon ranks are swelling. Indeed, during the 1990s, the LDS Church grew 19.2 percent, faster than any other denomination in the United States with more than 1 million members (Jones et al. 2002).

In addition to their size and growth rate, the geographic concentration of Mormons in many western states makes LDS voters a potentially formidable electoral bloc. Utah, settled by Mormons and home of the LDS Church's world headquarters, has a population that is two-thirds Latter-day Saints. Mormons also constitute 24.1 percent of the population in Idaho, 9.5 percent in Wyoming, 5.9 percent in Nevada, and 4.9 percent in Arizona. Even in areas where Mormons are not as numerous, they nonetheless have a considerable share of the religious market (Jones et al. 2002).

The potential potency of a Mormon electoral bloc is not merely a theoretical proposition. Mansbridge (1986), for example, credits Mormon voters as instrumental in the defeat of the Equal Rights Amendment in some key states near the end of its ratification period. In particular, Mormons have played an important role in the politics of various western states. In California, for example, LDS Church members were urged by their leaders not only to vote for Proposition 22 (a ban on gay marriage) in 2000 but also to become actively involved in the campaign (Coile 1999; Salladay 1999). Latter-day Saints in other states have also been involved in advocating ballot initiatives banning same-sex marriage, including active support for efforts in Hawaii, Alaska, and Nevada. Mormon political involvement has also been observed outside of the western states; the Mormon Church has supported an anti–gay marriage initiative in Nebraska and opposed riverboat gambling in Ohio. Attention to Mormons is further warranted by the prominence of Mormon politicians on the national stage. Harry Reid (D-Nev.), the Senate majority leader, is a member of the LDS Church, as is the former Massachusetts Republican governor and current presidential candidate Mitt Romney.

In general, scholars working on religion and politics have had little to say about Mormons. This is in spite of the fact that as the literature on how religion and politics intersect in the United States has burgeoned, scholars have become increasingly sophisticated in distinguishing among different religious groups. In seeking to explain how politically relevant attitudes and behavior are affected by religious involvement, a number of systems to classify denominations have been developed (Kellstedt et al. 1996; Kohut et al. 2000; Layman 2001; Steensland et al. 2000). However, these classification systems generally group Mormons with other, very different faiths in a catch-all "other" category or ignore them entirely. This is generally because too few Mormons show up in most national surveys to conduct reliable or meaningful analyses of their behavior. In addition, despite their cultural conservatism, Mormons have not been a high-profile component of the Christian Right, the movement that has drawn the most attention from scholars investigating religion's imprint on contemporary American politics.

We seek to contribute to the expanding literature on America's religious mosaic by presenting a political profile of American Mormons, with a particular focus on how the LDS Church mobilizes members on select political issues. At the outset, let us be clear on how we define "mobilization." Borrowing from Rosenstone and Hansen, we mean "the process by which candidates, parties, activists, and groups induce other people to participate. We say that one of these actors has mobilized somebody when it has done something to increase the likelihood of her participation" (Rosenstone and Hansen 1993, 26). Our focus is thus on the potential for the LDS Church to spur political participation among its membership.

Our discussion of Mormon mobilization relies on a metaphor—what we call the "dry kindling" effect. By this we mean that Mormons have great potential for political activity. Like kindling, they can be lit, ignited by the spark of explicit direction from their Church leaders. However, much of the flammability is due to the relative infrequency with which Mormons are mobilized by their leaders.

The dry kindling effect derives from three characteristics of Mormons, each of which is necessary but not sufficient to explain their political mobilization. First, Mormons are politically and culturally distinctive. Second, their intensive church involvement builds social capital and civic skills, both of which contribute to their capacity for political mobilization. Third, both the organization and teachings of the LDS Church facilitate adherence to the instructions of Church leaders, including on political matters.

A Politically Peculiar People

We begin by profiling the partisanship and voting patterns of Latter-day Saints over the last three decades. In two words, Mormons are conservative and cohesive. For example, in the 2000 presidential election, the Third National Survey of Religion and Politics found that 88 percent of Mormons voted for George W. Bush, exceeding the 84 percent of observant white evangelicals who voted for Bush (Green et al. 2001). The 2004 National Election Poll exit poll conducted for the major networks included Mormons as a separate category and showed that 81 percent of them voted for Bush (two-party vote).

There is great historical irony in the fact that contemporary Mormons are such loyal Republicans. When it was founded in the 1850s, the Republican Party had as its aim the elimination of what the 1856 party platform called the "twin relics of barbarism"—slavery and polygamy. The reference to polygamy was a direct attack on the Mormons, because they were reviled nationally for this practice (which was officially repudiated by the Church in 1890). Today, that all seems to be water under the bridge, as Mormons have become increasingly Republican in both their partisanship and voting patterns. Using data from the American National Election Studies (ANES), figure 5.1 displays the percentage of Mormons who identified as Republicans in three periods: 1972–78, 1980–88, and 1990–2000.[2] The data are aggregated over multiple years because of the relatively small number of Mormons in any single survey in the ANES series. For comparison's sake, we also present the percentage of Catholics and Southern Baptists who identified as Republicans over this same period.[3] We do so because, as we will elaborate upon below, Mormons share similar characteristics with both of these groups. In institutional structure, the LDS Church has much in common with the Catholic Church. In their cultural worldview, however, Mormons are more like Southern Baptists.

From figure 5.1, we see that in the 1970s roughly half of Mormons identified as Republicans, a number that climbed to 60 percent in the 1990s. Though Catholics and Southern Baptists show a similarly sloping upward line, the proportion of Republicans in both groups is about 25 to 30 percentage points lower than among Mormons in all three decades.

Mormons not only identify as Republicans; they vote for them, too. Figure 5.2 displays the percentage of each religious group voting for

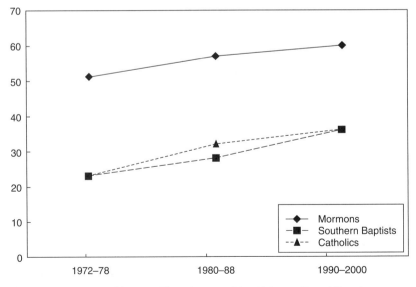

Figure 5.1   Partisanship over Time (percent identifying as Republican)

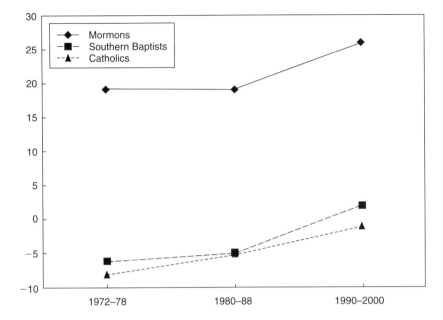

Figure 5.2 Presidential Vote over Time (percent voting for Republican candidate, subtracted from national average)

Republican presidential candidates in the 1970s, 1980s, and 1990s, subtracted from the national average. For example, in the 1990s, 65 percent of Mormons voted for Republican candidates, while nationally the average was 39 percent. The difference, 26 percentage points, is displayed in figure 5.2. We see, therefore, that even though the proportion of Mormons voting for Republican presidential candidates fell from 75 to 65 percent between the 1980s and 1990s, Republican support in the general electorate fell even more sharply (which should be obvious from the fact that a Democrat won the presidential elections in 1992 and 1996, and the popular vote in 2000). Though Catholics and Southern Baptists, relative to everyone else, also became more likely to vote Republican, again we see that Mormons lean much more heavily than members of these other groups toward the Republican Party.

Although it is perhaps a historical irony that contemporary Mormons favor Republicans, history teaches us that we should not be surprised to see that Mormons are homogeneous in their political leanings. Political unity among Mormons has deep historical roots. In the 1830s and 1840s, one of the charges leveled at Mormon settlers in

Missouri and Illinois was that they voted as a bloc. In fact, in 1838 fears of LDS bloc voting led non-Mormons to thwart Mormon attempts to cast ballots in Gallatin, Missouri. The resulting riot led the governor of Missouri, Lilburn W. Boggs, to issue an order that the Mormons must be driven from the state or "exterminated" (Arrington and Bitton 1979, 51).

Faced with this choice, the Mormons opted to leave the state, crossing the Mississippi River to found the city of Nauvoo, Illinois. But their bloc voting continued. In the 1840s Mormon leaders, Church founder Joseph Smith particularly, were courted by candidates of different parties vying for the cohesive Mormon vote. When the Mormons settled in Utah, the Church actually had its own political party (the People's Party), which dominated state politics until it was disbanded in 1891 by Church leaders who saw that Utah's unique political landscape was an impediment to achieving statehood. Owing to the historical antipathy many Mormons felt toward the Republican Party, Utah became a predominantly Democratic state. Concerned that the one-partyism of Utah was still an obstacle to becoming a state, LDS Church leaders "encouraged the development of the Republican party among church members" (Barrus 1992, 1102; see also Lyman 1986).

These efforts were quite successful, and the Church, as reflected in the politics of Utah, enjoyed a relatively healthy balance between the two parties throughout much of the twentieth century. Prominent church leaders were affiliated with both parties. For example, Ezra Taft Benson, one of the Church's governing authorities and eventually its president, was a conservative Republican of national stature, serving as agriculture secretary in the Dwight D. Eisenhower administration. Conversely, Hugh B. Brown, a high-ranking Church official in the 1950s and 1960s, openly identified as a Democrat, even speaking at the Utah party's state convention in 1958.

As we have seen, this period of relative political diversity among Mormons did not last. Others have documented how, over the last twenty to twenty-five years, social issues have become increasingly salient to the electorate, with the Republican Party positioning itself as the party of cultural conservatism (Kohut et al. 2000; Layman 2001; Miller and Shanks 1996). As a socially conservative group, Mormon voters have generally found themselves in accord with positions taken by the Republicans during this period.

One clear indication of the current political homogeneity among Mormons is that Church leaders, echoing times past, have expressed concern about it. Just as LDS leaders took steps to counter the political homogeneity of Mormons in the 1890s, the 1990s also saw public encouragement of more bipartisanship. In a 1998 interview with the *Salt Lake Tribune*, Marlin K. Jensen, an LDS Church leader and a Democrat, spoke candidly about the Church leadership's desire for greater political diversity among Mormons. In referring to a letter released by LDS Church leaders encouraging greater political involvement among their members, he remarked:

> One of the things that prompted this discussion . . . was the regret that's felt about the decline of the Democratic Party and the notion that may prevail in some areas that you can't be a good Mormon and a good Democrat at the same time. . . . So I think that it would be a very healthy thing for the church—particularly the Utah church—if that notion could be obliterated. . . . I think we regret more than anything that there would become a church party and a non-church party. That would be the last thing we would want to have happen. (*Salt Lake Tribune* 1998)

Although LDS Church leaders may wish to see greater partisan diversity among Mormons, their conservative leanings on social issues make the Republican Party their natural home. As one example of their conservatism on an issue that has resonated in the so-called culture war, Latter-day Saints generally take a traditionalist view regarding the role of women in society. Since 1972, the ANES survey has asked respondents their opinion on whether women should work outside the home. Specifically, respondents are asked to place themselves on a 7-point scale where 1 indicates that "women should have an equal role with men" and 7 means that "a woman's place is in the home." Nationally, the percentage expressing a traditionalist opinion (a 5, 6, or 7 on the scale) has dropped over the three decades that the ANES has included this question.

However, among Mormons, Southern Baptists, and Catholics, only the Mormons became—relative to the rest of the nation—more culturally conservative from the 1970s to the 1990s. In the 1970s, 38 percent of Mormons chose a traditionalist view of gender roles, but by the 1990s that had dropped to 29 percent. In contrast, the national average fell from 27 to 12 percent. In other words, the mean for Mormons in the 1990s was about the same as the national average during the 1970s. Mormons are slowly liberalizing their views of gender roles, but at a slower rate than Southern Baptists or Catholics. This change among Mormon Church members mirrors statements by church leaders that carefully reaffirm the traditional ideal while accommodating changing women's roles (Iannaccone and Miles 1990).

Another gauge of cultural conservatism consists of attitudes regarding abortion, perhaps the most salient issue driving the cultural divide between the parties (Adams 1997). Table 5.1 displays the distribution of opinions on abortion among Mormons, Southern Baptists, and Catholics. In this table, responses from 1980 to 2000 are aggregated, to ensure a reasonable number of Mormons in the sample.[4] To account for differences in the rate of church attendance across the three groups, we have chosen to report the responses only for those who attend church a few times per month or more, although the results do not change substantively when we do not make this restriction. In comparing Mormons, Southern Baptists, and Catholics, there is little difference in the percentage who report that abortion is never justified. Sixteen percent of committed Mormons and Southern Baptists take this position, with 19 percent of Catholics doing so. The big differences arise when we move to the next category—the position that abortion should be permitted only when the mother has been raped, is the victim of incest, or when delivery of the baby will endanger her life. Far more Mormons (60 percent) take this position than Southern Baptists (45 percent) or Catholics (38 percent). The difference in means for Mormons compared with both Southern Baptists and Catholics easily achieves statistical significance. Though there are few differences in the percentage choosing "when need has been established" as a justification for abortion, far fewer Mormons indicate that they believe abortion is purely a personal choice—only 10 percent, compared with 23 percent of Southern Baptists (a difference that is not statistically significant) and 26 percent of Catholics (a difference that is).

Mormons appear particularly adherent to their Church's official teachings, from the data in table 5.1. When we add the percentage of respondents who would never permit abortion to those who would permit it only in the case of rape, incest, and danger to the mother, we see that Mormons are the most consistently pro-life group among the three. Among frequently attending Mormons, 76 percent take at least a "pro-life with limited exceptions" position, compared with 61 percent of Southern Baptists and 57 percent of Catholics who attend church regularly. The explanation for the large number of Mormons

TABLE 5.1   Attitudes toward Abortion (percent choosing each
position—frequent church attenders only)

Attitude	Mormon	Southern Baptist	Catholic
By law, abortion should never be permitted	16	16	19
The law should permit abortion only in cases of rape, incest, and when the woman's life is in danger	60	45***	38***
The law should permit abortion for reasons other than race, incest, or danger to the woman's life, but only after the need for the abortion has been clearly established	14	17	17
By law, a woman should always be able to obtain an abortion as a matter of personal choice	10	23***	26***
N	154	1,230	2,892

Sources: American National Election Studies, 1980–2000.
Note: t-test, *p < .10, **p < .05, ***p < .01 (two-tailed). For the purpose of determining statistically significant differences, "Mormon" is the comparison category.

willing to permit abortion under some limited circumstances is presumably the fact that this is the official position of the LDS Church. Though the Church's opposition to abortion dates back to at least 1884 (Daynes and Tatalovich 1986), the LDS position has never been absolute. Exceptions are justified. For example, the LDS First Presidency, the church's highest governing body, issued a statement in the wake of the landmark *Roe v. Wade* decision in 1973 that stated:

> The Church opposes abortion and counsels its members not to submit to or perform an abortion except in the rare cases where, in the opinion of competent medical counsel, the life or good health of the mother is seriously endangered or where the pregnancy was caused by rape and produces serious emotional trauma in the mother. Even then it should be done only after counseling with the local presiding priesthood authority and after receiving divine confirmation through prayer. (Lee, Tanner, and Romney 1973, 29)

This policy has not changed since and has periodically been given renewed emphasis by current Mormon Church general authorities (Nelson 1985; Oaks 2001).[5]

Thus far, we have seen the first line of evidence for the dry kindling hypothesis: Mormons are a politically and culturally distinctive group. They are overwhelmingly Republican, even to the point of bucking the national trend in their preference for Republican presidential candidates. In a pattern that tracks their voting in presidential elections, there is a widening gap between their opinions on gender roles and those of the rest of the nation. Furthermore, they largely adhere to their Church's official position on abortion.

The fact that Mormons are distinctive politically is at least partly due to their distinctive beliefs and lifestyle. This includes a health code that prohibits coffee, tea, alcohol, and tobacco. Additionally, the Mormons' emphasis on traditional families means that they are encouraged not to delay marriage and having children; as a result, their average family has far more children than the national average (Utah has the nation's highest birthrate).[6] In one analysis of General Social Survey data pooled from 1972 to 1988, a majority (54 percent) of Mormons said that they thought the ideal number of children was four or more. The mode for every other religious group was two (Bahr 1992).

Clearly, the teachings of the LDS Church and the practices of individual Latter-day Saints regarding social and cultural issues are generally conservative. Therefore, it is not surprising that in a political environment characterized by partisan conflict over cultural issues, Mormons would gravitate to the party that has stressed moral conservatism. This is, however, quite different from an explicit endorsement of the Republican Party or individual Republican candidates by the Church hierarchy, which is not the practice of contemporary Mormon leaders.

Religious Participation and Political Activity

The social distinctiveness of Mormons goes hand in hand with the distinctive level of commitment Latter-day Saints make to their Church. The Mormon Church imposes a lot of "costs" on its members. In a sense, however, these costs may actually be the benefits of Mormonism. Scholars of religion employing the assumptions and methods of economists have advanced a compelling theory regarding the institutional advantages of what are called "strict" churches—churches that ask a lot of their members in behavioral restrictions and financial commitment

(Finke and Stark 1992; Iannaccone 1994). The members of these strict churches are able to overcome dilemmas about collective action because the distinctive lifestyle expected of them—abstinence from alcohol, regulation of sexual behavior, and the like—screens out free riders.

To ensure compliance with their behavioral guidelines, these strict churches "penalize or prohibit *alternative* activities that compete for members' resources. In mixed populations, such penalties and prohibitions tend to screen out the less committed members. They act like entry fees and thus discourage anyone not seriously interested in buying the product. Only those willing to pay the price remain" (Iannaccone 1994, 1187). The members of strict churches are thus expected to devote significant amounts of time and energy to volunteer activity for their faith, reinforcing these social networks (Wuthnow 1999). Indeed, the LDS Church is a quintessentially strict church (Campbell 2004).

Even a brief description of the expectations placed upon members of the LDS Church underscores the level of commitment required within the Mormon faith. First, Mormons are expected to spend a significant amount of time at church meetings—members of the LDS Church attend three consecutive meetings on Sundays, lasting for a total of three hours. Mormons may also spend considerable time traveling to and worshiping in LDS temples, which are distinct from the Sunday meetings held in the more numerous church meetinghouses. In addition to the time spent attending these church meetings, adult Mormons usually receive an assignment within the local congregation. This might include rising at the crack of dawn to teach high school students about LDS doctrine before they go to school. It might be organizing local proselytizing efforts, or participating in one of the church's welfare activities.

On top of these specialized assignments, each Mormon is also assigned a set of other members of the local congregation to visit every month, to ensure that their needs are being met by the Church. Furthermore, many Mormons spend up to two years in full-time missionary work while young or when retired. This list, which is far from exhaustive, should provide a sense that the Mormon Church has high expectations for the amount of time its members invest in the Church's activities. Mormons are also taught that they must pay a literal tithe, or 10 percent of their income, to the Church as well as contribute to other church funds, particularly one set aside for assistance to the poor in their local communities.

The high level of commitment that Mormons are asked to make to their church is why we characterize Latter-day Saints as dry kindling for political mobilization. We hypothesize that Mormons' church involvement feeds their political activism by providing them with the civic skills and social networks that facilitate engagement in public affairs. An alternative hypothesis, however, is that Mormons' voluntarism for their church crowds out any political activity by limiting the amount of time available for involvement in politics. Fortunately, the 2000 Social Capital Community Benchmark Survey (SCCBS) allows us to test these competing hypotheses. Conducted under the direction of Robert Putnam, the SCCBS consists of representative samples collected in forty communities across the United States, as well as a sample drawn nationally. The result is an N of almost 30,000 cases, including 219 self-identified Mormons.[7] Using these data, we are thus freed from the inferential hazards of aggregating surveys over multiple years in order to have a critical mass of Mormons in our analysis.

Church Involvement

We begin by detailing the "costs" of membership in the Mormon Church by reporting the level of church membership and attendance among Latter-day Saints, again in comparison with Southern Baptists and Catholics. Table 5.2 displays the percentages of Mormons, Southern Baptists, and Catholics who attend church "almost every week" or more. Of the three groups, Mormons are the most frequent attenders of religious services, with 67 percent reporting that they attend church weekly. In a pattern that will become familiar, Southern Baptists (58 percent) fall in between Catholics (47 percent) and Mormons. The difference between Mormons and Catholics easily exceeds the standard threshold for statistical significance, whereas the gap between Southern Baptists and Mormons is right on the threshold ($p < 0.10$).

Table 5.2 also includes another type of cost by displaying two measures of the resources that members of these three religious groups invest in their churches: money and time. A simple tabulation of financial donations by denomination reveals that Mormons have the highest giving rate. Mormons report giving more than Southern Baptists and Catholics in absolute dollars, but a more informative comparison accounts for differences in household income across the three groups. Table 5.2 thus displays a Religious Giving Index, which divides religious contributions by family income.[8] Using this measure, Mormons

TABLE 5.2 Levels of Religious and Political Participation

Measure	Mormon	Southern Baptist	Catholic
Attend church "almost every week" or more (percent)	67	58*	47***
Religious Giving Index (mean)	1.05	.93	.67***
Participate in church activity (percent)	78	53***	36***
Volunteered for church (percent)	60	36***	27***
Political Activity Index, 0–7 (mean)	2.27	1.91***	1.85***
N	168–218	720–1,147	6,210–7,204

Source: Social Capital Community Benchmark Survey.
Note: t-test, *p < .10, **p < .05, ***p < .01 (two-tailed). For the purpose of determining statistically significant differences, "Mormon" is the comparison category.

still have the highest giving rate, although only the difference between Mormons and Catholics achieves statistical significance. The third row of table 5.2 reports the extent to which members of the three religious groups have, over the previous year, participated in an activity with people at their place of worship other than attending services. The survey specifically mentions that such activities "might include teaching Sunday school, serving on a committee, attending choir rehearsal, retreat, or other things." By this measure, Mormons have the highest rate of religious participation, with 78 percent indicating that they have taken part in an activity with members of their church. This is in comparison to 53 percent of Southern Baptists and 36 percent of Catholics. As another indication of their faith-based voluntarism, a higher percentage of Mormons (60 percent) than either Southern Baptists or Catholics (36 and 27 percent, respectively) report having volunteered for a religious group in the previous year. In all these cases, differences between Mormons and the others are significant at levels well beyond conventional thresholds.

An implication that follows from the intensive church involvement of Mormons is that their church activity provides training in what Verba, Schlozman, and Brady (1995, chap. 15) call "civic skills." These are the quotidian tasks that constitute the practice of civic involvement—holding meetings, giving speeches, writing letters, and so on. Verba, Schlozman, and Brady find that training in these skills is an important resource leading to political activity, and that such training is often provided by churches. Data from the Citizen Participation Study confirm that Mormons are well trained in civic skills at church.[9] For example, 53 percent of Mormons report having given a speech or presentation at church within the previous six months, compared with 14 percent of Southern Baptists and 4 percent of Catholics. Similarly, 48 percent of Mormons report having attended a meeting where they took part in making decisions within the last six months, whereas 28 percent of Southern Baptists and 8 percent of Catholics have done so.

Political Involvement

Having quantitatively confirmed the behavioral commitment Mormons make to their Church, we can test whether their Church involvement sparks or extinguishes their political involvement. To do so, we again turn to the SCCBS, which included numerous measures of political engagement. We have constructed a simple index of political involvement with the following components: (1) voting in the previous presidential election; (2) signing a petition within the past twelve months; (3) attending a political rally within the past twelve months; (4) participating in a demonstration, protest, boycott, or march within the past twelve months; (5) having worked on a community project within the past twelve months; (6) belonging to an organization that has taken local action for social or political reform within the past twelve months; and (7) belonging to a public interest group, political action group, political club, or party committee.[10]

We have simply added up the number of these activities in which each respondent engages. The final row of table 5.2 displays the mean score on this participation index for Mormons, Southern Baptists, and Catholics. Mormons score moderately higher on the participation scale than the two other religious groups (all these differences are statistically significant).[11] Nor are these differences simply the result of demographic differences among the groups, because Mormons maintain their higher level of political involvement even controlling for potentially confounding factors like education, marital status, and political interest (for which results are not given). Prima facie, therefore, it seems that Church involvement does not push Mormons out of political involvement.

But does their religious involvement pull them *into* political activity, as the dry kindling hypothesis suggests? To test whether it does, we have created an index of religious participation that includes three behavioral measures: frequency of attendance at religious services, participation in a church-based activity outside worship services, and working as a volunteer for one's place of worship in the previous year.[12] We then employ a multivariate model that interacts being Mormon with this index of religious participation: Mormon x religious participation. If the dry kindling hypothesis is correct, this interaction term should be positive, which would mean that the more Mormons are involved in their church, the more they are involved in politics. We also include interactions between religious affiliation and religious involvement for both Southern Baptists and Catholics, to test whether the relationship we observe for Mormons is parallel to these other denominations. In addition, we control for a host of other potentially confounding variables, including education, age, marital status (currently married or not), gender, political ideology (coded so that a higher number indicates a more liberal ideology), and general level of political interest.[13]

Table 5.3 displays the results. As expected, we see that the coefficient for religious participation is positive, with one of the larger effects in the model. The interaction between Mormon and religious participation is also positive and statistically significant, meaning that we find support for our hypothesis. The more Mormons are involved in their church, the more they are involved in politics. Furthermore, though the other denominations' interaction terms are positive, their magnitude is smaller than what we observe for Mormons. In other words, for all three groups there is a positive relationship between religious and political participation, but the relationship is strongest for Mormons.

The differences among the three denominations are graphically presented in figure 5.3, where we see how each religious group's mean score is affected by religious participation. The level of predicted political activity for each religious group was calculated using the regression coefficients from table 5.3 and changing the Religious Participation Index from its minimum to its maximum while holding other values constant at their means. Interestingly, Mormons with the lowest level of religious participation have a slightly lower rate of political activity than Southern Baptists or Catholics at the same level of religious involvement. Mormons have the steepest sloping line, however, and so at the highest level of religious participation, they have the highest level of political involvement.

TABLE 5.3   Religious Participation and Political Activity

Variable	Coefficient	Standard Error	Significance
Mormon	0.019	(0.125)	
Southern Baptist	−0.068	(0.040)	
Catholic	−0.112	(0.022)	***
Education	0.409	(0.017)	***
Age	−0.000	(0.001)	
Married	0.105	(0.023)	***
Female	0.004	(0.019)	
Ideology	0.164	(0.018)	***
Political interest	0.506	(0.014)	***
Religious participation	0.217	(0.018)	***
Mormon x religious participation	0.264	(0.127)	**
Southern Baptist x religious participation	0.106	(0.040)	**
Catholic x religious participation	0.068	(0.026)	**
Constant	2.066	(0.051)	***
Observations	21,631		
R^2	0.28		

Source: Social Capital Community Benchmark Survey.
Note: $*p < .10$, $**p < .05$, $***p < .01$. The dependent variable is the political participation index and ranges from 0 to 7. Robust standard errors are in parentheses. Education, ideology, political interest, and religious participation have been standardized to have a mean of 0 and standard deviation of 1.

In sum, analysis of data from the SCCBS provides evidence of the second condition for the dry kindling effect, namely, that the intensive church involvement of Mormons facilitates their capacity to be politically involved. It is important to note, however, that the high rate of political activity of Mormons fully engaged with their church is not generally due to explicit mobilization on the part of LDS leaders. As we will explain in detail below, such direction comes infrequently. Instead, the high rate of political activity among participating Mormons is likely due to the civic skills and social networks they foster through their church activity.

Political Mobilization

The third component of the dry kindling effect centers on the emphasis within Mormonism on adherence to the instructions of the Church's leaders. These instructions are generally affirmations of LDS doctrine.

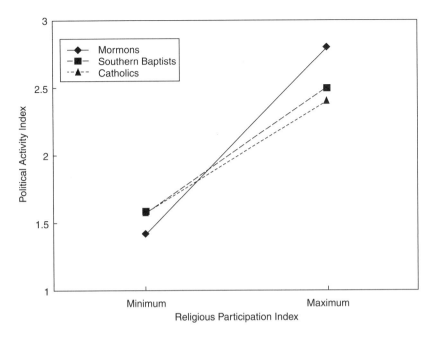

Figure 5.3   The Impact of Religious Participation on Political Activity

But on rare—and thus significant—occasions, they also include direction on political matters.

Strictly in its organizational structure, the LDS Church is reminiscent of the Catholic Church; it is centralized and hierarchical, with clear lines of authority. Like Catholics, Mormons have a single leader for the entire organization. The LDS Church is led by a president, a position that is simultaneously ecclesiastical and administrative. In Mormon parlance, the president of the church is a "prophet, seer, and revelator," the only person entitled to receive divine instruction pertaining to the Church as a whole. Adherence to the prophet's instructions in all matters is a hallmark of Mormon religious observance, *including with regard to political questions*. For example, in an oft-cited 1980 address to students at the Church-owned Brigham Young University, Elder Ezra Taft Benson—at the time next in line to become president of the LDS Church and someone who had long been visibly active in political causes—emphasized that the Church president's counsel is not necessarily restricted to spiritual matters but may extend to political issues as well (Benson 1980). Speaking of the LDS Church's role in legislative and electoral politics, current LDS Church president Gordon B. Hinckley more recently explained the reasoning behind the Church's occasional involvement by saying, "We deal only with those legislative matters which are of a strictly moral nature or which directly affect the welfare of the Church. . . . We regard it as not only our right but our duty to oppose those forces which we feel undermine the moral fiber of society" (Hinckley 1999, 52).

The president of the LDS Church is at the apex of an organization with a clearly defined chain of command. He and his two "counselors" (which are somewhat like vice presidents) together make up the First Presidency, the Church's highest governing body. Immediately below the First Presidency in both stature and decision-making authority is a group of twelve officials known as the Quorum of the Twelve Apostles. Collectively, these church officials are known as General Authorities or, more colloquially, as "the Brethren."[14] The General Authorities oversee the global operations of the LDS Church, which is divided into geographic units. Their role is administrative as well as pastoral, because they are the key policymaking body for the entire Church. Individual congregations, known as wards, are run entirely by lay members, under the close oversight of the General Authorities. Local leaders receive instruction through periodic visits by the General Authorities and training sessions broadcast on the church's satellite network. Day-to-day operations are governed by a handbook of instruction and policies, which local leaders consult regularly. In short, within the LDS Church, the doctrinal principle that church members should "follow their leaders" is not merely an abstract platitude—it is embodied in both doctrine and institutional structure.

The centralized organization and small, cohesive congregations that characterize the LDS Church mean that members can be rapidly mobilized when necessary. When natural disasters strike, for example, the LDS Church is often among the first groups within a community to render aid (Arrington, Fox, and May 1976). In theory, this same type of mobilization could be applied to political causes. In practice, however, it rarely has been applied to politics, at least in contemporary times. Though its members may be predominantly Republican, the LDS Church itself is scrupulously nonpartisan. Indeed, though it may appear that the Mormon emphasis on adherence to the Church's leaders would mean that they wield great political influence, in reality the General Authorities have not made public statements advocating specific candidates or parties for several decades. Before every major election, the First Presidency issues a letter that is read during Sunday meetings to every congregation in the United States, emphasizing the strict political neutrality of the Church.[15] And this neutrality is not simply a formality, honored only in the breach. Candidates are not to give political speeches in LDS meetings, campaign literature is not supposed to be distributed in church buildings, and voter guides are not to be distributed to LDS members at church.

That the political neutrality advocated by the LDS Church's general leadership is largely honored by its leaders at the local level can be confirmed with data from the ANES. The ANES surveys asked respondents about whether any political information pertaining to the current campaign was provided at their places of worship, or whether their clergy encouraged them to vote in a particular way.[16] We compare Mormons, Southern Baptists, and Catholics from 1994 to 2000 and we restrict our analysis to frequent church attenders to ensure that if respondents report that they did not hear any political cues at church, it was not because they were absent from the pews and thus unable hear the message. We see that of these three religious groups, Mormons are by far the least likely to receive political cues at church. Only 8 percent report receiving information about candidates, parties, or issues at church, compared with 14 percent of Catholics and 18 percent of Southern Baptists (differences that are both statistically significant). Similarly, only 1 percent of Latter-day Saints report that their clergy urged them to vote for a particular candidate, contrasted with 6 percent of Catholics and 11 percent of Southern Baptists.[17] Again, these differences clear the bar for statistical significance, although the Mormon/Catholic gap only achieves a p value of about 0.10.

Although Mormons rarely receive political direction from their leaders, there are nonetheless occasions when such guidance is given. The Church officially maintains partisan neutrality, but its leaders emphasize that they will take a public stand on issues deemed "moral" and not "political." Thus, there are occasions when the LDS General Authorities speak on public issues and channel the organizational energy of Mormon Church members to specific causes. For example, in 1976 LDS leaders announced the Church's official opposition to the Equal Rights Amendment. In response, Church members actively worked to defeat the amendment in a number of states, including Florida, Illinois, Maryland, Nevada, and Virginia (Magleby 1992;

Quinn 1997). Typically, the LDS Church has taken official stances on issues raised by ballot initiatives, rather than campaigns for elected office. This is presumably because of the Church's reluctance to intervene in a partisan contest, as well as the fact that this is often the vehicle by which controversial social issues are brought before the electorate. In recent years, LDS Church involvement has been observed in many state initiative campaigns opposing gambling (Arizona, Idaho, Ohio, and Utah) and gay marriage (Alaska, California, Hawaii, Nebraska, and Nevada).

The extensive involvement of the Mormon Church leading up to the March 2000 primary election in California is an instructive case study of LDS political engagement. Local church leaders were intensely involved at all levels of the campaign to mobilize Mormon Church members to actively support Proposition 22, an initiative to ban gay marriage. The official involvement by LDS Church leaders included two letters in May 1999. The first outlined the justification for supporting the initiative and gave fund-raising instructions to the leaders of local congregations. A second letter was read over California pulpits during Sunday worship meetings, encouraging church members to donate money, volunteer for the campaign, and otherwise support the initiative. The grassroots involvement of Church members included participation as precinct walkers in a sophisticated voter identification effort and in subsequent telephone bank and mailing operations staffed by LDS volunteers to mobilize voters. It is difficult to estimate the precise impact of Mormon Church members on the campaign, for there are no public records that record the religion of campaign donors or workers, but press accounts indicate that the pressure brought to bear on Mormons in California was intense and that the subsequent level of participation in both fund-raising and grassroots political activity, especially among church-attending Mormons, was quite high (Coile 1999; Salladay 1999).[18]

We have good reason to believe that the official involvement of the LDS Church exerted a significant influence on the voting behavior of its membership. In previous research regarding Mormon voting behavior on ballot initiatives, we outline two necessary conditions for Mormons to respond to their leaders on political questions (Campbell and Monson 2003). First, the position must receive the official endorsement of the Church. Second, the position of the leadership must be unified and widely known among Church members. Both conditions were clearly met in the case of Proposition 22. It is also interesting to note that the model of LDS Church involvement in the Proposition 22 campaign follows closely tactics used in a 1988 Idaho lottery initiative campaign. In both cases, this included using local leaders to solicit contributions from members as well as to actively recruit them as campaign workers (Popkey 1988). The efforts to support these ballot initiatives, in turn, provided LDS officials with a template to encourage Mormons' involvement in an anti–gay marriage campaign in Nevada in 2000 (Damore, Jelen, and Bowers 2005).

Although the example of Mormon mobilization in favor of California's Proposition 22 is illustrative of the potential impact of the Church's efforts to stir its members to political activity, we stress that the Church picks its battles carefully—even on the issue of gay marriage. For example, responding to a press inquiry after the election, a Church spokeswoman said that the Church was not actively involved in the gay marriage ballot proposition campaigns in 2004 (Neff 2005). It is possible that church leaders closely monitored each of the thirteen states with gay marriage ballot propositions and were confident of victory and thus reluctant to spend the political capital necessary to become heavily involved in the campaign.

Even in the absence of mobilization efforts coordinated by the LDS hierarchy, however, Mormons nonetheless have been periodically reminded that their Church opposes gay marriage and encouraged to work as individuals to thwart it. In July 2004, LDS Church leaders issued a one-sentence statement generally supporting an amendment to the federal Constitution prohibiting gay marriage but not endorsing the language of any specific proposed amendment. In October 2004, the Church issued another statement indicating general opposition to gay marriage. In May 2006, LDS leaders went a little further and had a letter read from every pulpit across the United States implying that the Church endorses the specific anti–gay marriage amendment to the Constitution that was soon to come before the U.S. Senate and encouraging Church members to "express themselves on this urgent matter to their elected representatives in the Senate."[19] Statements such as these have reinforced Mormons' opposition to marriage for homosexuals, as suggested by exit poll results in Utah demonstrating that Mormons who perceived the LDS Church as being in favor of a gay marriage ban there were much more likely to support it as well (Monson et al. 2006). Undoubtedly, their Church's opposition to gay marriage has also led individual Mormons to work on anti–gay marriage campaigns. For example, during 2004, press accounts in Oregon noted Mormons' involvement in support of that state's ballot initiative to codify a ban on homosexual marriage in the state constitution (Graves 2004). However, numerous inquiries have confirmed the lack of a Church-organized campaign to support that particular initiative (Graham 2005).

Conclusion

The metaphor of Mormons as dry kindling is meant to evoke an image of a group with great potential for political mobilization by their religious leaders. The uniquely Mormon capacity to spark intense activity among the membership is highlighted by a final comparison to attempts at mobilization among evangelical Protestants and Roman Catholics. Christian Right organizations like the Christian Coalition, which target evangelical Protestant churches (including Southern Baptists), expend great efforts to mobilize voters. Without the organizational advantages of a single centralized church, however, the Christian Coalition is less able to tap into channels of communication within a religious community the way the Mormons have done. Conversely, a hierarchical organization is clearly not sufficient for intense mobilization. The Catholic Church has just such an institutional structure, and yet without intensive voluntarism among the laity to foster social networks, civic skills, and intragroup trust, Church-directed political activity often meets with limited success. In the Proposition 22 case, Catholic leaders in California also endorsed the effort, but there is no evidence of a broad mobilization of lay Catholics by their leaders that compares to the mobilization of Mormons.

The metaphor of dry kindling is also meant to evoke periods of dormancy, punctuated by periodic bursts of intense mobilization, followed again by dormancy. That is, the potential for Mormon mobilization largely lies latent. Though there was a time when LDS leaders regularly spoke out on political issues, that has not been the case since the middle of the twentieth century. Since World War II, Mormon General Authorities have offered formal endorsements on only a select few public controversies, opposition to gay marriage being the most recent. Our intention has been to demonstrate that Mormons have an explosive capacity to muster their troops on behalf of these causes—with enough firepower to tip the balance in a close contest.

Yet as we have stressed, it is the very infrequency of Mormon mobilization that accentuates its effectiveness. Because LDS Church leaders rarely speak out on explicitly political questions, when they do, Mormons sit up and take notice. If their leaders spoke out on politics more frequently, Latter-day Saints might respond in smaller numbers or with less vigor. The result is a delicate balance between frequency and potency. We began this chapter by asserting that in American politics, Mormons matter. In light of this balance, perhaps we should amend that statement: Mormons potentially matter a lot, but not too often.

Notes

1. We use "Mormons" to refer to members of the Church of Jesus Christ of Latter-day Saints (the official name of the church) although at times we also use "Latter-day Saints." We employ the terms "Mormon Church" and "LDS Church" interchangeably.

2. In addition to strong and weak Republicans, this includes respondents who lean toward the Republicans. Results are substantively unchanged when the leaners are excluded.

3. The Ns for each group in each decade are as follows:

	1972–78	1980–88	1990–2000
Mormons	156	93	131
Southern Baptists	804	985	1,000
Catholics	2,075	2,253	2,752

4. Though we concede that twenty years is a long stretch of time, we have no reason to believe that abortion attitudes changed substantially within these three groups over this period.

5. Contrast this with the Southern Baptist position (see www.sbc.net/aboutus/pssanctity.asp) and the Catholic position as stated in article 5 of the Roman Catholic catechism.

6. However, note that birth control is not formally proscribed by church policy.

7. The SCCBS consists of representative samples drawn in forty communities across the United States, as well as a national sample. A detailed explanation of the methodology can be found at www.cfsv.org/communitysurvey/index.html. The data set itself has been archived at the Roper Center, www.ropercenter.uconn.edu/dataacq/scc_bench.html.

8. Note that in neither measure are the categories in equal intervals, so this index has no real meaning beyond comparisons across denominations. I.e.,

you cannot determine the religious donations of each group as a percentage of their income. The categories for donations to religious organizations are (1) none, (2) less than $100, (3) $100 to less than $500, (4) $500 to less than $1,000, (5) $1,000 to less than $5,000, and (6) more than $5,000. The income categories are (1) $20,000 or less, (2) over $20,000 but less than $30,000, (3) over $30,000 but less than $50,000, (4) over $50,000 but less than $75,000, (5) $75,000 but less than $100,000, and (6) $100,000 or more.

9. This is based on authors' analysis of the Citizen Participation Study. Note that these results are based on a sample of 45 Mormons, 242 Southern Baptists, and 681 Catholics.

10. The Cronbach's alpha index of this scale is 0.65. Exploratory factor analysis reveals that the components of the index all load cleanly on a single dimension. The index has a mean of 2.1, with a standard deviation of 1.6.

11. The difference between Mormons and the combination of remaining groups is also statistically significant (not shown).

12. The Cronbach's alpha of the index is .60, and exploratory factor analysis shows that these three activities load on a single dimension. The mean is 4.2 and the standard deviation is 2.1.

13. Education, ideology, political interest, and religious participation have been standardized to have a mean of 0 and a standard deviation of 1, in order to facilitate comparisons among them. Because the SCCBS data are not based on a probability sample of the U.S. population, but rather representative samples in a series of communities (which were not randomly chosen), we report robust standard errors, accounting for clustering within communities. Alternative strategies, including estimations with fixed effects for each community and hierarchical linear modeling, produce substantively identical results.

14. In addition to the First Presidency and the Twelve Apostles, there is another layer of General Authorities—the Seventies. Some of these officials serve for life, others for a fixed term.

15. Following is an excerpt from the letter read in LDS meetings in October 2000; a nearly identical letter is read before every election. For the full text of the letter see "First Presidency Reaffirms Political Neutrality" (www.lds.org/newsroom/showrelease/0,15503,3881-1-2947-666,00.html): "In this election year, we reaffirm the Church's long-standing policy of political neutrality. The Church does not endorse any political party, political platform, or candidate. Church facilities, directories, and mailing lists are not to be used for political purposes. Candidates for public office should not imply that their candidacy is endorsed by the Church or its leaders, and Church leaders and members should avoid statements or conduct that may be interpreted as Church endorsement of any political party or candidate."

16. "Was information about candidates, parties, or political issues made available in your place of worship before the election?" and "Did the clergy

or other church leaders at your place of worship encourage you to vote for a particular candidate or party?" Note that the second question is not included in the ANES cumulative file distributed by the Interuniversity Consortium for Political and Social Research.

17. Owing to the small number of Mormons in this sample, the 1 percent figure for Latter-day Saints reflects a grand total of *one* respondent.

18. Voluminous anecdotal evidence has been collected in a narrative about Mormon Church involvement in Proposition 22 at www.lds-mormon.com/doma.shtml. The website includes a set of documents that are referred to in some of the press accounts including precinct walking instructions, voter identification forms, and the letters from church leaders mentioned above.

19. For the full text of each statement, see "First Presidency Statement on Same-Gender Marriage," www.lds.org/newsroom/showrelease/0,15503,4044-1-20336,00.html; "First Presidency Issues Statement on Marriage," www.lds.org/newsroom/showrelease/0,15503,4044-1-19733,00.html; and "Letter from First Presidency of the Church to Church Leaders in the United States," www.lds.org/newsroom/extra/0,15505,3881-1-1-963,00.html.

SIX

From Liberation to Mutual Fund: Political Consequences of Differing Conceptions of Christ in the African American Church

Melissa Harris-Lacewell

W HEN STUDYING THE INFLUENCE of religion on political behavior, the social science literature has tended to approach the black church as a social, political, and religious organization. Investigating the connection between the church and political action, this research either stresses the organizational resources that accrue to black churchgoers, such as the networks, skills, mobilization, and contact opportunities nurtured in the church (Morris 1984; Verba, Schlozman, and Brady 1995) or seeks to map the psychological resources that contribute to the political actions of black church congregants, such as self-esteem and internal efficacy (Harris 1999; Calhoun-Brown 1996; Ellison 1993). This research tends to think of the church as a structure that brings actors into contact with one another; it has paid less attention to the church as a place that brings actors into contact with ideas. Social science has rarely investigated the political implications of black *theology*.

This chapter addresses this omission by exploring the connection between black theology and political action. It investigates two traditions of black ministry: Black Liberation Theology, emerging from the 1960s' Black Power movement, and the prosperity gospel, popular in many contemporary megachurches. Specifically, the chapter asks: How do these theological traditions define Jesus Christ and his relationship with the body of believers, and what are the political implications of these understandings of Christ within a black religious tradition?

Politics and the African American Church

The study of African American religiosity and political behavior has largely centered on one defining question: Does Christianity encourage or discourage political activism among African Americans? Lincoln and Mamiya (1990) review the literature on black churches and claim that several models dominate our understanding of the black church. The assimilation model advanced by scholars like Frazier (1963) argues that the church hampers ethnic assimilation into the American state and criticizes black religion as anti-intellectual and authoritarian. Isolation model scholars such as Orum (1966) argue that the church is isolated from civic affairs, is lower class, and is otherworldly in focus. The urban researchers Drake and Clayton (1962) see the church as a compensatory institution that allows the masses to flirt with power and acclaim unavailable in daily life. Assimilation, isolation, and compensatory models are all what the political scientist Fred Harris would call opiate models, arguing that black religiosity discourages political action through an otherworldly focus on divine restitution in the afterlife: "Opiate theorists argue that religion works as a means of social control, offering African Americans a way to cope with personal and societal difficulties and undermining their willingness to actively challenge racial inequalities" (Harris 1999, 5).

Alternatively, some researchers claim that the black church acts as an inspiration for political action by galvanizing black people to work toward political righteousness. This work claims that the black church was crucial in initiating and sustaining the civil rights movement. Morris (1984, 4) articulates this position, stating that "the black church functioned as the institutional center of the modern civil rights movement; churches provided the movement with an organized mass base leadership of clergymen, an institutionalized financial base, and meeting places where the masses planned tactics and strategies and collectively committed themselves to the struggle." Scholars of the black church like Lincoln and Mamiya (1990), and researchers of black political behavior such as Tate (1994), continue to find empirical evidence linking black churches to the political mobilization of African Americans.

Working in this tradition, Harris (1999) takes a multidimensional approach that looks at the multiple structures and influences within the black Protestant tradition and ultimately uncovers both macro- and micro-level resources that support a variety of political activities by African Americans. Similarly, Ellison (1993) finds that religious involvement fosters self-esteem and personal empowerment among African Americans through networks, socioemotional support, and tangible aid. He argues that the church allows African Americans to see themselves through a lens that asserts their inherent uniqueness as individuals and emphasizes spiritual qualities, such as wisdom and morality, over material possessions as a standard for self-evaluation. Also in this tradition, Calhoun-Brown (1996) makes an important distinction between political and nonpolitical churches. Reflecting the diversity that exists within the black religious tradition, she finds little evidence supporting a general connection between political mobilization and church attendance, but she does find an important link with political churches. "These political churches have the capacity not only to coordinate tangible and intangible resources needed for political action but to impact the motivations and consciousness of individuals as well" (Calhoun-Brown 1996, 946).

Although there is still debate about whether the black church discourages political action by encouraging followers to focus on the rewards of an afterlife, there is a good deal of respected, empirical evidence that many black churches are actively committed to providing worshippers with the organizational and psychological resources necessary for political action. The historical and empirical evidence indicates that whether through organizational contact or psychological resources, religiosity and church attendance generally encourage a more politically engaged African American electorate.

In this chapter, I take up a related but slightly different line of inquiry. Rather than explaining the church as a place where individuals come into contact with resources, both organizational and personal, I explain it as a place where people come into contact with ideas. I ask: What are the important *ideas* in contemporary black churches? That is, what is the content of African American theology and ministry? Then I question the political implications of those ideas. How might we expect black Christians to behave in the political world as a result of contact with these ideas? I present two schools of black religious thought, Black Liberation Theology as it emerged in the 1960s, and the prosperity gospel as it is practiced in some of today's largest black congregations. To constrain the discussion, I focus specifically on notions of Christ as they emerge in these two theological traditions and then argue for the political implications of each understanding of Christ.

The chapter first provides a brief history of Black Liberation Theology, lays out its central tenets, and explores its fundamental understandings of Christ. The same is done for the prosperity gospel. I then work through the political implications of each tradition and offer ideas about how the future of black politics might be influenced by each. Finally, I offer initial empirical evidence through an analysis of data from the 1994 National Black Politics Study.

Christ as Liberator: Black Power and Black Theology

The African American church developed as a distinct institutional structure as early as the antebellum period. Blacks living as freedmen in the North and newly emancipated African Americans in the South constructed the church as a central institution in black life. But the organizational separation of the black church did not necessarily reflect the creation of a separate black religion. Cone and Wilmore (1993, 89) argue that "when blacks separated themselves from White denominations and organized their own churches in the late eighteenth and early nineteenth centuries they did not perceive their actions as being motivated by theological differences. They accepted without alteration the church doctrines and politics of the White denominations from which they separated." In some ways, this assertion is an overstatement, one that does not credit the distinct worship styles and religious emphases that distinguished slave religion from the Christianity of white Americans, but it does reflect the lack of a fully articulated, distinct theological perspective to guide black Christian worship.

In 1964 Joseph Washington, an African American professor of theology, leveled a harsh and controversial critique, arguing that black churches are not Christian because they lack the guidance of an overarching theological approach. Asserting a derisive view of black religious traditions, Washington (1964, 97) writes: "There is little theology in Negro Protestantism. Past alienation from the theological roots of Protestantism, social separation from white Protestants and their historical and cultural extensions of the European tradition, addiction to religion as personal salvation by means of moral purity, worship as the primary means of release and the occasion for class identification—these are the bases for the religion of the Negro." Although Washington acknowledged unique patterns of worship among blacks, he places these practices outside Christian tradition because they are not guided by an articulated theology.

By the late 1960s, a group of African American ministers and theologians offered a corrective to this lack by developing a distinct Black Liberation Theology. Emerging out of the Black Power movement, Black Liberation Theology began as a response to the challenge of making Christianity relevant for African Americans engaged in a political and cultural struggle against racism. Black Theology addressed the need "not only to vindicate the young civil rights workers laboring in the rural South, . . . but also to galvanize the left wing of the Southern-based civil rights movement and reassemble it within the province of the Black Christians who lived in the urban North" (Cone and Wilmore 1993, 16). The Black Theology movement began with a statement by the National Committee of Negro Churchmen, published in the *New York Times* on July 31, 1966. This group of ministers responded to the emergence of Black Power by writing, "From the point of view of Christian faith, there is nothing necessarily wrong with concern for power. . . . At issue in the relations between whites and Negroes in America is the problem of inequality of power. . . . This is a fundamental root of human injustice in America" (NCNC 1968, 20). From these beginnings emerged a fully articulated Black Theology by the early 1970s.

Albert Cleages's *The Black Messiah* (1968), James Cone's *Black Theology and Black Power* (1969), and J. Deotis Roberts's *Black Political Theology* (1974) are foundational texts in Black Liberation Theology. At its core, Black Theology is predicated on the assertion that God has a unique relationship with African Americans. God is not a passive bystander in human history, but rather an active participant in the struggles of oppressed and dispossessed people. In the American context, this means that God is on the side of blacks as they struggle against the social, political, and economic marginalization caused by the legacy and persistence of white racism. Liberation is the theological center of this approach. It is the struggle for liberation that defines the ministry of Christ and the experience of Africans in America.

Cleage (1968, 20) asserts, "The purpose of Christianity is to free black people, to rid black people of injustice." Cone (1969, 39) argues, "It would seem that Black Power and Christianity have this in common: the liberation of man! If the work of Christ is that of liberating man from alien loyalties, and if racism is an alien faith, then there must be some correlation between Black Power and Christianity." Roberts (1971, 115) assures that "God is aware of centuries of undeserved Black suffering. He is aware of our experience of oppression. . . . Black hope stems from the assurance that God seeks the liberation of the oppressed."

Black Liberation Theology emerges from a specific historical moment. It articulates the political and spiritual yearning for a black-centered and Christian-inspired understanding of black suffering and resistance. However, it would be incorrect to think of Black Theology as entirely historically constrained. Black Theologians trace their ancestry to liberatory elements of slave religion. Black Theologians argue that while slave masters talked of the meek inheriting the earth, slaves spoke of God's delivering the Israelites from bondage. Even in these early articulations, there is the beginning of a Black Liberation Theology: "African and African American enslaved workers constructed a new religion drawing on three sources—memories of African religious beliefs, commonsense wisdom from everyday life, and a reinterpretation of the white-supremacy Christianity introduced to them by their Christian slave masters. The cornerstone of a black theology of liberation was thus a slave religion of freedom (Hopkins 1999, 16)." Although Black Liberation Theology was first fully articulated in response to the Black Power movement, it was not created out of whole cloth in the mid–twentieth century; rather, it is indelibly linked to an organic, folk theological tradition apparent in the freedom narratives of slave religion.

Black Liberation Theology must be understood within the context of its emergence, but also appreciated within its tradition and trajectory. Black Theology continues to inspire the work of a new generation of academics and preachers. In the 1980s and 1990s, a new generation of black seminarians built on the work of Black Theology to convey its continued relevance to black religiosity (Young 1986; Evans 1992; Hopkins 1993). Hopkins (1999) traces the emergence of second-generation scholars to the publication of Jacquelyn Grant's

(1979) "Black Theology and Black Women" and Cornel West's (1979) "Black Theology and Marxist Thought." From these texts emerged a second generation of black theologians interested in reevaluating Black Theology in light of popular culture, ordinary religious experiences of the black poor, Afrocentrism, and globalization (Spencer 1990; Hopkins 1993; Felder 1989; Young 1986). At this same time, a unique tradition emerged within Black Theology focused on the intersections of race, gender, class, and sexual orientation within the black church and religious experience. These womanist theologians are arguably the most important contributors to contemporary Black Theology (Grant 1989; Cannon 1995; Weems 1988; Williams 1993).

Images of Christ in the Black Liberation Theology Tradition

Perhaps the most important element of Black Liberation Theology is the centrality of a black Christ, first articulated by Albert Cleage, a theologian, preacher, and founder of the Shrine of the Black Madonna in Detroit. Cleage was a long-time friend of Malcolm X. Though he was a revolutionary black nationalist, he refused to concede Christianity to whites and join Malcolm X in the assertion that Islam was the only spiritual home for blacks. Cleage's *The Black Messiah* (1968) is a collection of sermons aimed at reclaiming Christianity for the eager young revolutionaries of the Black Power movement. In this volume, Cleage argues that Jesus of Nazareth was ethnically black. Using biblical genealogy, he traces Jesus' maternal ancestry to provide evidence of an African bloodline. "Jesus was a revolutionary black leader, a Zealot seeking to lead a Black Nation to freedom" (Cleage 1968, 4). Cleage was a practicing minister in the trenches of an urban church during a crisis in black Christianity as it sought to redefine its relationship with African Americans in the context of nationalist political struggle. Black Jesus restored the dignity of black Americans and gave them a sense of connection to the divine: "We issue a call to all black Churches. Put down this white Jesus who has been tearing you to pieces. Forget your white God. Remember that we are worshipping a Black Jesus who was a Black Messiah. God must be black if he created us in his own image. You can't build dignity in black people if they go down on their knees every day worshipping a white Jesus" (Cleage 1968, 98).

The Black Christ image is also central to James Cone's articulation of Black Liberation Theology. For Cone, however, Jesus' blackness is ontological rather than biological. Cone reasons that Christ aligns himself with those who struggle against oppression. Christ takes on the position of the poorest and most despised in any historical moment. Thus, in the American context, Christ must be understood as black. Blackness is therefore redefined as a gift of God, rather than a despised condition. "In a world which has taught blacks to hate themselves, the new black man does not transcend blackness, but accepts it, loves it as a gift of the Creator" (Cone 1969, 53). Although Cleage's assertion is of ancestral blackness, whereas Cone's is of ontological blackness, each sees the Black Messiah as a necessary element of Black Theology because African Americans can only develop a full respect for their own dignity if they see themselves as reflections of a black Jesus. Black theology calls African Americans to remember that "Jesus was born in a barn, wrapped in a blanket used for sick cattle, and placed in a stall" (Johnson 1993, 208), and to envision "black Jesus walking the dark streets of the ghettos of the North and the sharecropper's farm in the Deep South, without a job, busted, and emasculated" (Johnson 1993, 206). These are the images of a black Christ that link Jesus indelibly to the black American experience.

Black Liberation Theology not only asserts that Christ is black but also that his essential character is that of a liberator. Cone reasons: "If the gospel is a gospel of liberation for the oppressed, then Jesus is where the oppressed are and continues to work his liberation there. Jesus is not safely confined in the first century. He is our contemporary. . . . Christianity is not alien to Black Power; it is Black Power" (Cone 1969, 38). Johnson similarly argues for the modern significance of Christ by linking Christian identity with political liberation:

We must recognize that to be Christian is to be contemporaneous with Jesus, the Liberator. To be sure, to be Christian is not to hold views about Jesus but rather to become a contemporary with Jesus in his ministry of suffering and humiliation and of love and liberation. . . . To be a Christian is to stand with Jesus and participate in his ministry of love and liberation at the crossways of the world where men are crucified on the crosses of poverty, racism, war, and exploitation. (Johnson 1993, 213)

Black Liberation Theology defines Christ as liberator. This is an important theological departure from much of European Christology, for which the essential nature of Christ is manifest in his Incarnation. In the Nicene Creed, what is important about Christ is that he was divinely conceived, born of a virgin, crucified for human sin, and resurrected according to scriptural prophecy. Scholars in the Black Theology tradition argue that this understanding of Christ asserts that it is his birth, death, and resurrection that make Jesus the Christ; his ministry thus becomes secondary for understanding his divinity. Black Theology instead asserts that it is not the Incarnation but the work of liberation that is most relevant for understanding the nature of Jesus. "It does not begin with abstract speculation about Jesus' metaphysical nature. Instead it starts in history with Jesus' ministry as that is recorded in the Gospels. What Jesus did is what it means for him to be the Christ" (Douglas 2001, 113). By focusing on the ministry of Jesus, Black Theology asserts the centrality of the liberation work for modern Christians.

The understanding of Jesus in Black Liberation Theology is unique in two important ways. First, black theology constructs Christ as the Black Messiah with a specific connection to and message for African Americans. Second, Black Theology claims that it is in his role as liberator that Jesus becomes Christ. His ministry to the poor and dispossessed is the central message of Jesus for Christians. Although Black Theology is itself an internally contested field of inquiry, these two elements of Christ as black and as liberator are consistent across three decades of theology.

Christ as Investment: Prosperity Theology and the Politics of Uplift

Across America, thousands of black Christians pour into megachurches on Sunday mornings. *Emerge* magazine first reported on this phenomenon in 1997. Churches with two thousand or more members are a fast-growing segment of black religion in America. These churches can be found in traditional migration-destination cities like Philadelphia and Chicago and in Californian enclaves like Oakland, but they are mostly concentrated in Sunbelt cities like Atlanta and Dallas. Black megachurches tend to be located in or near large African American suburban communities (Smith and Tucker-Worgs 2000).

These black megachurches are attracting increased journalistic and scholarly attention and criticism from observers who question whether they have retained the African American church's historic commitment to broad-based community engagement and struggle against racial injustice.

For the most part, it is not Black Liberation Theology that is attracting these massive congregations. In fact, after thirty years of serious theological engagement with the academy, Black Theology has largely failed to penetrate the ministry of black churches. Lincoln and Mamiya (1990) produce both survey data and qualitative responses to show that Black Theology has a relatively limited influence upon the urban clergy. They find that ministers under forty and educated ministers were most likely to have an engagement with and positive view of Black Theology, but that only a little more than one-third of black pastors interviewed claimed to be influenced at all by Black Theology. A decade later, Pinn (2002, 24) argues that Black Theology never penetrated black churches very deeply and that "most black churches are not significantly influenced by academic discussions."

If it is not Christ the Liberator that thousands of black people meet on Sunday morning, who is the Jesus they come to worship? In many cases, black megachurches are preaching a prosperity gospel rather than Black Liberation Theology.[1] Many observers argue that in the focus on building bigger, slicker congregations, these churches have lost sight of a black religious tradition. "Amidst the euphoria and excitement over their new ventures there's real worry that many black ministers have developed terminal amnesia over the titanic historic role many black churches played in the struggle for civil rights and social justice" (Hutchinson 2001, 1).

The prosperity gospel is a constellation of beliefs variously grouped under the titles "Health-Wealth," "Word-Faith," and "Name It–Claim It." In its crudest form, the prosperity gospel teaches that followers who tithe regularly and maintain positive, faithful attitudes and language will reap financial gains in the form of higher incomes and nicer homes and cars. In more subtle forms, the prosperity gospel connects God's mission for his people to financial freedom and security for individual Christians. Visualization and positive confession are advanced as part of a spiritual law that encourages God to bless individuals. Wealth is seen as evidence of God's blessing, and Christians who fol-

low certain formulas in their personal and spiritual lives are expected
to reap substantial material rewards. It is not a uniquely black religious tradition. The major figures in the American prosperity gospel
are charismatic white evangelicals such as Oral Roberts, Kenneth
Copeland, Kenneth Hagin, and Robert Tilton.[2] Further, the prosperity
gospel is an international phenomenon that is also prevalent in Africa
and Latin America.

Many observers and critics of the American Christian faith use the
term "prosperity gospel" as a derogatory description of the relationship
between manipulative, wealth-seeking pastors and docile, naive congregants willing to tithe themselves into financial ruin hoping for greater
economic returns promised by God. This is certainly one variation of the
prosperity gospel. The Reverend Creflo Dollar of the World Changers'
Church International in College Park, Georgia, is probably the most
egregious example of a black minister in this tradition.[3] His ministry
asserts that those who tithe and have sufficient faith will be rewarded
with money and property. Dollar tells his followers "You ain't gonna
have no love and joy and peace until you get some money" and claims
that all those who critique him are "operating by a spirit of poverty"
(Dollar on the television program *Praise the Lord*, July 20, 1999). However, I hope to avoid the all-encompassing denunciation of prosperity
gospel ministries as heretical. Unlike theologians, I am not interested in
the biblical accuracy of the doctrine per se; rather, I want to claim the
prosperity gospel as an important development in the contemporary
black church and to investigate the consequences of this theological
position for the political action of African Americans.

Unlike Black Theology, which has been articulated by two generations of academic theologians, the prosperity gospel is folk theology.
Some may argue that the prosperity gospel should not rightly be
understood as theology, because it is not tied to a scholarly tradition
of inquiry. However, there is an important reason to understand this
ministry tradition as a kind of folk theology. In making a claim for the
creation of Black Liberation Theology in 1969, the National Committee of Black Churchmen asserts that theology is not the exclusive
domain of intellectual elites in academic seminaries—it is experiential.
"Black Theology was already present in the spirituals and slave songs
and exhortations of slave preachers and their descendants. All theologies arise out of communal experience with God. At this moment in

time, the black community seeks to express its theology in language that speaks to the contemporary mood of black people" (NCBC 1969, 37). A similar claim can be made for understanding the prosperity gospel as a contemporary theology. It arises from the work of preachers in their ministries, out of a communal experience with God, and it seeks to speak to the contemporary mood of churchgoers.

Other critics may concede that the prosperity gospel should be studied as an organic theology but may question the relevance of studying the prosperity gospel within the African American religious tradition. Unlike Black Liberation Theology, which has been explicitly developed to speak to African American Christians, the prosperity gospel appears to be little more than a derivate of a white evangelical movement. I maintain that the prosperity gospel is relevant to the study of black religion and politics, for two reasons. First, hundreds of thousands of African Americans are consumers of various forms of the prosperity gospel, whether as members in ministries or as consumers of books, videotapes, and audiotapes produced by prosperity gospel preachers. The very breadth of its influence on contemporary black Christians makes the prosperity gospel a meaningful field of inquiry for scholars of the African American religious experience.

Second, I maintain that although the prosperity gospel is closely linked to its white counterpart, it also has roots in indigenous black traditions. It is not an entirely derivative theology. Specifically, the black prosperity gospel can be understood as a contemporary form of the uplift ideology. The historian Kevin Gaines (1996, 2) describes this tradition, writing that "for many black elites, uplift came to mean an emphasis on self-help, racial solidarity, temperance, thrift, chastity, social purity, patriarchal authority, and the accumulation of wealth." Prosperity theology, as it is practiced by many black ministers, reflects these same themes and concerns. Just as elements of slave religion operate as a black historical tradition underlying Black Liberation Theology, uplift ideology ties the prosperity gospel to an indigenous black tradition.

The prosperity gospel is not a cohesive set of articulated religious concerns. There is no body of literature that contains the canonical thought of the movement. It is a folk theology, alive in practice and action. Therefore, the evidence for its theological content must come from the preaching and writings of the ministers in this tradition, rather than from scholars developing an approach within the academy. To focus the discussion, I have chosen one prominent minister in this tradition, T. D. Jakes, who is widely popular among African Americans—his church outside Dallas boasts a membership of 26,000. He is also a prolific writer. He has written five books that have become bestsellers on Christian lists. Moreover, he has a somewhat more nuanced message than other prosperity preachers. His definition of prosperity is broader than cash and property; he is also concerned with a personal and familial prosperity. Thus, he is less easily dismissed than some of his counterparts.

Images of Christ in the Prosperity Gospel: The Case of T. D. Jakes

Christ appears sparingly in the writings of T. D. Jakes. The nature of Jesus and his relationship to God's people is implicit in the advice and prescriptions offered to readers rather than explicitly articulated as it is in Black Liberation Theology. The two central characteristics of Jesus in Black Theology are Christ's blackness and his role as Liberator. In the prosperity gospel, Christ is an investment strategy and a personal life coach. Jakes's *The Great Investment: Balancing Faith, Family, and Finance to Build a Rich Spiritual Life* (2000) is representative of the approach to Christ taken by prosperity gospel ministers. Jakes suggests that Christians have been deceived by Puritan notions and monastic traditions that encourage material denial. Though he warns that poverty does not necessarily indicate a lack of faith, he does suggest that with enough faith and the right tools, wealth is available to all Christians. He reinterprets the Exodus narrative that has been central to African American religion since slavery as salvation from scarcity into a land of prosperity. Though it is seen by Black Liberation Theologians as evidence of God's role as a liberator, Jakes argues that the story of the Israelites is an indication of God's desire to make his people self-sufficient and prosperous. "God delivered them from scarcity. . . . This is where God wants us to be as well. . . . God wants you to have more than enough. He wants you to be financially independent" (Jakes 2000, 37). Jakes claims that as slaves the Israelites had become dependent on their Egyptian captors. When God led his people into the wilderness, it was to "wean them from the breast milk of dependency to the strong nutrition of self-reliance" (p. 34). By this reading, God frees his people from dependency, not oppression. Christ then becomes a fulfillment of this same mission, a messiah of self-sufficiency and wealth.

In the prosperity gospel, Jesus is a route to financial and personal fulfillment. Jakes normally eschews reference to Jesus and speaks more generally of God. He makes frequent use of the Old Testament and of the epistles of Paul, downplaying the gospels that are central to Black Liberation Theology. But when he does speak of Jesus, it is as a strategy or tool for personal gain. He does not claim that all gains will be financial. He stresses the importance of strong family connections and personal authenticity. Jesus is a path to all these things, but this relationship with Christ is always constructed as an individual investment strategy. It is not simply that believers have a *personal* relationship with Christ; they have an *individual* relationship.

To understand how Jakes perceives Christ, it is instructive to assess his advice about how believers should make use of Jesus. Jakes directs followers to cover their families in the blood of Jesus. "You simply pray the blood of Jesus will cover their hearts, minds, spirits, and bodies. . . . Christ's blood prayed daily over your family will keep the destroyer at bay. If you fail to pray and cover your family, through prayer, in Jesus' blood you leave them open to potential spiritually destructive influences that can tear the family apart" (Jakes 2000, 122). By this formulation, Jesus is a kind of talisman that can be invoked for strategic personal purposes. African-inspired religions such as voodoo and voodun claim a similar "magical" role for blood. In Jakes's formulation, Christ acts as a kind of individual good luck charm who can be used to gain wealth, protect one's family, and achieve one's goals. Also, those whose families do meet with misfortune can look to themselves for blame because they have failed to invoke the necessary incantation to protect their family from demonic forces. Christ is a tool to be wielded by believers, rather than an independent agent working on behalf of his people as a collective. Both prosperous and tragic family circumstances can be traced back to the ways that believers either used or failed to use the power of Jesus.

Jesus also takes on the role of personal life coach in the prosperity gospel. Jakes asserts that Christ's primary role is to allow his followers to reach their full potential as individuals. Jakes interprets the story of the Samaritan woman's encounter with Christ, writing that "Jesus knew all that this woman had done in her life, but focused not on her sins, but on her need. It's not that God doesn't judge us or want us to know our mistakes, but He sent His Son because He loves us and wants to see us whole" (Jakes 2002, 157). The prosperity gospel understands Christ as engaged in the everyday lives of his followers—he is concerned with their well-being. Whereas in Black Theology Christ is a liberator working on behalf of the race, in the prosperity gospel he is counselor and comforter engaging in a personal relationship with individual men and women.

Jakes stresses that Christ is a kind of personal trainer who gives his people exercises to strengthen their faith. "The best way to exercise a weak muscle is to expose it to resistance. Trials and tribulations are the training tools of faith. When you face a difficult time and God brings you through it, you develop faith that He will bring you through the next crisis. The more resistance training, the stronger the muscle of faith" (Jakes 2000, 171). For the prosperity gospel, faith is necessary because it is faith that allows access to personal and financial reward. Christ is a personal trainer of the faith muscle, which, when strong, allows believers to claim their prosperity. Jakes looks to the example of doubting Thomas to show how Christians often fail to recognize the importance of using faith as the evidence of things not seen. "Many times we, too, are required to bypass our senses and embrace our conviction. We must believe without the crutch of sensual perception. . . . We will be required to believe, without the benefit of our senses, against all odds, that we will achieve whatever we set out to do" (Jakes 2000, 164). Strong faith is necessary to access blessings, and Christ is the coach who strengthens that faith.

In the prosperity gospel, Christ is instrumental. His power can be accessed and used by believers to improve their finances, protect their families, strengthen their faith, and achieve personal authenticity. He is a benevolent and powerful friend who is engaged with the personal choices and trials of individual Christians. He expects obedience indicated through adherence to sound financial practices, kind intimate relations, and convicted professions of faith.[4] He is predictable and generous. Once believers tap into the formula for success and faith, God is certain to reward their efforts with boundless blessings of material gain and personal happiness.

Theorizing on the Consequences
for Political Activism

It is tempting to take on a theological critique of Black Liberation Theology and the prosperity gospel. We could line them up next to one another, compare them to biblical texts, and asses them in the light of canonical Christian theology. Yet as important as such an evaluation might be to Christian scholars, it is not the goal of this analysis. Instead, I argue that these differing conceptions of Christ have potentially powerful implications for African American politics. Social science has provided empirical evidence that religiosity, church attendance, and exposure to politics in church affect the likelihood that blacks will participate in electoral, communal, and protest action. It is thus reasonable to hypothesize that black religious ideas, or theology, influence the direction and shape of black political action. Black Liberation Theology and the prosperity gospel are particularly interesting because both of these religious traditions fall on the same side of the otherworldly/this-worldly divide. Critics of black religion have often suggested that the otherworldly focus of traditional black religion hampers political involvement by encouraging African Americans to remain meek and await their heavenly reward. Both Black Theology and the prosperity gospel encourage believers to focus on the requirements and rewards of this world, but the way that they direct that focus is radically different. How might these two approaches to Christ affect the ways that black Christians approach politics?

Black Liberation Theology was born out of the political ideology of Black Power, and it was inherently political in its inception. That the theology of a people would have to be reconsidered and rearticulated in the light of changing political realities is an assertion of the centrality of the sacred, spiritual world to African American political action. In the Black Theology tradition, Christ is black. One of the justifications for advancing a black Christ is the psychological impact of religious symbols on those who worship with their assistance. To the extent that the Black Messiah translates into greater self-esteem and a greater sense of mastery or efficacy, we would expect the Black Messiah to act as a psychological resource that can be accessed for political action. Developmental theories frequently suggest that positive role models are important for developing a sense of personal esteem and connection for young people. It is difficult to imagine a better role model than Christ! If Christ is black, then African Americans must by extension be worthy human beings, crafted in the image of God. Work by Harris (1999) and Ellison (1993) links self-esteem to political participation. Those who are introduced to the Black Messiah may develop psychological resources important for encouraging political participation.

But the question of the theology's political influence goes beyond frequency of participation and moves in the direction and spirit of political action. Through the narrative of Christ as liberator, Black Theology mandates a collective approach to politics and critiques a system of inequality. Christians are called by Jesus' example not just to serve the poor but also to destroy the structures that create and reproduce poverty. Black Theology asserts a relationship between Jesus and a community and argues for a moral imperative to progressive political action. In this tradition, Christianity is not primarily a matter of affective attachment to God or the traditional practice of religious ritual; Christianity is action on behalf of and in conjunction with Jesus for the purpose of changing the structures that perpetuate racial inequality.

This is not to say that Black Liberation Theology is the only ideological corrective necessary for a progressive black politics. First-generation Black Theology has been rigorously critiqued by both leftist and womanist theologians as being insufficiently engaged with nonracial systems of oppression like those based on gender, class, and sexual identity. There is little reason to believe that Cleage's Black Messiah inspires African Americans to act on behalf of black gay communities being ravaged by AIDS. It is not clear that a black Jesus has the same psychological impact on black women as he does on black men. Second-generation Black Theology, especially the contributions of womanists, is addressing these critiques. A fully articulated Black Liberation Theology sensitive to the interlocking systems of oppression by race, class, gender, and sexuality seems an ideal motivating ideology for progressive political action on behalf of African Americans.

But it is not Cone or Cannon who sells millions of books to black Christians, preaches to thousands of black men and women in enormous arenas, and is broadcast on weekly television programs to millions. It is the prosperity gospel that has won the allegiance of millions of contemporary African Americans. What are the potential political implications of such an alignment?

The answer is unclear. In *The State of Black America 2000*, R. Drew Smith and Tamelyn Tucker-Worgs released some of the first available data on black megachurches. On the basis of surveys of more than fifty black churches with memberships over two thousand, these preliminary data suggest that megachurches outperform their smaller counterparts in both political activity and community development. Ninety-six percent of black megachurches indicate that they have helped in voter registration drives, 87 percent have provided rides to the polls, 63 percent have advocated on behalf of ballot issues, and 10 percent report participating in protest rallies or marches. "Black megachurches may not be as apolitical as they have sometimes been thought to be. The apolitical image is possibly a problem of perception, created by the fact that the political aspects of black megachurches have not been as conspicuous as other aspects of their ecclesiastical and community activities" (Smith and Tucker-Worgs 2000, 187).

Although these data are useful in refuting the claim that black megachurches are unengaged politically, they cannot fully respond to the question of the political implications of prosperity theology, for several reasons. First, megachurches are a common organizational vehicle for the prosperity gospel, but the two are not equivalent. These data tell us what happens in big churches, but nothing about the theological content of these churches, reflecting the bias present in political science scholarship that tends to emphasize the organizational components of the church over the ideological ones.

Second, much of prosperity theology is disseminated through books, audiotapes, videotapes, and television rather than through traditional church membership. By focusing only on the activities of churches, we cannot know the impact of these ideas on the thousands of African Americans who consume prosperity theology outside church walls.

Third and finally, these data are highly aggregated. They ask about the activities of churches, not of individuals in the church. It is possible that a church can be classified as politically active, even if only a hundred of its ten thousand members are involved in political action. There is no way to discern from these data whether thousands of African Americans are being mobilized for action or not.

In the absence of this kind of empirical evidence, it is important to theorize about the political implications of the prosperity gospel. In this tradition, Christ is an investment strategy and a personal coach. Christ wants his people to prosper financially and personally. This is a pervasively individualistic conception of Christ. Faith is individual; rewards are individual. The individualistic tenor of the prosperity gospel reduces even the history of black social action to a series of individualistic successes. Thus, Jakes offers an unconventional interpretation of Rosa Parks's pivotal refusal to yield her seat on an Alabama bus. "Little did Rosa Parks know that when she refused to surrender her seat and move to the back of the bus, more was at stake than a ride home. She was moving center stage by being herself. No games, no lines, no makeup—this was the real Rosa, and God shined a light on her soul that made history" (Jakes 2002, 9). Parks is offered as an example of a woman who, in Jakes's words, has become one of "God's Leading Ladies." Her role in the Montgomery bus boycott and subsequent civil rights movement is defined as a great personal achievement rather than as a culmination of decades of resistance to segregation in public transportation.

Jakes (2002, 156) similarly casts Martin Luther King as an example of word-faith at work:

> There is a simple equation that applies to all of life. Conviction + Confession = Change. When you have belief planted firmly in your heart and you speak that belief, you will effect change. It adds up only when both elements are present. . . . If the mouth confesses what the heart is convicted of, it produces a strong elixir that will bring about change. It changed the country when Dr. Martin Luther King Jr. opened his mouth and spoke what his heart believed. It changed how the world viewed civil liberties. Dr. King combined convictions with confession and he changed the world.

This interpretation reduces the civil rights movement to the accomplishment of a single, faithful individual working in conjunction with Christ. Though King's articulation of the mood, demands, and spirit of the movement was undeniably critical to its success, Jakes's narrative renders the mass protest, sacrifice, and struggle of thousands of black men and women secondary to the words of a single religious leader.

Without the identity of Christ as liberator, there is no moral imperative for social action. This is especially true when we consider that the prosperity gospel's audience is largely middle-class and suburban blacks with a lot at stake in the status quo. Without a moral imperative, why should they risk their tenuous and newly won material comforts to address the continuing issues of racial inequality? To the extent that the prosperity gospel promotes an individualized, dispositional understanding of the world, it could discourage collective political action aimed at addressing the material circumstances of racial inequality.

Empirical Evidence

The preponderance of social science research on the black church focuses on its organizational rather than its theological components. But, in the mid-1990s, one national survey of African Americans provided a unique opportunity to connect specific African American religious beliefs with a broad range of political action. The 1994 National Black Politics Study (NBPS) asks a battery of questions about perceptions of God and Christ and includes measures of political activity. The data from the NBPS come from a probability sample of all African American households, yielding 1,206 respondents eighteen years of age or older.[5] The survey was conducted between November 20, 1993, and February 20, 1994, with a response rate of 65 percent. The survey was administered through the University of Chicago with Ronald Brown and Michael Dawson as principal investigators. I use data from the NBPS to ask several questions. First, which African Americans are most likely to adhere to a conception of Christ that reflects Black Liberation Theology, and which are most likely to understand God in a way consistent with the prosperity gospel? Second, do these beliefs have an independent influence on black political participation once we have accounted for other aspects of the black church? Third, what are the directions of these effects?

I use two measures from the 1994 NBPS to model understandings of Christ that are consistent with Black Liberation Theology and the prosperity gospel. The NBPS asked respondents: "When you speak or think of Christ, do you imagine Christ as being black or white?" Two hundred respondents (22 percent) report that they imagine Christ as black.[6] This measure is an unambiguous indication of belief in a black Christ, a central tenet of Black Theology. The measure for the prosperity gospel is less obvious. The NBPS asks respondents to agree or disagree with this statement: "The humiliation and oppression experienced by black people is surely a sign that God is almost totally removed from the problems that confront black people." Two hundred seven respondents

(22 percent) reported agreement with this belief. This measure is not a perfect indicator of the prosperity gospel, but it does capture an instrumental understanding of God. The prosperity gospel is centered in the belief that God's presence is manifested in tangible health, happiness, and wealth. Those who believe that oppression indicates God's absence are subscribing to a similarly instrumental notion of God. If God brings good things, then bad things mean that God is absent. Though imperfect, this measure does offer some leverage in understanding the prevalence and influence of these ideas within black religious thought.

Who Believes? Result from the Analysis

To analyze Black Liberation Theology and the prosperity gospel, each of these conceptions of God is measured as a dichotomous variable, where 1 indicates agreement and 0 indicates disagreement with the concept. From the NBPS data, the belief that Christ is black and the belief that African American racial problems indicate God's absence are separate dimensions of belief that are virtually uncorrelated (–.02). Only 3 percent of respondents express agreement with both statements, and the majority of the sample disagrees with both.

To determine the individual characteristics that contribute to these theological understandings, I model each as a function of gender, age, education, income, urban dwelling, denomination, and frequency of church attendance. Gender is a dichotomous variable with female coded as 1. Age is coded in years, with forty-three the average age of the sample. Education is measured as the highest grade completed, with high school diploma as the modal response category. Income is annual household income measured in nine income categories ranging from under $10,000 to over $75,000. Urbanity is a dichotomous variable where those who report living in a city are coded as 1. Frequency of church attendance is coded on a unit range, where 0 indicates never attending religious services and 1 indicates attending religious services at least once a week. Each equation is estimated using a maximum likelihood logistical estimation procedure.

The results, presented in table 6.1, indicate that black men are significantly more likely than black women to believe that Christ is black. Young people and those with higher levels of education are also far more likely to imagine a black Christ. Black Baptists (the majority of

TABLE 6.1   Models of Differing Notions of Christ

Variable	Christ Is Black		God Is Absent	
	Coefficient	Standard Error	Coefficient	Standard Error
Female	−.53**	.16	−.27	.17
Age	−.02**	.005	.004	.004
Education	.14**	.03	−.10**	.02
Income	.06	.04	−.10**	.04
City dweller	.36*	.17	−.11	.15
Baptist	.38*	.17	.04	.16
Frequency of church attendance	−.89**	.34	−.33	.33
Constant	−2.55**	.54	.37	.48

Source: 1993–94 National Black Politics Study.
Note: $*p < .05$, $**p < .01$. Coefficients are derived from a maximum likelihood logistical estimation in STATA.

respondents) and urban dwellers are substantially more likely to envision a black Christ. Those who attend church frequently, however, are less likely to perceive Christ as black. The pattern of effects is quite different when the same model is estimated with the instrumental conception of God as the dependent variable. There is no discernable effect of gender, age, urban residence, denomination, or frequency of church attendance. The belief that African American oppression is a sign of God's absence is more prevalent among African Americans with lower levels of education and with lower incomes, but the magnitude of these effects is modest.

Logit analysis allows us to translate these coefficients into predicted probabilities. The coefficients allow us to predict the likelihood that an individual with certain characteristics will hold particular religious beliefs. For example, the model predicts that the average female respondent—a forty-three-year-old Baptist with average education, income, and church attendance who lives in the city—has about a 16 percent likelihood of perceiving Christ as black. This same respondent has about a 14 percent likelihood of perceiving God's absence from black oppression. Her average male counterpart has a 24 percent likelihood of believing in Christ's blackness and an 18 percent likelihood of believing that God is absent. A twenty-one-year-old male, city-dwelling Baptist with average education, income, and church attendance has about a 31 percent likelihood of seeing Christ as black, but only about half that likelihood (17 percent) of citing black oppression as a reason to perceive God as absent. A sixty-five-year-old black woman of average characteristics has only about a 12 percent likelihood of envisioning a black Christ, but a greater probability (16 percent) of seeing black oppression as a reason to believe God is absent. However, if this older black woman is college educated and at the top of the income scale, her likelihood of perceiving God as absent from black discrimination is halved to 8 percent.

Political Consequences

These results offer some leverage in understanding the individual characteristics associated with differing conceptions of God. But a different analysis is necessary to determine the political consequences of these beliefs. The NBPS asks respondents about their involvement in a number of political activities. I construct a scale of political participation from responses to the following questions: (1) Did you vote in the last presidential election? In the past five years, have you (2) contacted a public official? (3) Attended a protest meeting or demonstration? (4) Taken part in a neighborhood march? (5) Signed a petition in support of or against something? The scale is coded on a unit range, so 0 means that the respondent did not engage in any of these activities and 1 indicates that the respondent engaged in all of them. The scale serves as a dependent variable in an ordinary least squares regression.

The estimated model accounts for several alternative hypotheses. The model tests the main hypotheses through the two measures of perceptions of Christ: the belief that Christ is black and the idea that black oppression indicates that God is absent. Three other theological variables are included in the model. Denomination is included to capture some of the variation in religious teachings across denominations. The NBPS also asked respondents to indicate if religion provides guidance in their day-to-day living. This variable is coded on a unit range, where higher values indicate that religion is more important as a daily guide. This measure is included to distinguish between those who compartmentalize their religiosity and those who perceive it as infusing other aspects of their lives. Finally, the model includes a measure that asked respondents "How important is it that all images and pictures of Christ in black churches show him as being black?" Although only

200 respondents report that they believe Christ is black, nearly 450 reported that it was important that images of Christ in black churches be black. Though the vast majority of those who believe Christ is black also believe it is important to represent him as black, there is nothing like perfect convergence on these two measures.[7] Both measures are included to account for the difference between a personal belief in a black Christ and more general belief that black images of Jesus are important.

In addition to these theological indicators, the model includes measures of the organizational elements of the black church that social scientists have more frequently explored. Verba, Schlozman, and Brady (1995) and Rosenstone and Hansen (1993) argue that African Americans who regularly attend church develop skills for political participation and are more likely to be mobilized than those who do not attend. Therefore, the model includes a measure of frequency of church attendance as a test of these hypotheses. Harris (1999) and Calhoun-Brown (1996) find that politicized black churches bring individuals into contact with personal and institutional resources that can be used in political participation. Using the measures available in the NBPS, it is possible to model participation in politicized churches.

Nearly half the respondents reported engagement with some form of church-based political discussion. Thirty-four percent reported talking to people about political matters at church. Fifty percent heard a clergy member talk about the need for people to become involved in politics. Thirty-eight percent heard a political leader speak at church, and 23 percent heard a church official suggest voting for or against certain candidates. Respondents were somewhat less likely to be engaged in political activity at church than in church-based political discussion, but nearly a quarter reported some involvement with church-based political action. Twenty-three percent helped in a voter registration drive; 25 percent gave people a ride to the polls on election day; 24 percent gave money to a political candidate; 27 percent attended a candidate fund raiser; 23 percent handed out campaign materials; and 42 percent signed a petition supporting a candidate as a part of their regular religious duties in the past two years. For the majority of African Americans, church is not a site of political conversation or action, but a substantial portion of blacks do encounter political ideas and opportunities for involvement in their religious lives. These measures are combined into additive scales of church-based political discussion and church-based political action, and they are included to account for ear-lier findings about the centrality of politicized black churches.

The model also includes two important measures of racial attitudes. Dawson (1994) and Tate (1994) show that individuals who perceive their own fate as linked to the fate of the race are more likely to partic-ipate politically. The NBPS asks respondents if "what happens to black people affects what happens in my own life." This measure of black-linked fate is coded on a unit range where higher values indicate stronger connection with the fate of the race. The model also includes a measure of support for racial self-reliance. Black Liberation Theology emerged from the black nationalist projects of the late 1960s. It is possible that those who believe Christ is black are more likely to be black national-ists, and that any differences in political participation will be due to nationalist disposition rather than religious beliefs. A measure of support for black self-reliance is coded from agreement with the statement "Black people should rely on themselves, not on others." This measure is included to control for the effect of black nationalist sentiment. Finally, the model includes a number of demographics shown in earlier research to have an impact on political participation: gender, age, income, education, and urban dwelling. The results from an ordinary least squares estimation of the model are reported in table 6.2.

The results confirm earlier findings about African American politi-cal participation. Socioeconomic status, measured as education and income, positively influences political action. Consistent with the find-ings of Shingles (1981), Tate (1994), and Dawson (1994), those with a sense of black-linked fate and those who support racial self-reliance are more likely to be politically involved. Further, the organizational resource model is supported. Those who attend church more fre-quently are more likely to engage in political action. When elected offi-cials make appeals from the pulpit and clergy encourage political involvement, participation among worshippers increases. Most impor-tant, there is a strong connection between church-based political action and the likelihood of engaging in political activity outside the church. Clearly, the black church is an important site for gathering resources that can then be used for political action.

Although earlier notions of political participation are confirmed, this analysis also shows an independent role for black theology in influ-encing African American political action. Even after controlling for demographic variables, racial attitudes, and organizational resources,

TABLE 6.2   Model of Political Action

Aspect of Model	Coefficient	Standard Error
Theology		
Christ is black	.06**	.02
Images of black Christ important	–.01	.02
Problems mean God is absent	–.04*	.02
Religion provides daily guidance	–.01	.02
Baptist	.001	.001
Organizational resources		
Frequency of church attendance	.08*	.03
Political action in church	.46**	.03
Political discussion in church	.02*	.01
Racial attitudes		
Black-linked fate	.07**	.02
Racial self-reliance	.06*	.02
Demographics		
Female	–.01	.01
Income	.01**	.002
Education	.005*	.002
Age	.0004	.0004
Urban dweller	.01	.01

Source: 1993–94 National Black Politics Study.
Note: $*p < .05$, $**p < .01$. $R^2 = .37$. Coefficients are derived from ordinary least squares regression performed in STATA.

key tenets of African American theology have a discernable impact on black political participation. Those who perceive Christ as the Black Messiah are significantly more likely to participate politically. Conversely, those who see God more instrumentally, asserting that black oppression is a reason for perceiving God as absent, are less likely to be politically engaged. Both the black Christ of Black Liberation theology and the instrumental Christ of the prosperity gospel thus have a discernable (though opposite) impact on black political action.

The Political Future of Black Churches

The church is a place where African Americans learn important civic skills. Those who are active learn about running meetings, passing motions, organizing groups, and mediating competing interests. All those skills can be used in the political realm. The church is a place where black people become available for mobilization by political entrepreneurs and groups. Candidates, parties, and organizations go to black churches to find voters, campaign workers, and community organizers. The church is a place where African Americans develop the psychological resources of self-esteem and efficacy. They learn about their intrinsic worth as human beings and use those psychological resources to bolster their capacity to engage with an often hostile American state. Political science has largely concerned itself with documenting these civic skills (Verba, Schlozman, and Brady 1995), psychological resources (Harris 1999), and mobilizing opportunities (Rosenstone and Hansen 1993).

But the church is also a place where black people come into contact with ideas. When African Americans meet a black Christ, they are more likely to engage in political participation. Black Liberation Theology is prophetic. It is meant to provide a theological grounding for a marginalized people struggling for equality. By introducing African Americans to Christ the Liberator, Black Theology supports the continuing struggle of African Americans by bolstering their participatory action. Conversely, when blacks encounter instrumental ideas of God that perceive black inequality as evidence of God's absence, they are less likely to engage politically.

This research suggests that social scientists should not leave the work of theology only to scholars in divinity schools and seminaries. Theological understandings are not simply private opinions; they represent potentially influential public opinions as well. In many ways, these findings open up more questions than they resolve. If Black Liberation Theology and the prosperity gospel are potentially influential in the political realm, it is important to determine the extent to which these theologies are operating among African Americans. The measures available in the NBPS are rough (but powerful) approximations of much more complicated theological stances. A next step would involve the creation of more carefully constructed scales for measuring these and other theological positions within the African American electorate. Though some aggregate research has attempted to categorize the theological position of churches, with more accurate, individual-level measures of theology, social scientists can more accurately pinpoint the effects of these positions on political action and participation.

We are brought back again to the question of whether Christianity encourages or discourages political activism among African Americans. Part of the answer lies in how black Christians understand the political implications of their relationship with Christ. Two traditions of black ministry, Black Liberation Theology and the prosperity gospel, have very different notions of Christ and therefore exert different influences on political action. Black Liberation Theology seeks to make Christianity relevant for African Americans engaged in a struggle against racism. It asserts that God has a unique relationship with African Americans and is centered on a belief in a black Christ who sides with African Americans as they struggle against social, political, and economic marginalization. Black Liberation Theology reasons that Christ takes on the position of the poor and despised; thus, in the American context, Christ must be understood as black.

The prosperity gospel offers a radically different interpretation of Christ, asserting God's desire to help his people become financially secure. It teaches that Christ helps individuals who follow certain formulas in their personal and spiritual lives. Christ is an investment strategy and a life coach whose power can be accessed by believers to improve their finances, protect their families, strengthen their faith, and achieve personal authenticity.

This instrumental view of Christ has implications for the future of black politics. The prosperity gospel is a fast-growing theology among black Americans. Preachers like Creflo Dollar and T. D. Jakes have congregations, viewers, and readers numbering in the tens of thousands. There is some evidence that their individual and instrumental message dampens political activism among African Americans. This effect can have significant consequences for the Democratic Party, which relies heavily on African American turnout in local and national elections. However, this effect is countered to the extent that other congregations advance Black Liberation Theology's understanding of a God who sides with the oppressed, the vulnerable, and the poor.

Soon after the 2004 presidential election, two major conferences highlighted the political consequences of these divergent black theological positions. On January 24, 2005, the four black Baptist conventions joined for a momentous meeting that brought these historically antagonistic groups together for a week in Nashville. They agreed on an extensive platform reflecting a progressive social and political agenda. Their plan called for an end to the Iraq war and the George W. Bush administration's tax cuts, an extension of the Voting Rights Act, opposition to the confirmation of Alberto Gonzales as attorney general, an end to the prison-industrial complex, a commitment to public education and health care, a national living wage, and development activities in Africa and the Caribbean.

A few days later, more than a hundred black clergy met in Los Angeles to craft a Black Contract with America on Moral Values. Calling themselves the High Impact Leadership Coalition, these ministers developed a platform centered on the conservative political agenda of the Republican Party. This group makes opposing gay marriage central, and it calls for the protection of marriage and family, home and business ownership, and education and prison reform.

These two meetings reinforce the earlier empirical evidence about the political consequences of different theological positions within the black church. Both groups derived their political agendas from interpretations of biblical texts. The Baptist conventions focused on a theology steeped in social justice. The High Impact Leadership Coalition, conversely, met at the Reverend Fred Price's Crenshaw Christian Center. Price and his 16,000-member church are solidly within the prosperity gospel tradition.

It is worth asking what all this means for the future of black politics. In truth, too much has been made of the increased share of the black vote won by President Bush in 2004. African Americans have traditionally given 10 to 12 percent of their votes to the Republican presidential candidate. The Republican Party's anti–gay marriage initiatives only returned the black Republican vote to historic norms after a precipitous decline in 2000. There has been no major exodus of black voters to the Republican Party. However, these two meetings of black churches reflect political possibilities. When the black church offers a theology rooted in the Social Gospel tradition, emphasizing the alleviation of poverty, racial and gender equality, and world peace as moral values, it leads to a progressive political agenda among African Americans. When black churches advance an individualistic conception of the gospel that breaks the link between moral reasoning and structural inequality, it leads to a conservative political agenda focused on private morality.

There has never been a single black church or a monolithic black politics. African American religious traditions have always blended concerns for social justice and personal righteousness. Black political attitudes have often combined political progressivism with personal conservatism. But in the current context of highly partisan politics,

African Americans may find it difficult to combine these traditions. The very different agendas of these two church summits suggest that we may be at a crossroads in both black religious thought and black political practice.

Notes

1. This is not always true. The megachurch structure and the prosperity gospel approach are not synonymous. There are Black Liberation Theology megachurches like Trinity United Church of Christ in Chicago, and there are countless small congregations whose theology is prosperity gospel. However, many of the black megachurches are prosperity gospel ministries. I will focus particularly on T. D. Jakes of the Potter's House in Dallas.

2. Black Entertainment Television drew a great deal of criticism when it made Robert Tilton's ministry a regular programming feature in 2000.

3. Creflo Dollar is the founder and pastor of World Changers Church International in College Park, Georgia. His ministry is broadcast on TBN and he is the author of several books, including *The Miracle of Debt Release.* Another popular African American prosperity gospel minister is Fredrick K. C. Price, the pastor and founder of Crenshaw Christian Center in California. Price's television ministry, *Ever Increasing Faith*, airs in fifteen of the largest markets in the United States.

4. Jakes peppers his text with shadowboxes containing important insights such as "If you cannot handle the temptation to overextend your credit, get rid of all your credit cards" (p. 35); "When a woman appreciates what her husband does, she is, in essence, appreciating him" (p. 100); and "Faith is believing in things when common sense tells you not to" (p. 166).

5. Because I am specifically interested in the impact of these ideas on black Christians, this analysis retains only the 925 respondents who indicate that they are Protestant or Catholic.

6. Only forty-seven respondents indicated that they thought of Christ as white. Most asserted that their vision of Christ was neither white nor black.

7. These items are positively correlated with a magnitude of 0.41.

SEVEN

Power in the Pews? Religious Diversity and Latino Political Attitudes and Behaviors

Louis DeSipio

Dɪscᴜssɪᴏɴs ᴏғ ᴀᴍᴇʀɪᴄᴀɴ ᴄᴀᴛʜᴏʟɪᴄɪsᴍ often marginalize the importance of Latinos to the dynamism of the faith.[1] That most Latinos are Catholics is taken as a truism. At the same time, however, the experiences of Latinos as Catholics and the Latino relationship with non-Latino Catholics is largely neglected. In scholarly analysis of contemporary Catholicism, the category "Catholic" often refers to Catholics of European ancestry. In some cases, a separate Catholic group is mentioned—"Latino Catholics" (e.g., Kohut et al. 2000). Though this division recognizes that there are some significant social and political differences between Latino and non-Latino Catholics, it masks the important role that Latinos play in the continuing dynamism and political importance of Catholics in the American electorate.

In some ways, this categorization reflects the marginal status of Latinos within American Catholicism. By failing to analyze either the unique contribution of Latinos to American Catholicism or Latino community tensions over faith and religious practice, traditional analysis of American Catholicism neglects the important role that Latinos are playing in revitalizing the faith and building its numbers. The failure to assess Latino contributions to American Catholicism also reflects a second failure by scholars of American religion. Because most Latinos have always been Catholic, there has been a consistent failure to examine the religious diversity of the Latino experience and the impact that this diversity is having on the process of Latinos' adaptation in the United States both culturally and politically. It is this adaptation that I examine in this chapter, with a particular focus on the impact of religious diversity on Latinos' political attitudes and behaviors.

My objective in this chapter is threefold. I begin with a brief history of the relationship between Latinos and the Catholic Church and offer some measurements of contemporary Latino religious affiliation based on survey data. These data indicate that Latinos remain strongly Catholic and that, despite Protestant inroads in parts of Latin America and in some Latino communities, Latino Catholicism is likely to remain the dominant pattern for the foreseeable future. Second, I look at the role of religion generally, and Catholicism more specifically, in Latino electoral participation. Finally, I look at differences in Latino political attitudes and behaviors that can be attributed to religion. Though differences in mobilization, attitudes, and behaviors that can be attributed to differential religious practices are relatively few, they are potentially significant as more political actors seek to win Latino support.

Latino Religiosity and Religious Practice

The great majority of Latinos are Catholics, and this has been the case throughout the Latino presence in the United States. Though the share of Latino populations made up of Catholics has declined slightly during the past decade, Catholic Latinos continue to outnumber Latinos of other faiths by a factor of at least two to one (see table 7.1).[2] Moreover, Latinos are distinctive not only in their high rates of Catholicism; among non-Catholic Latinos, mainline Protestants are a small minority, whereas evangelical Protestant Christianity has grown dramatically among Latinos during the past decade (Hunt 2000).

Latinos of Mexican origin or ancestry report the highest rates of Catholicism, with Catholics outnumbering other faiths three to one. Cubans and Latinos who trace their origin or ancestry to countries of Latin America and the Caribbean other than Mexico, Puerto Rico, or Cuba have the lowest rates of Catholicism. Even in these populations, however, more than 60 percent of Latinos report that they are Catholics.

Cubans and Puerto Ricans (resident in the continental United States) have seen declines in the past decade in self-reported Catholicism. In a 1989 survey, 65 percent of Puerto Ricans and 78 percent of

TABLE 7.1 Latino Religious Preference, 1989–2002 (percent)

1989	Mexican	Puerto Rican	Cuban	
Catholic	77.1	65.2	77.6	
Protestant	8.7	17.8	10.9	
"Christian"	3.2	4.6	3.0	
Other religious tradition	0.3	0.0	0.4	
None/Other/Refused	10.8	12.3	8.0	
n	1,550	589	679	

1999	Mexican	Puerto Rican	Cuban	Other Latino
Catholic	77	70	66	60
Protestant	5	11	5	12
Other religious tradition	11	14	21	13
Jewish	—	—	1	
None	6	6	5	7
n	2,417			

2001	Mexican	Puerto Rican	Cuban	Other and Mixed Latin American/ Caribbean
Catholic	74.6	58.3	62.7	61.8
Protestant	4.1	13.9	6.9	8.9
"Christian"	10.0	11.8	12.7	10.1
Other religious tradition	6.8	11.1	11.8	10.1
None/other/refused	4.4	4.9	5.9	7.2
n	958	144	102	505

2002	Latino
Catholic	70
Protestant	8
Other religious tradition	14
None	8
n	2,929

Sources: Author's calculations based on: 1989 data, Latino National Political Survey; 1999 data, *Washington Post* / Henry J. Kaiser Family Foundation / Harvard University National Survey of Latinos in America; 2001 data, Hispanic Churches in American Public Life National Survey; 2002 data, Pew Hispanic Center / Henry J. Kaiser Family Foundation 2002 National Survey of Hispanics.

Note: Puerto Rican category includes people of Puerto Rican–origin or –ancestry populations residing in the continental United States.

Cubans reported that they were Catholic. A 2001 survey, with smaller Puerto Rican and Cuban respondent pools (and thus larger sampling error) found lower rates of Catholicism. Just 58 percent of Puerto Ricans and 63 percent of Cubans in this survey reported that they were Catholics. Later in the chapter, I discuss some factors that are increasing the share of Protestants in the Latino population. For now, it is important to note these exceptions to the pattern of overwhelming Catholicism among Latinos, and to recognize that changing demographics may presage a slow change in the high rates of Latino Catholicism.

The non-Catholic Latinos include a mix of mainline Protestants, evangelical and nondenominational Christians, people of other faiths, and a handful of atheists and agnostics. The most dramatic growth increase over the 1990s appeared among individuals identifying simply as "Christian" or reporting membership in another religious tradition.

To put these numbers in context, approximately 70 percent of Latinos are Catholic. The Latino population in the United States is approximately 43 million, of whom approximately 30 million are Catholic. Thus, approximately four in ten Catholics nationwide are Latino. High Latino birthrates and continued migration from the other countries of the Americas ensure that the Latino share of the U.S. Catholic population will continue to grow for the foreseeable future.

Roots of and Tensions in Latino Catholicism

This bond between Latinos and the Catholic Church can be traced to the pervasiveness of Catholicism among new immigrants from Latin America and, until recently, to the dearth of proselytizing among Latinos by non-Catholic faiths. One of these characteristics—migration—has been on a continued upward trajectory for the past forty years and shows no sign of abating, reinforcing high levels of Latino Catholicism. The other characteristic—low competition for Latino religiosity—is very much in flux. Evangelical churches are expanding in Latino communities and creating a connection among many Latinos alienated from the Catholic Church.

It is generally a risky proposition in the study of Latinos to attribute too much of contemporary Latino political and social behavior to practices of new migrants. Although the majority of Latinos are immigrants or the children of immigrants, Latinos have been present in the

United States since its first days. These early waves of Latino residents and their children established the norms and created the communities where subsequent migrants until quite recently moved. This is particularly true in the case of Latino religious practice. The roots of the Latino presence in the Southwest can be traced to religious and colonial expansion from Mexico and to the early population concentrations surrounding Catholic missions (Gómez-Quiñones 1994). The earliest Latino migrants from the Caribbean in the nineteenth century also brought a Catholic faith with them, though one that was more infused with indigenous religious practice.

These early Mexican and Caribbean migrants saw the Church as a focus, and often *the* focus, of community social and political organization. Community identity was often defined in terms of the parish, and early efforts to shape life in the United States tapped bonds formed there. Through the early twentieth century, Latinos were overwhelmingly a rural and small-town population, and parish boundaries reinforced social barriers between ethnic populations. In communities with both Latino and non-Latino residents, religious practice further distinguished Latinos. In the Southwest, non-Latino Catholics generally did not worship with Latinos. As the non-Latino population in the Southwest grew, Anglos came to control leadership roles in the Church, and often institutionalized religious practice in a way that distanced it from Latino populations.

The Southwest in this era also saw a massive influx of white Protestants, who brought with them racially exclusionary attitudes and had little desire to share their institutions with Mexican American Catholics (Montejano 1987). Protestant efforts to proselytize among Latinos were much more common in New York and, consequently, shaped the experience of Puerto Rican and other Caribbean Latinos more than that of Mexican Americans.

As the Latino population began to grow, diversify, and urbanize in the twentieth century, the Catholic Church served as an anchor in often segregated Mexican American and Latino neighborhoods. These Catholic churches served more of a cultural than a political role (Sanchez 1993). They hosted cultural celebrations, educated some of the community's young, and assisted parishioners in times of need. Community members used the local church as a locus for civic or political organizing, but examples of priests or lay church leaders leading such organizations are rare.

Though they were Spanish speaking, many of the priests in the churches were not Mexican American or Latino. Many were Mexican, from other parts of Latin America or the Caribbean, or from Ireland. As a result, these non–Mexican American priests were unable to serve as ethnic leaders in times of political need, and the Catholic Church did not provide a resource for leadership development and upward mobility among Mexican American youth. Thus, the Church in the Southwest emphasized cultural activities linking Mexican American parishioners to Mexican culture and to the Church, but it rarely served as a locus for political organizing and leadership development.

Despite this historical faith-based bond, the Catholic Church and Latino communities have a long history of cultural tensions that always create the potential for distance between Latinos and the Church. American Catholicism has traditionally been dominated by European-ancestry Catholics. In many cases, these Church leaders applied majority anti-Latino biases (see Gordon 1999 for one notorious nineteenth-century example). Though respecting the humility and faithfulness of Latinos, American Catholic leaders did not know much of the Latino experience and came to take Latino Catholicism for granted. The distance of most Latinos from the centers of U.S. Catholicism until the 1950s reinforced this bias with neglect.

The Catholic Church also tended to reflect a paternalistic attitude toward Mexican Americans and other Latinos. In the 1910s and 1920s, it served as an agent and advocate of Americanization efforts, which tended to undervalue Latino cultural practices and solidarity. In California, the Church often reflected majority biases that the Mexican immigrants were sojourners who would sooner or later return to Mexico. Consequently, it served as an agent for the Mexican government in its efforts to organize and represent Mexicans in the United States. The Mexican government–led efforts treated the Mexican immigrant community with little respect, assuming that the immigrants themselves were incapable of acting politically (Sanchez 1993).

Perhaps more important, Church leaders did not invest in ensuring that Latinos themselves rose in the priesthood or in lay positions within the Church. Often, churches in heavily Latino areas would have as priests non–Latino Americans, Europeans, or Latin Americans who migrated once they had joined the priesthood (and often brought with them Mexican or Latin American biases against Latinos, émigrés from their own countries and often émigrés of a lower social status).

This dearth of Latino leadership within the Catholic Church had several effects. Over time, the parish diminished in importance as a locus for political and social organization. Mexican American civic organizations began to emerge in the 1920s and political organizations in the 1940s, supplanting parishes as focuses for community life. These newly emergent community organizations certainly made symbolic connections to the Catholic Church, but the Church's teachings and practices were not central to their activities. Though there have certainly been exceptions, Mexican American and other Latino political movements in the twentieth century were largely secular (though they tapped religious iconography, e.g., the Virgin of Guadalupe). Although Latinos have continued to attend church more regularly than the population as a whole, their political attitudes have distanced more from Church teachings than have those of other churchgoing Catholics. I discuss Latino political attitudes in greater depth later in the chapter, but here it is important to note a divide between Latinos' religious practice and other aspects of their lives.

The Catholic Church's failure to promote a Latino leadership within the American Catholic hierarchy has had an unmeasurable effect on the decisions of individual Latinos on how to use their professional energies. In the modern (post-1965) era, as Latinos have moved into leadership positions in politics, the corporate and philanthropic worlds, the academy, and other institutions of American life, they have not achieved similar prominence in the Catholic Church. Because opportunities for Latinos in other sectors of American society are relatively newly achieved, their absence from leadership roles in the Catholic Church could just be seen as a function of time. It could also reflect, however, decisions made by individual Latinos over the past twenty to thirty years not to enter the priesthood.

The contemporary era (roughly since the 1950s) has seen a greater investment by Catholic Church agencies and resources in some aspects of Latino community organizing. Some of the first waves of Latino organizing to elect Latinos to office built on parish-level networks, such as Los Angeles' Community Services Organization (Chávez 2002). In the 1960s, the United Farmworkers tapped the Catholic religious faith of Mexican and Filipino farmworkers to facilitate agricultural union organizing. Some of the early Cuban émigré activity, particularly that focused on Operation Pedro Pan's efforts to facilitate the migration of children in the early years of the Cuban Revolution, used the good offices of the Catholic Church and a Miami monsignor (Torres 2003). Ernesto Cortes, following the Industrial Areas Foundation model of Saul Alinsky, has constructed several Texas-based community-level organizations made up primarily of Mexican Americans that are formed around parish structures (Rogers 1990; Warren 2001).

Although this list of activities is significant (and not necessarily exhaustive), it should suggest that relative to the volume of Latino political and social organizing over the past several decades, the role of the Catholic Church in facilitating this organization or in serving at its core has been limited. Certainly, Latino leaders have tapped a symbolic tie to Catholicism (e.g., seeking a benediction from a priest at the beginning of a meeting or using the imagery of the Virgin of Guadalupe), but the link between the Catholic Church and Latino political organizing rarely goes beyond this symbolic connection. This disjuncture can be explained, in part, by the relative dearth of Latinos in pastoral positions in the Catholic Church.

Protestant churches also offered some foundation for political mobilizing in contemporary Latino communities. One of the early leaders of the Chicano Movement, Reies López-Tijerina, who led the land rights movement in New Mexico, was a Protestant pastor. His organizing style and early successes were shaped by his religious training (López-Tijerina 2000). But until recently, Protestant churches did not invest extensive energies in outreach to Latinos. Ironically, they reflected the same assumptions as those of Catholic leaders—that Latinos were overwhelmingly Catholic and would be for the foreseeable future.

The impact of Catholic neglect of the Latino community can be seen in religious conversion and attitudinal data among Latinos. According to the Hispanic Churches in American Public Life (HCAPL)[3] National Survey conducted by the Tomás Rivera Policy Institute in 2000, 26 percent of Latino mainline Protestants are former Catholics. Thirty-nine percent of Latino evangelical Christians and Latinos of other religious traditions are former Catholics. Few Latino Catholics (less than 10 percent) report conversion to Catholicism from other faiths.

Non-Catholic Latinos have neutral to negative attitudes toward the Catholic Church, which suggests that they are unlikely to become Catholics in the future. The HCAPL survey found that the majority of Protestant Latinos and a near majority of Latinos of other faiths view the Catholic Church in either a very unfavorable or somewhat unfavorable light. It should be noted that this survey was conducted well before the publicity surrounding the scandal in the Catholic Church over the sexual practices of some priests.

Undeniably, the comparative conversion rates may well reflect non-Catholic Latinos' evaluations of the faith-based dimensions of these different religious practices, different levels of community and structure offered by Catholic and non-Catholic faiths, and different types of outreach or proselytism by different faiths. But they also must, to some degree, reflect the long-term failure of the Catholic Church to move Latinos into positions of leadership and to make the Church a home for Latino civic and political organizing. The attitudes of non-Catholic Latinos toward the Church suggest that it would have limited short-term success if it tried to convert non-Catholics.

Latino Migration and Religious Diversity

Despite the potential for a growing gulf between the Latino community and the Catholic Church, the Latino population will remain predominantly Catholic for the foreseeable future because of the sustained effect of new immigration to the United States. Each year, approximately 350,000 Latinos immigrate as permanent residents, and another 400,000 migrate without legal status. Though there has been an expansion of Protestant missionary work in Latin America over the past forty years and a commensurate growth in Protestant church membership, Latin America remains overwhelmingly Catholic. As a result, Latino immigrants are somewhat more likely than U.S.-born Latinos to be Catholics (see table 7.2). The HCAPL survey and a Pew Hispanic Center / Henry J. Kaiser Family Foundation survey find that about three-quarters of Latino immigrants are Catholic.

These new Latino immigrants may bring with them a more contested religion than did Latino immigrants of earlier eras. Evangelical Protestant faiths recently have been much more active in parts of Latin America, particularly the Caribbean and Central America, than they have in the past. Thus, many Latino immigrants have been exposed to faiths other than Catholicism and may well be more open to conversion once in the United States, particularly if they find the practice of Catholicism more hollow or alien in the United States than in their home countries. Religious options are also more plentiful than they have been in the past. Spanish-language television and radio broadcasts bring a number of faiths into the living rooms of Latino immigrants in a way that they did

TABLE 7.2   Nativity and Latino Religious Preference,
2001 and 2002 (percent)

Tradition	U.S. / Puerto Rican Born	Immigrant
United States, excluding Puerto Rico, 2001		
Catholic	61.7	75.4
Protestant	8.1	4.9
"Christian"	13.8	7.1
Other religious tradition	10.8	6.2
None/other/refused	5.6	6.3
n	835	870
Puerto Rico, 2001		
Catholic	61.6	
Protestant	10.8	
"Christian"	15.6	
Other religious tradition	6.0	
None/other/refused	6.0	
n	250	

Tradition	Latino Native Born	Latino Foreign Born
2002		
Catholic	59	76
Protestant	11	6
Other religious tradition	21	11
None	8	7
n	915	2,014

Sources: 2001 data, Hispanic Churches in American Public Life National Survey; 2002 data, Pew Hispanic Center / Henry J. Kaiser Family Foundation 2002 National Survey of Hispanics.

not in the past. Perhaps as important, today's immigrants, much more than immigrants of previous eras, are able to maintain an ongoing connection with nonmigrant family members and with their home communities. One institution around which this transnationalism organizes is the church (Levitt 2001).

New Latino immigrants bring more than numbers to American churches, particularly the Catholic Church. They bring energy and the experience of a more participant-directed Catholicism. This certainly has the potential to revitalize Church institutions if the hierarchy is open to these changes (Burke 2002). Some dioceses have demonstrated more openness to such changes than others. New immigrants also bring needs that can often be met most effectively through church institutions, particularly when the government is reducing its role in meeting service needs in immigrant communities (Pardo 1998). Again, this opportunity for churches to serve as loci of civic as well as spiritual life can revitalize them as community institutions. Certainly, many forces would impede such efforts, but the volume of new Catholic immigrants offers a major challenge and opportunity for Church leaders.

Religion and Latino Electoral Participation

Latinos have lower rates of participation in electoral and nonelectoral politics than do other populations. These differences remain, though they are narrowed considerably, when analysis accounts for sociodemographic differences between Latinos and non-Latinos (de la Garza and DeSipio 1993; DeSipio 1996a, 1996b, 2006). The most plausible explanation for the remaining gap between Latino and non-Latino participation has to do with differences in mobilization (de la Garza, Menchaca, and DeSipio 1994; Shaw, de la Garza, and Lee 2000). This dearth of mobilization is reinforced by the high numbers of "new" participants who join the Latino adult population annually: people turning eighteen; approximately 700,000 Latino adults who migrate to the United States; and approximately 275,000 Latinos who are naturalized.

For previous waves of migrants from Europe, churches have played an important role in providing networks that allow immigrants to become political and, in some cases, to push immigrants toward electoral participation. Whether they will play this role for contemporary Latino migrants (and for the Latino community more broadly) has recently been called into question. On the basis of their analysis of the 1989 Citizen Participation Study, Verba, Schlozman, and Brady (1995) argue that lower levels of Latino participation in a range of civic and organizational activities can be explained in part by their Catholicism. They argue that because of the hierarchical nature of the Catholic Church, Latinos do not develop skills in their church-based activities that can be applied to other civic and political activities. So, according to this account, Latinos are disadvantaged politically by their lower rates of Protestantism.

This finding has been challenged by scholars with more research experience in Latino communities. Jones-Correa and Leal (2001) tap a Latino-specific source (the Latino National Political Survey) to measure Latino participation in community and electoral politics. They find that, controlling for demographic predictors of Latino participation, Latino Catholics are *more* likely to participate than Latino non-Catholics. Lee, Pachon, and Barreto (2002) take this analysis a step further. Among Latinos, they find very limited differences in voting, contacting government, or protest based on religious affiliation or practice. Where they do find an effect—on voting—they find that evangelical Christians are *less* likely than Catholics to vote. Perhaps their more important finding, however, is that churches can play a role in promoting Latino participation through active efforts to promote mobilization and to develop civic skills among their parishioners. They find that this mobilization and skill development is rare, but it is no more or less likely to be found in Catholic or non-Catholic churches attended by Latinos.

I want to push this step a step further by assessing whether the impact of religious practice or preference shapes the likelihood of electoral participation over and above the impact of demographic factors that have long been shown to influence Latino participation and immigration and the nativity characteristics of Latinos. To test this relationship, I report a logistic regression model of U.S.-citizen respondents to the HCAPL survey; see table 7.3. The HCAPL survey asked about electoral participation in the 1996 election, and I use this as my dependent variable.

The results of the model both largely reinforce existing findings on the impact of demography and nativity on Latino political participation *and* further call into question the Verba, Schlozman, and Brady findings of a dampening effect of Catholicism on Latino participation. Increasing levels of education dramatically increase the likelihood of electoral participation. Respondents with higher levels of education are between three and five times as likely to have voted as the control group (those with a grade school education or less). Increasing age has a small, statistically significant negative effect. Though this finding is a bit unusual, it perhaps reflects older respondents who were politically socialized in an era when Latinos were excluded from politics. Income has a slight positive impact on voting, though these findings only marginally reach acceptable levels of statistical significance. As has been found in the past, the U.S. born are somewhat more likely to vote than the foreign born (DeSipio 1996b).

TABLE 7.3   Voter Participation among U.S.-Citizen Latinos

Independent Variable	Voted 1996 β	Election S.E.
Demographics		
Age	–0.071***	0.006
Education (grade school or less)		
Some high school	1.081***	0.310
High school graduate	1.135***	0.300
Some college	1.760***	0.310
College graduate and beyond	1.925***	0.326
Household income ($15,000 or less)		
$15,000–$24,999	–0.194	0.265
$25,000–$34,999	0.008	0.263
$35,000–$49,999	0.530*	0.289
$50,000–$79,999	0.851*	0.319
$80,000 or more	0.709*	0.389
Don't know / refused	–0.486*	0.263
Gender (males as control)	0.245**	0.119
Immigration characteristics		
Origin/ancestry (Mexico)		
Puerto Rico	0.482**	0.239
Cuba	0.508	0.376
Dominican Republic	0.106	0.417
Central America	0.920**	0.462
Other Latin America / mixed	0.268	0.189
Nativity (born abroad as control)	0.502***	0.174
Religious preference or practice		
Preference (Catholic)		
Other religious tradition	–1.355**	0.683
No preference / atheist / agnostic	–0.518	0.373
Constant	137.635***	12.098
Total cases	1,012	
Predicted correctly	72.7%	
	Pseudo R^2 = .326	

Source: Hispanic Churches in American Public Life Survey.
Note: *p < .10, **p < .05, ***p < .01. S.E. = standard error.

   Controlling for all these factors, however, religious practice has a statistically significant impact on voting. Compared with Catholics, Latinos who practice other faiths are *less* likely to have voted by a margin of about 30 percent. There is no statistically significant difference between Catholics and those Latinos who do not practice an organized religion.

The cumulative impact of these findings points to an important lesson. Undeniably, Latino participation is lower than that of other racial and ethnic groups in U.S. society. The cause of this gap, however, is not the overwhelming practice of Catholicism among Latinos. Instead, Latino Catholics vote, and engage in other political activities, at rates higher than Latinos who practice other faiths.

Verba, Schlozman, and Brady may have failed to examine closely the religious practices of non-Catholic Latinos when they used lower rates of Protestantism to explain lower levels of civic engagement among Latinos. Though they find a pattern of increased participation among Protestants in the population as a whole, they look primarily at the impact of membership in mainline Protestant churches and, consequently, do not account for the high rates of evangelical Protestantism among Latinos. Only a small minority of Protestant Latinos are members of mainline Protestant denominations. Thus, Latinos do not benefit from the positive effect that mainline Protestant churches have had on the mobilization of other racial and ethnic groups.

Religion and Latino Political Attitudes and Behavior

In this final section, I look at three dimensions of Latino political attitudes and behavior to see if religious preferences and practices have a predictable impact on the way Latinos view and act in the political world. First, I assess the degree to which Latinos of various faiths connect their belief systems to politics. Second, I look at attitudes toward several public policy issues where religious or moral values are likely to shape attitudes. Finally, I evaluate attachment to each of the parties to assess whether religion influences Latino partisanship.

The Influence of Religious Beliefs on Latino Political Activities

The variation in voting by religious faith raises the question of whether denomination also influences how Latinos use their political power. Tapping the HACPL survey data, I examine three measures of Latino political practice disaggregated by religious affiliation. In answer to a general question that is not specifically focused on politics, Protestant respondents reported that they received somewhat more guidance from religion than did Latino Catholics and Latinos of other religious faiths (see table 7.4). Though the differences between Latinos of different religions affiliations did achieve statistical significance, it should

TABLE 7.4   Influence of Latino Religious Beliefs on Political
Practice, by Religious Tradition (percent)

Measure of Influence	Catholic	Protestant	"Christian"	Other Practice
Guidance received from religion, by religious affiliation				
A great deal	48.3	69.7	66.5	56.3
Quite a bit	22.8	15.6	18.5	15.5
Some	21.3	11.0	8.7	16.9
None	7.6	3.7	6.4	11.3
Degree of involvement in social and political issues among religious organizations to which respondent belongs, by religious affiliation				
More involved	64.5	60.4	60.3	46.4
Less involved	35.5	39.6	39.7	53.6
Relevance of candidate's faith and morals to voting decisions, by religious affiliation				
Very relevant	40.8	67.6	52.0	37.0
Somewhat relevant	33.0	16.7	27.5	31.5
Not very relevant	9.9	8.3	9.4	3.9
Not relevant at all	16.2	7.4	11.1	27.6

Source: Hispanic Churches in American Public Life Survey.

be noted that the majority of Latinos in all groups reported receiving "a great deal" or "quite a bit" of guidance from religion.

A second measure of the potential for a differential role for religion based on religious affiliation appears in an assessment of Latino evaluations of whether their churches have become more or less involved in social and political issues than they were in the past. Again, there is little variation across religious faiths. But, confirming the differential impact of membership in a Catholic Church, Catholics are more likely than Latinos who practice Protestant faiths to report that their churches have become more socially and politically involved in recent years.

The last individual-level measure of the role of religious affiliation in Latino political activity assesses the relevance of the faith or morals of candidates for elective office to Latinos' voting decisions. A candidate's faith and morals matter most for Protestants. More than two-thirds report that a candidate's faith and morals are very relevant to their voting decisions. At the other extreme, more than a quarter of non-Christian Latinos report that a candidate's faith and morals are not relevant at all, as do 16 percent of Catholics.

These data on the influence of religious affiliation on Latino political activities indicate that there are small but statistically significant differences between Latinos of different religious faiths. Mainline Protestants appear to get the most guidance from their faith. They are followed closely by evangelical Protestants. Catholics, conversely, have seen the most growth in the involvement of their churches in social and political issues and non-Protestant and non-Catholic Latinos derive the least guidance about voting decisions from a candidate's faith and morals.

Issue Preferences

Previous studies of Latino issue preferences have focused primarily on the question of whether one can speak of *a* set of Latino issue preferences or whether one must instead examine the issue preferences of Latino national origin groups individually. With some exceptions, scholars have found a great deal of commonality across Latino populations when it comes to attitudes on domestic policy issues. In fact, it is issues, more than a broadly recognized Latino pan-ethnicity or shared partisanship, that holds the potential for building a unified Latino politics of the future (DeSipio and de la Garza 2002; DeSipio 2006). In an effort to examine whether religion plays a role in Latino attitudes toward key issues, I examine six contemporary policy issues that have at their core a moral or religious dimension—undocumented immigrant eligibility for government assistance, the death penalty, organized prayer in public schools, the teaching of human origins in the schools, abortion, and homosexuality (see table 7.5).

Unlike study of policy differences across Latino national-origin groups, the analysis of positions on these policies held by Catholics, Latinos who practice another religion, and Latinos who are not members of an organized religion shows differences, sometimes dramatic ones. The least difference appears in attitudes toward government services to the undocumented and toward the death penalty. Latinos of all religious traditions support government assistance to the undocumented. Latinos are divided on the death penalty, with a slight

TABLE 7.5 Latino Attitudes toward Policy Issues with Moral and Religious Dimensions, by Religious Tradition (percent)

Attitude	Catholic	Other Religious Tradition	No Preference/ Agnostic/Atheist
"People who have immigrated to this country illegally should be eligible for government assistance, such as Medicaid or Welfare"			
Strongly agree	20.0	18.2	20.0
Agree	41.0	41.3	43.2
Disagree	21.8	21.4	15.8
Strongly disagree	8.8	10.7	11.6
Neither agree nor disagree	8.5	8.4	9.5
Attitude toward death penalty for persons convicted or murder			
Favor	37.1	34.6	39.2
Oppose	46.4	51.5	49.5
Neither favor nor oppose / no opinion	16.5	13.9	11.3
Attitude toward having organized prayer in public schools			
Approve	71.4	75.2	55.7
Disapprove	22.7	20.9	33.0
Neither approve nor disapprove/ no opinion	5.9	3.9	11.3
How should human origins be taught in the schools?			
Creation story in Bible	22.4	50.0	20.5
Evolution	14.0	7.2	26.1
Both	63.7	42.8	53.4
Attitudes toward abortion			
Should never be permitted	24.1	38.4	25.3
Only in cases of rape or incest	39.9	34.1	32.6
Should be permitted if the need is clearly established	9.5	6.7	9.5
Women should be able to obtain abortions	24.9	19.7	31.6
Not sure	1.5	1.2	1.1
Attitude toward sexual relations between two people of the same sex			
Always wrong	59.2	76.8	55.8
Almost always wrong	5.3	3.5	7.4
Wrong sometimes	6.6	3.8	5.3
Not wrong at all	21.2	12.9	23.2
Not sure	7.8	3.1	8.4

Source: Author's calculations based on Hispanic Churches in American Public Life National Survey.

plurality opposing it for people convicted of murder (the position of the Catholic Church).

Perhaps not surprisingly, respondents who did not practice an organized religion are somewhat less likely to support having organized prayer in public schools. Yet the majority even of these nonreligious Latinos support school prayer. Among Catholics and Latinos who practice other religious traditions, more than seven in ten support having organized prayer in public schools. Here again, there is a consensus majority position with somewhat more variation among Latinos who do not practice religion.

The final three policy issues see more dramatic differences between Catholics and other Latinos. Catholics are much more likely to state that both evolution and creationism should be taught in the schools. Half of Latinos who practice other religions say that only creationism should be taught. The majority of Latinos, regardless of religious tradition or practice, oppose abortions in most cases. The Latinos who practice religions other than Catholicism are the most likely to take the most strident antiabortion positions. Just over 30 percent of Latinos who state no religious preference support a woman's right to an abortion. The majority of Latinos oppose sexual relations between people of the same sex; this position is most common among Latinos who practice religions other than Catholicism. Slightly more than 20 percent of Catholics and Latinos who expressed no religious preference stated that homosexuality was "not wrong at all."

Although preliminary, this analysis of these six issues with moral overtones offers an indication that the broad agreement that has been found among Latinos on policy issues may not be as consistent across religious affiliations as it is across national origin groups. With the exception of the question of teaching human origins in the schools, the majority or plurality of Latinos agree, regardless of religious practice. That said, however, some consistent variations merit further analysis. Latinos practicing religious traditions other than Catholicism generally take more socially conservative positions. Because their share of the Latino population is relatively small, their impact on overall Latino attitudes is small. It is reasonable, however, to expect that they will make up a larger share of the Latino population, and particularly the Latino electorate, in the future and may have more of an impact over time.

Partisanship

Just as the great majority of the Latino population is Catholic, an equally strong majority is Democratic.[4] Unlike the story with issue attitudes, there is a consistent national-origin difference in partisanship. Cuban Americans developed an attachment to the Republican Party in the 1960s and 1970s that grew throughout the 1990s and may be in slight decline now. Aside from this national-origin-based difference, there has been relatively little study of what drives variation in Latino partisanship. Traditional explanations of movement from the Democrats to the Republicans as income and education increase have been tested for Latinos but have not proved reliable as predictors. In other words, wealthy Mexican Americans and Puerto Ricans are not dramatically less likely to be Democrats than their lower income co-ethnics. There is some state-by-state variation. These variations, however, follow the majority populations in the states, with some states having relatively higher rates of registration as independents. Unlike majority populations, Latinos who identify as neither Democrats nor Republicans include some who are outside American party politics altogether, not somewhere between the two parties (Hajnal and Lee 2006).

The role of religious affiliation and practice in shaping partisanship has not been rigorously tested. In table 7.6, I present a simple model that adds religious preference or practice to other factors—specifically demographic and immigration characteristics, previously shown to affect individual partisanship—to test whether there is an independent impact of religion on Republican and Democratic partisanship.[5] The comparison in each case is Latinos who identify as Democrats or Republicans to all other respondents.

As would be predicted from existing studies of Latino partisanship, age, education, and income shape partisan preferences. Older Latinos are less likely to affiliate with either party and more educated Latinos are more likely. Upper-income Latinos are more likely to be Republicans, but income has little impact on Democratic partisanship. Women are somewhat more likely to be Democrats. Cubans are more likely than Mexicans to be Republicans and Puerto Ricans and Dominicans more likely to be Democrats. The native born are more likely to be Democrats. Finally, controlling for all these characteristics, Latinos who practice religions other than Catholicism are significantly different from Catholics. The non-Catholics are approximately 40 percent

TABLE 7.6 Partisanship in Latino Communities

Independent Variable	Republican Partisans β	Republican Partisans S.E.	Democratic Partisans β	Democratic Partisans S.E.
Demographics				
Age	−0.023***	0.005	−0.026***	0.004
Education (grade school or less)				
Some high school	−0.137*	0.370	0.475**	0.203
High school graduate	0.594**	0.315	0.587***	0.196
Some college	0.762*	0.316	0.737***	0.204
College graduate and beyond	0.622*	0.324	0.734***	0.215
Household income ($15,000 or less)				
$15,000–$24,999	0.737**	0.323	0.198	0.189
$25,000–$34,999	0.627*	0.340	0.057	0.195
$35,000–$49,999	1.026***	0.344	−0.055	0.225
$50,000–$79,999	1.237***	0.349	−0.297	0.234
$80,000 or more	1.571***	0.394	−0.455	0.288
Don't know / refused	0.343	0.311	−0.492***	0.179
Gender (male as control)	−0.216	0.171	0.247**	0.117
Immigration characteristics				
Origin/ancestry (Mexico)				
Puerto Rico	−0.542	0.376	0.898***	0.217
Cuba	2.312***	0.273	−1.236***	0.289
Dominican Republic	−0.265	0.545	0.718***	0.280
Central America	−0.576	0.618	0.504*	0.295
Other Latin America / mixed	0.256	0.202	0.171	0.142
Nativity (born abroad as control)	−0.016	0.187	0.547***	0.125
Religious preference or practice				
Preference (Catholic)				
Other religious tradition	0.360**	0.183	−0.464***	0.135
No preference / atheist / agnostic	−0.041	0.425	−0.265	0.274
Constant	42.305***	10.727	50.974***	7.921
Total cases	1,619		1,425	
Predicted correctly	88.4%		64.1%	
Pseudo R^2	220		143	

Source: Hispanic Churches in American Public Life Survey.
Note: *$p < .10$, **$p < .05$, ***$p < .01$. S.E. = standard error.

more likely to be Republicans than the Catholics. They are 37 percent less likely to be Democrats.

Latino voting in the 2004 elections confirms these findings, though widespread doubt about the accuracy of the Latino component of the National Election Poll makes these findings somewhat tentative (Leal et al. 2005). Bush saw an increase in his share of Latino voters from the 31 to 35 percent earned in 2000 to between 37 and 44 percent in 2004. The change in Latino preferences between these two elections appears almost exclusively in Protestant voters, who made up approximately one-third of the Latino electorate.

According to the National Exit Poll, Bush increased his share of Latino Protestant votes from 44 to 56 percent (Suro, Fry, and Passel 2005). In both 2000 and 2004, Bush earned just 33 percent of Catholic Latino votes. This increased level of support among Protestant Latinos, in part, reflected a greater congruence between President Bush's morally conservative message and the policy agenda of Latino Protestants. Just as important, however, it reflected a very skilled use by the Bush campaign of targeted outreach to Protestant churches, including Latino ones. This outreach was done nationally but focused particularly on the competitive states. New Mexico Latinos, for example, appear to have moved in greater numbers into the Republican camp, and the most comprehensive Latino outreach in the state was done through the churches (Catholic as well as Protestant). Latinos in the Orlando area also saw Bush outreach through the Protestant churches. Doubts about the point estimates in the National Exit Poll and the degree to which this newly achieved level of support is idiosyncratic to President Bush and not to Republicans in general should provide some caution about extrapolating these findings to 2008 and beyond. That said, the Republicans have demonstrated that targeted outreach to Protestant Latinos can move them, at least temporarily, into the Republican camp with the right candidate. If Democrats expect to maintain their traditional dominance over the Latino vote, they will need to target Protestant Latinos more effectively to demonstrate that their policies speak more to Latino needs than do messages of moral conservatism.

These findings reinforce the analysis of issue attitudes to suggest that non-Catholic Latinos are more conservative than Catholic Latinos. As I have indicated, non-Catholic Latinos make up a minority of the overall Latino population, so their impact may be obscured when discussing "Latino politics." However, they have clearly translated their social conservatism on the issues discussed in the previous section into a tentative attachment to the political party that is more likely to advocate these positions at the state and national levels. Considering the long-term attachment of non-Cuban Latinos to the Democrats, this movement of religious, socially conservative Latinos to the Republicans could reflect the beginning of a new division within the Latino community, a theme to which I return below.

Conclusion

To the extent that Latino political behavior is discussed in the mainstream media at all, the discussion tends to focus on a rather narrow question, though one with potentially significant national consequences in close elections such as those in 2000 and 2004. That question is whether President Bush, or Republican candidates more broadly, can make significant inroads among Latino voters, often noted as the nation's most rapidly growing electorate. To a significant degree, unrecognized by most who raise the question, the answer is found in the issues raised in this chapter on the intersection of Latino religious practice and political attitudes and behaviors.

From the perspective of Republican leaders, there is a hope that President Bush has created a personal bond to Latinos that will reward not just him but the party as a whole. This bond will, they hope, overcome the long history of Democratic partisanship among non-Cuban Latinos and the recruitment of many newly registered Latino voters into the Democratic Party in the 1990s. This recruitment appeared in the aftermath of what was widely perceived to be a pattern of anti-immigrant and anti-Latino initiatives on the part of Republican Party leaders, including former California governor Pete Wilson, Pat Buchanan, former House speaker Newt Gingrich, and, to a lesser degree, the 1996 presidential candidate Bob Dole. If this personalistic bond builds, Republican leaders expect and Democratic leaders fear that other Republican candidates can potentially make the same sort of appeal to Latinos as Bush has done and go on to win strong minorities or even majorities of the Latino vote. Over time, this connection could transcend the individual and link Latinos to Republican positions on key issues. No national Republican leader has invested as much time or energy in winning Latino support as Bush. Nor has any had the cultural resources that Bush can tap to connect to Latinos (limited fluency in Spanish, cultural connections to the Texas Latino experience, Latino family members, and a comfort level with and interest in Mexico). These political resources might well have allowed Bush to bring new Latino voters into the Republican fold and to convert some Latino Democrats to Republican partisanship by 2008 had the president not lost control of the immigration reform debate in 2006. For many Latinos, the rhetoric of many Republican leaders, particularly in the House of Representatives, returned to the more nativistic tone of the mid-1990s, undercutting the more moderate tone that Bush had used to make inroads among Latinos.

The findings presented here should indicate a path for future outreach once the tensions and nativist rhetoric of the immigration reform debate decline. Socially conservative Latinos who practice religious faiths other than Catholicism share issue positions with many Republicans and are more likely to affiliate with their party. And there are many more Latinos like these who are currently not involved in politics but could be brought in through targeted mobilization.

Although a more focused Latino outreach targeting socially conservative, non-Catholic Latinos is a more modest objective than bringing Latinos as a whole into the Republican fold, it would appear to be achievable. The political reward would be smaller—these Latinos vote at lower rates than do their Catholic co-ethnics—but if broadly successful, it would give more substantiation to Republican claims that their outreach to Latinos can succeed. Such success might serve as a foundation for a more community-wide outreach that could also incorporate Latino Democrats and Latino Catholics who, though also socially conservative, do not currently select their party or their candidates based on these socially conservative positions.

In the interim, however, Latino Catholics will likely remain Democrats and will likely not respond to Republican entreaties, even if many of them do share Republican positions on some social issues. This finding highlights the gap with which I began this chapter. Although non-Latino Catholics are generally moving away from the Democratic Party, Latino Catholics are not. Thus, discussions of the political significance of Catholicism that do not account for ethnic variation fail to tell the full story of the American Catholic experience and marginalize Latinos' contribution to it.

Notes

1. I use the terms "Latino" and "Hispanic" interchangeably to refer to U.S. residents who trace their ancestry to the Spanish-speaking nations of Latin America. Where possible, I identify political attitudes, behaviors, and practices of individual national-origin groups, e.g., Mexican Americans.

2. The earliest comprehensive national data on Latino religious practice were collected in 1989. One earlier (1965) survey shows a dramatic increase in Mexican American Protestantism in the intervening years. This survey, conducted in Los Angeles and San Antonio, found that just 5 percent of urban Mexican Americans were Protestant (Grebler, Moore, and Guzman 1970).

3. For general descriptions of the survey, see Tomás Rivera Policy Institute (2000) and Espinosa, Elizondo, and Miranda (2003). I would like to acknowledge Jesse Miranda of the Alianza de Ministerios Evangelicos Nacionales, Virgilio Elizondo of the Mexican American Cultural Center, and Gastón Espinosa of the Hispanic Churches in American Public Life Office for use of these data. They, of course, bear no responsibility for what is presented in this chapter. The interpretation of the data is strictly my own.

4. Although it is not the topic for this chapter, it could be argued that Latinos (or, at least, non-Cuban Latinos) have similar relationships to the Democratic Party and the Catholic Church. Each institution depends on Latinos but does not invest sufficiently to maintain their loyalty.

5. These models are of *all* Latinos, including noncitizens, so they include more respondents without a party preference. Models just for citizen respondents produce similar, though more muted results (not reported). Among U.S. citizen respondents, religion is a statistically significant predictor of Democratic partisanship. It marginally slips out of significance for predicting Republican partisanship, though it is signed in the same direction as reported in the models reported here.

EIGHT

The Evolution of Jewish Pluralism: The Public Opinion and Political Preferences of American Jews

Paul A. Djupe

W HAT ARE THE POLITICS OF American Jews in the new millennium, and how have they changed? Jews have been stalwart components of the fading New Deal coalition and have retained their Democratic affiliations while other erstwhile partners in that coalition have fragmented (e.g., Catholics) or changed teams (e.g., southern Evangelical Protestants). Jews remain one of the most liberal groups in American society and continue to vote for Democrats at high rates. The question asked over and over again is why. More specifically, how has the Jewish community been able to resist assimilation and the fragmentation of opinion that follows? Does Jewish public opinion shift in response to larger political trends? What is at the root of the opinion differences that do exist among Jews?

In this chapter, I take a common tack, examining Jewish public opinion over time for evidence of the social forces operating underneath. It is a common strategy because the data available are limited either in the extent to which political topics are covered or in the inclusion of questions tapping the social forces affecting the Jewish community. Few studies, however, have had access to or employed a time series of significant length and identical questions to look for evidence of pluralism. I begin with a discussion of the data used in the chapter, which is followed by an analysis of Jewish public opinion on a variety of topics over the past thirty years, and then I explore some of the major causes of social fragmentation and their political consequences.

A Group Defying Study

Because Jews in America have played such an important role in shaping the currents of American politics, one would assume that studies of Jewish public opinion abound. On the contrary, however, relatively few systematic studies of Jewish public opinion exist, and many utilize surveys of Jews in particular urban communities (the North American Jewish Databank holds sixty-eight such community studies). Because of their small numbers—just under 2 percent of the population is a common estimate—typical surveys of 1,000 to 1,500 people will not include enough Jewish respondents to sustain analysis. Fortunately, the extended time series from 1972 to 2004 of the General Social Survey (GSS, obtained from the Interuniversity Consortium for Political and Social Research; Jewish n = 973), and the large-n surveys conducted by Wuthnow (2000; total n = 5,603, Jewish n = 104) and Kohut and others (1996; total n = 9,652, Jewish n = 217), both obtained from the American Religion Data Archive, allow a fairly reliable analysis of American Jewish public opinion.

The number of Jewish respondents per survey in the GSS is rather small (typically around 30 to 50). To aggregate enough cases for analysis, I combine two to three surveys, which gathers in the range of 75 to 150 Jewish respondents per survey grouping. This decision trades the number of time points for more reliable time point estimates and an (admittedly limited) ability to examine within-group differences over time.

Although advances have been made in surveying American Jews, the primary focus of such surveys has been communal, religious, and, if public policy stances are included at all, Israel-centric. The Annual Survey of American Jewish Opinion, sponsored by the American Jewish Committee, surveys the Jewish contingent (1,001 respondents) of the Market Facts mail panel. It includes some domestic political questions but focuses on foreign policy. Other telephone survey efforts employ enormous screening samples to find enough Jewish respondents—the 1990 National Jewish Population Study, for example, screened 125,813 people to amass a Jewish sample of 2,441 households and 6,514 individuals. The study asks very few political questions, however. Greenberg and Wald (2001) take advantage of data collected through

Knowledge Networks ($n = 1,498$), an Internet survey company, and exit poll data from 1972 to 2000 to examine voting and party identification trends. Sigelman (1991) likewise uses exit poll data in his investigation of Jewish distinctiveness concerning pocketbook voting in presidential elections in the 1980s.

Political Ideology

A common starting place for analysis is an ideological orientation that helps to structure more specific opinions toward government policies. In figure 8.1, the distribution of ideology in the Jewish population from 1972 to 2004 is displayed, collapsed into liberal, moderate, and conservative categories. Though there is little movement from the beginning to the end of the time series, there is a considerable amount in between. Overall, about 9 percent fewer Jewish respondents are liberal in 2000 compared with 1972 (when 54 percent identified as liberal), 7 percent fewer are moderate in 2000 (down from 35 percent), and there are almost three times as many conservatives as in 1972—now up over a quarter. The shifts have not been steady through time. Instead, liberal identification plunged through the mid-1980s, then sharply rebounded, with a mirror trend in conservative identification. The decline in moderates has been more steadily linear over the thirty-year period.

Is this an anomalous trend, or does it tell us something about how Jews have responded to the political system over time? First, we can have some confidence in the data because the ideology trend comports with analyses by other researchers with different data, including exit polls, which have much larger numbers of Jews (Himmelfarb 1985; Greenberg and Wald 2001). Assuming the data are reliable, figure 8.1 shows us how malleable ideology can be, and that Jews appeared to be moving toward some new pattern of alignment up until the mid-to-late 1980s. Large portions of the Jewish community were moving into the conservative camp, perhaps as "neo-conservatives" following elites such as Norman Podhoretz and Irving Kristol.

Something caused an abrupt shift, and when we pinpoint the shift matters quite a bit for its possible explanation. Essentially, the forces working on Jewish connections to the political system have been summarized as race and religion. The Jewish community has had a tricky relationship with the black community (Berman 1994; Greenberg and Wald 2001). Jews are a very liberal group, are ardent backers of civil

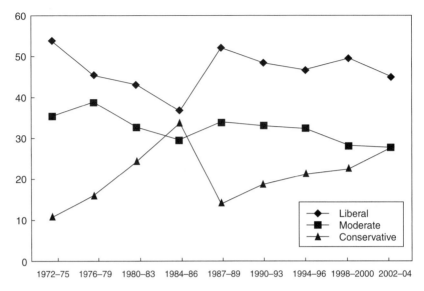

Figure 8.1 The Ideological Identification of American Jews, 1972–2004

rights, and support a generous welfare system. Like many whites, however, many Jews blanched at more strident black demands in the 1970s and have often opposed affirmative action quotas, with which Jews have an unfortunate history.

Nationally, a backlash against a Democratic Party "captured" by its more potent constituents (read: blacks and liberals), along with a troubled economy and a hostage crisis, brought Ronald Reagan to the presidency in 1981 with surprisingly strong Jewish support. A sensible explanation of Jewish retrenchment in the mid-to-late 1980s is reaction to Reagan's courtship of evangelical Protestants. The same forces that compelled George H. W. Bush to declare himself a chimeric born-again Episcopalian repelled Jews from conservative identification. As the label "conservative" came to be identified with social issues, Jews retreated from it (Greenberg and Wald 2001; Levey 1996). That state did not last long, however, and President Bill Clinton's "me-too" politics allowed more Jews to begin to shift rightward again.

Domestic Policy Opinions

If ideology does indeed structure how people view the propriety of more specific actions of government, then the distribution of such opinions should fluctuate similarly. As the discussion above intimates, however, the meaning of ideological labels can change over time, suggesting the opposite relationship. Political opinions may remain relatively constant, but how they aggregate into an ideological identification may change.

The GSS asks respondents if the United States is "spending too much money, too little money, or about the right amount" on improving and protecting the environment; solving the problems of big cities; improving and protecting the nation's health; improving the nation's education system; improving the conditions of blacks; military, armaments, and defense; foreign aid; and welfare. An analysis of Jewish responses over time to these issues is instructive.

The pattern across these issues is a bit surprising. Jews are not uniformly liberal and do not want to spend more on every issue. About three-quarters of Jewish respondents across the thirty-two-year span from 1972 to 2004 want to spend more on education, health, and the environment. Just below half think the United States spends too much on defense and too little to improve the conditions of blacks. Roughly a quarter want to spend more on welfare, and despite Israel being the largest recipient of U.S. foreign aid, less than a tenth think the United States spends too little on foreign aid.

The trend over time for most issues resembles that for ideology, though with much more muted shifts. Most liberal responses dip in the late 1970s, rebound throughout the 1980s, but never recover to their 1972 values. These trends follow the larger American public mood shifts chronicled by Stimson (1991). The public turned against an activist federal government in the late 1970s but recovered a more liberal outlook in reaction to the Reagan administration's excesses.

The exceptions include foreign aid, which shows a small secular increase; welfare, which does recover to just above its 1972 value; and spending on the problems of cities. The opinion that too little is being spent on big city problems is cut almost in half over the thirty-year span, from 84 percent in the 1972–75 period to 54 percent in the 2002–4 surveys. The 20-point bump in the early 1990s may be attributable to several riots. Blacks and Hasidic Jews clashed in Crown Heights, New York, in August 1991 after a Lubavitcher Jewish man killed a black child in a car accident; riots also broke out in Los Angeles in April 1992 after police officers charged with beating Rodney King were acquitted. By the time of the 1994–96 surveys, the increased concern for big city problems had worn off. The huge declines in concern for big cities may reflect the changing geography of the American Jewish population, which has been moving away from the heavily urban Northeast and out of urban cores to suburbia.

Are the opinions of American Jews moving in the same directions as other Americans' opinions? Table 8.1 shows correlations between spending attitudes and time for Jews and non-Jews; a positive correlation signifies a move over time to favor increased spending in the program. The non-Jewish population has by and large moved in a liberal direction to favor increases in spending across the board, save the military, where more favor cuts in 2002–4 than in 1972–75. The Jewish population, if it has moved at all, has followed suit, favoring increases in spending on education, welfare, the military, and foreign aid. Jews have only moved toward cutting spending on big city problems. We can conclude with some confidence that Jewish opinion on federal spending is moving in the same direction as that of other Americans— leftward.

Stances on Moral Issues

Next, we examine Jewish opinion on moral issues, some of the most divisive issues in American politics over this period: abortion, homosexuality, sex education, capital punishment, legalization of marijuana,

TABLE 8.1   The Correlation of Spending Opinions and Time for Jewish and Non-Jewish Respondents, 1972–2004

Government Spending Opinions	Jewish Respondents Only	Non-Jewish Respondents
Improving and protecting the environment	0.036	0.046**
Improving and protecting nation's health	0.007	0.084**
Solving problems of big cities	−0.095*	0.026**
Improving the nation's education system	0.131**	0.159**
Improving the condition of blacks	0.037	0.066**
Welfare	0.133**	0.046**
The military, armaments, and defense	0.106*	0.006
Foreign aid	0.141**	0.082**
Number of cases	~570	~27,000

Sources: General Social Surveys, 1972–2004.
Note: *$p < .05$, **$p < .01$. The correlations involve the opinion and the study year. A positive correlation signals opinion moving toward increasing spending from 1972 to 2004; a negative correlation signals a move toward desiring spending cuts.

and gun control. A large majority of Jews continues to support the death penalty, Jews have become significantly more tolerant of homosexuality, and on balance they oppose the legalization of marijuana, a position that has liberalized since the mid-1990s. The Jewish community is strongly in favor of maximum choice on abortion, the provision of sex education in public schools, and more restrictive gun control laws.

Jewish opinion on these issues has not changed much, with the exception of a growing tolerance of homosexuality and a slight increase in support for gun rights. As we would expect, on all issues, the Jewish population is more liberal than other Americans, though in varying degrees. Jews are only slightly more likely to oppose the death penalty and favor sex education, are somewhat more likely to favor legalizing marijuana and gun control, and are much more likely to favor access to abortion services and to find homosexuality acceptable.

Civil Liberties Positions

American Jews have long been supporters of civil liberties for unpopular groups, largely because Jews have been subject to discriminatory practices in the United States and abroad. The Jewish community has formed and backed a variety of groups dedicated to preserving and expanding civil liberties protections, including the American Civil Liberties Union, the American Jewish Committee, the American Jewish Congress, and the Anti-Defamation League (Chanes 2001). Jewish public opinion has also been strongly in favor of civil liberties protections (Cohen 1989; Levey 1996; Lipset and Raab 1995; Svonkin 1997).

It is a common finding that Americans unanimously favor civil liberties in principle. In practice, support drops in proportion to the aversion felt toward the target group, and thus support for civil liberties *application* is a much better measure of support. Fortunately, the GSS has included a battery of questions about civil liberties throughout the time series, asking whether respondents would allow several unpopular groups (communists, militarists, homosexuals, atheists, and racists) to speak in public (see figure 8.2), to teach in a college, and to have books espousing their beliefs in a public library.

Despite historically strong support for civil liberties, Jewish respondents' application of protection for these five target groups varies across time and venue. One constant emerges—Jews' application of civil liberties protections for these groups has been increasing since a

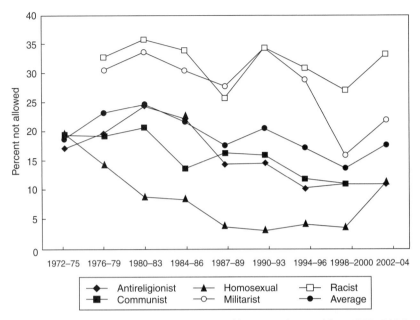

Figure 8.2   Should Unpopular Groups Be Able to Speak in Public? 1972–2004

nadir of tolerance in the early 1980s. In some cases, upward of 15 percent more favor protection of liberties since the 1980s, though the more common increase is in the range of 5 to 10 percent.

In each case—public speech, teaching, and publishing—Jews have the most tolerance for homosexuals. This is not a surprising difference because gays and lesbians do not necessarily hold antidemocratic views or engage in hate speech—homosexuality is a lifestyle rather than a belief. The other unpopular groups are engaging in ideologically charged, unpopular speech, and Jews have far less tolerance for them. Interestingly, Jews have less tolerance for militarists and racists than for atheists and communists. In the public speech venue, the difference of the latter over the former is almost a factor of two, though the differences are less in the teaching and library examples (roughly 10 percent). Espousing the genetic inferiority of certain races and urging the replacement of democratic governance with military rule can invoke images or even memories of Nazi Germany and, historically, ethnic Jews have been overrepresented among communist sympathizers and atheists.

Moreover, the levels of tolerance vary by mode of communication of the unpopular belief. The highest rates of intolerance are leveled against unpopular groups teaching in a college setting—over two-fifths would not allow racists to teach college in the 2002–4 time period, whereas just under a quarter would not allow racists to keep books in the library and a third would prohibit them from making a public speech (the general public would grant the most protection to racists making a speech and the least protection to racist books in the library). Though conventional wisdom suggests near unanimous support for civil liberties, the Jewish community has found room to become more supportive of liberties protections over time, paralleling but staying ahead of general trends in society.

Foreign Affairs Opinions

Prominent among the concerns of the American Jewish community has been the establishment and then the protection of Israel; many see it as a refuge for Jews persecuted worldwide as well as restoration of a divine promise (for some). After some initial divisions about the establishment of Israel, Jews rallied around the new state. Support for Israel was bolstered by the 1967 Six-Day War between Israel and its Arab neighbors, including Egypt. However, until the 1990s, most foreign affairs of the U.S. government revolved around concerns dictated by the Cold War and efforts by the Soviet Union to extend its global sphere of influence.

Since President Harry Truman recognized the state of Israel in 1948, American support for it has been bipartisan among elected officials. The only criticisms of a pro-Israel policy, largely from the left, stem from a concern for the plight of Palestinians. As such, the Jewish community may be divided, on the one hand, by a concern for the security of Israel and, on the other, for the human rights of those under Israeli occupation after the Six-Day War.

To test this, we are fortunate that the GSS has included several relevant measures over a good portion of the time series, from 1972 until 1994. The GSS has asked how respondents feel about several countries, including Israel, Egypt, and Russia. Though a blunt instrument, feelings toward countries can capture a sense of unity around principal objects of U.S. foreign policy, especially concerning the Middle East.

It is clear that Jewish respondents in the GSS have liked and continue to like Israel very much. In the early GSS surveys, not long after the Six-Day War, opinion was nearly unanimous and pegged at the positive pole. Since then, as others have found (e.g., Waxman 1999),

positive feelings have eroded slightly, though significantly (in a correlation of the opinion with time: $r = -0.153$, $p = 0.00$, $n = 344$). Egypt
was not well liked in the early 1970s, though not disliked as much as
Israel was liked. Feelings toward Egypt bounced considerably in the
early 1980s, no doubt the result of efforts to reconcile relations
between Egypt and Israel in the Camp David Accords in 1979 that led
to a treaty between the two shortly thereafter. Feelings toward Egypt
then dipped a bit, but remain in net positive territory into the 1990s.
Feelings toward Russia have followed a more secular road to positive
territory, though the low point occurred in the early 1980s when
Ronald Reagan labeled the Soviet Union an evil empire.

The GSS also included several general measures about U.S. involvement in world affairs and the United Nations. Interestingly, but not surprisingly, the trend in respondent sentiment about whether the United
States should stay in or pull out of the United Nations resembles the
ideology trend—support dipping in the early 1980s before rebound-
ing. Support for remaining in the United Nations dropped from 95 percent in the early 1970s to the low 80s in the early 1980s before
regaining lost ground by the late 1980s. Over time, more respondents
have come to see U.S. involvement in world affairs as in the best interests of the country, moving 10 points higher from its starting place of
82 percent support in the early 1970s. As Republicans regained Congress in 1994 and campaigned against the UN, Jewish support
dropped, though still remained quite high.

What do these results tell us? Jewish citizens favor a strong U.S.
world presence (though evidently not increased foreign aid), are still
highly favorable to Israel, and are far less hostile toward Israel's once
primary adversary—Egypt. The bluntness of these instruments, however, does not allow us more than a superficial sense of these feelings—
how deep do they go? What do Jews think about specific policies Israel
adopts or how the peace process is evolving? Though we cannot
answer these questions with the time series, there are snapshots available. They generally suggest that support for Israel is fragmenting
along religious lines (e.g., Greenberg and Wald 2001), with the more
orthodox showing greater support for Israel and the less observant
supportive, but caring less and less. The other barrier to addressing
issues of realignment around foreign affairs is that the time series only
extends until 1996 on these questions, and serious events since then
could have affected Jewish opinion about Israel, the Middle East, and

foreign affairs generally. Still, with weakening cohesion around Israel and strong bipartisan support for the Jewish state, it seems unlikely that the Middle East will spark any significant realignment among Jews.

Electoral Leanings

In a now-famous quip, Milton Himmelfarb once commented that Jews earn like Episcopalians and vote like Puerto Ricans. Has the Jewish community, once at the core of the New Deal Democratic coalition, remained in the Democratic camp? From an economic status perspective, Jews might be expected to be Republicans, though federal protections against discrimination have helped make possible that economic status. This reality, among other things, has kept Jews reliable Democrats (Greenberg and Wald 2001). Perhaps in an era in which discrimination against Jews is very low, the connection between activist government and economic progress will be lost. Though many other religious groups are being targeted for realignment along various axes of conflict (Layman 2001; Green et al. 1996), Jews might be moved from their traditional partisan moorings as well.

With what political party have Jews identified over the past thirty years? Figure 8.3 shows considerable secular change in the Jewish community, though it remains quite distinctive from the rest of the population. Whereas the general population is split nearly evenly between Democrats, Republicans, and independents, the Jewish population is heavily Democratic. At its nadir in the 1998–2000 period, about three-fifths of Jews identified as Democrats (including leaners), 14 percent as independents, and just under a quarter as Republicans. The chief beneficiary of declining Democratic affiliation early on was the Republican Party. However, Jewish Republican identification has been cut in half since its mid-1980s peak of 29 percent, and Democratic affiliation has rebounded since the 2000 election. I can only surmise that the evangelical tenor of the Bush presidency and the low priority given to peace in the Middle East have shocked American Jews back to their historically strong Democratic affiliation.

Can the pattern before George W. Bush signal a potential realignment? The Jewish community is still firmly in the Democratic camp, for now, though it could move to join Catholics in electoral limbo. Core public policy concerns could land Jews in either party. How that

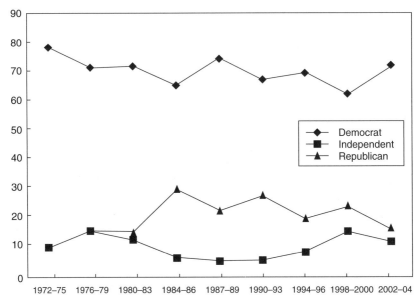

Figure 8.3 Jewish Party Identification, 1972–2004 (percent)

calculation is made depends on how the parties handle the concerns of their other constituent groups, especially Christian conservatives for the Republicans and blacks for the Democrats.

For instance, Jews are not terribly fond of welfare, but they are ardent supporters of civil rights. Most Jews are not comfortable with the intermingling of church and state, nor with restrictive laws policing private sexual behavior and its consequences; instead, most Jews are individualists and respect the liberty to practice religion. Though Jews are significant portions of the electorate in electoral-vote-rich states (primarily New York, Illinois, California, and Florida), many of those states are increasingly Democratic and Jews are under 2 percent of the population nationwide. Those facts conspire against the importance of the Jewish community to parties attempting to maintain already uncomfortably diverse electoral coalitions.

At the same time, some black politicians have alienated Jews by criticizing Israel's relations with the Palestinians—one famous example is former representative Cynthia McKinney of Georgia, who lost a 2002 Democratic primary after $1.3 million poured in from out of state to her opponent. The donors are widely believed to have been Jewish (Torpy and Cook 2002).

Figure 8.4 displays the presidential vote of Jews over the thirty-year period. Overall, support for the Democratic presidential nominee has remained over 70 percent. That story, however, misses considerable movement in between. The 1980 and 1984 elections stand out, as Democratic support plunged to 50 percent in 1980 and 59 percent in 1984. This marked the Republican high-water mark among the Jewish population, with 39 percent voting for Reagan. It has since been cut in half, as Democratic support rallied in 1988 to the highest levels since 1968.

Clearly, this is no evidence of realignment, but the pattern shows a willingness among Jews to change sides under the right conditions. Some Jews could safely support Ronald Reagan, who squeaked into office in 1980 with the support of southern religious conservatives but was then able to evade responsibility to them; Reagan then faced a weak challenger and was buoyed by a recovering economy in 1984. Moreover, many Jews were opposed to President Jimmy Carter's approach to the Middle East. By 1988, religious conservatives were in the ascendancy, shaping the agenda enough to alienate 1984's Reaganite "Morning in America" Jewish voters.

No discussion of Jewish electoral behavior would be complete without a mention of the effect of Joseph Lieberman's historic run on the Democratic ticket for president in 2000—voting for the Gore-Lieberman ticket did climb a few points over 1996 support for Clinton-

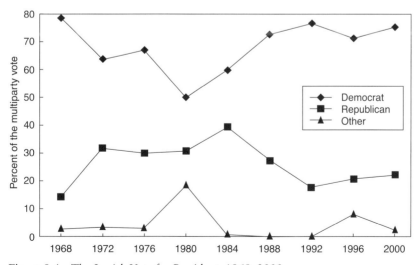

Figure 8.4   The Jewish Vote for President, 1968–2000

Gore. Though John F. Kennedy's campaign was the first to crack the "Protestant barrier," Lieberman's candidacy was no mean feat. Picked for his centrist politics and ready use of religious rhetoric, Lieberman raised the profile of Orthodox Judaism. His easy acceptance by society, however, also suggests the lack of impact he likely had and will have on Jewish voting behavior. Kennedy jolted Catholics back into the Democratic camp after many had drifted off after Franklin Delano Roosevelt. In part, Kennedy signaled that Catholics had finally arrived and would be considered full citizens. Though no Jewish person has yet been president, by 2000 there was little question of acceptance to be answered by Lieberman's candidacy. Moreover, his Orthodoxy and very public religious expression surely did not play well among the large portion of the Jewish community that prefers more private expressions of faith; at the same time, he is not Orthodox enough for others. Further, already robust Democratic affiliations and voting among Jews have little room to grow. So, though Lieberman's candidacy was an important and positive marker in the history of the American Jewish community, it is unlikely to have major, lasting political effects.

Jewish Political Fragmentation

The list of factors that promote the fragmentation of the Jewish community is long, though most are not unique to the Jewish community and occur in essentially all immigrant communities. There is a wealth of studies (e.g., Freedman 2000; Goldstein 1993; Greenberg and Wald 2001; Levey 1996; Lipset and Raab 1995—the following discussion relies heavily on Lipset and Raab's work) and now systematic data with which to examine the growing divisions within the Jewish community. We can catalogue with care the weakened communal connections of American Jews and their political consequences. The most commonly cited trends are a majority of Jews marrying non-Jewish spouses by 1990, knowledge of Judaism slackening, slipping attendance at synagogue (with less than half of younger Jews joining synagogues), and less frequent religious practice. The birthrate among Jews is declining (as is common for more educated populations), with estimates that Jews will soon constitute less than 2 percent of the American population. Moreover, the population depletions caused by a low birthrate and intermarriage losses will not be replaced by immigration as they were in earlier times. In fact, Lipset and Raab (1995) argue that these trends of communal fragmentation have existed perennially for Jews in America and have only been obscured and offset by immigration.

A common assumption among scholars of the Jewish community is that unity is preserved, in part, through participation within the religious community. Though religious participation may indeed assist in maintaining communal ties, its role in promoting political cohesion may be less than once suspected. A recent study of rabbis of the four primary American Jewish movements has found considerable diversity in many political opinions and behaviors important to Jewish unity (Djupe and Sokhey 2003). For instance, few rabbis show significant public concern about anti-Semitism, few rabbis feel close to or are members of the Jewish advocacy organizations (e.g., American Jewish Committee and Anti-Defamation League), and rabbis have quite diverse views on the role the United States should play on the path to peace in the Israeli/Palestinian conflict. Not surprisingly, though, rabbis are overwhelmingly Democratic and liberal, as they report their congregations are. Even Orthodox rabbis, of whom a third identify as Republicans (a trend to watch), almost unanimously report majority-Democratic congregations.

Greenberg and Wald (2001) add several factors that round out an understanding of the forces buffeting the Jewish community. Over the long run, they and others argue, the group prosperity allowed by the openness and opportunities of American society will sow the seeds of Jewish diversity, undermining historic ties to the Democratic Party and liberalism more generally (see also Moore 1986). Further, political movements since the civil rights movement in the 1960s have encouraged Jewish voters to seek other options. Many Jews have little support for affirmative action, which reminds many of the quotas that capped Jewish economic participation, but which is a core issue for the African Americans who are crucial to the Democratic coalition.

Underlying many of the communal trends discussed above is the geographical dispersion of once tightly knit immigrant communities. Hoge, Johnson, and Luidens (1994), for instance, show that for a sample of Presbyterian baby-boomers, moving 100 miles away from the childhood home is one of the strongest predictors of religious disaffiliation. Geographic dispersion also makes unity of opinion difficult to sustain (Huckfeldt and Sprague 1995). For example, Fuchs (1956a) found that Jewish women who remained in a Jewish neighborhood during the day had quite unified Democratic voting intentions, but the men who left to work outside the neighborhood had political affiliations resembling the wider community's, meaning a greater Republican propensity.

Nevertheless, the Jewish community remains politically distinctive, and Sigelman (1991, 990) suggests why: "The real key to Jewish support of Democratic nominees is that the proportion of liberals and Democrats is so much higher among Jews than gentiles in the first place. In this persistent adherence to the Democratic Party in general and the liberal wing of the party in particular, the Jewish community is indeed distinctive."

Sigelman is coy about *how* Jews have fended off the forces that have frayed the political cohesion of other ethnoreligious groups, but it is certainly not because Jews are immune to those forces: "Jews, like Catholics and Protestants, do respond politically when tickled or pricked" (1991, 991). One answer is provided by Chanes (2001, 117): "No self-identifying group in the United States offers as many institutions that provide opportunities for advocacy [and communal identity] as does the American Jewish community. The multiplicity of Jewish organizations . . . is the strength . . . of the Jewish community." If organizational life is key to sustaining identity, shaping opinions, and generating participation, then the Jewish community is in a position of relative strength from which to resist the forces that strain communal bonds.

Empirical Evidence

In this section, I explore some of the common explanations to see where cracks in the Jewish community are appearing and how they relate to Jewish political attachments. The two variables of interest here are partisanship and ideology—the two strongest and most stable attachments that structure best how citizens' political views are aggregated. I examine what have been identified as the major culprits of fragmentation: religious observance, geography, religious intermarriage, social class, and political opinions and values.

Religious Observance

For observers of American politics, the political attachments of American Jews have remained anomalous. Most groups follow their economic self-interest, to a greater or lesser extent. There are exceptions, but there *are* general class divisions in the American electorate. What explains the exceptions? Whites lower on the economic ladder in the South, who are also largely evangelical Protestants, now vote strongly Republican; as mentioned above, Jews have been said to have incomes like Episcopalians but political affiliations like Hispanics (Himmelfarb 1968, 1985). Some of the exceptional patterns thus appear to be generated by religious attachments.

The most prominent proponent of a religious explanation for Jewish political distinctiveness is Lawrence Fuchs (1956b), who in his study of Jewish political behavior in the 1950s suggested that a concern for the unfortunate, called *tzedakeh*, led Jews to take liberal social policy positions. Jews had few qualms about government pursuing policies to benefit the poor because of the value placed on learning. Higher education instills an appreciation for grand social policy initiatives, but also support for government upholding civil liberties—two important liberal planks after the New Deal. Moreover, Jews find some common bond with postmillennial Christians, who are called to shape the world in God's image to prepare for the second coming of Christ. Of course, the return of Christ is not high on Jewish priority lists, but Jews do embrace the world and are not motivated to separate the world from God. According to Fuchs, these three Jewish values help to explain the place of Jews in the liberal camp.

The balance of opinion among scholars of the Jewish community, however, suggests that religion actually plays little role in sustaining Jewish exceptionalism. Jewish opinions differ little from those of other liberal religious groups, controlling for other factors (Cohen and Liebman 1997), and Greenberg and Wald (2001) argue that Jewish religious values have several possible applications to salient political issues. Others find few differences in opinion between observant and nonobservant Jews, sure signs that other factors are at work.

Examining GSS data, there is no discernable trend in Jewish religious attendance through the last thirty years. It appears to move higher through the 1980s and then settle back down in the 1990s to levels common in the 1970s. Of course, there are many other components of Jewish religious observance, such as dietary restrictions, though none are measured in the GSS over time. Moreover, any differences within the Jewish community are confounded by the different movements. Greater attendance at religious services is most likely standing in for the effects of being more Orthodox. Keeping in mind these many weaknesses in what the attendance measure can yield, table 8.2 suggests that Democratic Jews attend services at the same rate as non-Democrats. Table 8.3 shows that those who attend more often are more conservative, but that greater attendance does not affect partisan identification. Essentially, we see that personal thoughts about how government should be run (ideology) are starting to change, but the public expression of those beliefs (partisanship) is held in line by a mixture of forces: the cues of Jewish communal groups, the public agenda of the Republican Party, and surely some social coercion. Over time, however, social fragmentation may weaken the potency of social networks and loosen ties to Jewish interest groups, allowing diverse political orientations to flower.

It is important to realize that the evidence is mixed about the Jewish communal forces maintaining traditional Jewish political attachments. Those with the strongest connections to the Jewish community *and* those with the weakest are most Democratic (the traditional political attachment of the Jewish community). That is, those in the western United States, who are generally younger and more likely to intermarry, are more Democratic, as are older Jews, females, and those with children (see table 8.2). Indeed, this portrait of Democratic affiliations sounds much like the pattern among the American public. What is distinctive in the Jewish community is that religious attendance does not appear to structure partisan affiliation, at least for now.

Geographic Dispersion

On the basis of the full GSS time series, the probability of living in the Northeast for American Jews changed from 1 in 2 in 1972 to 1 in 4 by 2000. American Jews have followed the great migration to the Sunbelt—the South and West. The greatest beneficiary is the South, followed by the West. The probability of a Jewish person living in the South doubled from 1 in 7 to over 1 in 4; the probability of living in the West rose from 1 in 14 to 1 in 6 over the same thirty-year period. Of course, as Jews choose where to live based on work, schools, and safety, the maintenance of religious tradition may become much more difficult (Fishman 1999). Residential relocation may make it more difficult to obtain kosher foods, to attend a synagogue, and to associate with other Jews (compounding the other issues).

Table 8.2 compares the traits of Democrats and non-Democrats to get a sense of the demographic trends, if any, that generate partisan divisions among Jews. Greater percentages of non-Democrats reside in the South,

TABLE 8.2 Demographic, Geographic, and Media Use Differences between Jewish Democrats and Non-Democrats

Descriptor	Kohut and others 1996			General Social Surveys (GSS), 1990–2004		
	Democrats	Non-Democrats	Significant Difference?	Democrats	Non-Democrats	Significant Difference?
Education (mean)	5.5	5.2	No	15.7	15.7	No
Age (mean)	3.3	3.0	No	51.1	47.4	Yes
Income (GSS = 1991–96) (mean)	4.7	5.5	Yes	17.6	18.3	No
Income (GSS = 1998–04) (mean)	—	—		19.3	19.5	No
Female (mean)	1.6	1.5	No	1.4	1.6	Yes
Religious attendance (mean)	3.7	3.8	No	2.7	2.8	No
Newspaper readership (mean)	1.3	1.2	Yes	1.7	1.8	No
Television use (mean)	1.2	1.2	No	—	—	
Radio use (mean)	1.4	1.4	No	—	—	
Talk radio use (mean)	2.5	2.6	No	—	—	
Large city (percent)	38.3	39.0	No	48.6	46.4	No
Married to another Jew (percent)	—	—		74.4	77.3	No
Married (percent)	54.2	63.0	No	63.8	61.3	No
Divorced (percent)	2.7	10.4	No	12.0	11.3	No
Own home (percent)	65.0	69.5	No	69.4	64.0	No
Have kids under 18 (percent)	27.4	38.7	No	32.4	29.6	No
Union household (percent)	12.3	11.8	No	14.4	16.0	No
Own a gun (percent)	—	—		8.0	22.0	Yes
South (percent)	27.8	23.3	No	16.9	27.4	Yes
West (percent)	20.8	15.1	No	30.1	16.8	Yes
Northeast (percent)	41.7	53.4	Yes	41.6	40.7	No
Midwest (percent)	9.7	8.2	No	11.4	15.0	No

Sources: Diminishing Divide Surveys (Kohut 1996; $n \sim 217$) and General Social Surveys, 1990–2004 ($n \sim 430$). The specific number of cases for each entry varies.

Note: $p = .117$. GSS = General Social Survey. "Yes" means that the difference is statistically significant at least at the $p < .10$ level (t-test results).

TABLE 8.3   Contributing Factors to Party Identification and
Political Ideology among American Jews (ordinary least squares
regression estimates)

Variable	Political Ideology		Party Identification	
	Coeff.	*(S.E.)*	*Coeff.*	*(S.E.)*
Age	0.003	(0.004)	−0.015	(0.004)***
Education	−0.052	(0.021)**	−0.008	(0.026)
Sex	−0.223	(0.120)*	−0.509	(0.149)**
Has kids	−0.023	(0.025)	−0.061	(0.030)**
Social class	−0.002	(0.110)	−0.084	(0.135)
Owns a gun	0.635	(0.171)***	0.705	(0.215)***
South	0.004	(0.157)	0.123	(0.198)
West	−0.257	(0.163)	−0.494	(0.202)**
Midwest	−0.466	(0.182)**	−0.041	(0.226)
Religious attendance	0.106	(0.030)***	0.012	(0.047)
Religious intermarriage	−0.460	(0.241)*	0.111	(0.294)
Survey year	−0.003	(0.008)	−0.003	(0.010)
Constant	11.933	(15.678)	−11.314	(19.747)
Adjusted R^2	0.084		0.067	
S.E.E.	1.296		1.647	
Number of cases	500		520	

Sources: General Social Surveys, 1972–2004.
Note: *$p < .10$, **$p < .05$ ***$p < .01$. Full coding information is available from the author.
Coeff. = coefficient; S.E. = standard error. S.E.E. = standard error of the estimate.

whereas more Democrats are in the West. The Midwest and Northeast
have the same proportions of Democrats and non-Democrats. In table
8.3, multiple demographic factors are used to predict both political ideology and partisanship. In contrast to the bivariate results in table 8.2,
these results suggest that, all else being equal, there are more liberals in
the Midwest, whereas the other regions do not have effects on ideology.
The western United States is more likely to host Jewish Democrats—
the other regions have no effect on partisan identifications.

Another related, interesting finding is that non-Democratic Jews are
three times more likely to own a gun than Democrats (22 vs. 8 percent
of Democrats). Jewish gun owners are three times more likely to live
in the South, far less likely to live in the Northeast, and attend religious services less often, which suggests a libertarian orientation. Gun
owners are slightly more likely to be male, but not significantly so.

There is no difference in the proportion of either partisan group that lives in a big city, which raises a challenge to the mobility hypothesis. This lack of effect is complicated, and is most likely produced by the concentration of Orthodox living in cities who have more conservative tendencies, while some religiously liberal Jews living in suburbia or elsewhere may be becoming more politically conservative.

Religious Intermarriage

Much has been made about the rise in intermarriage and the threat it poses to the Jewish community (e.g., Bayne 1999; Freedman 2000; Lipset and Raab 1995; Sklare 1964). The trends are truly severe. Over the near thirty-year period covered by the GSS, intermarriage rates among Jews have increased from roughly one-fifth in 1972 to nearly two-fifths by 2000. Marrying a non-Jew is much more common among the young, but also among women and the less educated, who are also less likely to have some Jewish education (Fishman 2000). Because an inherited Jewish identity for a child depends on having a Jewish mother (incontestable by any movement), perhaps the pressure is not as great on women to marry within the faith. There are also regional differences—marrying a Jew is less likely in the western United States. As one would expect, those who attend synagogue more often tend to marry within the faith.

A statistically equivalent proportion of Democrats and non-Democrats are married to another Jewish person (table 8.2); those married or divorced are not differently partisan from everyone else. In the multivariate testing in table 8.3, those married to another Jewish person are more liberal, the roots of a Democratic identification, though they are neither more nor less Democratic. The long-term effects of rising intermarriage rates are only starting to wash over the Jewish community, however.

Social Class

Moore (1986) shows that the opportunities for advancement in the United States, which is comparatively free from discrimination, ironically were the reason for the fragmentation of many minority groups. For Catholics, for instance, economic advancement allowed adherents to move to new suburbs that were not organized along religious lines, weakening the social cohesion of Catholics and eroding religious adherence. Declining anti-Semitism in the United States has allowed the Jewish community to flourish economically, and Jews continue to earn more than almost all other religious groups (Roof and McKinney 1987). It is undeniable that fewer social norm restraints on Jewish economic and social mobility have helped to weaken Jewish communal bonds. But do status differences now drive political differentiation?

There are certainly high-profile Jewish Republicans who are also quite wealthy, and many hypothesize that rising status will break the attachment of Jews to liberalism and the Democratic Party. In the 1990s, however, there was no systematic class difference between Jewish Democrats and non-Democrats (tables 8.2 and 8.3), but those with more education were more liberal (table 8.3). On average, both partisan camps have completed a college education and earn indistinguishably high incomes. Of course, there are many factors with which social status overlaps, such as gender, age, and geographic mobility, but they have mixed effects. A higher proportion of Democrats are women and are also a few years older than non-Democrats—and older people are generally richer, while women are poorer. At the same time, a much greater proportion of Democrats have children under the age of eighteen.

Political Issues and Agendas

Most explanations of differences in political ideology and partisanship can be attributed to stances on political issues and how much weight individuals give those stances in making their evaluations. Consistent ideological stands across issues are highly likely among the best educated and most engaged of the electorate (Flanigan and Zingale 2002), descriptors that fit the Jewish community well. It behooves us, therefore, to take a more direct look at the link that individual respondents make between their issue preferences and their political affiliations.

For this analysis, I employ the 1994–96 Pew survey, which asked 217 Jewish respondents (out of a total sample of 9,652) detailed political issue questions. It is important to examine this link between issues and partisanship on a shorter time span, because at other times partisanship may have been interpreted with different criteria. Table 8.4 shows responses to ten domestic policy questions among Jews and the rest of the sample for comparison. On each issue, Jews are more liberal than the rest of the American electorate, with two exceptions. The Jewish sample is no different than the rest on whether businesses make too much money (just about half of each agrees) and have too much power (about 70 percent of each group agrees).

TABLE 8.4   The Issue Positions of American Jews and the Differences between Jewish Democrats and Non-Democrats, 1996 (percent)

| | Statement A#1 | | Neither/ | Statement A#2 | | Jewish Democrats vs. Non-Democrats |
	Agree Strongly	Agree	Both	Agree	Agree Strongly	Difference?
	Government is always inefficient			*Government does a better job than it is credited for*		
Jewish	38.0	19.2	2.3	14.1	26.3	Yes
Total	54.7	11.5	1.5	13.7	18.7	
	Regulations do more harm than good			*Regulations in public interest*		
Jewish	31.9	12.6	3.9	18.8	32.9	Yes
Total	40.2	14.9	1.9	17.2	25.8	
	Poor get benefits too easily			*Poor don't get enough benefits*		
Jewish	22.8	18.0	13.1	20.4	25.7	Yes
Total	37.7	16.3	6.2	11.4	28.4	
	Government shouldn't do more for the poor			*Government should do more for the poor*		
Jewish	22.3	15.5	5.3	22.3	34.5	No
Total	32.2	14.4	3.0	12.7	36.3	
	Blacks have gained recently			*Blacks have not progressed recently*		
Jewish	47.9	21.6	1.9	9.9	18.8	No
Total	53.4	19.0	1.2	7.3	19.1	
	Blacks are responsible for lack of progress			*Discrimination prevents blacks' progress*		
Jewish	28.9	19.1	8.8	17.6	25.5	No
Total	42.7	16.1	6.2	12.2	22.8	
	Military strength best way to peace			*Diplomacy best way to peace*		
Jewish	23.6	9.7	7.4	13.4	45.8	Yes
Total	29.3	7.9	4.7	11.2	47.0	
	Everyone should be willing to fight for the United States			*One can refuse to fight for the United States*		
Jewish	19.3	11.3	1.4	12.3	55.7	No
Total	41.8	9.9	1.6	10.0	36.7	

TABLE 8.4   (continued)

	Statement A#1			Statement A#2		Jewish Democrats vs. Non-Democrats Difference?
	Agree Strongly	Agree	Neither/ Both	Agree	Agree Strongly	
	Companies do not have too much power			Companies have too much power		
Jewish	9.2	15.0	2.9	20.3	52.7	No
Total	9.6	10.3	1.2	16.8	62.1	
	Businesses earn a fair profit			Businesses earn too much profit		
Jewish	29.4	22.1	2.0	6.4	40.2	Yes
Total	27.7	17.1	1.3	9.8	44.0	

Sources: Diminishing Divide Surveys (Kohut et al. 2000).
Note: N = 210. "Total" refers to the entire sample, not including the Jewish component. The total sample data are weighted; the Jewish responses are not. "Difference" refers to the difference in mean scores between Jewish Democrats and non-Democrats. "Yes" means that the difference is statistically significant at least at the $p < .10$ level (t-test results).

One would expect significant differences between Jewish Democrats and non-Democrats on these core issues dealing with poverty programs, government regulations, national security, and programs concerning race. In fact, there are significant differences on only half of the ten issues. Democrats are more likely to agree that "government does a better job than it is credited for," "regulation is in the public interest," "the poor don't get enough benefits," "diplomacy is the best way to peace," and "businesses earn too much money." There are no differences on questions dealing with business power, conscientious objectors, the role of discrimination in the progress of blacks, whether blacks have in fact progressed, and government efforts for the poor.

This pattern of results suggests some need to revise arguments about the role of political issues in dividing the Jewish electorate. Previous work has argued that the politics of race have driven a wedge between Jews and the Democratic Party. Of course, those arguments were made to explain patterns in the past, when many more Jews supported Ronald Reagan. Here, Jews are both more liberal than the population on racial issues and Jewish Democrats and non-Democrats do not hold appreciably different stands on these racial issues. The results seem to suggest that Jewish partisanship hews to more conventional lines—the role of government in solving problems society faces, not necessarily whether those problems are serious.

Because there are fewer differences on policy stances than we might expect, perhaps Jewish partisans differ in the emphasis they give certain issues. The Pew study did not include agenda items, so I turn to a third data source—Wuthnow's (2000) Religion and Politics Survey, with 104 Jewish respondents and eleven political agenda questions (see table 8.5). Despite a lower sample size, Jewish Democrats consistently differed from non-Democrats in the importance they attach to public policies. In fact, on every issue Democrats attach greater significance to the issue than non-Democrats, which is not surprising given the liberal tint of the items.

Further analysis suggests some cross-pressures at work among Jews. There is a tendency for more Democratic Jews to say that leaders of religious organizations should express their views on social and political issues rather than keep silent. Moreover, Democratic Jews are more likely to say that it is right for clergy to discuss political issues from the pulpit. Non-Democratic Jews are more hesitant to take the same stands, though the difference is not great (10 percent for the first question and 20 percent for the second one). As Berelson, Lazarsfeld, and McPhee (1954) found long ago, the cross-pressured (here Jewish Republicans) downplay the importance of politics. Furthermore, they downplay the political role of the synagogue, which is the source of the cross-pressure.

Conclusions

Observers have expended considerable effort studying and thinking about the incidence and effects of pluralism within the American Jewish community. Periodic reports, sponsored by Jewish advocacy organizations, blare across the news media about such indicators as growing intermarriage rates and declining religious practice that some suggest threaten the continuity of the Jewish community. How have these long-term trends affected the politics of the Jewish community? Are the dire warnings from Jewish groups warranted? I cannot comment on whether the growing pluralism is "dire"; the diversification of

TABLE 8.5 The Agendas of American Jews and the Differences between Jewish Democrats and Non-Democrats, 2000

Agenda Item	Percent Quite Interested	Percent Fairly Interested	Percent Not Very Interested	Democrat/ Non-Democrat Difference in Means	Significant Difference?
Legislation to protect the environment	63.5	31.7	4.8	.30	Yes
Overcoming discrimination against women in our society	69.2	23.1	7.7	.43	Yes
Reducing intolerance toward homosexuals	50.0	32.7	15.4	.54	Yes
Achieving greater equality for racial and ethnic minorities in our society	71.2	23.1	5.8	.27	Yes
Social policies that would help the poor	69.2	26.0	3.8	.26	Yes
Campaign finance reform	48.1	24.0	27.9	.42	Yes
Maintaining strict separation between church and state	70.2	18.3	8.7	.39	Yes
Government policies to promote international peace	67.3	26.9	4.8	.31	Yes
Relief and development programs for people in Third World countries	29.8	51.0	19.2	.28	Yes
International human rights issues	49.0	41.3	8.7	.23	No
Social responsibilities of corporations	49.0	37.5	13.5	.36	Yes

Source: 2000 Religion and Politics Survey (Wuthnow 2000).
Note: Number of cases = 104. "Yes" means that the difference is statistically significant at the $p < .10$ level or better (t-test results).

the Jewish community is only starting, and it is certainly not cracking in two. Indeed, the fragmentation trends witnessed are quite complicated and at times contradictory.

Largely, Jewish public opinion has grown more liberal, which few thought was possible. The evidence is mixed or opposite on moral issues, but it is robust on government spending and civil liberties. How these opinions aggregate into an ideology and partisan attachment has shifted considerably over time, moving toward a distinctly conservative and Republican position in the 1980s and then returning to near previous levels in the 1990s. Even these severe shifts in ideology and partisanship mask drastic social shifts inside the Jewish community, however.

The Jewish community appears to be splintering along political lines parallel to the rest of society, unless the Bush era's effects are lasting. To be sure, levels of liberalism and Democratic affiliation and electoral support mean that the Jewish community is still quite distinctive in the American electorate. The exact pattern of that splintering is still not especially clear, but most likely it will follow the more general pattern described by Wuthnow (1988). Wuthnow argues that a steady decline in denominationalism has led to an alignment of traditionalists in one camp and nonbelievers and religiously liberal believers in another camp.

Some evidence from the partisan affiliations of rabbis from the four movements suggests change along these lines. Djupe and Sokhey (2003), for instance, report that Reconstructionist, Reform, and Conservative rabbis nearly unanimously identify with the Democratic Party (98, 96, and 95 percent, respectively). However, a third of Orthodox rabbis are non-Democratic—5 percent independent and a quarter Republican. The distribution of presidential voting in the 2000 election among rabbis was nearly identical.

This story fits with a host of anecdotal evidence and journalistic accounts of upheaval in the Jewish community. For instance, Samuel Freedman (2000, 23) writes: "From the suburban streets of Great Neck to the foot of the Western Wall, I have witnessed the struggle for American Jewry. It is a struggle that pits secularist against believer, denomination against denomination, gender against gender, liberal against conservative, traditionalist against modernist even within the same branch."

At the same time, the evidence examined in this chapter does not support a clean "culture wars" style break within the Jewish community. Jews are divided ideologically by at least one religious measure—but not in terms of their partisanship. The great fear, intermarriage, does not seem to have serious political consequences as of yet. Younger, western, female liberals are more likely to intermarry. At the same time, older Jews, women, and westerners are more likely to be Democrats. Therefore, though grave threats to Jewish communal attachments are raging, many of those same groupings more likely to stray from the community are also those most likely to adhere to traditional Jewish partisan attachments. In the aggregate, there appears to be little change, though the dynamics driving the overall pattern are enduring immense changes.

However, the 1990s appear to have been transitional for American Jewish politics, and the future key is the pattern of social, religious, and political attachments of younger Jews. Younger Jews are more independent and just as liberal; they are more likely to intermarry; they are more likely to live in areas with low concentrations of Jews; and they are less likely to observe religious practices and attend religious services. Without evidence of widespread attachment to the Jewish community, it appears that momentum is currently sustaining traditional attachments (Sigelman 1991). Perhaps in the next generation, status, values, and regional diversity may result in the diversity of political viewpoints that many have anticipated.

Working to sustain that momentum, the Republican Party has also failed to entice more independent Jews into the fold. The repeated statements of such figures as former attorney general John Ashcroft and former House majority leader Tom Delay (R-Tex.) that the United States is a Christian nation and efforts by Republican leaders to push an agenda drawn from the playbook of Protestant conservatives have given Jews pause, despite select Jewish elite calls for cooperation (e.g., Podhoretz 2000). Because the Democratic Party moved toward the center throughout the 1990s, it seems unlikely that the Republican Party will budge much in the near future, especially since winning the presidential election in 2004. That stasis will also likely keep Jewish political attachments in the same place, retaining for the Jewish community an appellation for their politics of "exceptional."

NINE

The Politics of American Muslims

Paul A. Djupe and John C. Green

Islam represents a largely new addition to American religious pluralism. A small but rapidly growing group, American Muslims have attracted considerable attention in the wake of the terrorist attacks of September 11, 2001, and the subsequent wars on terrorism and in Afghanistan and Iraq. But these special circumstances aside, Muslims are just the most recent religious minority confronting the promise and peril of becoming American.

This chapter fills a void in the literature with a description of American Muslims, using two special surveys of Muslim attitudes and behavior. We begin with an overview of this community's demography, including its ethnic and religious diversity. American Muslims are no less diverse than Christians or Jews, though like the latter, their minority status has recently produced a high degree of political solidarity. Keeping this diversity in mind, we then review American Muslims' attitudes on domestic and foreign policy, self-identified partisanship and ideology, and views on civic engagement. Here we find that Muslims hold liberal views on economic and foreign policy but more conservative positions on moral issues. On balance, they are Democrats and moderates, with a strong commitment to civic engagement.

Next we turn to the type and level of reported political participation by American Muslims, including estimates of Muslims' 2000 and

2004 presidential vote. This community appears to be quite active politically, and although it gave a plurality of its votes to George W. Bush in 2000, it overwhelmingly backed Democrat John Kerry in 2004. One reason for this dramatic change is reported discrimination since September 11 and a sense of hostility from the American government.

We conclude with multivariate analyses of selected issue positions and ideology, the presidential vote, and the level of political participation by American Muslims. We find that American Muslims' politics are explained by many of the same factors that matter for other Americans, especially ideology and religious commitment. In addition, however, Muslims' political behavior is shaped by their recent negative experiences in American society.

The Size of the American Muslim Population

There is considerable debate over the size of the American Muslim population. Because the U.S. government keeps no official statistics on religion, the size of religious communities must be ascertained by other means, none of which is entirely satisfactory. These problems are exacerbated when a religious community is small, dispersed, and potentially unpopular. Thus, it is hardly surprising that estimates of the size of the Muslim population vary widely, despite the consensus that it is rapidly growing.

The American Muslim Council and other Muslim organizations have offered the largest estimates for the number of Muslims in the United States—7 to 8 million—based on immigration figures, local studies, and congregational canvasses (see Ba-Yunus and Kone 2004 for a comprehensive review). Such figures translate into around 3 percent of the total population. However, no independent estimates support such figures. For example, the 2000 Census of Religious Congregations and Membership estimated 1.6 million Muslim adherents, or about 0.6 percent of the total population (Jones et al. 2002). These lower estimates have been supported by survey researchers. For example, Tom Smith of the National Opinion Research Center estimated 1.8 million Muslims or 0.67 percent of the population (Smith 2001). He concluded that American Muslims were unlikely to make up more than 1 percent of the population, so a high estimate of their size is 2.8 million. To put these estimates in perspective, the 7 to 8 million estimate is roughly equal to all Lutherans, while the 1 percent figure is about the same size as Episcopalians.

Of course, for political purposes the most important figure is the number of Muslim adults. Smith's best estimate is 1.4 million, or about 0.7 percent of the voting-age population. This figure is supported by the 2004 exit polls, where Muslims made up 0.7 percent of voters. The 2001 American Religious Identification Survey found 1.1 million Muslim adults, or about 0.5 percent of the voting-age population (ARIS 2001); the 2004 National Survey of Religion and Politics, 0.5 percent; and the 2004 Zogby postelection survey and pooled 2004 Pew Research Center surveys, each 0.4 percent.[1] These multiple data sources give considerable validity to the smaller estimates offered by scholars. These figures suggest that the politically active, visible part of the Muslim community is between one-quarter and one-third the size of its American Jewish counterpart.

Although Muslims make up only a small portion of the electorate overall, like other religious minorities they can matter in politics due to geographic concentration and high levels of political activity. American Jews, for instance, constitute about 2 percent of the adult population, but they are heavily engaged in politics and are concentrated in electoral-vote-rich states such as New York, Florida, Illinois, and California (see chapter 8 in this volume). Muslims are also concentrated in vote-rich states, including New York, California, and Illinois (Smith 1999). However, the most notable concentration is in Michigan, a battleground state in the 2000 and 2004 presidential elections. Moreover, there is considerable evidence that Muslims were becoming more fully engaged in politics, at least until September 11, 2001 (Leonard 2003).

The Project MAPS Surveys

In this chapter, we plumb two surveys commissioned by Project Muslims in the American Public Square (Project MAPS), funded by the Pew Charitable Trusts, and conducted by Zogby International. Completed in 2001 and 2004, these innovative surveys, the only attempts to obtain nationally representative samples of Muslims to date, are worth describing in some detail.[2]

The most difficult barrier to surveying a small, dispersed population is identifying an appropriate sampling frame—the set of people that can be contacted and that corresponds to the population of interest. For example, the General Social Survey randomly sampled 46,000 individuals across thirty-two years and found an unimpressive grand total of fifty-four respondents who self-identified their religion as "Moslem/Islam." For the Project MAPS surveys, Zogby International began by constructing a sample with a random selection of Islamic centers, matching the zip code to local telephone exchanges, and then calling individuals within these areas with common Muslim surnames (Project MAPS 2001). Because many African American Muslims do not have common Muslim surnames, face-to-face interviews were conducted in and around four cities (Detroit, New York, Washington, and Atlanta). In the end, 1,781 self-identified Muslims over the age of eighteen years were surveyed in November and December 2001; in 2004, 1,846 respondents were surveyed in August and September. The two samples have very similar demographic traits, revealing a high degree of consistency in the sampling methodology.

Although the Project MAPS surveys are a great resource, it is important to note the limitations of these data. The most significant limitation is that the "mosqued" population of Muslims is probably overrepresented. As Leonard (2003) reviews the literature, the most quoted figure of those who are "mosqued" is a strikingly low 10 to 20 percent (Haddad and Lummis 1987), though she notes that this figure is controversial. The proportion of the Project MAPS samples affiliated with a mosque is significantly higher—one-half reported attending *weekly* or more often. Because religious commitment varies by ethnicity, groups like Turks and Iranians, who tend to have lower levels of religiosity, may well be underrepresented (Leonard 2003). Furthermore, the data set pegs the proportion of African American Muslims at 20 percent of the total without any clear empirical justification.[3] Nevertheless, these systematically gathered data provide an unequaled opportunity to explore the politics of American Muslims.

Ethnicity, Demography, and Religiosity

At the turn of the twenty-first century, most Muslim Americans were not born in the United States—just under two-thirds of the 2001 and 2004 Project MAPS respondents are immigrants. More than two dozen nationalities were found in the Project MAPS surveys, and each may have a distinctive culture, language, set of religious practices, motivation for immigration, and experience once in the Unites States. Following a fairly common practice, we have separated American Muslims into five categories based on race and national origin: African

Americans, South Asians (e.g., Pakistanis and Indians), Africans, Arabs (e.g., Saudis and Yemenis), and a catch-all "other" category.

African American Muslims first came to the United States as slaves (Diouf 2004), though Islam really took hold in the African American community in the early decades of the twentieth century in urban areas, spurred by contact with immigrant Arab and South Asian Muslims. Still, the character of Islam was altered to fit African American culture, with traditions and symbols borrowed from other American religions. Early African American Muslims, such as members of the Nation of Islam, were part of a Black Nationalist movement seeking out identities independent from connections to a history of slavery. True to their roots, African American Muslim organizations have an agenda rooted in eradicating racism and its legacy of poverty, crime, and drug use, and supporting rights for prisoners, because prisons remain important recruiting grounds for their movement (Leonard 2003).

Although there were early immigrants to America from colonial India, the rate was heavily circumscribed by U.S. immigration laws. After the laws were liberalized in 1965, much larger numbers came to the United States, particularly after Bangladeshi independence in the early 1970s and the Soviet invasion of Afghanistan in 1979. Though South Asian immigrants are divided by the politics that created their homelands, they are united in their high social class and probably constitute the largest group within the American Muslim community (Leonard 2003).

Arab Muslims, too, are divided by their national histories, languages, and Muslim sects, though these have been considered until recently to be more national than religious groups. Early Arab Muslims left the Ottoman Empire when freedoms were limited and before access to the United States closed after World War I. Family members of these early immigrants largely defined the immigration from World War I to 1965, when immigration policy was relaxed. Many post-1965 Arab immigrants were educated and looking for economic opportunities and advancement (Leonard 2003), a pattern reflected in the Project MAPS data.

Less is known about African Muslims—Diouf (2004) suggests they are largely invisible—except that they were the first American Muslims (as slaves) and also the newest immigrants. In addition, they generally do not have the stereotypical Islamic appearance—veils, headscarves, long dresses, skullcaps. Some are students and many are not well off;

most studies of African Muslims describe the lives of day laborers and other low-wage workers (see Leonard 2003).

African Americans were set at 20 percent in both of the Project MAPS samples, which made them the third largest ethnic group. South Asians were the most numerous, with one-third of the samples (or about two-fifths, excluding African Americans), followed by Arabs (one-fourth of the sample, and one-third, excluding African Americans). The least numerous were Africans (one-twelfth and one-tenth, respectively) and the other Muslims (one-sixth overall and about one-fifth, respectively).

As table 9.1 shows, four-fifths or more of the South Asians, Africans, and Arabs were immigrants to the United States, compared with two-fifths of the other Muslims, and just one-twentieth of African Americans. Overall, most of the immigration has been recent, with two-thirds arriving since 1980 and less than one-quarter before 1970. However, there was considerable variation in the date of immigration, with about two-thirds of Africans coming in the 1990s, compared with one-third of South Asians and just one-fifth of Arabs.

There is also a clear regional pattern of Muslim residence in the United States. Overall, more than one-third live in the Northeast, one-quarter in the Midwest, about one-fifth in the West, and the remaining one-sixth in the South. South Asians and the other Muslims are most common in the Northeast (two-fifths), while Africans are most likely to live in the Northeast and Midwest (less than one-third each). Arabs were most concentrated in the Midwest (almost two-fifths). African Americans were also most numerous in the Northeast, followed by the South.

These samples of Muslims had relatively high social status compared with other Americans, with almost three-fifths holding college degrees and one-third reporting household incomes of more than $75,000 a year.[4] On both counts, South Asian and Arab Muslims had the highest status (more than three-fifths had college degrees and two-fifths had incomes above $75,000), while the Africans and African Americans were less well educated and affluent (about two-fifths had college degrees and roughly one-sixth were in the highest income bracket). However, there was less variation in occupation than one might imagine given these education and income differences. Overall, roughly one-tenth each were business managers or in a medical profession, while one-fifth held a professional or technical job. South

TABLE 9.1   American Muslim Demography and Religiosity, 2004 (percent)

Demographic Category	All	African American	South Asian	African	Arabs	Other
Immigrant	64.0	5.4	84.6	100.0	83.7	39.4
Northeast	36.4	41.6	39.7	32.8	28.9	37.1
South	22.9	28.4	23.0	24.1	20.6	18.1
Midwest	26.1	18.6	21.4	30.7	37.3	24.6
West	14.6	11.4	15.9	12.4	13.2	20.3
Percent college graduates	59.1	38.7	71.2	40.9	63.4	59.8
Percent over $75,000	33.2	16.8	41.3	12.3	40.0	36.2
Managerial	10.1	11.3	10.5	4.5	11.3	7.8
Medical	9.0	7.7	10.1	10.5	8.0	9.1
Professional/ technical	22.8	18.2	25.4	21.1	24.5	20.4
Student	8.5	5.2	11.1	18.8	6.0	5.7
Homemaker	10.2	3.6	11.6	6.0	12.8	13.9
Mean age (years)	43.6	46.8	41.8	35.5	44.5	46.6
Male	58	57	59	74	61	44
Spouse is Muslim	88.6	82.6	93.6	86.7	87.0	85.6
Converted to Islam	20.4	67.9	0.8	2.2	1.4	47.8
Religion very important	81.7	93.5	79.3	91.9	76.8	72.7
Weekly mosque attendance	54.3	72.9	57.3	67.2	41.0	36.7
Attended a mosque in past week	50.6	73.7	50.1	63.2	35.4	33.8
Pray all 5 *salah* daily	49.9	59.7	40.6	64.2	53.2	43.3
Mosque has one ethnic group majority	21.5	46.1	14.5	11.7	15.5	16.3

TABLE 9.1   (continued)

Demographic Category	All	African American	South Asian	African	Arabs	Other
Very involved in mosque beyond *salah* and *Jum'ah*	18.3	47.2	10.8	14.6	8.8	14.3
High religious commitment	50.0	77	48	59	38	36

Source: Project MAPS (2004).

Asians and Arabs were most likely to hold the top three highest-status occupations (more than two-fifths).

Interestingly, many Africans and South Asians were students, a fact reflected in the mean age of the groups. Overall, these samples are relatively young, with a mean age of 43.7 years. Africans and South Asians were considerably younger, and African Americans were the oldest group. Less than one-tenth of these samples was sixty-five years or older.[5]

Perhaps because of traditional gender roles brought from their country of origin, more South Asians, Arabs, and other Muslims reported being homemakers. Indeed, immigrant women were more likely to be homemakers, as were those with higher levels of religiosity. As one might expect, well-educated women were less likely to have a domestic occupation. Overall, these samples were nearly three-fifths male, a figure that rises to almost three-quarters of Africans and falls to less than one-half of the other Muslims. About seven in ten reported being married and nearly nine in ten were married to another Muslim.[6] These figures were highest among South Asians and lowest among African Americans.

There was a modest correlation ($r = .108$) between age and likelihood of being married to another Muslim. This relationship may not bode particularly well for the future of the American Muslim community, because the inclination to marry within the same faith fades from one generation to the next. Eventually, American Muslims may mirror the current American Jewish community, in which the high rate of intermarriage (around 50 percent) is labeled a "crisis" (see chapter 8 in this volume). But for the moment, these patterns reveal the conservative impact of immigration on Muslim American culture (see Leonard 2003).

Unfortunately, the Project MAPS surveys lack a measure of denominational affiliation, so it is not possible to investigate major distinctions, such as between Sunni and Shiite Muslims, let alone smaller or regional subtraditions. It may be that the ethnic categories capture these distinctions in a crude way. It is likely, for example, that many of the African American Muslims belong to the Nation of Islam, an American denomination. It is worth noting that only about one-fifth of these respondents attended a mosque where a single ethnic group was a majority (table 9.1). African American Muslims reported the highest proportion of ethnically homogenous mosques (nearly one-half), far above all the other groups. It may well be that immigration has produced a "melting pot" within the Muslim community itself.

One-fifth of these samples reported being converts to Islam. The largest number of converts occurred among African Americans, at two-thirds, followed by the other Muslims, at almost one-half. Here there were two distinct patterns: African Americans reported more conversions before 1980 and the other Muslims reported more recent conversions, with almost half since 1990. The mean age of conversion was twenty-six and the standard deviation is eight and a half years. However, there were virtually no converts among the other three ethnic groups.

Overall, these samples of Muslims scored high on measures of religious commitment. For example, more than four-fifths reported that religion was "very important" in their lives. More than one-half reported weekly Mosque attendance (and only slightly fewer claimed to have attended a mosque in the past week). About one-half reported praying all five *salah* daily, and almost one-fifth claimed to be "very involved" in the mosque beyond *salah* and *Jum'ah* (Friday prayers). On all but one of these measures of religious commitment, African Americans scored the highest, followed by Africans (the exception was daily prayer, where the Africans were most observant). The other Muslims typically scored lowest, with the South Asians and Arabs falling in between (the latter also reported a high level of daily prayer).

This pattern is summarized at the bottom of table 9.1, where the percentage found in the top half of a religious commitment scale is reported.[7] On this composite measure, African Americans and Africans showed the highest level of commitment, followed by South Asians, Arabs, and other Muslims.

It may be that the largely African American mosques have taken on some of the character of black Protestant churches, in which opportunities for individual involvement abound. African American Muslims have been less bound by traditional Islamic strictures and more open to their own interpretation (Lincoln 1997). Of course, the overlay of conversion, race, and religious distinctiveness may also encourage higher rates of participation in the religious institution. Houses of worship are often noted as the center of the black community (Lincoln and Mamiya 1990; Morris 1984), meaning that churches and mosques may incorporate significant social and communal functions in addition to religious purposes. In contrast, Muslim immigrants may participate less in their more ethnically heterogeneous mosques, instead focusing on private devotions. Perhaps greater ethnic concentration would produce higher levels of participation.[8]

In summary, the Project MAPS surveys reveal considerable diversity among American Muslims. Most are immigrants from around the world, with a large group of African Americans. On balance male, middle aged, and middle class, there was considerable variation in the level of religious commitment. We will initially focus on the ethnic distinctions, and then consider the impact of demography and religious commitment on Muslims' political attitudes and behavior.

Issue Positions, Political Identification, and Views on Civic Engagement

American Muslims hold very similar views on some issues and diverse opinions on others. Table 9.2 looks at opinions on eleven social welfare and cultural issues included in both Project MAPS surveys (here reporting the 2004 results). Muslim Americans were nearly unanimous (overall and across the ethnic groups) in favoring universal health care, eliminating racism, stricter environmental laws, increased after-school programs for children, more aid to poor people, and foreign debt relief for poor countries.

A bit more variation occurred on the remaining policy questions, with a distinctive pattern among the ethnic groups. Overall, four-fifths supported limits on gun purchases, where African Americans and other Muslims were the least supportive and the three immigrant groups more so. About two-thirds of the respondents favored stronger laws to fight terrorism. Here African Americans and other Muslims were the least supportive, while the South Asians, Africans, and Arabs were much more so. On this issue there was considerable change between 2001 and 2004, with support for such laws falling by 15 percentage points overall (we

TABLE 9.2   American Muslims' Favorable Stances on Social
Welfare and Cultural Issues, 2004 (percent)

Issue Favored	All	African American	South Asian	African	Arabs	Other
Social Welfare Issues						
Universal health care	96.3	97.8	96.3	97.8	96.1	93.5
Eliminating racial discrimination	94.7	96.2	94.4	94.1	94.6	93.5
Stricter environment laws	94.0	90.3	95.5	94.1	95.9	91.8
Increased after-school programs	93.7	93.5	93.2	97.8	94.6	90.5
More aid to poor people	92.4	91.1	94.7	95.6	92.6	85.7
Increased foreign aid	88.4	89.5	89.1	95.6	88.9	79.2
Debt relief for poorer countries	88.2	85.2	89.9	91.9	90.3	81.8
Limits on buying guns	81.1	73.9	84.3	79.6	86.0	74.9
Stronger laws to fight terrorism	68.9	48.0	78.1	85.4	73.8	57.1
More income-tax cuts	65.0	57.7	64.6	67.2	72.6	60.6
Requiring fluency in English	52.3	30.2	61.1	56.9	57.9	49.4
Eliminating affirmative action	37.1	21.6	41.6	38.7	43.4	35.9
Cultural Issues						
Banning sale of pornography	75.8	79.2	73.8	73.5	77.0	74.5
Faith-based initiatives	69.9	80.1	67.2	75.7	70.0	57.1
School vouchers	65.6	80.1	61.1	65.4	63.9	58.4
Death penalty	60.8	41.1	66.9	65.4	67.7	58.7
Research on stem cells	59.9	48.8	65.0	52.9	61.2	65.4

TABLE 9.2   (continued)

Issue Favored	All	African American	South Asian	African	Arabs	Other
Limiting abortions	55.0	53.9	55.0	56.9	58.2	48.9
Ten Commandments in public	51.1	50.9	47.4	56.9	55.1	48.9
School prayer	47.9	53.4	45.8	44.9	47.9	46.3
Doctor-assisted suicide	31.4	18.3	33.3	34.6	34.6	39.0
Research on cloning	28.2	11.1	35.9	22.6	30.7	33.0
Same-sex marriage	15.0	4.6	17.0	5.9	16.3	28.6

Source: Project MAPS (2004).

will return to this topic below in more detail). Almost two-thirds also favored more income-tax cuts, and here the three immigrant categories were most favorable (although this support declined by 8 percentage points from 2001). Overall, one-half of the sample supported requiring residents to be fluent in English, a policy also supported by the three immigrant groups and much less so by African Americans and other Muslims. Finally, less than two-fifths supported eliminating affirmative action, with African Americans the most opposed.

This strong social welfare liberalism may reflect the minority status of the respondents, in one or another sense of the term. These patterns are interesting given the relatively high social status of these samples, but high status may also explain support for increased tax cuts and law-and-order policies among South Asian and Arab Muslims.

There was considerably more variation on eleven "moral" issues, including policies pertaining to sexuality and public expression of religion (table 9.2). Overall, Muslim Americans tended to hold conservative views on these issues. For example, three-quarters favored banning the sale of pornography, with only modest variation by ethnicity. Roughly two-thirds favored faith-based social services and school vouchers. Here African Americans showed the highest level of support, with other Muslims and South Asians the least. The reverse pattern occurred on the death penalty for those convicted of murder. Overall, about three-fifths had favorable views, but it was the three immigrant groups with the highest support and African Americans with the least.

A similar pattern held for stem cell research, except that Africans showed a lower level of support and the other Muslims a higher one.

A little more than one-half of Muslim Americans favored restricting abortion, and there was relatively little variation by ethnic group. A similar pattern held for posting the Ten Commandments in public schools and school prayer: About one-half of the samples were in favor, with only small variations across the groups. Muslim Americans did not favor doctor-assisted suicide, research on cloning, or same-sex marriage. On these issues, African Americans had the most conservative views (joined by Africans on same-sex marriage).

On these moral issues, there were a few changes between 2001 and 2004, including a 22-percentage-point increase in support for school vouchers, and an 8-percentage-point drop in support for the death penalty and displaying the Ten Commandments. These changes may reflect the post–September 11 situation. For instance, school vouchers for Muslim children could offer a safe haven from the intolerance experienced in public schools or wider society—a strategy once employed by American Catholics to avoid Protestant-dominated public schools (Dolan 1992). Likewise, weakened support for display of the Ten Commandments and the death penalty may reflect a growing sense of discrimination.

What about Muslim American views on foreign policy? Table 9.3 shows that Muslim Americans were quite critical of U.S. policy. Just two-fifths of the sample supported the war in Afghanistan, and there was even less backing for the war in Iraq. On the latter, one-sixth or less believed the Iraq war was worth the cost, supported the war effort, or backed sending more U.S. troops. These patterns reflect the view that the Iraq war could destabilize the region (88 percent), encourage more terrorism in the United States (87 percent), and not bring democracy to the Middle East (71 percent). American Muslims clearly prefer a nonmilitary approach, believing that terrorism is best combated by reducing inequalities in the world (93 percent), a view consistent with the social welfare liberalism shown in table 9.2. There was not a lot of variation on these issues across the ethnic groups, except for the very low level of support for the Afghanistan and Iraq wars by African Americans.

On the Israeli-Palestinian conflict, American Muslims overwhelmingly (more than 90 percent) believed that the United States should reduce its financial support of Israel and support the creation of a

TABLE 9.3   American Muslims and Foreign Affairs, 2004 (percent)

Support/ Agree	All	African American	South Asian	African	Arabs	Other
Support Afghanistan war	39.7	19.9	47.5	55.2	40.4	41.0
Support Iraq war	13.9	9.4	15.7	16.5	12.9	17.1
Iraq war was worth it	16.0	10.3	17.6	23.3	16.2	16.4
More troops to Iraq	10.7	3.6	12.9	22.6	8.2	13.9
Iraq war could mean more terrorism in United States	86.7	86.4	87.2	78.1	87.5	89.0
Iraq war could destabilize Middle East	87.6	89.0	87.4	81.7	89.4	85.6
Iraq war will bring democracy to Middle East	30.7	37.2	30.2	40.0	26.3	26.3
Terrorism is best combated by reducing inequalities in world	92.7	93.0	92.1	91.4	92.6	94.9
United States should reduce financial support of Israel	89.6	90.9	87.4	80.7	92.1	92.9
United States should support a Palestinian state	94.3	90.8	95.0	93.0	97.0	92.6
United States should reduce support of undemocratic regimes in Muslim world	76.8	67.0	78.2	82.6	82.0	72.0
Kashmir is central dividing issue between Pakistan and India	77.7	65.6	87.8	66.7	75.6	74.2

Source: Project MAPS (2004).

TABLE 9.4   American Muslim Party Identifications and Political
Ideologies, 2004 (percent)

Party Identification or Political Ideology	All	African American	South Asian	African	Arabs	Other
Party identification, 2001						
Democrat	43.3	59.5	38.2	46.4	32.4	49.3
Independent	30.7	28.0	31.8	23.8	34.9	25.0
Republican	25.1	11.4	28.9	28.6	32.4	25.0
Party identification, 2004						
Democrat	53.4	59.7	51.8	63.4	46.6	56.3
Independent	33.0	34.2	34.0	28.2	34.8	26.8
Republican	12.7	4.4	14.2	8.5	17.5	14.7
Political ideology, 2001						
Liberal	31.2	30.1	38.1	33.3	22.9	31.4
Moderate	41.9	38.9	41.2	30.6	47.7	42.8
Conservative	24.2	27.4	18.9	32.4	27.3	22.7
Political ideology, 2004						
Liberal	33.3	37.5	34.9	25.6	29.3	35.1
Moderate	44.6	38.2	47.6	43.8	48.2	38.6
Conservative	19.9	23.4	15.5	25.6	20.5	22.3

Source: Project MAPS (2001, 2004).

Palestinian state. And more than three-quarters supported a reduction in U.S. support for undemocratic regimes. Similarly, there is agreement with former secretary of state Colin Powell that the main conflict between India and Pakistan is the claim over the state of Kashmir.

How do these patterns aggregate into broader political attachments? Table 9.4 reports the self-identified party and ideology of Muslim Americans. Partisanship shows a substantial change between 2001 and 2004. In 2001, more than two-fifths of Muslim Americans identified as Democrats, a little under one-third as independents, and the remaining one-quarter as Republicans.[9] A majority of African Americans were Democrats, as was a plurality of every group. Arabs and South Asians were the most Republican. However, these figures were relatively low for recent immigrant groups, which historically have tended to identify strongly with the Democrats.

By 2004, Muslim American partisanship had changed substantially, so that a clear majority (54 percent) identified as Democrats. Meanwhile, Republican identification was cut by one-half, falling to 12 percent. The

Democrats made major gains in all the ethnic groups except African Americans, who were already heavily Democratic. The biggest gain was some 20 percentage points among Africans. No doubt these changes reflected the policies of the Bush administration after September 11. In addition, this change reveals how malleable partisan identification can be, especially among recent immigrants.

Ideology differs from party affiliation and shows less change over time. In 2001, two-fifths of Muslim Americans identified as "moderates," a figure that was only slightly higher than in 2004. In both years, about one-third identified as "liberal." But some change occurred in "conservative" identification, which fell from almost one-quarter to about one-fifth overall. Indeed, every group showed at least a small shift away from conservatism toward liberalism. Interestingly, the most Republican ethnic group was not the most conservative: By 2004, Arabs were the most moderate and South Asians, the second most Republican, were the *least* conservative. In all, the distribution of Muslims on these two key political attachments can be best described as unsettled.

A final set of politically relevant attitudes were views toward civic engagement. Democratic citizenship requires individuals to value civic engagement, and table 9.5 reveals that such values are common among Muslim Americans. Large majorities (four-fifths or more) agreed that Muslims should participate in politics, support social service programs sponsored by non-Muslims, and join interfaith activities. Two-thirds agreed that Muslims should support worthy non-Muslim candidates in elections. Interestingly, agreement with these civic values was always weakest among the groups with large numbers of converts, African Americans and other Muslims, which suggests that conversion may foster greater insularity than immigration.

Overall, more than one-half of Muslim Americans claimed that it was "very important" for them to be active in politics. More impressive still, more than three-fifths claimed that it was very important for their *children* to be politically active. In contrast to the other civic values, here African Americans scored the highest. South Asians scored the lowest on these measures.

To what degree do American Muslims want their religion and religious organizations involved in politics? Table 9.5 reveals strong support for the mixing of religion and politics. For one thing, a large majority agrees that the "influence of religion and values in the United States should increase" (71 percent). This positive view of the role of religion

TABLE 9.5   American Muslim Views about Democracy
and the United States and Religion and Political Participation,
2004 (percent)

Issue	All	African American	South Asian	African	Arabs	Other
Strongly Agree						
Very important to be active in politics	53.9	58.8	49.3	64.7	54.2	52.0
Very important for children to be active in politics	62.7	68.6	58.4	63.4	63.5	62.6
Muslims should participate in politics	85.6	80.3	88.1	83.6	89.5	80.4
Muslims should support worthy non-Muslim candidates	68.2	59.9	69.4	69.7	75.2	62.4
Muslims should participate in interfaith activities	80.3	72.7	82.3	85.8	84.3	76.1
Muslims should donate to non-Muslim social service programs	85.5	76.8	88.5	93.4	87.9	81.1
Agree						
Influence of religion and values in United States should increase	71.5	82.0	69.3	72.5	69.3	63.8
Mosques should express their political views	60.6	90.5	47.2	52.3	59.5	56.3
Muslims should vote in a bloc	59.7	66.0	58.1	59.8	62.6	48.3
Being Muslim is very important to vote choice	51.1	66.9	47.2	45.8	50.1	39.9

TABLE 9.5   (continued)

Issue	All	African American	South Asian	African	Arabs	Other
Right for *Khatibs* to discuss politics in the *Khutbah*	43.6	64.5	32.5	36.7	45.5	41.1
American Muslim Taskforce endorsement is very important to vote choice	42.1	52.1	40.2	47.8	43.1	26.1

Source: Project MAPS (2004).

in politics extends to Muslim institutions as well. Overall, three-fifths agree that mosques should express their political views and that Muslims should vote in a bloc. However, there were limits to this political role. For example, fewer respondents were willing to define themselves as part of such a Muslim voting bloc, with just a bare majority agreeing that being a Muslim should be important to how one votes. Further, only two-fifths agreed that Muslim preachers (*Khatibs*, who can deliver a Friday sermon) should discuss politics during their sermon. And just two-fifths saw endorsement by the American Muslim Taskforce on Civil Rights and Elections (AMT, a coalition of the ten largest Muslim organizations) as very important for choosing a candidate.

The greatest support for mixing religion and politics comes, not surprisingly, from African Americans, paralleling the view of black Christians (Kohut et al. 2000). South Asians once again showed the least support for acting in concert with other Muslims; they are the most educated, which tends to encourage individualism. Interestingly, African Americans were the least willing to entertain the influence of a group outside their Muslim community—they displayed comparatively anemic support for the AMT endorsement. Other ethnic groups were less enthused with the idea of politicking during worship services. A near-majority of Africans, for instance, appreciated AMT's recommendation but did not believe in political preaching.

Political Behavior and the Presidential Vote

How active are American Muslims in politics? Table 9.6 provides a snapshot of various kinds of political activity other than voting in

TABLE 9.6   American Muslim Political Participation, 2001 and
2004 (percent)

Measure of Participation	Year	All	African American	South Asian	African	Arabs	Other
"Mostly" follow politics	2001	60.3	72.0	50.4	54.7	64.0	63.3
	2004	64.3	72.1	60.1	44.5	65.2	72.2
Contacted politician/media	2001	50.0	62.7	42.3	41.9	48.3	57.4
	2004	54.5	73.6	44.1	31.3	54.2	66.1
Attended a rally	2001	40.2	61.0	29.4	32.3	41.3	38.1
	2004	45.9	67.4	33.8	32.8	46.0	51.7
Discuss politics "always"	2001	35.2	42.8	25.9	32.3	42.1	35.3
	2004	41.7	45.5	31.4	39.6	49.8	47.6
Visited political website	2001	34.1	38.4	30.3	22.5	39.7	32.5
	2004	41.0	32.9	40.4	43.1	42.0	52.4
Boycotted	2001	30.2	51.3	18.5	17.2	31.6	32.3
	2004	36.7	67.5	20.2	10.4	37.6	45.8
Contributed to candidate	2001	33.7	46.1	27.0	32.6	33.2	33.0
	2004	35.6	40.8	31.8	28.5	35.1	43.2
Active member of party	2001	25.9	33.8	22.9	26.6	25.7	21.8
	2004	25.1	31.6	18.8	38.2	21.9	30.4

Source: Project MAPS (2001, 2004).

2001 and 2004. First, it is worth noting that the reported level of activity increased or stayed the same for the samples as a whole. This pattern of increased activity held on balance for all the ethnic groups, although there were a number of exceptions. The other Muslims reported increased participation rates on all activities, while South Asians and Arabs reported an increase in all but one.

Overall, more than one-half of American Muslims reported having contact with a politician or the news media in 2004, and a little less than one-half reported attending a campaign rally in 2004. About two-fifths of the 2004 respondents claimed to discuss politics "always" with family and friends and to have visited a political website. And a bit more than one-third reported participating in a boycott or making a campaign contribution to a candidate in 2004. Finally, one-quarter overall said they were an "active member" of a political party.

In 2004, African American Muslims were the most active of the groups, leading in contacting public officials, attending rallies, and participating in a boycott. The other Muslims were likely to "mostly" follow politics, and the Arabs were the most likely to report discussing politics "always" with family and friends. Although their overall level of activity was low, the Africans scored highest on visiting political websites and being active party members. South Asians did not specialize in any activities, though they did score a bit above Africans overall.[10]

Table 9.7 lists the reported voting behavior among American Muslims. In 2004, four-fifths of respondents claimed to be registered to vote, up a bit from 2001.[11] As before, African Americans scored highest and Africans lowest. Nearly nine of ten Muslims said they were likely to vote, a figure that also increased from 2001 and held across the ethnic groups. Note, however, that the reported turnout in the 2000 and 2004 elections followed a different pattern. For one thing, the turnout was *down* in 2004 compared with 2000. The decline was uneven, with African Americans, Africans, and Arabs showing the largest reductions. These differences could result from the survey's measure of turnout, but it could also be that the post–September 11 environment discouraged some Muslims from voting or that Muslims in noncompetitive states were less inclined to participate.[12] Although these data must be viewed with some caution, they do suggest that American Muslims are engaged in the political process.[13]

Turnout aside, the estimated presidential vote choice showed a dramatic change in the Project MAPS surveys.[14] In 2000, almost one-half of Muslim Americans voted for the Republican George W. Bush, just over one-third for the Democrat Al Gore, and about one-sixth for Ralph Nader (who is of Arab descent) or another candidate. These numbers were impressive for several reasons. As we have seen, most Muslims in 2001 regarded themselves as Democrats. Also, African American Muslims voted heavily for Gore, giving him two-thirds of their votes. Though this was a good bit lower than African Americans as a whole (who voted over 90 percent for Gore), it was quite different than the other Muslim groups: Arabs voted two-thirds for Bush (and nearly one-fifth for Nader), and South Asians backed Bush at nearly the same rate. Nearly one-half of Africans supported Bush, while the other Muslims almost broke even (with a slight edge for Gore). Surely the 2000 Bush campaign's aggressive courting of the Muslim vote explains the pattern.

TABLE 9.7   American Muslims and Voting Behavior, 2001 and
2004 (percent)

Measure of Behavior	Year	All	African American	South Asian	African	Arabs	Other
Registered to vote	2001	78.7	87.7	74.7	74.2	79.2	76.9
	2004	82.6	91	78.8	56.9	85.5	88.7
Very likely to vote	2001	85.3	82.7	87	85.1	85.4	85.5
	2004	89.2	89.2	90.1	88.2	88.2	88.7
Reported	2000	86.7	90.4	84.2	81.1	89.5	85.6
presidential vote	2004	77.1	81.7	81.1	49.3	80.7	84.8
Reported vote choice							
Gore	2000	36.0	61.4	31.0	35.6	18.1	42.6
Bush		47.6	22.4	57.7	46.6	60.0	40.5
Nader		13.9	13.3	9.3	15.0	19.3	13.3
Other		2.5	2.9	2.0	2.8	2.6	3.6
Kerry	2004	82.3	85.4	86.7	86.8	75.5	79.5
Bush		6.7	4.6	7.7	8.7	5.5	9.2
Nader		10.0	8.2	5.3	4.5	17.5	10.7
Other		1.0	1.8	0.3	0.0	1.5	0.6

Source: Project MAPS (2001, 2004).

The 2004 election was strikingly different: President Bush received about 7 percent of the Muslim vote, some 40 percentage points less than in 2000. Meanwhile, the Democrat Kerry received more than 80 percent (with the remaining one-tenth going to Nader and others). Arabs and the other Muslims voted a little less strongly for Kerry, but Bush did not reach double digits among any group. The main reason for this turnaround was the Bush administration's policies after September 11. Although Bush's positive statements about Islam were no doubt appreciated in the Muslim community, they did little to prevent his sharp decline at the polls.

Reported Discrimination and Views of American Society

Muslim Americans had a particular interest in the U.S. response to the September 11 attacks. How would the United States and its citizens treat

Muslims (and people thought to be Muslims because of their appearance)? According to table 9.8, the answer was "not particularly well."

By October 2001, a majority of the respondents to the Project MAPS survey reported that they or someone they knew had experienced some form of discrimination. Slightly more African American and Arab Muslims reported such negative experiences than South Asians or Africans. In the 2004 survey, the question was separated, asking about discrimination experienced against themselves and against others they knew. Fully two-fifths reported discrimination after September 11, and three-fifths reported knowing a victim of discrimination. Thirty-seven percent reported no discrimination against themselves or others they knew, suggesting a slight increase in such problems since the 2001 survey. By any standard, these figures are shockingly high.

Table 9.8 also lists a breakdown of the types of discrimination the respondents reported after September 11. Verbal abuse was common, suffered by one-quarter in 2001 and by another one-fifth by the 2004 survey. Physical abuse, though less common (6 percent), doubled by the 2004 survey (12 percent), while reports of racial profiling tripled from 8 to 24 percent. In addition, just under one-fifth of the respondents believed they had been denied a job because of their religion. Given this reported discrimination, how did Muslims feel about American society? Is the whole society prejudiced or just a part of it? Table 9.9 reports relevant answers from the 2001 and 2004 Project MAPS surveys. In 2001, two-fifths of Muslim Americans agreed with this statement: "In my experience and overall, Americans have been respectful and tolerant of Muslims." On this response, there was some variation by ethnic group. More than one-half of South Asians agreed with this statement, but less than one-third of African Americans. By 2004, agreement with this statement had fallen to less than one-third overall and had declined in every ethnic group (although the intergroup differences remained). By 2004, a plurality of Muslims agreed that "Americans have been respectful and tolerant of Muslims, but American society overall is disrespectful and intolerant of Muslims." One-sixth located the problem in a subset of America, while 12 percent said Americans in general were intolerant.

Table 9.9 also contains a measure of dissatisfaction with American society. Overall, two-thirds of the 2004 sample was dissatisfied, and many of those were very dissatisfied, particularly African Americans (84 percent) and the other Muslims (70 percent). South Asians were

TABLE 9.8 American Muslim Experience with Discrimination, 2001 and 2004 (percent)

Strongly Agree	All	African American	South Asian	African	Arabs	Other
I or others experienced discrimination since 9/11 (2001 data)	56.0	61.1	50.0	53.0	60.0	57.7
I have experienced discrimination since 9/11 (2004 data)	40.1	46.8	35.6	36.8	39.3	45.0
Others have experienced discrimination since 9/11 (2004 data)	58.5	61.8	56.2	54.1	58.4	61.9
Type of discrimination						
Verbal abuse, 2001	25.3	22.0	22.5	23.6	30.9	27.0
Verbal abuse, 2004	43.7	49.3	41.4	33.6	44.4	46.2
Physical abuse, 2001	6.2	5.6	6.3	7.3	5.8	7.1
Physical abuse, 2004	11.9	11.3	10.4	12.7	11.9	16.2
Racial profiling, 2001	8.3	14.2	6.5	4.9	8.0	6.2
Racial profiling, 2004	24.0	22.9	22.7	24.8	25.3	25.7
Denied employment, 2001	2.8	4.5	2.3	2.4	1.6	4.0
Denied employment, 2004	18.0	20.6	17.0	16.4	16.7	20.2

Source: Project MAPS (2001, 2004).

TABLE 9.9   American Muslim Summary Views of American Society and Discrimination, 2001 and 2004 (percent)

Those Who Agree	All	African American	South Asian	African	Arabs	Other
Please tell me which statement best reflects Americans' attitudes toward Muslims since the September 11 attacks:						
A. In my experience and overall, Americans have been respectful and tolerant of Muslims.						
2001	43.2	32.6	51.7	45.1	39.5	43.7
2004	32.1	18.6	39.5	38.7	31.5	31.0
B. In my experience, Americans have been respectful and tolerant of Muslims, but American society overall is disrespectful and intolerant of Muslims.						
2001	34.8	41.9	30.4	33.6	36.6	32.1
2004	34.7	34.0	34.6	28.5	37.2	34.5
C. In my experience and overall, Americans have been disrespectful and intolerant of Muslims.						
2001	8.2	11.1	5.7	7.4	8.7	9.8
2004	11.9	28.3	5.3	5.8	9.5	12.1
D. In my experience, Americans have been disrespectful and intolerant of Muslims, but American society overall is respectful and tolerant of Muslims.						
2001	13.8	14.4	12.2	13.9	15.2	14.4
2004	16.2	12.7	15.1	22.6	17.9	17.7
Overall, how satisfied are you with things in U.S. society today?						
(Dissatisfied)	64.5	83.5	54.3	59.5	61.9	70.0
The American media is fair in its portrayal of Muslims and Islam	26.6	18.5	34.8	26.0	19.0	33.5
Hollywood is fair in its portrayal of Muslims and Islam	14.4	9.1	22.6	11.8	9.7	14.7
United States fighting a war on:						
Terrorism?	33.0	19.9	42.9	39.0	30.3	29.1
Islam?	38.2	53.9	28.3	34.6	39.4	39.1
It is a good time to be a Muslim in America	50.7	57.1	47.9	54.7	49.8	47.0

Source: Project MAPS (2001, 2004).

the least dissatisfied (54 percent). This dissatisfaction may reflect Muslim perception of the American news media; just one-quarter of Muslims felt the media portrays Muslims fairly. There was some variation between groups, with African Americans the least supportive (18 percent) and South Asians the most (34 percent). However, there was an even more negative perception of Hollywood's portrayal of Muslims and Islam; just 14 percent of respondents said Hollywood's portrayal was fair, with the same distribution of ethnic group support as with the media.

American Muslims also have real doubts about the character and goals of the war on terrorism. When asked if the U.S. effort was a war on "terrorism" or a war on "Islam," one-third of the 2004 sample chose the former and nearly two-fifths the latter (the rest had no opinion). A majority of African Americans felt it was a war on Islam, a view held by a plurality of Arabs and other Muslims, and by a substantial minority of South Asians and Africans.

Despite the experience of discrimination, perceptions of a lack of tolerance and respect, and dissatisfaction with the state of American society and government, American Muslims were still fairly optimistic. One-half agreed with the statement "It is a good time to be Muslim in America." Interestingly, African Americans were the most positive in this regard, followed by Africans, Arabs, South Asians, and the other Muslims. As with many minorities in U.S. history, the promise of America appears to exceed the perils of becoming an American.

Multivariate Analyses

In this section, we take a more systematic look at American Muslims' issue positions, voting behavior, and political participation. We start with the effect of religiosity added to ethnicity. To what extent are American Muslims' issue positions, political attachments, and community involvement driven by their religious commitment? In table 9.10, we correlate a measure of religious commitment with these sets of variables within each ethnic group, measured as in table 9.1. We expect that the effects of being more religious should vary somewhat for each ethnic group; but on moral and cultural issues, we expect to see more consistent effects of religion across groups.

The results largely conform to our expectations, and the first two listed issues tell that story well. Overall, there is no relationship between

TABLE 9.10   Correlations between Religious Commitment, Public Policy Support, and Political Attachments for the Major Ethnic Groups, 2004

Variable	All	African American	South Asian	African	Arabs	Other
Death penalty	.030	−.090*	.131***	.263***	.135***	.072
Abortion restrictions	.202***	.129**	.204***	.111	.122***	.156**
Gay marriage	−.318***	−.197***	−.308***	−.073	−.293***	−.327***
Stem cell research	−.222***	−.138***	−.107**	−.230***	−.218***	−.219***
School prayer	.130***	.081	.009	.277***	.179***	.191***
School vouchers	.270***	.223***	.031	.271***	.265***	.314***
Income tax cuts	−.002	−.217***	.092**	−.001	.087*	.091
Government assistance to poor	.088***	.097*	.071*	.144*	.012	.233***
Gun control	−.014	.015	.025	.073	−.027	−.026
Debt relief	.114***	.153***	.063	.050	.122***	.146**
Stronger anti-terrorism laws	−.080***	−.157***	−.034	.130	.079*	−.089
More troops to Iraq	−.119***	−.013	−.139***	.002	−.112**	−.159**
Political ideology	−.104***	.031	−.160***	−.092	−.180	−.130*
Partisan identification	.053*	−.040	−.052	.227*	.068	.061
Community organizations	−.281***	−.228***	−.278***	−.158*	−.129***	−.315***
Mosque involvement	.775***	.807***	.737***	.760***	.720***	.781***
Political participation	−.156***	−.165***	−.125***	−.378***	−.055	−.128*
Approximate number of cases	1745	340	580	123	460	222

Source: Project MAPS (2004).
Note: $*p < .10$, $**p < .05$, $***p < .01$. The shaded cells show the absence of statistical significance; cells with asterisks signify significant relationships between religious commitment and the included variables.

religiosity and support for the death penalty, but that is because committed African American Muslims take a different stance than others—being more opposed to the death penalty—whereas committed Muslims in the other ethnic groups are more likely to support it. African Americans are more opposed to the death penalty than other Americans because of the high concentration of blacks on death row. Many Muslim countries also still administer the death penalty, which might explain high support among the immigrant groups. There are other issues on which religious commitment produces varying stances across groups, including support for income-tax cuts, legalizing drugs, ending affirmative action, and stronger antiterrorism laws (committed African Americans take opposite stances from those committed to Islam in most of the other ethnic groups).

On the second issue, support for expanding stem cell research, the religious community is united against it. The effect varies just a bit across the ethnic groups but remains significant in all cases. Stem cell research is a more abstract moral issue inviting the application of religious teachings. Likewise, on gay marriage, there is a similar effect of commitment across groups—all are statistically significant, except for Africans (which may be due to a smaller sample size and a lack of variance), and report that the more religious they are the more they oppose gays and lesbians marrying. School vouchers, faith-based initiatives, and euthanasia are examples of other issues with similar effects of religious commitment across groups.

On others matters, the issue may not be salient in all ethnic communities or the group may simply not be divided on it. For instance, there is unanimity across groups in favor of gun control and hence little variation to explain.

Political partisanship and ideology appear not to be driven by religious commitment for American Muslims. Overall, committed Muslims are more conservative and slightly more Democratic, though the effect varies considerably across groups. On ideology, there is no relationship for Africans and African Americans, but similarly sized correlations (if not all significant) for South Asians, Arabs, and other Muslims, showing a relationship between religious commitment and conservatism. There is no relationship between commitment and partisanship for any group but Africans, where high levels of religious commitment are associated with Democratic partisanship. Though insignificant, the sign is reversed for African Americans and South Asians.

One would expect strong relationships between community involvement and religious commitment, which is what table 9.10 shows. Here all relationships were moderate to strong and in the expected direction. The only variation comes for Arabs and South Asians, who show weaker tethers between religious commitment and community engagement, perhaps because of a large number of immigrants. Africans, who one would expect to display patterns similar to South Asians and Arabs, show a strong relationship between commitment and participation, perhaps assisted by African Americans.

Determinants of Issue Opinions

In table 9.11, we use ordinary least squares regression to estimate the effects of a variety of explanations for ideology itself and three issue opinions: debt relief for poor nations, abortion restrictions, and aid to poor people. These three questions, which cover a range of issue types, can give us a good sense of the most potent forces shaping political opinion in the Muslim community.

Overall, it is clear that political ideology and religious commitment are the dominant forces. Ideology works consistently, so that self-identified conservatives take the more "conservative" positions on these issues—against debt relief and government aid to poor people and in support of abortion restrictions. Predictably, religious commitment produces support for making abortions harder to obtain, but more committed Muslims are also more supportive of aid to the poor and debt relief, both of which are normative in the Muslim community, but certainly not "conservative" positions in the American context.

Numerous factors are at work beyond the two workhorses of ideology and religious commitment. Converts are more likely to oppose debt relief, while immigrants are significantly more in favor of aid to the poor, referencing their struggles to jump-start the American dream. On a related note, some measure of socioeconomic status affects all three opinions, as those who oppose debt relief are more educated, whereas those who oppose aid to the poor and favor abortion restrictions have higher incomes.

Ethnic group membership has only a modest effect once other variables are taken into account. That is, the ethnic effects we have seen throughout this chapter appear to stem in large part from the differing status and norms of group members. That does not mean that

TABLE 9.11 Determinants of American Muslim Public Policy Stances: Support for Debt Relief for Poor Nations, Abortion Restrictions, Government Aid to Poor People, and Ideology (ordinary least squares regression estimates)

Variable	Debt Relief Coeff.	(S.E.)	Abortion Coeff.	(S.E.)	Aid to the Poor Coeff.	(S.E.)	Ideology Coeff.	(S.E.)
Religious commitment	.098	(.023)***	-.220	(.038)***	.074	(.019)***	-.090	(.030)***
Ideology	.099	(.022)***	.135	(.037)***	.138	(.019)***	—	
Convert	.180	(.081)**	.025	(.138)	.041	(.069)	-.065	(.109)
Immigrant	-.091	(.072)	.072	(.122)	-.266	(.061)***	.145	(.096)
War on terror or Islam?	-.036	(.050)	.064	(.084)	-.048	(.042)	-.090	(.066)
Experienced anti-Muslim discrimination	.057	(.050)	-.026	(.084)	-.060	(.042)	-.017	(.066)
Education	.059	(.033)*	.042	(.055)	.017	(.028)	-.041	(.044)
Income	-.013	(.016)	-.049	(.027)*	.045	(.013)***	.043	(.021)**
Age	-.002	(.002)	.003	(.003)	.002	(.001)	-.002	(.002)
Female	.027	(.050)	-.028	(.084)	.004	(.042)	-.010	(.066)
South Asian	-.001	(.059)	.071	(.098)	-.031	(.049)	-.162	(.077)**
African American	-.102	(.086)	.043	(.144)	-.157	(.073)**	.003	(.114)
African	-.121	(.101)	-.424	(.169)**	-.112	(.085)	.066	(.136)
South	-.062	(.060)	.029	(.101)	-.113	(.051)**	.021	(.080)
Midwest	.071	(.057)	.167	(.095)*	.009	(.048)	-.018	(.075)
Constant	.866	(.213)	2.747	(.358)	.807	(.180)	3.164	(.263)
Number of cases	975		957		992		975	
Adjusted R^2	.047		.058		.104		.010	
S.E.	.729		1.212		.622		.962	

Source: Project MAPS (2004).
Note: *$p < .10$, **$p < .05$, ***$p < .01$. See the appendix to the chapter for variable coding. Positive coefficients (coeff.) indicate a more conservative stance on the issues—oppose debt relief, favor abortion restrictions, and oppose aid to poor people. S.E. = standard error.

242   *Paul A. Djupe and John C. Green*

ethnicity does not matter—the groups are different in important ways that profoundly shape members' political views. As further evidence of this notion, there are no age and gender effects, which would indicate greater individualism within ethnic groups.

The significant differences by region could simply stand in for ethnic differences (recall table 9.1), but they could also be an indication that the Muslim community is assimilating. Southern Muslims are more likely to oppose government aid to the poor, as would be typical of other American southerners, while midwestern Muslims support abortion restrictions at greater rates. These patterns suggest that over the long run, Muslims are likely to follow the social integration pattern of Jews and Catholics.

The model for ideology performs weakly, suggesting the shallow roots of political attachment among American Muslims. Those with a lower religious commitment are, predictably, more liberal; well-off Muslims are more conservative; and South Asians are more liberal. No other variables attain significance.

Determinants of the Vote

In table 9.12, we use logistic regression to estimate what factors distinguish Bush voters from others in both 2001 and 2004—combining non-Bush voters for the sake of simplicity and because the 2004 election was surely a referendum on the administration. In the 2000 election, few explanations distinguish themselves, except for partisanship and ideology, working as expected. Converts and African Americans were more likely to vote for a Bush opponent along with those who opposed further restrictions on access to abortion. Even in the 2000 election, those who experienced discrimination were more likely to vote against Bush, though many of those who believed that the United States was waging a war against Islam instead of terrorism admitted that they had voted for Bush in 2000.

This was absolutely not the case in 2004, when those reporting discrimination and believing there was an American war against Islam voted against Bush. Partisanship and ideology still worked in the expected directions in 2004. We also see a rationalization in the vote with the appearance of a flurry of demographic and ethnic effects. The educated were more likely to vote against Bush, whereas older, South Asian, and African Muslims were more likely to support him. Interestingly, Muslims living in the South were more likely to vote against him.

TABLE 9.12   Determinants of the Muslim Presidential Vote, 2000 and 2004 Elections (logistic regression estimates)

	2000 Election		2004 Election	
Variable	Coeff.	(S.E.)	Coeff.	(S.E.)
Convert	−.796	(.332)**	.206	(.589)
Immigrant	.072	(.295)	−.636	(.469)
Religious commitment	.018	(.106)	.249	(.171)
Partisanship	1.609	(.162)***	1.379	(.241)***
Ideology	.313	(.102)***	.685	(.176)***
Importance of being Muslim to vote choice	—		−.129	(.218)
Importance of American Muslim Taskforce endorsement	—		.268	(.221)
War on terror or Islam	.497	(.288)*	−2.932	(.513)***
Experienced anti-Muslim discrimination	−.508	(.230)**	−.873	(.371)**
Stem cell research	−.002	(.096)	−.007	(.162)
Abortion restriction	−.159	(.092)*	.108	(.137)
Stronger environmental laws	.027	(.144)	.117	(.245)
Education	.141	(.130)	−.419	(.209)**
Age	−.008	(.008)	.023	(.011)**
South Asian	−.387	(.272)	.948	(.413)**
African American	−.886	(.329)***	.228	(.652)
African	−.659	(.489)	2.143	(.771)***
South	−.230	(.290)	−.858	(.467)*
Midwest	.283	(.247)	−.244	(.403)
Constant	−2.322	(.903)	−2.672	(1.579)
Number of cases	610		670	
Cox and Snell R^2	.325		.220	
Percent correctly predicted	80.6		93.4	

Source: Project MAPS (2001, 2004).
Note: *p < .10, **p < .05, ***p < .01. See the appendix to the chapter for variable coding. The dependent variable is coded 1 if the respondent voted for George Bush and 0 if they voted for anyone else: 45.3 voted for Bush in 2000 (he won a plurality among the sample), and 7.6 percent in 2004. Coeff. = coefficient; S.E. = standard error.

However, African Americans were no longer the only anti-Bush group, as other ethnic groups came to join them in their opposition to Bush's agenda. Clearly, the personal experiences and mobilization of American Muslims since 2001 determined their votes in 2004. Taken together, these patterns suggest that the Muslim community will most likely vote as a bloc in the near future.

Determinants of Political Participation

In table 9.13, we consider explanations for political participation among Muslims, examining first the 2001 data and then the 2004 data. Participation includes several activities that were included in both surveys: being an active member of a political party, contributing time or money to a candidate, visiting a political website, contacting the media or a politician on an issue, attending a rally for a politician or cause, and participating in a boycott of a product or business. We are concerned mainly with the extent to which ethnicity, traditionally important factors such as interest group mobilization, and their experiences and thoughts about America after September 11 explain Muslim participation in politics. There are quite a few differences between the 2001 and 2004 surveys that highlight the extent to which the events of September 11 changed the dynamics of political involvement of the American Muslim community.

In 2001, we see strong effects from traditional causes of political participation—those who believe it is important to participate, discuss politics often, and follow politics in the media participate in more political activities than others. Immigrants are less likely to participate, showing the difficulty of navigating the American political system and the inefficacy noncitizens must feel about politics. On the other side, those active in various kinds of community organizations participate at high levels. We see some similar effects in the 2004 data—immigrants participate less, while those psychologically engaged with politics participate more.

There is a basic contradiction in that those who are dissatisfied with the way things are going in America participated less in 2001, but those who see the United States waging a war on Islam participated more. This contradiction appears in the 2004 data through a dramatic reversal: the more dissatisfied the respondent with America, the more they participated. Those experiencing discrimination by 2004 participated more than those who did not, showing a mobilization of and an outlet for personal experience.

Other demographic differences are worth noting. In 2001, women participated less, while African Americans and those with higher incomes participated more. In 2004, income and gender were insignificant predictors, though we see significant effects for greater education and having children at home. In 2004, African Americans participated less often, showcasing the widespread mobilization of the other ethnic

TABLE 9.13 Determinants of Muslim Political Participation, 2001 and 2004 (ordinary least squares regression estimates)

Variable	Participation, 2001		Participation, 2004	
	Coeff.	(S.E.)	Coeff.	(S.E.)
Convert	−.060	(.170)	.286	(.210)
Immigrant	−.618	(.150)***	−.526	(.179)***
Religious commitment	.068	(.078)	.071	(.081)
Mosque involvement	−.119	(.080)	−.213	(.082)***
Important to participate	−.582	(.081)***	−.646	(.090)***
Political discussion	−.280	(.080)***	−.167	(.103)
Follow politics	−.166	(.071)**	−.200	(.092)**
Community organizations	.240	(.024)***	.206	(.028)***
Satisfied with the way things are going in American society	−.155	(.059)***	.168	(.068)**
War on Islam or terror	.482	(.134)***	.023	(.133)
Experienced discrimination	−.083	(.108)	.270	(.132)**
Education	.040	(.064)	.177	(.080)**
Children under age 17	.045	(.043)	−.184	(.048)***
Age	−.005	(.005)	−.004	(.006)
Gender	−.319	(.108)***	−.044	(.125)
Income	.069	(.036)*	.038	(.040)
South Asian	−.010	(.123)	−.238	(.144)*
African American	.374	(.175)**	−.503	(.219)**
African	.220	(.197)	.078	(.226)
South	−.012	(.133)	.011	(.153)
Midwest	.135	(.119)	.383	(.140)***
Constant	3.280	(.513)	3.025	(.582)
Number of cases	672		582	
Adjusted R^2	.464		.441	
S.E.E.	1.286		1.356	

Source: Project MAPS (2001, 2004).
Note: *$p < .10$, **$p < .05$, ***$p < .01$. See the appendix to the chapter for variable coding. S.E.E. = standard error of the estimate.

Muslims since 2001. One venue was involvement in a mosque, insignificant in 2001 but strongly significant in 2004, reflecting a common pattern in other religious communities (Djupe and Grant 2001).

Conclusion: Diversity and Unity

We have reviewed a wealth of data about the politics of American Muslims using the 2001 and 2004 Project MAPS surveys, and it is useful to summarize the results. On the one hand, we found that American Muslims are quite diverse in ethnic, demographic, and religious terms. But on the other hand, Muslim Americans are remarkably united in politics—far more, in fact, than most religious communities in the United States. Muslims tend to hold liberal views on social welfare issues and conservative views on moral issues. On foreign policy, they are almost uniformly critical of American foreign policy under the Bush administration. Muslims report strong support for civic engagement and are open to an active role for religion in politics.

However, Muslims' broader political identifications do not seem yet to be firmly rooted in American politics. They tend to be moderate in ideological terms, shifting a bit to the left between 2000 and 2004. A greater change occurred in partisanship, with Muslims moving from a Democratic plurality to a Democratic majority by 2004. And, of course, the most dramatic change was at the ballot box, where solid support for George W. Bush in 2000 turned into a nearly unanimous vote for John Kerry in 2004.

The major source of these political changes was, of course, September 11 and its aftermath. The foreign policy of the Bush administration was a factor, but of even greater importance was the discrimination Muslim Americans reported at the hands of other American citizens and the hostility they felt from the American government. These experiences produced considerable dissatisfaction with American society. Our multivariate analysis reveals that these negative experiences and concerns were important factors in accounting for Muslims' issue positions, presidential vote, and level of participation. But these problems have not apparently reduced (much) the political activity of Muslims nor dimmed their hope for a better future in this country. Indeed, the most powerful factors explaining Muslim politics are ideology and religious commitment, things that matter to the rest of the American public as well.

These facts lead us to conclude that Muslim political unity is circumstantial and that in the absence of an external threat, they would go their separate ways politically—much as they did in the 2000 election. The political networks do not seem to be in place to construct and maintain a monolithic American Muslim electorate. Thus, the typical pattern of decaying unity in immigrant communities because of their economic and educational success will surely occur in the American Muslim community over time (e.g., Moore 1986). For the moment, however, Muslim Americans remain distinctive in the face of the peril and promise of becoming American. And like other small and distinctive religious communities, they can have an important impact on the nation's closely divided politics.

Appendix: Variable Coding

Religious commitment: 1, lowest quartile on religious commitment scale; 2, second-lowest quartile; 3, second-highest quartile; 4, highest quartile.

Ideology: "Which description best represents your political ideology?" 1 = progressive / very liberal, 2 = liberal, 3 = moderate, 4 = conservative, 5 = very conservative. Libertarians were excluded.

Convert and *Immigrant:* 1 = yes, 0 = no.

War on terror or Islam? "Do you feel the U.S. is fighting a war on terrorism or a war against Islam?" 1 = terrorism, 2 = Islam.

Experienced discrimination: Coded 1 if either the respondent and/or friends and family experienced discrimination after September 11 and coded 0 if neither did.

Education: 1 = non–high school graduate, 2 = high school, 3 = some college, 4 = college graduate.

Income: 1 < $15,000; 2 = $15–25,000; 3 = $25–35,000; 4 = $35–50,000; 5 = $50–75,000; 6 < $75,000.

Female: 1 = male, 2 = female.

Importance of being Muslim to vote choice: "How important is being Muslim in your decision for whom to vote?" 1 = very important, 2 = important, 3 = not important.

Importance of AMT endorsement: "If the American Muslim Taskforce (AMT) endorses one of the presidential candidates, how important would it be in your decision for whom to vote?" 1 = very important, 2 = important, 3 = not important.

Partisanship: 1 = Democrat, 2 = independent, 3 = Republican.

Mosque involvement: "Excluding *salah* and *Jum'ah* prayer, how involved are you in the activities of the mosque? Would you say that you are" 1 = very involved, 2 = somewhat involved, 3 = not very involved, 4 = not at all involved.

Important to participate: "How important is it for you to participate in politics?" 1 = very important, 2 = important, 3 = not important.

Political discussion: "How often do you discuss politics with family and friends?" 1 = always, 2 = sometimes, 3 = hardly ever, 4 = never.

Follow politics: "How often would you say you follow what's going on in government?" 1 = most of the time, 2 = some of the time, 3 = only now and then, 4 = hardly at all.

Community organizations: An additive index ranging from 0 to 10, giving 1 point for some participation (the options are donated time, donated money, served as an officer, and a combination of these) in each of the following groups: school or youth programs; any arts or cultural organization; any neighborhood, civic, or community group; any organization to help the poor, sick, elderly, or homeless; any professional organization; any mosque or religious organization; any trade or labor union; any veteran's or military service organization; any ethnic organization; any Muslim political action or public affairs organization.

Satisfied with the way things are going in American society: "How satisfied are you overall with the way things are going in American society today?" 1 = very satisfied, 2 = satisfied, 3 = somewhat dissatisfied, 4 = very dissatisfied.

Political participation: An additive index giving one point (range is 0 to 6) for participation in each of the following activities: active member of political party, contribution of time or money to candidate, visiting political website, contacting the media or a politician on an issue, attended a rally for a politician or cause, participated in a boycott of a product or business.

Children under 17: Ranges from 0 to 6 (where 6 stands for 6 or more).

Notes

1. The Zogby 2004 Post Election Survey had 10,000 cases and the Muslim figures were made available by Tom Perriello of Progressive Faith Media. The National Surveys of Religion and Politics were conducted at the University of

Akron 1992 to 2004 (with a total of some 14,000 total cases and 4,000 in 2004). According to Scott Keeter, survey director for the Pew Research Center, the Muslim figures came from pooling the 35,000 cases in the 2004 surveys.

2. The 2001 and 2004 Project MAPS surveys were made available at cost by Zogby International. We owe a special thanks to John Zogby and Zogby International for allowing access to these data.

3. The American Religious Identification Survey (ARIS) found that 62 percent of American Muslims claimed Mosque membership, a figure supporting the Project MAPS sampling strategy. However, ARIS also found that African Americans were 27 percent of American Muslims, more than the Project MAPS assumption of 20 percent.

4. ARIS found that 52 percent of Muslim Americans had college degrees and 21 percent had incomes over $75,000 a year. Thus, the Project MAPS samples may overrepresent higher status people. By way of comparison, ARIS also found one-third of Americans to be college graduates and one-quarter to have income greater than $75,000 a year (ARIS 2001).

5. ARIS found the mean age of American Muslims to be twenty-eight years, higher than in the Project MAPS data (ARIS 2001). The ARIS mean estimate for the entire U.S. population was forty-three years.

6. ARIS found 52 percent of American Muslims to be male, 49 percent married, and 73 percent married to another Muslim (ARIS 2001). This difference with Project MAPS may reflect a higher "mosqued" population.

7. The religious commitment scale combines frequency of worship attendance, frequency of prayer, religious salience, and participation in a Mosque beyond worship into a single factor with an eigenvalue greater than 1; a factor score was then produced from this analysis, and divided into quartiles. The top two quartiles were added together for ease of presentation in table 9.2 (see Kohut et al. 2000 and Green et al. 1996 for information on religious commitment measures).

8. In the 2004 data, there is a weak relationship between ethnic concentration of the mosque and religious commitment for the whole sample ($r = .092$) that varies by ethnicity—stronger for African Americans ($r = .135$) and Africans ($r = .154$), insignificant for South Asians ($r = .019$) and other Muslims ($r = .036$), and weakly negative but significant for Arabs ($r = -.086$).

9. ARIS found that 35 percent of Muslim Americans were Democrats in 2001, 39 percent Independents, and 19 percent Republicans. However, the ARIS data, unlike Project MAPS, were collected before September 11.

10. The low rate of African participation may reflect the fact that the 2004 sample contained more recent immigrants than the 2001 sample.

11. ARIS found that 80 percent of the U.S. population was registered in 2001, but just 44 percent of Muslims. The higher levels may reflect overreporting and/or the higher social status of Project MAPS samples.

12. For the 2001 Project MAPS survey, the measure of turnout was a recall measure of 2000 turnout; for 2004 it was anticipated turnout in 2004. Like many other survey measures of turnout, these figures certainly contain a high level of overreporting.

13. All these reported levels of activism are high compared with the population at large, and this may reflect some overreporting on the part of the respondents. However, the questions asked if the respondent *ever* participated in these ways, and in addition, these individuals have high social status, a factor strongly associated with political participation.

14. For the 2001 Project MAPS survey, recall of 2000 presidential vote choice was used. The 2004 Project MAPS survey had a measure of anticipated presidential vote because the survey occurred before the 2004 election. These data were adjusted to reflect the presidential vote in the Zogby 2004 post-election survey.

TEN

Secularists, Antifundamentalists, and the New Religious Divide in the American Electorate

Louis Bolce and Gerald De Maio

ONE OF THE MORE INTERESTING developments in American politics during the past decade has been the appearance of a new type of voter: the "anti–Christian fundamentalist" (Bolce and De Maio 1999a). Antifundamentalists, of course, have been on the cultural scene since the split between theologically conservative and liberal Protestants during the third great awakening (Marsden 1980). But only relatively recently have anti–Christian fundamentalists become a force in national electoral politics. Today, anti–Christian fundamentalism is not just pervasive among self-identified Democrats and an important consideration in the party evaluations and voting preferences of culturally liberal and secular political independents—it is also present among Republicans. Thus, reaction against the perceived clout of Christian fundamentalists in the Republican Party has on occasion touched off factional infighting between Republican moderates and conservatives, exemplified, for example, by Senator John McCain's widely quoted denunciation of the "southern fundamentalist" supporters of then–Texas governor George W. Bush as "agents of intolerance" after his defeat in a blistering campaign for delegates in the 2000 South Carolina primary.

More recently, Republican representative Christopher Shays of Connecticut, in the wake of the Terri Schiavo controversy, worried aloud that the "Republican Party of Lincoln" was turning into "a party of theocracy," a concern also echoed by a former Republican senator from Missouri, John Danforth, and the former Republican governor of New Jersey, Christine Todd Whitman (Mitchell 2000; Danforth 2005; Benson 2005; Nagourney 2005). There is little doubt that the rise of political antifundamentalism on the national level since the 1990s reflects deepening religious and cultural divisions within the American electorate and a restructuring of national party coalitions along a secularist/religious divide (cf. Kellstedt et al. 1994; Bolce and De Maio 1999b; Layman 2001; Pew Forum 2005).

However broadly one wants to interpret the meaning of modern anti–Christian fundamentalism, there is little question that the reemergence of religious outgroup antipathy as a significant force in political conflict during the last decade of the twentieth century is an extraordinary development. In most situations, as Converse (1964, 238) observed, "Contextual information giving a group clear political relevance is lacking." One has to reach back to pre–New Deal America—when political divisions between Catholics and Protestants also encapsulated local ethnocultural cleavages over Prohibition, immigration, public education, and blue laws—to find significant occasions in the past when the partisanship and/or vote choice of identifiable social groups could be characterized as overt expressions of religious outgroup antipathy (McCormick 1974). The question, then, is why Christian fundamentalists became politically relevant to significant secularist segments of the electorate during the 1990s: What new information about Christian fundamentalists transformed their status in the political thinking of the nonfundamentalist public to the extent that the antifundamentalists felt motivated to use their feelings toward this religious group to guide their political perceptions and voting decisions?

The Culture Wars and the Rise of Political Antifundamentalism

There are no good data on how ordinary nonfundamentalists felt about Christian fundamentalists before 1988, when the Center for Political Studies at the University of Michigan first began testing respondents' attitudes toward this religious group in the biennial American National Election Studies (ANES). There are, however, a variety of sources—newspaper and magazine stories, fiction and nonfiction, historical and

social science literature, college texts, polemics by scientific popular-
izers and secularists, and so on—from which we can get a picture of
what cultural elites have thought about Christian fundamentalists and
communicated to their students, readers, viewers, and audiences. Overall, the elite take on Christian fundamentalists and the fundamentalist movement in the Protestant churches has been negative. Much of
the antagonism has tended to cluster around beliefs that Christian fundamentalists are narrow-minded, hickish, and intolerant, and pose
threats to progress and "enlightened" or "educated" opinion.

The popularization of anti–Christian fundamentalism dates back to
the famous 1925 Scopes "monkey trial" and the sensationalized press
coverage of the clash between traditional Christians and the forces of
modernity and cosmopolitanism (Larson 1997; Hunter 1991). Those
who got to know fundamentalist and evangelical Christians through
the militantly secularist pen of H. L. Mencken (1926) would find it difficult not to think of them as "half-wits," "yokels," "ignoramuses,"
"bigots," "anthropoid rabble," and otherwise "menaces to Western
Civilization." Mencken's caricatures of rural and small-town Protestantism found a receptive audience in the more urbane and secular populations inhabiting the big cities outside the South. Since Scopes,
Menckenesque stereotypes of fundamentalists have become reinforced
and indeed embellished in American literature and cinema. In the
works of Sinclair Lewis, William Alexander Percy, and in *Inherit the
Wind*, Jerome Lawrence and Robert E. Lee's popular play and subsequent movie about the Scopes trial, for example, fundamentalists turn
up as uneducated, backward, lower class, gullible, intolerant, odd, and
hypocritical. They are the sort of folks, as the Southern Bourbon Percy
put it, "who attend revivals and fight and fornicate in the bushes after-
wards" (1941, 149).

Antifundamentalist stereotypes have also received the imprimatur of
social science. Students whose views of Christian fundamentalists were
shaped by the landmark social science literature of the post–World
War II era on the cultural origins of right-wing extremist movements
would have learned that religious orthodoxy—particularly (although
not exclusively) of the white evangelical Christian variety—was an
essential component undergirding prejudiced and antidemocratic belief
systems (Adorno et al. 1950; Allport 1954; Stouffer 1955; Hofstadter
1955; Glock and Stark 1966; Selznick and Steinberg 1969; Lipset and
Raab 1970). In such works, Christian fundamentalism was singled out

as particularly dangerous to the body politic, even being characterized by one prominent historian as akin to a "virus" (Hofstadter 1955, 288).[1]

Clearly, antifundamentalism has resonated in elite circles, and it still does today—among secular intellectuals, Christian fundamentalism is the antithesis of the civilized or democratic mind. (E.g., see Lewis 1994; Rich 1994; Weisskopf 1993; Dowd 2004; Friedman 2004; Reich 2005; and Blumenthal 2004. For a critical analysis of journalistic coverage of religious Christians, see Byrd 1993. For an analysis of Hollywood's take on fundamentalists, see Goodman 1999.) There is no hard evidence, however, that antifundamentalism figured prominently in the political belief systems of ordinary nonfundamentalists before the 1980s. Christian fundamentalists, as a religious group, were not *politically* salient to the antifundamentalists (as, say, Catholics were to anti-Catholics throughout the nineteenth and early twentieth centuries) because the partisan orientations of fundamentalists lacked distinct and discernable qualities that could be contextualized in ways that would be comprehensible and politically meaningful to those who intensely disliked or feared them. When fundamentalists were not tuning out from national politics, their voting behavior tended to reflect sectional patterns: Democratic in the southern states, particularly at the congressional and local levels, and class-based partisanship outside the South (Smidt 1987; Layman 2001; for an alternative view, see Manza and Brooks 1999).

Though antifundamentalism before the 1980s might have contained an ideological dimension (anticonservative) along with some sectional and issue components (anti-South, anti–school prayer, anticreationism), because the cultural stereotype or schema of Christian fundamentalists did not include a partisan dimension, partisan animus was generally absent in elite attacks on Christian fundamentalists. It was not until the cultural upheavals and religious realignments in the party system during the last quarter of the twentieth century that politically relevant contextualizing information became available, enabling antifundamentalists to draw partisan implications from the antipathy they felt toward this religious group. A negative cultural referent now became a full-blown political referent to secularists and other antifundamentalists (for expositions of reference theory, see Merton 1968 and Conover 1988).

Ethnocultural historians argue that during the nineteenth century, religious identities were transformed into political ones when an outgroup was perceptually linked to clashes over local customs and cultural practices (McCormick 1974). Such "culture wars" typically arise when a religious or cultural group organizes to use political means to impose its customs and values on individuals beyond the group's boundaries, or, alternatively, when the group politically mobilizes to protect its values and local cultural practices from attacks by outside forces (Leege et al. 2002). Ethnocultural historians have employed this explanatory model to account for negative voting triggered by religious divisions over temperance and blue laws during the nineteenth century (McCormick 1974). Of course, negative reference group feelings are politically heightened when lifestyle conflicts are nationalized—for example, by Supreme Court decisions—and during times when political parties make appeals to adherents of competing religious worldviews. Both factors—political conflicts over lifestyles and values, and new religious divisions rooted in a secularist/traditionalist split in the electorate—were instrumental in launching the anti–Christian fundamentalist phenomenon in contemporary politics.

The genesis of political antifundamentalism has its origins in secularists' reaction to the mobilization of evangelical Christians during the middle and late 1970s to undo social changes set in motion by a cultural revolution that began a decade earlier. What later became known as the "Christian Right" movement was itself a defensive reaction against threats to traditional values brought about by the secularization of national culture starting in the turbulent 1960s (see Wilcox 2000 for an analysis of the origins and various transformations of the Christian Right movement). Supreme Court decisions such as *Engel v. Vitale* (1962) and *School District of Abington Township v. Schempp* (1963) directly challenged long-standing local practices such as school prayer and Bible reading associated with the Protestant cultural hegemony in the United States.

Traditionalists, moreover, saw the rise of a counterculture that included a feminist movement, a new sexual morality, the growing acceptance of recreational drug use, and the flouting of traditional authority as threats to their core beliefs and values. Events such as the struggle for the Equal Rights Amendment (1972–82), the polarization of public opinion over *Roe* v. *Wade*, Anita Bryant's anti–gay rights campaign in Dade County, Florida, and the Kanawha County, West Virginia, school wars in the 1970s marked the first stirrings of the contemporary cultural wars (Hunter 1991; Martin 1996). On the front lines of these battles were religiously committed Catholics and evangelical Protestants, in opposition to secularists and cultural modernists (who would eventually form the core of antifundamentalism in the electorate). Most of these clashes during the counterculture era, however, occurred on the periphery of partisan politics or involved confrontations between factions within the Democratic Party.

The New Religious Divide among Party Elites and Activists

The first substantial presence of secularists as a political force within a major party was at the Democratic National Convention in 1972. Before then, neither party contained many secularists nor showed many signs of moral and cultural liberalism. Moreover, before the late 1960s, there was something of a tacit commitment among elites in both parties to traditional Judeo-Christian values regarding authority, sexual mores, and the nuclear family (Kirkpatrick 1976; Layman 2001). This consensus was shattered in 1972 when the Democratic Party was captured by a faction whose cultural reform agenda was perceived by many (both inside and outside the convention) as antagonistic to traditional religious values. The largest "religious" bloc represented at the convention was made up of "secularists," that is, self-identified agnostics, atheists, religious "nones," and persons who never or seldom attended religious services (Layman 2001). More than a third of the white delegates fit this description, a remarkable figure when, according to Hunter (1991), only about 5 percent of the population in 1972 could be described as secularists.

The ascendancy of secularists in the Democratic Party had long-term consequences for the relative attractiveness of the two major parties for adherents of different religious outlooks. The Democratic Party became more appealing to secularists and religious liberals and less attractive to traditionalists. Party stalwarts and influential New Deal cultural traditionalists (many of whom were Catholic)—such as Mayor Richard J. Daley of Chicago, the labor leader George Meany, and a host of ethnic members of Congress like New York representatives John Rooney and James Delaney—found themselves isolated and their power and influence in the party waning. Representatives and senators from the party's more conservative southern wing found the cultural liberalism of the national party even more unpalatable and more difficult to defend and explain to their constituents. Many withdrew from active participation in national Democratic Party gatherings, and some bolted to the Republican Party. The increased importance of secularists in the Democratic Party had the opposite effect on the Republicans, who over time came to be seen as more hospitable to traditionalists and less appealing to religious liberals. What was at first an intraparty culture war was becoming, albeit in fits and starts, a full-blown interparty culture war.

By 1992, there were clear signs of religious and cultural polarization in the composition and attitudes of the delegates attending the Democratic and Republican national party conventions, events that launched what one team of political researchers dubbed the first "electoral cultural war" (Kellstedt et al. 1996, 286). According to the 1992 Convention Delegate Study (CDS)—which was carried out by Richard Herrera and Warren E. Miller and made available from the Interuniversity Consortium for Political and Social Research—first-time white delegates at the 1992 Democratic convention in New York City were twice as likely as their Republican counterparts at the 1992 Houston convention (61 to 30 percent) to describe themselves as "irreligious" or minimally attached to religion (i.e., attended worship services "a few times a year" or less, or reported that religion was unimportant in their lives). Between 1972 and 1992, the percentage of nominal mainline Protestants among first-time Republican delegates declined from over a third to a fifth, while the proportion of religiously committed evangelical and fundamentalist delegates in this group tripled to 18 percent. Two-thirds of white Republican delegates attended religious services at least once a month; only two of five white Democratic delegates demonstrated their faith with this degree of commitment. The overall trends for the twenty-year span surveyed by CDS are summed up by Layman (2001, 107): "The Democratic Party now appears to be a party whose core support comes from secularists, Jews, and the less committed members of the major religious traditions . . . [The Republican Party] is becoming a party of the traditionally religious and religiously committed, whose core of support consists of the highly active members of the evangelical Protestant, mainline Protestant, and Catholic traditions."

Increased religious polarization is also apparent in how Democratic and Republican national convention delegates have come to view various core constituent groups of the opposing party. Democratic and

Republican activists in the CDS surveys are significantly more negative toward groups associated with the newer religious and cultural divisions in the electorate than toward groups associated with older political cleavages based on class, race, ethnicity, party, and ideology. In 1992, for example, the average thermometer rating of Republican delegates for union leaders, liberals, blacks, Hispanics, and Democrats was 17° warmer than their mean rating for feminists, environmentalists, and pro-choice groups (44° vs. 27°). Similarly, the mean thermometer rating of Democratic delegates that year was 21° warmer for conservatives, the rich, big business, and Republicans than their average rating for pro-life groups and Christian fundamentalists (34° vs. 13°). Of the 18 groups tested by CDS, the most negatively rated group by Democratic delegates was Christian fundamentalists. More than half the Democratic delegates gave Christian fundamentalists the absolute minimum score they could, 0°; the average Democratic thermometer score toward this religious group was a very cold 11°, marginally warmer than the 4° score they gave to Christian Coalition founder Pat Robertson.

Clearly, by 1992 Christian fundamentalists had become a salient political object to Democratic Party elites and activists—90 percent of the convention delegates thought they had enough information about Christian fundamentalists to form an intensely negative opinion about them. More important, by almost any conceivable criterion established by ethnocultural historians and social psychologists, Christian fundamentalists had become a negative political referent to an increasingly secularist and culturally liberal national Democratic Party.

The Secularist/Traditionalist Divide in the Electorate

To find out the extent to which the new religious cleavage and negative religious group associations have expanded beyond elites and party activists into the electorate, we classified ANES respondents according to their attitudes toward scriptural authority and levels of religiosity (see Bolce and De Maio 1999b for religious classifications). Persons who exhibited the minimum of religiosity (i.e., rejected scriptural authority, had no religious affiliation, never attended religious services or prayed, and indicated that religion provided no guidance in their day-to-day lives) were coded as secularists. Respondents who exhibited the highest levels of faith and commitment (i.e., prayed and attended religious services regularly, accepted the Bible as divinely inspired, and said that religion was important to their daily lives) were coded as traditionalists. Persons who fell between these poles were classified as religious moderates. In 2004, 69 percent of ANES respondents fell into the latter category, with the remaining respondents splitting 12 percent secularist and 19 percent traditionalist. Because the culture war is largely a clash in values among whites, we confined our analysis to whites in the ANES surveys (see Calhoun-Brown 1997 for a discussion of black perspectives on cultural issues and groups).

Answers to a battery of questions included in the ANES and the Pew Surveys on Religion and Public Life covering the past four presidential elections point to four important aspects of the secularist worldview (see table 10.1). First, it is associated with a moral outlook that may be described as relativistic. Second, it is an ideologically liberal worldview. Secularists were more than twice as likely to identify their politics as liberal than as conservative (53 vs. 23 percent); traditionalists (overwhelmingly) and religious moderates (to a lesser extent) described their politics as conservative. Third, secularism is no less powerful a determinant of attitudes on the contentious values issues than is a religiously traditionalist worldview. In most instances, secularists consistently and lopsidedly embrace the culturally liberal positions. Traditionalists generally line up on the opposite side, and religious moderates fall in between.

Secularists were most distinct with respect to the coolness they displayed toward the idea that the traditional two-parent family performs beneficial socializing functions, their greater willingness to accept nontraditional family forms (e.g., gay adoption, gay marriage), and their greater acceptance of post-1960s sexual mores. Secularists were significantly less likely to condemn marital infidelity and far more likely than the others to oppose any law restricting the right to abortion.

Fourth and finally, secularism embodies an antagonism toward religion in the public square and hostility toward theologically traditional religious groups. Secularists distinguished themselves from moderates and traditionalists, for example, by their belief that religious group involvement in the political process is divisive and harmful for society and by the antipathy they expressed toward evangelical Christians, the Catholic Church, and particularly Christian fundamentalists and Religious Right organizations such as the Christian Coalition (registering

TABLE 10.1   Religious Worldview, Moral Outlook, and Attitudes toward the Social Issues (percent)

Attitude or Ideology	Traditionalists	Moderates	Seculars
Agree that we should adjust our views of right and wrong to changing moral standards	24	44	62
Agree that new morals are causing societal breakdown	83	63	33
Agree that there would be less problems if the traditional family were emphasized more	93	78	49
Strongly agree that extra–marital sex is always wrong[a]	89	70	51
Ideology			
Liberal	9	22	53
Moderate	18	34	25
Conservative	73	44	23
Agree that a woman's right to abortion should be unrestricted	11	37	70
Favor a ban on partial birth abortion	81	64	34
Agree that gays should be allowed to serve in the military	60	79	87
Agree that gay adoption should be legally permitted	18	47	67
Allow gays to marry	9	33	75
Agree that the influence of religion in politics threatens to divide us as a nation[b]	20	45	71
Churches should stay out of politics[c]	34	49	71
Would not vote for a qualified atheist nominated by own party[c]	70	35	9
Would not vote for a qualified evangelical Christian nominated by own party[c]	13	13	48
Negative toward atheists[c]	76	49	8
Negative toward evangelical Christians[c]	20	26	61
Negative toward the Catholic Church[d]	24	20	53
Negative toward Christian fundamentalists[d]	14	22	68

Sources: 1992, 1997, and 2004 American National Election Studies (ANES); Religion and Public Life Survey (2003).
[a]This question was asked in the ANES 1992 Study.
[b]This question was asked in the ANES 1997 Pilot Study.
[c]Religion and Public Life Survey (2003). Members of group being evaluated were removed from the computation
[d] "Negative" is defined as evaluating the Catholic Church or Christian fundamentalists 40° or colder on ANES's 100° thermometer scale. Catholics and fundamentalists were excluded from the computations of thermometers toward the Catholic Church and Christian fundamentalists, respectively.

34° toward both groups on the 2000 ANES thermometer scale, the last time the Center for Political Studies tested feelings toward the Religious Right). Secularists were two and a half times more likely than religious moderates and traditionalists to exhibit antipathy toward these four groups representing traditional Christianity.

Political Antifundamentalism as Secularist Reaction to the Religious Right

As idea elements in political belief systems, Christian fundamentalists and the Religious Right have increasingly become interchangeable attitude objects; for many voters, the "Christian Right" symbol evokes not only "pictures in their heads" of fundamentalists but positive and negative reactions to those images as well. The increased fusion of Christian fundamentalists with the Religious Right in the political belief systems of white nonfundamentalists is strongly indicated by the trend in the correlation coefficients gauging the relationship between the ANES's feeling thermometers toward fundamentalists and the Religious Right (in 1988, "evangelical groups active in politics"; in 1996 and 2000, "the Christian Coalition"). The product-moment coefficients assessing the degree of constraint between anti–Religious Right affect and feeling antagonistic toward Christian fundamentalists increased from .46 in 1988 to an average of .65 since then. Although positive feelings toward the Christian Right do not necessarily translate into high regard for Christian fundamentalists, feeling intensely antagonistic toward the Religious Right almost assures feeling intensely negative toward Christian fundamentalists, particularly if one is a secularist. For this segment of the population, the two groups have become almost interchangeable cognitive elements. In the 2000 ANES data set, 87 percent of secularists who reported feeling animus toward the Religious Right also indicated that they felt intensely antagonistic toward fundamentalists (up from 70 percent in 1988). Although there is evidence that some nonsecularists also negatively associate Christian fundamentalists with the Christian Right in their political belief systems, neither religious moderates nor traditionalists do so to the same degree that secularists do.

To find out the sorts of images that nonfundamentalists have of Christian fundamentalists, we examined responses to a battery of questions included in the 1997 ANES Pilot Study. This survey instrument

262 Louis Bolce and Gerald De Maio

was designed to investigate the impact of group threat on prejudices about blacks and Christian fundamentalists. The data provide insights into how animus toward the Religious Right structures beliefs about and feelings toward Christian fundamentalists. Persons who feel antagonism toward the Religious Right view fundamentalists as culturally *and* politically threatening. More specifically, the data indicate that militant opponents of the Religious Right are significantly more likely than others to accept stereotypes of Christian fundamentalists as intolerant, ideologically extreme, culturally imperialistic, and intense opponents of women's equality. By almost any criterion, the anti–Religious Right segment of the populace views Christian fundamentalists as outside the bounds of mainstream American political culture and civility. For example, four in ten opponents of the Christian Coalition in the 1997 ANES Pilot Study considered fundamentalists untrustworthy; that is, they placed members of this religious group in categories 5, 6, and 7 on the 7-point trustworthy–untrustworthy scale. Seven of ten anti–Religious Right respondents rated fundamentalists at least 6 on the ANES 7-point tolerance–intolerance scale. More than a third rated fundamentalists 7 on the 7-point equal role for women scale (a "woman's place is in the home"); the mean attribution score that these respondents gave to fundamentalists on the women's role scale was 5.67. Respondents who did not feel intense animus toward the Religious Right located the political and cultural orientations of Christian fundamentalists not all that far from where fundamentalists placed themselves—as being ideologically and culturally somewhat to the right of whites in general, but not radically so. Intense opponents of the Religious Right, conversely, located the ideological thinking of fundamentalists nearly two ideological units to the right of the white generic norm, near the extreme conservative fringe (6.4 on the ANES 7-point scale).[2] With these sorts of notions about fundamentalists, it is not surprising that intense opponents of the Religious Right feel significantly more negative toward fundamentalists than do other respondents; the former rated fundamentalists at 21° on the 100° thermometer scale, whereas the average rating given to fundamentalists from all other respondents (excluding fundamentalists themselves) was 53°.

The results in table 10.2 reveal that Christian fundamentalists have become salient to intense opponents of the Religious Right in another respect—one with direct electoral implications. Militant secularists are not only more likely than others to view Christian fundamentalists negatively but also appear to be more disposed to notice and retain

TABLE 10.2   The Impact of Intensely Disliking the Religious Right on Respondents' Perceptions of Christian Fundamentalists (percent)

Perception of Christian Fundamentalists (CFs)	Anti–Religious Right	Others
CF leaders push too hard to have their beliefs written into law[a]	56***	17
N	(57)	(252)
CFs are untrustworthy[b]	41**	12
N	(54)	(244)
CFs are intolerant[c]	70***	19
N	(55)	(243)
CFs believe that women's place is in the home[d]	40***	9
N	(52)	(224)
CFs are extreme conservatives[d]	56**	15
N	(48)	(189)
CFs are a core Republican constituency	86***	44
N	(57)	(252)
Mean thermometer rating of CFs[f]	21***	53°
N	(57)	(255)

Source: American National Election Pilot Study, 1997.

Note: $*p < .05$, $**p < .01$, $***p < .001$. The entries are percentages unless otherwise noted. The significance tests were computed on the total N for each variable. Analyses include white non–Christian fundamentalists only. A member of the "anti–Religious Right" is defined as a respondent who evaluated the Christian Coalition 20° colder that this respondent's average for the other groups.

[a]"Strongly Agree response" on ANES V970184, V970185.

[b]Responses 5–7 on v970187.

[c]Responses 6–7 on v 970191.

[d]Response 7 on v970234, v970319.

[e]Response 1 on v970131 and v970132.

[f]Thermometer score ranging from 0°–100° on v971038.

information communicated in the mass media about the partisan affiliations of fundamentalists. Nearly nine in ten of them picked up and retained political news linking Christian fundamentalists with the Republican Party, while only 44 percent of the other respondents did so. The political significance of this is that voters with the most negative perceptions of Christian fundamentalists are also those who are most likely to identify this religious group as an intense Republican voting bloc.

Secularists and the Antifundamentalist Phenomenon in the Electorate

The increased interdependence of the Religious Right and Christian fundamentalist symbols since the late 1980s means that the cognitive representations that voters have formed about the Christian Right political movement, in varying degrees, have become cognitive representations of Christian fundamentalists. To the extent that a voter has come to believe that the Religious Right is an important (and influential) constituency of the Republican Party, the voter has also come to believe, more or less, that fundamentalists are an important constituency of the Republican Party. If the voter intensely dislikes fundamentalists, that voter has politically relevant information that can be utilized to make decisions about the political party associated with this disliked group. The voter, for example, might come to think that this party is taking on the cultural and ideological characteristics of the disliked group and decide to affiliate with a rival political party and oppose candidates supported by Christian fundamentalists.

Figure 10.1 displays the trends in party identification for secularists, antifundamentalists, and religious traditionalists over the last five presidential elections. The data show a clear-cut religious divide in party affiliation that has widened appreciably during the past decade, with secularists and antifundamentalists becoming increasingly Democratic in their affiliation, and religious traditionalists strengthening their loyalties to the Republicans. During this period, secularists switched from a modest pro-Republican bias in 1988 to a decidedly pro–Democratic Party preference by 2004.

Similarly, figure 10.1 shows that the 7-point advantage given to the Democrats by antifundamentalists in 1988 became a 32-point net plus sixteen years later. In contrast, the loyalties of religious traditionalists over this same period went toward the Republicans. The result of these divergent trends was that the religious gap in the party loyalties of secularists and traditionalists multiplied more than sixteenfold (from 4 to 67 percentage points) over the course of these five elections; in a similar vein, the partisan chasm separating antifundamentalists and traditionalists more than quadrupled, from 15 percentage points in 1988 to a 66-point gap sixteen years later.

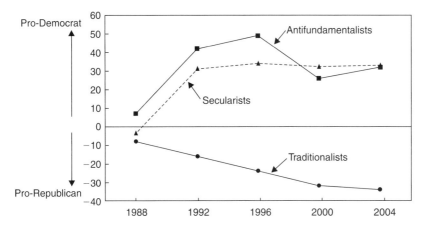

Figure 10.1   The Religious Divide in Party Identification, 1988–2004

The secularist/religious divide is also apparent in the voting patterns of these two groups during this same period (see figure 10.2). Throughout the period, when secularists and antifundamentalists were aligning with the Democratic Party, religious traditionalists were casting their votes in greater numbers for the opposing Republican Party's presidential tickets. Traditionalists began this era solidly in the Republican camp and ended it even more lopsidedly Republican; in both the 2000 and 2004 elections, three-quarters of traditionalists favored George W. Bush over Al Gore and John Kerry (figure 10.2). The result of these divergent trends was an electorate that was increasingly becoming split along a secularist/traditionalist dimension. In the four elections since the contentious Houston convention in 1992, the religious gap separating secularists and traditionalists was more important than other social and demographic cleavages in the electorate: It was much larger than the gender gap and more significant than any combination of income, education, marital status, age, and regional groupings.

The increased importance of antifundamentalists and traditionalists to the Democratic and Republican electoral coalitions is not just in their loyalty to these respective parties but also in the contribution they make to the total Democratic and Republican votes. For example, almost a third of Gore's and Kerry's white support in the 2000 and 2004 elections came from antifundamentalists; in contrast, roughly the same proportion of Bush's voters were drawn from religious traditionalists in these elections (30 percent). The religious polarization that began in the 1970s and early 1980s at the elite/activist level of

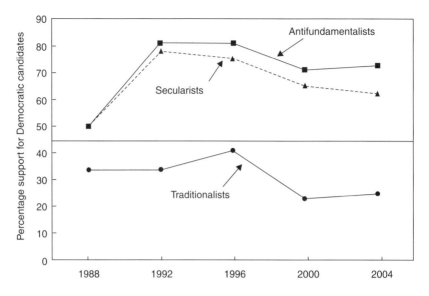

Figure 10.2   The Religious Divide in Presidential Elections, 1988–2004 (percent of two-party vote cast for Democratic presidential candidates)

the Democratic and Republican parties had by the 1990s filtered down to the mass electorate and become reflected in the opposing party evaluations and voting choices of antifundamentalists and traditionalists.

Political Antifundamentalism and Anti–Religious Right Animus

To assess the political impact of antifundamentalists when examined alongside the effects of other factors causally related to voters' choices in presidential elections, we computed logistic regression equations for all the presidential election years since the ANES first included a thermometer item toward fundamentalists in its survey instrument (1988–2004). Because we are also interested in finding out whether and to what extent the political effects of antifundamentalism on individual voting preferences are artifacts of anti–Religious Right animus, we computed a second logistic regression equation for each presidential election in which the ANES had thermometers assessing both anti–Religious Right and anti–Christian fundamentalist animus (1988, 1996, 2000).

The effects of antifundamentalism (operationalized by the ANES thermometer item) were assessed first by allowing antagonism toward the Religious Right to operate through this variable. A second equation was computed with the effects of anti–Religious Right animus removed from the item tapping antifundamentalism, and using the residual as the new antifundamentalist predictor variable in the model. The other independent variables are standard demographic indicators and attributes found in the voting literature to be predictors of vote choice in recent elections (i.e., respondent's political ideology, party identification, attitude toward government guarantee of jobs and a decent standard of living, retrospective assessment of the economy, abortion attitudes, racial liberalism, and the two dummies assessing the respondent's religiosity).

The logistic model for the 2004 election included two additional variables to assess the effects of two salient short-term forces that were in operation that year and not at work in previous elections—the war in Iraq and gay marriage, a new hot-button cultural issue precipitated by a Massachusetts Supreme Court decision expanding the legal definition of marriage to include homosexual couples; controversial same-sex weddings performed by the mayors of San Francisco and New Paltz, New York; and the presence of referenda on the ballot in eleven states limiting marriage to heterosexual unions. The dependent variable in each model was presidential vote choice, coded 0 = not Republican and 1 = Republican.

The results, reported in table 10.3, show that antagonism toward Christian fundamentalists has been an enduring predictor of voting against Republican presidential candidates since the first Bill Clinton presidential election, even when the effects of other potent explanatory factors—respondent's partisanship, retrospective economic judgments, symbolic racism, abortion position, religiosity, and attitudes toward the Iraq war and gay marriage in the 2004 election—are taken into account. The significant effects of abortion in the 1990s, secularism in the past two presidential elections, and animus toward fundamentalists throughout this era reflect the growth of religious and moral divisions in the electorate since the 1980s (see Abramowitz 1995 and Carmines and Stimson 1989 for analyses of the impact of abortion and race in this era). Although the bivariate effects of respondent abortion attitudes and political ideology remained powerful throughout this era—in 2004 both individually were significant at the $p < .001$ level, for example—the diminished importance of their partialed effects in the 2000 and 2004 elections reflects the increased association

TABLE 10.3 The Impact of Anti–Christian Fundamentalism in Recent Presidential Elections (with and without affect toward the Religious Right controlled)

Variable	1988 β	1988 S.E.	1992 β	1992 S.E.	1996 β	1996 S.E.	2000 β	2000 S.E.	2004 β	2004 S.E.
Region	-.44	.32	-.29	.23	-.49	.38	-.77***	.27	-.52	.62
Age	1.49	.80	.59	.47	1.92***	.85	-.88	.58	.01	.02
Gender	.35	.28	-.67***	.21	-.03	.37	-.31	.26	.49	.50
Education	.25	.58	1.24***	.43	1.48*	.60	-1.26****	.55	.10	.17
Income	.45	.63	.35	.47	1.62	.90	.05	.79	.01	.01
Party identification	-5.52**	.52	-4.20**	.37	-6.05**	.66	-6.32**	.51	-.91**	.16
Ideology	-2.24***	.77	-1.67**	.59	-3.02***	1.06	-.82	.59	-.17	.30
Jobs / decent living	-.43	.48	-.77	.40	-.46	.88	-.52	.42	-.10	.14
Economy	-1.24***	.39	-1.27**	.34	2.54**	.59	-.81	.47	-.50***	.17
Race attitudes	-.81	.61	-1.68***	.55	-2.31****	.95	-.15	.57	-.59***	.18
Abortion	-.28	.46	-.97***	.33	-1.14*	.56	-.58	.40	-.45	.27
Traditionalist	.11	.41	.32	.31	.33	.65	.99****	.40	.33	.94
Secularist	-.38	.44	-.25	.28	.01	.55	-1.10***	.35	-1.76***	.82

	Model 1 B	Model 1 S.E.	Model 2 B	Model 2 S.E.	Model 3 B	Model 3 S.E.	Model 4 B	Model 4 S.E.	Model 5 B	Model 5 S.E.
Antifundamentalism	-1.52	.93	-3.17**	.89	-5.42**	1.55	-1.18*	.61	-4.55****	1.94
(With effects of Religious Right removed)	-.93	1.01	N.A.		-1.34	1.26	-1.19	1.06	N.A.	
Iraq (oppose)									-1.23**	.20
Gay marriage (for)									-.12	.16
Constant	-.13**	1.05	-5.10**	.89	-10.32**	1.75	-2.46***	.82	-2.77***	2.52
N	585		940		544		835		481	
Model chi square	413.27		542.49		523.40		604.99		491.46	
Correct (percent)	88		83		91		83		93	
Nagelkerke R^2	.69		.60		.82		.73		.89	

Sources: 1988, 1992, 1996, and 2000 data from American National Election Studies.

Note: $*p < .06$, $**p < .05$, $***p < .01$, $****p < .001$. Entries are logit coefficients with standard errors. N.A. = not available. S.E. = standard error. The dependent variable was: 0 = not voting Republican; 1 = voting for Republican presidential candidate. All predictors were coded 0 to 1, with high poles for region: non-South; age: older; sex: female; education: postgraduate; income: high; religiosity: secularist; party identification: Democrat; ideology: liberal; government economic policy: decent standard of living; racial attitudes: liberal; economy: worse; racial attitudes: liberal: abortion: pro-choice; affect toward fundamentalists: antagonism. Analyses include whites only. A thermometer item for the Religious Right was not included in the 1992 and 2004 survey instrument.

of these two variables with one another and with some of the other predictors during this period (for a discussion of expanded ideological conflict during this period, see Layman and Carsey 2002).

The results of the second regression equation indicate that the political effects of antifundamentalism are not unrelated to a respondent's evaluation of the Christian Right. When the effects of the latter are removed from the thermometer rating of Christian fundamentalists, antifundamentalism is no longer a significant predictor of voting behavior in presidential elections. This suggests that one important reason why antifundamentalists have been voting increasingly against Republican presidential candidates since the 1990s is their conflation of fundamentalists with the Christian Right movement. Overall, these results indicate that the quality of antifundamentalism that has colored secularist perceptions of the Republican Party since the 1990s is fear of the cultural agenda of the Religious Right, with whom Christian fundamentalists have been prominently linked in national political news, not necessarily animus toward Christian fundamentalists per se.

The Secularist Bases of Antifundamentalism

The Religious Right was born out of lifestyle conflicts arising from the opposing religious and moral worldviews of secularists and religious traditionalists. These religious and moral differences were politicized, beginning in the 1970s, when Democratic and (later) Republican elites made respective appeals to secularists and religious traditionalists by embracing policies favored by these groups in their national platforms. It was the politicization of these preexisting religious and cultural cleavages that gave rise to political antifundamentalism. The fusion of anti–Christian Right animus with antifundamentalism, particularly among secularists, raises the question of whether antifundamentalism today reflects anti–Christian Right animus and nothing else (e.g., see Singer 2000). The evidence indicates the contrary.

Table 10.4 presents four regression models computed sequentially to identify the historical and more recent sources of anti–Christian fundamentalism. The coefficients reported in the table are product-moment coefficients assessing the simple bivariate relationships between each predictor and the dependent variable, as well as standardized regression coefficients comparing the relative importance of the pre-

TABLE 10.4 Predictors of Anti–Christian Fundamentalism

Predictor	r	Model I ß	Model II ß	Model III ß	Model IV ß
Region	.04	.03	−.02	.04	.03
Age	.02	.05	.09**	.09**	.05
Gender	.02	.01	.01	.04	.03
Education	.22	.24***	.22***	.22**	.13***
Family income	.03	−.05	−.03	−.03	−.01
Secularism	.26	.25***	.18***	.15**	.09**
Moral relativism	.29		.22***	−.10**	.04
Party identification	.19			.06	.03
Ideology	.30			.15***	.08*
Abortion attitude	.27			.12***	.05
Pro–gay rights	.19			.09**	.04
Animus toward the Religious Right[a]	.58				.43***
Adjusted R^2		.11	.16	.21	.34

Source: 2000 data from American National Election Studies.
Note: $*p < .05$, $**p < .01$, $***p < .001$. $N = 816$. The table shows rs and standardized regression coefficients. The dependent variable was coded 0 to 100, with positive affect coded to the midpoint of the variable. All predictors were 0 to 1, with high scores for non-South, female, moral relativist, Democrat, liberal, pro-choice, and anti–Religious Right. A positive sign indicates that the value of the independent variables predicts to feeling antagonistic toward Christian fundamentalism. The analysis includes white, non–Christian fundamentalists only.
[a]The Religious Right variable is the thermometer variable toward the Christian Coalition; positive affect was coded to the midpoint. The empty cells for this predictor are because it is only included in Model IV.

dictors in each of the four models. The data are from the 2000 ANES, the last time thermometer items for the Religious Right and Christian fundamentalists were included in the survey instrument.

Models I and II examine the contemporary relevance of traditional sources of antifundamentalism. The "old" sources of antifundamentalism reflect long-standing antipathies and suspicions rooted in cultural and religious cleavages dating from the Scopes trial era. The items included in Model I are education (as a surrogate for cosmopolitanism and rationalism) and a dummy variable assessing secularism. The age, region, gender, and family income of respondents are introduced as controls. Model II adds the respondent's moral outlook to the equation.[3]

The inclusion of this variable in a separate equation rests on the theoretical premise that moral worldviews are informed or conditioned by religion and formal education (Hunter 1991; Norris and Inglehart 2004). Model III adds variables tapping the post-1960s lifestyle conflicts—reflected by struggles over abortion and gay rights—that expanded into partisan and ideological divisions during this period. Because Christian fundamentalists have been prominent among abortion and gay rights opponents, it seems plausible that gay rights supporters and pro-choice advocates would be more inclined than their traditionalistic counterparts to feel antagonistic toward fundamentalists. Our indicator of anti–Religious Right affect was added to the other predictors in Model IV. The dependent variable is the thermometer item for Christian fundamentalists, adjusted to the nonfundamentalist respondent's group mean to control for positivity (and negativity) bias and folded to allow only negative sentiment to vary.

By comparing the results from Model I with those in Models II, III, and IV, we can trace what happens to the effects of the more "remote" sources of antifundamentalism when moral relativism and the more proximate causes are included in the subsequent models. We can find out, for example, the extent to which the historical sources of antifundamentalism are expressed today through variables capturing contemporary political and cultural conflicts.

The results for Model I point up the continuing importance of antagonisms arising from cleavages over religion and cosmopolitanism in structuring attitudes toward Christian fundamentalists. Both factors are significant predictors of feeling antagonistic toward Christian fundamentalists. The model accounted for 11 percent of the variance in the adjusted Christian fundamentalist thermometer item. As expected, secularists and highly educated respondents are significantly more likely than their opposites to express animus toward fundamentalists. When the item tapping moral relativism is added into the mix, it too is significant; this variable increases the explained variance by about a third—see Model II. The diminished influence of secularism indicates that moral relativism includes a secular worldview whose effects on the dependent variable are expressed indirectly through the respondent's moral outlook. Slightly less than a third of moral relativism's effect on antifundamentalism is due to secularism's influence on moral outlook.

Model III shows that the direct effects of moral relativism diminish appreciably (although they do remain significant) when variables tapping contemporary conflicts over lifestyle and ideology are added to the equation (compare Model II with Model III). Some of the effects of moral relativism are filtered through the respondent's abortion attitudes, political ideology, and attitudes toward gay rights, with the liberal position on these items predicting antifundamentalism. For example, about one-third of the direct effects of a respondent's ideological orientation and abortion attitude on that individual's view of fundamentalists can be traced to the indirect effects of a moral worldview working through these variables. The results show that historical cleavages growing out of religious and moral differences expand into conflicts over gay rights and abortion, which in turn trigger negative reference group feelings toward fundamentalists. The significance of ideology confirms Layman and Carsey's (2002) argument that ideological controversy now encompasses a cultural dimension—which in this regression model includes competing views on abortion and gay rights and opposing stances toward Christian fundamentalists—as well as the more historical cleavages over social welfare policy and race. The four variables in Model III added five points to the adjusted R^2.

Model IV underscores the centrality of anti–Religious Right animus in structuring feelings toward Christian fundamentalists. The addition of this variable to the equation added 13 points to the adjusted R^2 (accounting for 38 percent of total explained variance); the magnitude of its bivariate and multivariate effects overwhelms the effects of the other predictors. Clearly, a case can be made that a significant aspect of modern antifundamentalism can be attributed to the conflation of the fundamentalists with Christian Right groups in the political belief systems of intense opponents of the Religious Right. Yet the fact remains that 62 percent of the total explained variance for the item assessing antifundamentalism is attributable to antagonisms arising from competing religious and moral worldviews, differences in cosmopolitanism, opposing ideological perspectives, and antagonisms arising from contemporary conflicts over lifestyle issues (compare the adjusted R^2s in Models III and IV). And it should also be noted that the historically based sources of anti–Christian fundamentalism—secularism and cosmopolitanism (captured here by high educational attainment)—remain significant in the final, more complete model. In sum, the results from the four regression models point to contemporary political factors—as well as more historically based religious, moral, and cultural forces—as giving shape to modern antifundamentalism.

Conclusion

In his introductory essay to the *Almanac of American Politics 2002*, Michael Barone (2001) argues that the most important demographic variable accounting for how Americans voted in the 2000 election was religion. The religion gap separating Republican from Democratic voters in the 2004 election was even more noticeable.[4] This cleavage, one that polarizes more along secularist/traditionalist lines than denominational ones, has since the 1990s given rise to a new type of voter in the American electorate: the anti–Christian fundamentalist. Yet as we have seen, secularist antireligious animus is not restricted just to fundamentalism (see table 10.1). According to a 2003 Pew Religion and Public Life Survey, for example, three-fifths of secularists reported that they disliked evangelical Christians and almost half (48 percent) said that they would not vote for a qualified evangelical nominated by their party. A majority (53 percent) of secularists queried in the 2004 ANES survey expressed antagonism toward the Catholic Church, and 45 percent felt antagonistic toward both fundamentalists and the Catholic Church.

This is not to say that antagonists to traditional Christianity are newcomers to the American cultural landscape. Antifundamentalists have been inveighing against the Christian fundamentalist "menace" to enlightened progress since the days of Clarence Darrow and H. L. Mencken. And as recent scholarship reminds us, militant secularists, at the elite and activist levels, have been agitating against any accommodation of religion since the 1870s, the most prominent examples being the attempt to ban religious schools in Oregon and the adoption of state Blaine amendments prohibiting state aid to "sectarian" schools (Hamburger 2002; Smith 2003).

Only relatively recently, however, have militant secularists, antifundamentalists, and antagonists to the institutional Catholic Church begun to coalesce in a single party. According to analyses of data contained in the ANES 2004 survey, 43 percent of Kerry's white support came from antifundamentalists, more than a quarter (28 percent) of his supporters voiced antagonistic feelings toward the Catholic Church, and a fifth expressed animosity toward both the Catholic Church and Christian fundamentalists. More than 80 percent of anti-Catholic secularists went for Kerry over Bush, and 96 percent of antifundamentalist, anti-Catholic secularists supported the Massachusetts senator. In contrast, Bush carried almost three-quarters of nonsecularists who felt positively toward both the Catholic Church and Christian fundamentalists.

With the selection of Howard Dean—one of the most secular candidates to run for president in modern history—to chair the national Democratic Party, and the substantial presence of Dean supporters in the Democratic base, religiously based political divisions are unlikely to abate in the foreseeable future (Foer 2003). Dean's factually correct but derogatory characterization of the Republican Party as the "white Christian party" in a June 2005 speech to Democratic activists in San Francisco will more likely reinforce than lessen this polarization, despite the efforts of some prominent Democrats to bolster the party's image among religiously traditional Christians. Yet even if Democrats want to mute the current polarization based on religion by appearing to be more receptive to the concerns of religious traditionalists, views expressed by senators Hillary Clinton and Barack Obama, they run up against their party's secularist base who, according to 2004 ANES data, voted 71 to 29 percent to elect Democratic candidates to office. Even more constraining is the secularist core among the party's activists and primary voters, exemplified by committed Dean supporters. According to a Pew Survey Report (2005a, 23), 88 percent of these activists said that "blurring of the separation between church and state" is their top domestic policy concern. It is the substantial presence of secularists in the Democratic Party and the influence this bloc has on the party's cultural agenda that explain why, according to another Pew Survey Report (2005b), white religious Christians are much more likely to believe that the Democratic Party is hostile than friendly toward religion.

Notes

1. American social science at the time did suggest somewhat optimistically, however, that the deleterious effects of Christian fundamentalism could be combated with some healthy doses of college education and exposures to modern culture, along with, of course, proper elite monitoring. For a critical evaluation of the methodological flaws and intellectual and political biases in the literature cited in the text above, see Christie and Jahoda 1954, Brown 1965, and Wilcox 1992. See Busch 1998 for a recent empirical study that challenges the findings of earlier research linking intolerance and political extremism to religious orthodoxy and Christian fundamentalism.

2. Survey data on the actual cultural and political attitudes of Christian fundamentalists indicate that their social and political views are appreciably less extreme than militant secularists believe. According to the 2000 ANES survey, fundamentalists were divided over the abortion issue; 43 percent wanted to ban the procedure altogether, while the remainder favored permitting abortion under some circumstances. The ANES survey results also show fundamentalists opposed to government-sponsored prayer, opting instead for silent prayer, the modal position taken by the general population on the ANES school prayer item. Similarly, fundamentalists, though more culturally traditional and ideologically conservative than nonfundamentalists, have relatively egalitarian attitudes with respect to women's rights (they averaged "3" on the 7-point women's role scale) and they displayed a moderately conservative political ideology in terms of their mean self-placements (5.59 on ANES's 7-point ideology scale). A significant minority (40 percent) indicated that they support laws protecting gays from job discrimination; the same percentage said that gays should be allowed to serve in the armed forces. Their thermometer ratings for Catholics and Jews, respectively, were a relatively warm 62° and 68°, modestly warmer than the average ratings of non-Catholics and non-Jews for these two groups. Clearly, the Christian fundamentalist revealed in empirical data collected over the past decade is at some variance with the popular image of Christian fundamentalists reflected by the response patterns in table 10.2.

3. We included this variable in the model because of the prominence given to conflict arising from competing moral outlooks in both the ethnocultural literature and in Hunter's (1991) culture wars thesis. The moral relativism construct was created from factor scores from four ANES items in 2000: New morals are causing societal breakdown (v001530); we should adjust views to changing moral climate (v001531); there would be fewer problems if the traditional family were emphasized (v001532); and we should tolerate others' moral standards even if they disagree with our own (v001533). The index was created from principal components analysis using a varimax rotation. The items loaded on a single factor that accounted for 49 percent of the variance. The loadings ranged from −.727 to .732. The reliability coefficient (alpha) for the construct was .69.

4. E.g., a LEXIS-NEXIS search turned up just four stories appearing in the *Washington Post* and *New York Times* on party polarization along religious lines for the 2000 election cycle. In contrast, the two papers published thirty-six stories on the religion gap in 2004.

ELEVEN

Religion and American Political Life: A Look Forward

J. Matthew Wilson

As the preceding chapters in this volume have made clear, the interaction between religion and politics in America is profound. People from a rich variety of religious backgrounds seek to apply the teachings, principles, and moral wisdom derived from their traditions to their political life, to bring their faith out of the church, synagogue, or mosque and into the public square. At the same time, as Louis Bolce and Gerald De Maio point out in chapter 10, those with little or no attachment to religion are often resentful of these efforts and increasingly orient their politics toward opposing them. These realities have combined to generate considerable discussion, both normative and empirical, about the role of religious faith in American public discourse and electoral politics, often centered on the "culture wars" theme (Hunter 1991; Green et al. 1996; Leege et al. 2002; Fiorina 2005; Brewer and Stonecash 2006).

Yet as instructive as it may be in some respects to speak of an increasingly unified "religious America" pitted against its secularist counterpart, such a discussion can easily overlook the vast diversity of America's communities of faith in their methods and aims of political engagement. As the contributors to this volume point out, religious traditions in this nation range from significant reticence about politics to enthusiastic participation in partisan electoral campaigns. Moreover, the focus of religiously motivated political efforts extends well beyond the frequently discussed issues of abortion, homosexuality, and school prayer to also encompass economic redistribution, the welfare state, racial equality, the environment, and various foreign policy concerns. Historically, people of faith have bolstered (and often spearheaded) movements on both the political left *and* the political right, sometimes in ways that do not map neatly onto the programs and ideologies of secular political parties. This book makes clear that such diversity and nuance in political expression by religious Americans remains very much alive today.

The preceding chapters have provided a sense of that diversity by chronicling the unique features and challenges of religiously based political mobilization within each of America's major faith traditions. Among all the differences of theology, ideology, and history that serve to make these traditions distinctive, however, certain overarching questions emerge that must be confronted by all and that will shape the future of religious–political interaction in America. Foremost among these are two issues: attitudes toward the politicization of faith and approaches to the question of social and economic justice. The answers of religious people to these questions will go a long way toward determining whether the future of religion and politics in America looks like the status quo of the culture wars or something very different.

Faith in the Public Square: An Enduring Dilemma

Discerning and negotiating the proper role for religious faith in the public life of a liberal democracy is a difficult and controversial proposition. To make this assertion is, to a great extent, to state the obvious. For some time, but especially during the past few years, countless books, articles, and op-ed pieces have been written affirming this truth and offering various perspectives on it. The vast majority of these works focus on the issue from the standpoint of the state, asking how a liberal polity can balance separation and accommodation, or how the political system can "save" itself from religious zealotry. The central question seems to be how and to what extent the political system should be open to engagement with religion. For many religious leaders and their congregations, however, this issue is secondary. The more fundamental question with which they must grapple is the reverse: How and to what extent should their religion be open to engagement with politics?

This dilemma is made acute by two competing realities. First, the teachings and doctrines of all major religions have obvious implications for the political order; for instance, that a regime that practices genocide is morally inferior to one that does not, and thus should be opposed, would be a relatively uncontroversial application of moral values to politics. If religious faith leads an individual to support a ban on abortion, an increase in the minimum wage, prayer in public schools, or unilateral nuclear disarmament, then political action would seem natural (or perhaps even mandatory) in an effort to achieve these objectives. At the same time, however, the world of politics is full of half measures, sordid compromises, unsavory bedfellows, and endemic corruption. Is practical political engagement by people and communities of faith worth the descent into that mire, with a potentially attendant loss of religion's clear prophetic voice?

In a characteristic formulation of this dilemma (aimed at Christians but applicable to other faiths as well), the twentieth-century theologian Karl Barth asserts that "it is quite impossible for the Christian to adopt an attitude of complete indifference to politics" and that there can be no such thing as a "non-political Christianity" (Barth 1960, 162). Yet he cautions that much of the political realm is amoral (if not immoral) and that too close an engagement with practical electoral politics or with quests for partisan advantage "will inevitably bring discredit and disgrace on the Christian name" (p. 184).

How, then, are these competing imperatives—to engage political issues with a moral dimension while maintaining a distinct religious identity that is above politics—to be balanced and reconciled? As the preceding chapters point out, leaders and believers in America's various religious traditions have answered in different ways. For some, the answer has been an unambiguous "yes" to active political involvement by both clergy and laity, often in close association with a particular political party. White evangelical Protestants, who historically had been somewhat reticent about political participation, became actively politicized in response to the cultural upheavals of the 1960s and 1970s and have become key elements (some would say *the* key element) of the Republican electoral coalition (Clabaugh 1974; Noll 2001). Likewise, African American churches are known for their extensive politicization. Beginning in the New Deal era, but especially since the civil rights movement, black churches and clergy have provided active support to Democratic candidates, often allowing them to speak from the pulpit (for a few examples among many, see Mikkelsen 2000, Libit 2002, and Hallow 2003a).

Other religious groups have been much more ambivalent or reserved in their political activity. The Catholic Church in America, for example, has traditionally been very reluctant to take a role in electoral politics, in part because of its historically marginal position in American society (Byrnes 1991). As David Campbell and Quin Monson discuss in chapter 5, the Mormon Church has gone to great lengths to stress its nonpartisanship and to avoid endorsing particular candidates. Finally, the very strong separationist positions held by many Jews and liberal Protestants in America have limited the political mobilization of those religious traditions, as Paul Djupe and Laura Olson document in chapters 8 and 3, respectively.

Both the activist and the quiescent religious traditions are facing challenges to their established strategies, however. Those groups that have been heavily involved in politics, most notably black Protestants and white evangelicals, face a key question: Are the moral rewards of political engagement, in terms of concrete policy victories, worth the distractions, compromises, and seductions inherent in secular politics? As Clyde Wilcox and Carin Robinson suggest in chapter 1, believers, and especially leaders, who forge alliances with one of the two major parties are often significantly constrained in the exercise of their prophetic voice. Black clergy, many of whom are deeply opposed to abortion and same-sex marriage, are forced to soft-peddle those issues (or, in the case of nationally prominent figures like Jesse Jackson and Al Sharpton, to actually change their positions) to avoid friction with the Democratic Party and its candidates. Evangelical churches and groups like Focus on the Family offer very muted criticism of Republican misdeeds (even those, like the Mark Foley congressional page scandal, involving sexual predation) because of their desire to see Republican candidates elected. And, in the end, for what? After more than forty years of close alliance with the Democratic Party, African American Christians see an America with enduring and enormous racial disparities, where the welfare state actually became *less* generous under the last Democratic president. Likewise, after twenty-five years as the loyal foot soldiers of the "Republican Revolution," white evangelicals confront a society in which abortion is still legal and in which gay marriage seems on the cusp of becoming a reality.

These realities prompted Cal Thomas and Ed Dobson, in their widely acclaimed book *Blinded by Might* (1999), to argue that religious groups (and evangelical Christians in particular) need to acknowledge the limits and perils of political action and, to a significant extent, to *dis*engage from the political sphere. Though their argument is neither unassailable nor reflective of a consensus, it does point to an increasing reassessment and introspection among many religious Americans who have long trumpeted the imperative of political action.

Those religious groups that have traditionally eschewed political involvement face dilemmas and reassessments as well, however. Increasingly, many are realizing that basic moral principles about which they care deeply are profoundly affected by the policies that government does or does not enact. Given that, is it a morally defensible strategy to sit on the sidelines of politics? As Campbell and Monson point out in chapter 5, the Mormon Church has traditionally been very reluctant to involve itself in the political process. However, the Church also has a very strong commitment to traditional marriage and family structures that are imperiled by the growing push for same-sex unions. As a result, Mormons have begun to engage actively in campaigns over a variety of marriage-related state ballot propositions, a trend likely to continue and accelerate given the increased national prominence of the gay marriage issue.

Likewise, the Catholic Church has historically been very reticent about involvement in American politics but began in the 1980s to speak out in policy-specific terms on issues like abortion, poverty, and nuclear disarmament (Byrnes 1991). More recently, Catholic lay organizations have begun issuing voter guides stressing the primacy of the Church's pro-life teaching, often with the explicit or implicit blessing of local bishops (Steinfels 2006). At the same time, however, many Catholic clergy and lay leaders worry about being drawn into an apparent alliance with either major political party, because neither advances a platform that is completely consistent with Catholic social teaching.

Finally, as Olson notes in chapter 3, the religious left in America prides itself on its strong separationism, its skepticism about clergy as clergy or congregations as congregations engaging in political activity.

Yet this political quiescence has rendered the contemporary religious left a shell of the movement that historically spearheaded drives for the abolition of slavery, expanded workers' rights, the end of Jim Crow segregation, and a more pacifist foreign policy. It has also caused the religious left to cede the terrain of politics to forces with whose understanding of the moral dimensions of politics they profoundly disagree. Just as politically activist religious groups experience strains and dissatisfactions stemming from their engagement with politics, many politically reticent ones are increasingly dissatisfied with their *lack* of such engagement. How both sets of groups resolve these dilemmas will profoundly shape the interaction of American religion and politics in the years to come.

Economic Policy and the Welfare State: A Moral Issue?

Looking forward, some arenas for the engagement of religious groups in American politics are quite predictable. For the last several decades, religiously traditional forces have done battle with their liberal and secularist counterparts over human life issues (originally abortion, joined more recently by euthanasia and embryonic stem cell research), gay rights, and the place of religion in the public square (especially in schools). Though social and technological changes may shift the terrain somewhat, these battles are sure to continue—these questions' moral dimension is obvious and broadly acknowledged. What is much less certain, however, is the prospective nature of religious engagement with issues of poverty and inequality in America. Though antipoverty efforts have at times in American history been the central focus of religious groups' involvement in politics, they are not currently a prominent component of the set of widely recognized "moral issues." This omission—or "missing agenda," to borrow a term from Wilcox and Robinson—is one of the most striking features of religion's interaction with contemporary American politics.

There are many reasons to expect religiously based political activism on behalf of the economically disadvantaged. First, care for the poor is almost universally normative across religious traditions. It figures prominently in the Christian gospel message, and it is also central to Jewish and Muslim social teaching, as Paul Djupe in chapter 8, and Djupe and John Green document in chapter 9. Moreover, there is a long history of religious people, both in America and abroad, leading political fights for workers' rights and economic redistribution, including "conversionist" Christian socialists of the late nineteenth century like F. D. Maurice (Niebuhr 1951). Finally, as various chapters in this volume demonstrate, economic justice remains central to the political visions of many religious groups in America today, including Jews, Muslims, the religious left, and most African American and Latino Christians.

Yet these groups are relatively small, that history of activism is receding, and those teachings about charity can have ambiguous application in the world of public policy. The real story of religion and American economic policy in the years to come will be told by the actions of those belonging to America's two largest religious traditions, evangelical Protestantism and Roman Catholicism—which are both beset by conflict and ambivalence over these issues.

For evangelical Protestants, there is a real strain between their genuine desire to help the poor (Hart 1992) and their theological emphasis on individualism and an ethic of self-reliance. Evangelicals are very generous in their support of private charitable efforts, but they are deeply skeptical of the government programs that constitute the modern welfare state (Wilson 1999). Because of this ambivalence, evangelical political activism has tended to focus on a relatively narrow set of human life, family values, and church-state issues. Though some prominent evangelical voices (most notably Wallis 2005) are beginning to challenge this pattern and emphasize the moral dimensions of economic issues, it remains to be seen how much countervailing influence they will have against theological individualism and twenty-five years of habitual support for the Republican Party and its laissez-faire economic policies.

American Catholics face some of these same challenges to the political articulation of a social justice agenda. Though Catholic leaders have been explicit for some time about the political imperative to aid the poor and to guarantee basic rights such as access to health care and a living wage (U.S. Conference of Catholic Bishops 1986), it is not clear that those pronouncements have significantly affected the voting behavior of Catholics in the electorate. And whereas some scholars have stressed the communitarian dimensions of Catholic theology and asserted the existence of a distinctively Catholic political liberalism (Greeley 1990, 2000), others have argued that this economic liberalism is largely a clerical phenomenon with little political resonance among the lay faithful (Wilson 2004, 2007). Like evangelicals, Catholics in America have channeled the bulk of their faith-based political initiatives into a small—not to say unimportant—set of human life issues.

Evangelicals and Catholics alike confront two main challenges to presenting a politicized, faith-based vision of economic and social welfare policy in America. First, the specific policy implications of Christian teaching on poverty and charity are often ambiguous and open to debate. How does one translate "blessed are the poor" into a concrete position on the top marginal tax rate or the lowest morally permissible minimum wage? The policy positions associated with religious teachings against abortion, gay marriage, and the death penalty are clear: Don't allow those things. On economic policy, however, it is not clear that a sense of solidarity with the poor obligates one to fight to maximize the size and scope of the welfare state. Though the conventionally defined moral issues often concern essentially dichotomous policy choices (Will abortion be permitted or not? Will the government sanction same-sex unions or not?), economic policy differences between the parties in America seem more often to involve small questions of degree or emphasis (Should Medicare spending increase by 5 or 7 percent? Should the estate tax exemption be $3 million or $6 million?). It is much harder to galvanize religious groups over what often seems, rightly or wrongly, to be dickering at the margins than over what seem to be stark conflicts over fundamental social values.

In addition, the current configuration of the American political landscape does not permit many religious voters to cast a ballot fully in accord with their moral values. This dilemma is particularly acute for Catholic voters, whose Church teaches that the proper approach to politics is a "seamless garment" of respect for life, support for traditional marriage and the family, and solidarity with the poor and disadvantaged. These voters must in effect choose between their pro-life convictions and their social justice convictions. Presented with this choice, most religiously committed Catholics and evangelicals prioritize life and family issues and vote Republican, though not always with enthusiasm. As Wallis (2005, 298) argues, "Many moderate and progressive Christians . . . find it painfully difficult or even impossible to vote 'Democrat' given the party's highly ideological and very rigid stance on this critical moral issue [abortion]."

Ambiguous policy implications and an unfavorable partisan alignment certainly mitigate against a strong religious voice in the economic policy sphere, but they do not preclude it. President George W. Bush's "compassionate conservative" agenda, though submerged both financially and rhetorically by the wars in Afghanistan and Iraq, offers one possible way forward. The increased visibility of pro-life Democratic congressional candidates in the 2006 midterm election and the increased openness to pro-life perspectives (at least rhetorically) of several prospective Democratic 2008 presidential contenders also offer some tentative hope that the stark divide between "the human life party" and "the social justice party" may soften. A commitment to the poor and disadvantaged is the one thing that unites all the disparate religious traditions discussed in this volume, from Mormons to Muslims. The devil, as always, is in the details. What is the proper mix of government and private-sector activity in alleviating poverty? What is the right balance between charity and personal responsibility? Do parties and candidates exist that will allow religious people, particularly Catholics and evangelicals, to express a commitment to economic justice without compromising even more fundamental principles? The answers to these questions will be central in shaping the interaction of religion and politics in America in the years and decades to come.

References

Abramowitz, Alan I. 1994. Issue Evolution Reconsidered: Racial Attitudes and Partisanship in the U.S. Electorate. *American Journal of Political Science* 38:1–24.

———. 1995. It's Abortion, Stupid: Policy Voting in the 1992 Presidential Election. *Journal of Politics* 57:176–86.

Abramowitz, Alan I., and Kyle L. Saunders. 1998. Ideological Realignment in the U.S. Electorate. *Journal of Politics* 60:634–52.

Adams, Greg D. 1997. Abortion: Evidence of an Issue Evolution. *American Journal of Political Science* 41:718–37.

Adams, James L. 1970. *The Growing Church Lobby in Washington*. Grand Rapids: William B. Eerdmans.

Adorno, T. W., Else Frankel-Brunswik, Daniel J. Levinson, and R. Nevitt Sanford. 1950. *The Authoritarian Personality*. New York: Harper & Row.

Alinsky, Saul D. 1946. *Reveille for Radicals*. New York: Random House.

Allport, Gordon W. 1954. *The Nature of Prejudice*. Reading, Mass.: Addison-Wesley.

Alpert, Rebecca T., ed. 2000. *Voices of the Religious Left: A Contemporary Sourcebook*. Philadelphia: Temple University Press.

ARIS (American Religious Identification Survey). 2001. *Profile of U.S. Muslim Population*. ARIS Report 2. New York: Graduate School of the City University of New York.

Arrington, Leonard J., and Davis Bitton. 1979. *The Mormon Experience: A History of the Latter-Day Saints*. New York: Alfred A. Knopf.

Arrington, Leonard J., Feramorz Fox, and Dean L. May. 1976. *Building the City of God: Community and Cooperation among the Mormons*. Salt Lake City: Deseret Books.

Axelrod, Robert. 1986. Presidential Election Coalitions in 1984. *American Political Science Review* 80:281–84.

Ba-Yunus, Ilyas, and Kassim Kone. 2004. Muslim Americans: A Demographic Report. In *Muslims' Place in the American Public Square: Hopes, Fears, and Aspirations*, ed. Zahid H. Bukhari, Sulayman S. Nyang, Mumtaz Ahmad, and John L. Esposito. New York: Alta Mira.

287

Bahr, Stephen J. 1992. Social Characteristics. In *Encyclopedia of Mormonism*, ed. V. H. Ludlow. New York: Macmillan.

Barone, Michael. 2001. The 49% Nation. In *The Almanac of American Politics 2002*, ed. Michael Barone and Richard E. Cohen. Washington, D.C.: National Journal Group.

Barrus, Roger M. 1992. Political History. In *Encyclopedia of Mormonism*, ed. V. H. Ludlow. New York: Macmillan.

Barth, Karl. 1960. *Community, State, and Church: Three Essays*. Garden City, N.Y.: Doubleday.

Bayne, Steven. 1999. Jewish Organizational Response to Intermarriage: A Policy Perspective. In *Jews in America: A Contemporary Reader*, ed. Roberta Rosenberg Farber and Chaim I. Waxman. Hanover, N.H.: Brandeis University Press.

Bendyna, Mary E. 2000. The Catholic Ethic in American Politics: Evidence from Survey Research. Ph.D. diss., Georgetown University.

Benson, Ezra Taft. 1980. Fourteen Fundamentals in Following the Prophet. Speech at Brigham Young University in Provo, Utah, February 26.

Benson, Josh. 2005. Belatedly, Whitman Comes Out Swinging. *New York Times*, January 9.

Berelson, Bernard, Paul Lazarsfeld, and William McPhee. 1954. *Voting*. Chicago: University of Chicago Press.

Berman, Paul, ed. 1994. *Blacks and Jews: Alliances and Arguments*. New York: Delacorte Press.

Blumenthal, Sidney. 2004. The Lowest Ignorance Takes Charge. *The Guardian*, November 11. www.guardian.co.uk/usa/story/0,12271,1348261,00.html.

Bolce, Louis, and Gerald De Maio. 1999a. The Anti-Christian Fundamentalist Factor in Contemporary Politics. *Public Opinion Quarterly* 63:508–42.

———. 1999b. Religious Outlook, Culture War Politics, and Antipathy toward Christian Fundamentalists. *Public Opinion Quarterly* 63:29–61.

Brewer, Mark D., and Jeffrey M. Stonecash. 2006. *Split: Class and Cultural Divides in American Politics*. Washington, D.C.: CQ Press.

Brown, Clifford, Jr., Lynda S. Powell, and Clyde Wilcox. 1995. *Serious Money: Fundraising and Contributing in Presidential Nomination Campaigns*. Cambridge: Cambridge University Press.

Brown, Roger. 1965. *Social Psychology*. New York: Free Press.

Bummiller, Elisabeth. 2003. Evangelicals Sway White House on Human Rights Issues Abroad. *New York Times*, October 25.

Burke, John Francis. 2002. *Mestizo Democracy: The Politics of Crossing Borders*. College Station: Texas A&M University Press.

Busch, Beverly G. 1998. Faith, Truth, and Tolerance: Religion and Political Tolerance in the United States. Ph.D. diss., University of Nebraska.

Byrd, Joann. 1993. Coverage of Christians. *Washington Post*, November 14.

Byrnes, Timothy A. 1991. *Catholic Bishops in American Politics*. Princeton, N.J.: Princeton University Press.

Calhoun-Brown, Allison. 1996. African American Churches and Political Mobilization: The Psychological Impact of Organizational Resources. *Journal of Politics* 58:935–53.

———. 1997. Still Seeing in Black and White: Racial Challenges for the Christian Right. In *Sojourners in the Wilderness: The Christian Right in Comparative Perspective*, ed. Corwin E. Smidt and James M. Penning. Lanham, Md.: Rowman & Littlefield.

Campbell, David E. 2004. Acts of Faith: Churches and Political Engagement. *Political Behavior* 26:155–80.

Campbell, David E., and J. Quin Monson. 2003. Following the Leader? Mormon Voting on Ballot Propositions. *Journal for the Scientific Study of Religion* 42:605–19.

Campbell, David E., and Carin Robinson. 2007. Religious Coalitions For and Against Gay Marriage: The Culture War Rages On. In *The Politics of Same-Sex Marriage*, ed. Craig Rimmerman and Clyde Wilcox. Chicago: University of Chicago Press.

Campbell, Ernest Q., and Thomas F. Pettigrew. 1959. *Christians in Racial Crisis*. Washington, DC: Public Affairs Press.

Cannon, Katie. 1995. *Katie's Cannon: Womanism and the Soul of the Black Community*. New York: Continuum.

Carmines, Edward G., and Harold W. Stanley. 1992. The Transformation of the New Deal Party System: Social Groups, Political Ideology, and Changing Partisanship among Northern Whites, 1972–1988. *Political Behavior* 14:213–37.

Carmines, Edward G., and James A. Stimson. 1989. *Issue Evolution: Race and the Transformation of American Politics*. Princeton, N.J.: Princeton University Press.

Chanes, Jerome A. 2001. Who Does What? Jewish Advocacy and the Jewish Interest. In *Jews in American Politics*, ed. L. Sandy Maisel, Ira N. Forman, Donald Altschiller, and Charles W. Bassett. Lanham, Md.: Rowman & Littlefield.

Chappell, David L. 2004. *A Stone of Hope: Prophetic Religion and the Death of Jim Crow*. Chapel Hill: University of North Carolina Press.

Chávez, Ernesto. 2002. *"Mi Raza Primero": Nationalism, Identity, and Insurgency in the Chicano Movement in Los Angeles, 1966–1978*. Berkeley: University of California Press.

Christie, Richard, and Marie Jahoda, eds. 1954. *Studies in the Scope and Method of the Authoritarian Personality*. Glencoe, Ill.: Free Press.

Clabaugh, Gary K. 1974. *Thunder on the Right: The Protestant Fundamentalists*. Chicago: Nelson-Hall.

Cleage, Albert B., Jr. 1968. *The Black Messiah: The Religious Roots of Black Power*. New York: Sheed & Ward.

Cohen, Steven M. 1989. *The Dimensions of American Jewish Liberalism*. New York: American Jewish Committee.

Cohen, Steven M., and Charles S. Liebman. 1997. American Jewish Liberalism: Unraveling the Strands. *Public Opinion Quarterly* 61:405–30.

Coile, Zachary. 1999. Mormons Raise Funds to Stop Gay Marriage. *San Francisco Examiner*, August 8.

Coleman, Richard. 1980. *Issues of Theological Conflict*. Grand Rapids: Willam B. Eerdmans.

Cone, James H. 1969. *Black Theology and Black Power*. New York: Seabury.

Cone, James H., and Gayraud S. Wilmore, eds. 1993. *Black Theology: A Documentary History*. Maryknoll, N.Y.: Orbis.

Conover, Pamela Johnston. 1988. The Role of Social Groups in Political Thinking. *British Journal of Political Science* 18:51–76.

Converse, Philip E. 1964. The Nature of Belief Systems in Mass Publics. In *Ideology and Discontent*, ed. David Apter. New York: Free Press.

Conway, M. Margaret. 1991. *Political Participation in the United States*, 2nd ed. Washington, D.C.: CQ Press.

Cooperman, Alan. 2003. Bush's Comments Agitate Evangelicals. *Seattle Times*, November 22.

Corbett, Michael, and Julia Mitchell Corbett. 1999. *Politics and Religion in the United States*. New York: Garland.

Crawford, Sue E. S. 1995. Clergy at Work in the Secular City. Ph.D. diss., Indiana University.

Crawford, Sue E. S., Laura R. Olson, and Melissa M. Deckman. 2001. Understanding the Mobilization of Professionals. *Nonprofit and Voluntary Sector Quarterly* 30:321–50.

Cromartie, Michael. 1994. *Disciples & Democracy: Religious Conservatives and the Future of American Politics*. Grand Rapids: Willam B. Eerdmans.

D'Antonio, William V., James D. Davidson, Dean R. Hoge, and Katherine Meyer. 2001. *American Catholics: Gender, Generation, and Commitment*. Walnut Creek, Calif.: AltaMira Press.

Damore, David F., Ted G. Jelen, and Michael W. Bowers. 2005. "Sweet Land of Liberty": The Gay Marriage Amendment in Nevada. Working paper, Department of Political Science, University of Nevada at Las Vegas.

Danforth, John C. 2005. Onward, Moderate Christian Soldiers. *New York Times*, June 17.

Davidson, James D., Andrea S. Williams, Richard A. Lamanna, Jan Stenftenagel, Kathleen Weigert, William Whalen, and Patricia Wittberg. 1997. *The Search for Common Ground: What Unites and Divides Catholic Americans*. Huntington, Ind.: Our Sunday Visitor.

Dawson, Michael. 1994. *Behind the Mule: Race and Class in African-American Politics*. Princeton, N.J.: Princeton University Press.

Daynes, Byron W., and Raymond Tatalovich. 1986. Mormons and Abortion Politics in the United States. *International Review of History and Political Science* 23:1–13.

de la Garza, Rodolfo O., Martha Menchaca, and Louis DeSipio, eds. 1994. *Barrio Ballots: Latino Politics in the 1990 Elections*. Boulder, Colo.: Westview Press.

de la Garza, Rodolfo O., and Louis DeSipio. 1993. Save the Baby, Change the Bathwater, and Scrub the Tub: Latino Electoral Participation after Seventeen Years of Voting Rights Act Coverage. *Texas Law Review* 71:1479–1539.

DeSipio, Louis. 1996a. *Counting on the Latino Vote: Latinos as a New Electorate*. Charlottesville: University of Virginia Press.

———. 1996b. Making Citizens or Good Citizens? Naturalization as a Predictor of Organizational and Electoral Behavior among Latino Immigrants. *Hispanic Journal of Behavioral Sciences* 18:194–213.

———. 2006. Latino Civic and Political Participation. In *Hispanics and the Future of America*, ed. Marta Tienda and Faith Mitchell. Washington, D.C.: National Academies Press.

DeSipio, Louis, and Rodolfo O. de la Garza. 2002. Forever Seen as New: Latino Participation in American Elections. In *Latinos: Remaking America*, ed. Marcelo Suárez-Orozco and Mariela M. Páez. Berkeley: University of California Press.

Dionne, E. J. 2000. There Is No "Catholic Vote," and Yet It Matters. *Washington Post*, June 18. www.brook.edu/views/op-ed/dionne/20000618.htm.

———. 2003. When Presidents Talk of God. *Washington Post*, February 14.

———. 2006. A Shift among Evangelicals. *Washington Post*, June 16.

Diouf, Sylviane Anna. 2004. African Muslims in Bondage: Realities, Memories, and Legacies. In *Monuments of the Black Atlantic: Slavery and Memory*, ed. Joanne M. Braxton and Maria I. Diedrich. Munster, Germany: Lit Verlag.

Djupe, Paul A., and Christopher P. Gilbert. 2003. *The Prophetic Pulpit: Clergy, Churches, and Communities in American Politics*. Lanham, Md.: Rowman & Littlefield.

Djupe, Paul A., and J. Tobin Grant. 2001. Religious Institutions and Political Participation in America. *Journal for the Scientific Study of Religion* 40:303–14.

Djupe, Paul A., and Anand E. Sokhey. 2003. American Rabbis in the 2000 Elections. *Journal for the Scientific Study of Religion* 42:563–76.

Dolan, Jay P. 1992. *The American Catholic Experience: A History from Colonial Times to the Present*. Notre Dame, Ind.: University of Notre Dame Press.

Douglas, Kelly Brown. 2001. *The Black Christ*. Maryknoll, N.Y.: Orbis.

Dowd, Maureen. 2004. The Red Zone. *New York Times*, November 4.

Drake, St. Clair, and Horace R. Clayton. 1962. *Black Metropolis: A Study of Negro Life in a Northern City*. New York: Harper & Row.

Ebaugh, Helen Rose. 1991. *Vatican II and U.S. Catholicism*. Greenwich, Conn.: JAI Press.

Ebersole, Luke Eugene. 1951. *Church Lobbying in the Nation's Capitol*. New York: Macmillan.

Ellison, Christopher G. 1993. Religious Involvement and Self-Perception among Black Americans. *Social Forces* 71:1027–55.

Emerson, Michael O., and Christian Smith. 2000. *Divided by Faith: Evangelical Religion and the Problem of Race in America*. Oxford: Oxford University Press.

Espinosa, Gastón, Virgilio Elizondo, and Jesse Miranda. 2003. *Hispanic Churches in American Public Life: Summary of Findings*. Notre Dame, Ind.: Institute of Latino Studies.

Evans, James H. 1992. *We Have Been Believers: An African-American Systematic Theology*. Minneapolis: Fortress Press.

Felder, Cain Hope. 1989. *Troubling Biblical Waters: Race, Class and Family*. Maryknoll, N.Y.: Orbis.

Findlay, James F. 1993. *Church People in the Struggle: The National Council of Churches and the Black Freedom Movement, 1950–1970*. Oxford: Oxford University Press.

Finke, Roger, and Rodney Stark. 1992. *The Churching of America, 1776–1990: Winners and Losers in Our Religious Economy*. New Brunswick, N.J.: Rutgers University Press.

Fiorina, Morris P. 1981. *Retrospective Voting in American National Elections*. New Haven, Conn.: Yale University Press.

———. 2005. *Culture War? The Myth of a Polarized America*. New York: Pearson Longman.

Fishman, Sylvia Barack. 1999. The Changing American Jewish Family Faces the 1990s. In *Jews in America: A Contemporary Reader*, ed. Roberta Rosenberg Farber and Chaim I. Waxman. Hanover, N.H.: Brandeis University Press.

———. 2000. *Jewish Life and American Culture*. Albany: State University of New York Press.

Flanigan, William H., and Nancy H. Zingale. 2002. *Political Behavior of the American Electorate*, 10th ed. Washington, D.C.: CQ Press.

Foer, Franklin. 2003. Howard Dean's Religion Problem. *New Republic*, December 29. www.tnr.com/doc.mhtml?pt=u4BDXy1QP9wDtyBarRd Mvg==.

Fowler, Robert Booth. 1995. *The Greening of Protestant Thought*. Chapel Hill: University of North Carolina Press.

Fowler, Robert Booth, and Allen Hertzke. 1995. *Religion and Politics in America: Faith, Culture, and Strategic Choices.* Boulder, Colo.: Westview Press.

Frazier, E. Franklin. 1963. *The Negro Church in America.* New York: Schocken.

Freedman, Samuel G. 2000. *Jew v. Jew: The Struggle for the Soul of American Jewry.* New York: Touchstone.

Friedland, Michael B. 1998. *Lift Up Your Voice Like a Trumpet: White Clergy and the Civil Rights and Antiwar Movements, 1954–1973.* Chapel Hill: University of North Carolina Press.

Friedman, Thomas L. 2004. Two Nations under God. *New York Times,* November 4.

Fuchs, Lawrence. 1956a. American Jews and the Presidential Vote. *American Political Science Review* 49:385–401.

———. 1956b. *The Political Behavior of American Jews.* Glencoe, Ill.: Free Press.

Gaines, Kevin K. 1996. *Uplifting the Race: Black Leadership, Politics, and Culture in the Twentieth Century.* Chapel Hill: University of North Carolina Press.

Gilbert, Christopher P. 1993. *The Impact of Churches on Political Behavior: An Empirical Study.* Westport, Conn.: Greenwood.

Glock, Charles Y., and Rodney Stark. 1966. *Christian Beliefs and Anti-Semitism.* New York: Harper & Row.

Goldstein, Sidney. 1993. *Profile of American Jewry: Insights from the 1990 Jewish Population Study.* New York: Council of Jewish Federations.

Gómez-Quiñones, Juan. 1994. *Roots of Chicano Politics, 1600–1940.* Albuquerque: University of New Mexico Press.

Goodman, Walter. 1999. Survival of the Fittest, in Hollywood and the Heartland. *New York Times,* August 25.

Gordon, Linda. 1999. *The Great Arizona Orphan Abduction.* Cambridge, Mass.: Harvard University Press.

Graham, Nick. 2005. Telephone interview with Quin Monson, July 11.

Grant, Jacquelyn. 1979. Black Theology and Black Women. In *Black Theology: A Documentary History 1966–1979,* ed. Gayraud Wilmore and James Cone. Maryknoll, N.Y.: Orbis.

———. 1989. *White Women's Christ and Black Women's Jesus: Feminist Christology and Womanist Response.* Atlanta: Scholars Press.

Graves, Bill. 2004. Oregon Catholic Board Lends Support to Measure 36; Mormons Issue a Statement Endorsing the Proposal to Amend the State Constitution to Ban Same-Sex Marriage. *Portland Oregonian,* September 9. www.oregonlive.com/special/oregonian/gaymarriage/040909.html.

Grebler, Leo, Joan Moore, and Ralph Guzman. 1970. *The Mexican American People: The Nation's Second Largest Minority.* New York: Free Press.

Greeley, Andrew M. 1990. *The Catholic Myth: The Behavior and Beliefs of American Catholics.* New York: Scribner.

———. 2000. *The Catholic Imagination*. Berkeley: University of California Press.

Green, John C., James L. Guth, Lyman A. Kellstedt, and Corwin E. Smidt. 2001. How the Faithful Voted: Religion and the 2000 Presidential Election. *Center Conversations* 10:11–12.

Green, John C., James L. Guth, Corwin E. Smidt, and Lyman A. Kellstedt. 1996. *Religion and the Culture Wars: Dispatches from the Front*. Lanham, Md.: Rowman & Littlefield.

Greenberg, Anna, and Kenneth D. Wald. 2001. Still Liberal after All These Years? The Contemporary Political Behavior of American Jews. In *Jews in American Politics*, ed. L. Sandy Maisel and Ira Forman. Lanham, Md.: Rowman & Littlefield.

Guth, James L. 1996. The Bully Pulpit: Southern Baptist Clergy and Political Activism 1980–92. In *Religion and the Culture Wars: Dispatches from the Front*, ed. John C. Green, James L. Guth, Corwin E. Smidt, and Lyman A. Kellstedt. Lanham, Md.: Rowman & Littlefield.

Guth, James L., and John C. Green. 1993. Salience: The Core Concept? In *Rediscovering the Religious Factor in American Politics*, ed. David C. Leege and Lyman A. Kellstedt. Armonk, N.Y.: M. E. Sharpe.

Guth, James L., John C. Green, Corwin E. Smidt, and Lyman A. Kellstedt. 1995. Faith and the Environment: Religious Beliefs and Attitudes on Environmental Policy. *American Journal of Political Science* 39:364–82.

Guth, James L., John C. Green, Corwin E. Smidt, Lyman A. Kellstedt, and Margaret Poloma. 1997. *The Bully Pulpit: The Politics of Protestant Clergy*. Lawrence: University Press of Kansas.

Guth, James, Lyman A. Kellstedt, John C. Green, and Corwin E. Smidt. 2001. America Fifty/Fifty. *First Things* 116:19–26.

Guth, James L., Lyman A. Kellstedt, Corwin E. Smidt, and John C. Green. 1998. Thunder on the Right? Religious Interest Group Mobilization in the 1996 Election. In *Interest Group Politics*, 5th edition, ed. Alan Cigler and Burdett Loomis. Washington, D.C.: CQ Press.

Haddad, Yvonne Yazbeck, and Adair T. Lummis. 1987. *Islamic Values in the United States: A Comparative Study*. Oxford: Oxford University Press.

Hadden, Jeffrey K. 1969. *The Gathering Storm in the Churches*. Garden City, N.Y.: Doubleday.

Hajnal, Zoltan, and Taeku Lee. 2006. Out of Line: Immigration and Party Identification among Latinos and Asian Americans. In *Transforming Politics, Transforming America: The Political Incorporation of Immigrants in the United States*, ed. Taeku Lee, S. Karthick Ramakrishnan, and Ricardo Ramírez. Charlottesville: University of Virginia Press.

Hall, Mitchell K. 1990. *Because of Their Faith: CALCAV and Religious Opposition to the Vietnam War*. New York: Columbia University Press.

Hallow, Ralph Z. 2003a. Arnold, Davis Collect Endorsements. *Washington Times*, September 15. www.washtimes.com/national/20030914–115026-7572r.htm.

———. 2003b. Lieberman a Tough Sell among Jewish Donors. *Washington Times*, July 8. www.washtimes.com/national/20030708–121753-8252r htm.

Hamburger, Philip. 2002. *Separation of Church and State*. Cambridge, Mass.: Harvard University Press.

Hanna, Mary T. 1979. *Catholics and American Politics*. Cambridge, Mass.: Harvard University Press.

Harris, Fredrick C. 1999. *Something Within: Religion in African-American Political Activism*. Oxford: Oxford University Press.

Harris, John F. 2001. God Gave U.S. "What We Deserve." *Washington Post*, September 14.

Hart, Stephen. 1992. *What Does the Lord Require? How American Christians Think about Economic Justice*. Oxford: Oxford University Press.

———. 2001. *Cultural Dilemmas of Progressive Politics: Styles of Engagement among Grassroots Activists*. Chicago: University of Chicago Press.

Hertzke, Allen. 1988. *Representing God in Washington: The Role of Religious Lobbies in the American Polity*. Knoxville: University of Tennessee Press.

———. 1993. *Echoes of Discontent: Jesse Jackson, Pat Robertson, and the Resurgence of Populism*. Washington, D.C.: CQ Press.

Hetherington, Marc J. 2001. Resurgent Mass Partisanship: The Role of Elite Polarization. *American Political Science Review* 95:619–31.

Himmelfarb, Milton. 1968. Is American Jewry in Crisis? *Commentary*, March, 39–44.

———. 1985. Another Look at the Jewish Vote. *Commentary*, December, 39–44.

Hinckley, Gordon B. 1999. Why We Do Some of the Things We Do. *Ensign*, November, 52.

Hofrenning, Daniel J. B. 1995. *In Washington but Not of It*. Philadelphia: Temple University Press.

Hofstadter, Richard. 1955. *The Age of Reform*. New York: Alfred A. Knopf.

Hoge, Dean R., Benton Johnson, and Donal A. Luidens. 1994. *Vanishing Boundaries: The Religion of Mainline Protestant Baby Boomers*. Louisville: John Knox Press.

Hopkins, Dwight N. 1993. *Shoes That Fit Our Feet: Sources for a Constructive Black Theology*. Maryknoll, N.Y.: Orbis.

———. 1999. *Introducing Black Theology of Liberation*. Maryknoll, N.Y.: Orbis.

Huckfeldt, Robert, and John Sprague. 1995. *Citizens, Politics, and Social Communications*. Cambridge: Cambridge University Press.

Hunt, Larry L. 2000. Religion and Secular Status among Hispanics in the United States: Catholicism and the Varieties of Hispanic Protestantism. *Social Science Quarterly* 81:344–62.

Hunter, James Davison. 1991. *Culture Wars: The Struggle to Define America.* New York: Basic Books.

Hutchinson, Earl Ofari. 2001. New Worries about Mega-Black Churches. *Black World Today*, February 2, 1–5.

Iannaccone, Laurence R. 1994. Why Strict Churches Are Strong. *American Journal of Sociology* 99:1180–1211.

Iannaccone, Laurence R., and Carrie A. Miles. 1990. Dealing with Social Change: The Mormon Church's Response to Changes in Women's Roles. *Social Forces* 68:1231–50.

Jakes, T. D. 2000. *The Great Investment: Faith, Family and Finance to Build a Rich Spiritual Life.* New York: Berkeley.

———. 2002. *God's Leading Lady: Out of the Shadows and into the Light.* New York: G. P. Putnam's Sons.

Jelen, Ted G. 1991. *The Political Mobilization of Religious Beliefs.* New York: Praeger.

———. 1993. *The Political World of the Clergy.* Westport, Conn.: Praeger.

———. 1998. Research in Religion and Mass Political Behavior in the United States: Looking Both Ways after Two Decades of Scholarship. *American Politics Quarterly* 26:110–34.

Jelen, Ted G., and Clyde Wilcox, eds. 2002. *Religion and Politics in Comparative Perspective: The One, the Few, and the Many.* Cambridge: Cambridge University Press.

Johnson, Joseph A. 1993. Jesus, the Liberator. In *Black Theology: A Documentary History*, ed. James H. Cone and Gayraud S. Wilmore. Maryknoll, N.Y.: Orbis.

Jones, Dale E., Sherri Doty, Clifford Grammica, James E. Horsch, Richard Houseal, Mac Lynn, John P. Marcum, Kenneth M. Sanchagrin, and Richard H. Taylor. 2002. *Religious Congregations and Membership in the United States, 2000.* Nashville: Glenmary Research Center.

Jones-Correa, Michael, and David Leal. 2001. Political Participation: Does Religion Matter? *Political Research Quarterly* 54:751–70.

Kelley, Dean. 1972. *Why Conservative Churches Are Growing.* San Francisco: Harper & Row.

Kellstedt, Lyman A. 1989. Evangelicals and Political Realignment. In *Contemporary Evangelical Political Involvement: An Analysis and Assessment*, ed. Corwin Smidt. Lanham, Md.: University Press of America.

Kellstedt, Lyman A., John C. Green, James L. Guth, and Corwin E. Smidt. 1994. Religious Voting Blocs in the 1992 Election: The Year of the Evangelical?" *Sociology of Religion* 55:307–25.

———. 1996. Grasping the Essentials: The Social Embodiment of Religion and Political Behavior. In *Religion and the Culture Wars*: *Dispatches from the Front*, ed. John C. Green, James L. Guth, Corwin E. Smidt, and Lyman A. Kellstedt. Lanham, Md.: Rowman & Littlefield.

Kellstedt, Lyman A., John C. Green, Corwin E. Smidt, and James L. Guth. 1999. Faith and the Vote: The Role of Religion in Political Alignments. Paper presented at meeting of the American Political Science Association, Atlanta.

Kellstedt, Lyman A., and Mark Noll. 1990. Religion, Voting for President, and Party Identification, 1948–1984. In *Religion & American Politics*: *From the Colonial Period to the 1980s*, ed. Mark Noll. Oxford: Oxford University Press.

Kellstedt, Lyman A., Corwin E. Smidt, and Paul Kellstedt. 1991. Religious Tradition, Denomination, and Commitment: White Protestants and the 1988 Election. In *The Bible and the Ballot Box*: *Religion and Politics in the 1988 Election*, ed. James L. Guth and John C. Green. Boulder, Colo.: Westview Press.

Kenski, Henry C., and William Lockwood. 1991. Catholic Voting Behavior in 1988: A Critical Swing Vote. In *The Bible and the Ballot Box: Religion and Politics in the 1988 Election*, ed. James L. Guth and John C. Green. Boulder, Colo.: Westview Press.

Kinder, Donald R., and D. Roderick Kiewiet. 1981. Sociotropic Politics. *British Journal of Political Science* 11:129–61.

Kirkpatrick, Jeane. 1976. *The New Presidential Elite: Men and Women in National Politics*. New York: Russell Sage.

Knight, Kathleen, and Robert S. Erikson. 1997. Ideology in the 1990s. In *Understanding Public Opinion*, ed. Barbara Norrander and Clyde Wilcox. Washington, D.C.: CQ Press.

Kohut, Andrew, John C. Green, Scott Keeter, and Robert C. Toth. 2000. *The Diminishing Divide: Religion's Changing Role in American Politics*. Washington, D.C.: Brookings Institution Press.

Larson, Edward J. 1997. *Summer for the Gods: The Scopes Trial and America's Continuing Debate over Science and Religion*. New York: Basic Books.

Layman, Geoffrey. 2001. *The Great Divide: Religious and Cultural Conflict in American Party Politics*. New York: Columbia University Press.

Layman, Geoffrey, and Thomas M. Carsey. 2002. Party Polarization and "Conflict Extension" in the American Electorate. *American Journal of Political Science* 46:786–802.

Leal, David, Matt Baretto, Jongho Lee, and Rodolfo O. de la Garza. 2005. The Latino Vote in the 2004 Election. *PS: Political Science and Politics* 38:41–49.

Lee, Harold B., N. Eldon Tanner, and Marion G. Romney. 1973. Policies and Procedures: Statement on Abortion. *New Era*, April, 29.

Lee, Jongho, Harry P. Pachon, and Matt Barreto. 2002. Guiding the Flock: Church as a Vehicle of Latino Participation. Paper presented at meeting of American Political Science Association, Boston.

Leege, David C. 1996a. The Catholic Vote in '96: Can It Be Found in Church? *Commonweal* 123:11–18.

———. 1996b. Religiosity Measures in the National Election Studies: A Guide to Their Use, Part 2. *Votes and Opinions* 2: 6–9, 33–36.

———. 2000. Divining the Electorate: Is There a Religious Vote? *Commonweal* 127:16–19.

Leege, David C., and Lyman A. Kellstedt. 1993. *Rediscovering the Religious Factor in American Politics*. Armonk, N.Y.: M. E. Sharpe.

Leege, David C., and Paul D. Mueller. 2000. American Catholics at the Catholic Moment: An Analysis of Catholic Political Patterns, 1952–1996. Paper presented at meeting of American Political Science Association, Washington.

Leege, David C., Kenneth D. Wald, Brian S. Krueger, and Paul D. Mueller. 2002. *The Politics of Cultural Differences: Social Change and Voter Mobilization Strategies in the Post New Deal Period*. Princeton, N.J.: Princeton University Press.

Leege, David C., and Michael R. Welch. 1989. Religious Roots of Political Orientations: Variations among American Catholic Parishioners. *Journal of Politics* 51:137–62.

Leonard, Karen Isaksen. 2003. *Muslims in the United States: The State of Research*. New York: Russell Sage Foundation.

Levey, Geoffrey Brahm. 1996. The Liberalism of American Jews: Has It Been Explained? *British Journal of Political Science* 26:369–401.

Levine, Jeffery, Edward G. Carmines, and Robert Huckfeldt. 1997. The Rise of Ideology in the Post-New Deal Party System, 1972–1992. *American Politics Quarterly* 25:19–34.

Levine, Susan. 1997. A Place for Those Who Pray: Along Montgomery's "Highway to Heaven," Diverse Acts of Faith. *Washington* Post, August 3.

Levitt, Peggy. 2001. *The Transnational Villagers*. Berkeley: University of California Press.

Lewis, Anthony. 1994. Merchants of Hate. *New York Times*, July 15.

Libit, Howard. 2002. Black Church Group Starts Ad Campaign Attacking Ehrlich. *Baltimore Sun*, September 12. www.baltimoresun.com/news/elections/bal-md.ad12sep12,0,4733553.story.

Liebman, Robert C., and Robert Wuthnow, eds. 1983. *The New Christian Right: Mobilization and Legitimation*. Hawthorne, N.Y.: Aldine.

Lincoln, C. Eric. 1997. The American Muslim Mission in the Context of American Social History. In *African-American Religion: Interpretive*

Essays in History and Culture, ed. Timothy E. Fulop and Albert J. Raboteau. New York: Routledge.

Lincoln, C. Eric, and Lawrence H. Mamiya. 1990. *The Black Church in the African American Experience*. Durham, N.C.: Duke University Press.

Lipset, Seymour Martin, and Earl Raab. 1970. *The Politics of Unreason: Right-Wing Extremism in America, 1790–1970*. New York: Harper & Row.

———. 1995. *Jews and the New American Scene*. Cambridge, Mass.: Harvard University Press.

López Tijerina, Reies. 2000. *They Called Me "King Tiger": My Struggle for the Land and Our Rights*. Houston: Arte Público Press.

Lyman, Edward O. 1986. *Political Deliverance: The Mormon Quest for Utah Statehood*. Urbana: University of Illinois Press.

Magleby, David B. 1992. Contemporary American Politics. In *Encyclopedia of Mormonism*, ed. V. H. Ludlow. New York: Macmillan.

Mansbridge, Jane. 1986. *Why We Lost the ERA*. Chicago: University of Chicago Press.

Manza, Jeff, and Clem Brooks. 1999. *Social Cleavages and Political Change: Voter Alignments and U.S. Party Coalitions*. Oxford: Oxford University Press.

Marsden, George M. 1980. *Fundamentalism and American Culture: The Shaping of Twentieth-Century Evangelicalism 1870–1925*. Oxford: Oxford University Press.

Martin, William. 1996. *With God on Our Side: The Rise of the Religious Right in America*. New York: Broadway Books.

Marty, Martin E. 1970. *Righteous Empire*: *The Protestant Experience in America*. New York: Dial Press.

———. 1999. Who Is the Religious Left? *Sightings*, April 30. http://marty center.uchicago.edu/sightings/archive_1999/sightings-043099. shtml.

Marx, Gary T., and Douglas McAdam. 1994. *Collective Behavior and Social Movements: Process and Structure*. Upper Saddle River, N.J.: Prentice Hall.

McCormick, Richard L. 1974. Ethno-Cultural Interpretations of Nineteenth-Century American Voting Behavior. *Political Science Quarterly* 89: 351–77.

McLoughlin, William. 1968. The American Evangelicals: 1800–1900. In *The American Evangelicals, 1800–1900*, ed. William McLoughlin. New York: Harper & Row.

Mencken, H. L. 1926. *Prejudices: Fifth Series*. New York: Alfred A. Knopf.

Merton, Robert K. 1968. *Social Theory and Social Structure*. New York: Free Press.

Meserve, Jeanne. 2000. Bush Courts Catholic Vote, Gore Spends Day at School. CNN.com, May 26. www.cnn.com/2000/ALLPOLITICS/stories/05/26/campaign.wrap/.

Mian, Waffiyah. 2006. The American Crescent: Muslim American Party Identity Post 9/11. Senior thesis, Georgetown University.

Mikkelsen, Randall. 2000. Black Church Group Hails Clinton as One of Its Own. CNN.com, September 20. http://www.cnn.com/2000/ALLPOLITICS/stories/09/20/clinton.bishops.reut/index.html.

Miller, Arthur H., Patricia Gurin, Gerald Gurin, and Oksana Malanchuk. 1981. Group Consciousness and Political Participation. *American Journal of Political Science* 25:494–511.

Miller, Warren E., and J. Merrill Shanks. 1996. *The New American Voter*. Cambridge, Mass.: Harvard University Press.

Mitchell, Allison. 2000. One Party Quite Divisible: McCain's Attack on Robertson and Falwell Underscores Striking Split within GOP. *New York Times*, February 29.

Mockabee, Stephen T. 2001. Party Polarization in American Politics. Ph.D. diss., Ohio State University.

Mockabee, Stephen T., Joseph Quin Monson, and J. Tobin Grant. 2001. Measuring Religious Commitment among Catholics and Protestants: A New Approach. *Journal for the Scientific Study of Religion* 40:675–90.

Moen, Matthew C. 1992. *The Transformation of the Christian Right*. Tuscaloosa, Ala.: University of Alabama Press.

Monson, J. Quin, Leah A. Murray, Kelly D. Patterson, and Sven E. Wilson. 2006. Dominant Cue Givers and Voting on Ballot Propositions. Working paper, Department of Political Science, Brigham Young University.

Montejano, David. 1987. *Anglos and Mexicans in the Making of Texas, 1836–1986*. Austin: University of Texas Press.

Moore, R. Laurence. 1986. *Religious Outsiders and the Making of Americans*. Oxford: Oxford University Press.

Morris, Aldon D. 1984. *The Origins of the Civil Rights Movement: Black Communities Organizing for Change*. New York: Free Press.

Nagourney, Adam. 2005. GOP Right Is Splintered on Schiavo Intervention. *New York Times*, March 23. www.nytimes.com/2005/03/23/politics/23repubs.html.

NCBC (National Committee of Black Churchmen). 1969. *Black Theology*. Monograph.

NCNC (National Committee of Negro Churchmen). 1968. Statement by the National Committee of Negro Churchmen, July 31, 1966. In *The Black Power Revolt: A Collection of Essays*, ed. Floyd B. Barbour. Boston: Porter Sargent.

Neff, Lisa. 2005. Mormons on a Mission. *The Advocate*, April 12. www
.advocate.com/toc_w.asp?id=936.

Nelson, Russell M. 1985. Reverence for Life. *Ensign*, May, 11.

Niebuhr, H. Richard. 1951. *Christ and Culture*. New York: Harper & Row.

Noll, Mark A. 2001. *American Evangelical Christianity: An Introduction*.
Oxford: Blackwell.

Norris, Pippa, and Ronald Inglehart. 2004. *Sacred and Secular*. Cambridge:
Cambridge University Press.

Oaks, Dallin H. 2001. Weightier Matters. *Ensign*, January, 13.

Oldfield, Duane M. 1996. *The Right and the Righteous: The Christian Right
Confronts the Republican Party*. Lanham, Md.: Rowman & Littlefield.

Olson, Laura R. 2000. *Filled with Spirit and Power: Protestant Clergy in Politics*. Albany: State University of New York Press.

———. 2002. Mainline Protestant Washington Offices and the Political Lives
of Clergy. In *The Quiet Hand of God: Faith-Based Activism and the Public Role of Mainline Protestantism*, ed. Robert Wuthnow and John H.
Evans. Berkeley: University of California Press.

Orum, Anthony. 1966. A Reappraisal of the Social and Political Participation
of Negroes. *American Journal of Sociology* 72:32–46.

Pardo, Mary. 1998. *Mexican American Women Activists Identity and Resistance in Two Los Angeles Communities*. Philadelphia: Temple University
Press.

Penning, James, and Corwin E. Smidt. 2002. *Evangelicalism: The Next Generation*. Grand Rapids: Baker Books.

Percy, William Alexander. 1941. *Lanterns on the Levee: Recollections of a
Planter's Son*. New York: Alfred A. Knopf.

Petrocik, John R. 1981. *Party Coalitions: Realignment and the Decline of the
New Deal Party System*. Chicago: University of Chicago Press.

Pew Forum. 2005. *Religion and Public Life: A Faith-Based Partisan Divide*.
Washington, D.C.: Pew Forum on Religion and Public Life.

Pew Survey Report. 2003. *Religion and Public Life Survey*. Washington, D.C.:
Pew Research Center for the People and the Press.

———. 2005a. *The Dean Activists: Their Profile and Prospects*. Washington,
D.C.: Pew Research Center for the People and the Press.

———. 2005b. *Religion a Strength and Weakness for Both Parties*. Washington, D.C.: Pew Research Center for the People and the Press.

Pinn, Anthony B. 2002. *The Black Church in the Post–Civil Rights Era*. Maryknoll, N.Y.: Orbis.

Podhoretz, Norman. 2000. The Christian Right and Its Demonizers: A Curious Fear and Loathing. *National Review*, April 3, 30–31.

Poole, Keith T., and Howard Rosenthal. 1997. *Congress: A Political-Economic
History of Roll Call Voting*. Oxford: Oxford University Press.

Popkey, Dan. 1988. Mormons Take Active Role against Lottery. *Idaho States-man*, October 31.

Pratt, Henry J. 1972. *The Liberalization of American Protestantism*. Detroit: Wayne State University Press.

Prendergast, William B. 1999. *The Catholic Voter in American Politics: The Passing of the Democratic Monolith*. Washington, D.C.: Georgetown University Press.

Project MAPS (Project Muslims in the American Public Square). 2001. American Muslim Poll Nov/Dec 2001. www.projectmaps.com/pmreport. pdf.

———. 2004. Muslims in the American Public Square: Shifting Political Winds and Fallout from 9/11, Afghanistan, and Iraq. www.projectmaps .com/AMP2004report.pdf.

Quebedeaux, Richard. 1974. *The Young Evangelicals*. New York: Harper & Row.

Quinley, Harold E. 1974. *The Prophetic Clergy: Social Activism among Protestant Ministers*. New York: Wiley.

Quinn, D. Michael. 1997. *The Mormon Hierarchy: Extensions of Power*. Salt Lake City: Signature Books.

Reich, Robert B. 2005. Deepening the Religious Divide. *American Prospect Online*, May 6. www.prospect.org/web/page.ww?section=root&name= ViewPrint&articleId=9536.

Reichley, A. James. 1985. *Religion in American Public Life*. Washington, D.C.: Brookings Institution Press.

Rich, Frank. 1994. The North Crusade. *New York Times*, June 9.

Roberts, J. Deotis. 1971. *Liberation and Reconciliation: A Black Theology*. Philadelphia: Westminster Press.

———. 1974. *A Black Political Theology*. Louisville: Westminster John Knox Press.

Robinson, Carin, and Clyde Wilcox. 2007. The Faith of George W. Bush: The Personal, Practical, and Political. In *Religion and American Presidents*, ed. Mark J. Rozell and Gleaves Whitney. New York: Palgrave/MacMillan.

Robinson, Lynn D. 2002. Doing Good and Doing Well: Shareholder Activism, Responsible Investment, and Mainline Protestantism. In *The Quiet Hand of God: Faith-based Activism and the Public Role of Mainline Protestantism*, ed. Robert Wuthnow and John H. Evans. Berkeley: University of California Press.

Rogers, Mary Beth. 1990. *Cold Anger: A Story of Faith and Power Politics*. Denton: University of North Texas Press.

Roof, Wade Clark, and William McKinney. 1987. *American Mainline Religion: Its Changing Shape and Future*. New Brunswick, N.J.: Rutgers University Press.

Rooney, Jim. 1995. *Organizing the South Bronx*. Albany: State University of New York Press.

Rosenstone, Steven J., and John Mark Hansen. 1993. *Mobilization, Participation, and Democracy in America*. New York: Macmillan.

Rozell, Mark J. 2002. The Christian Right in the 2000 GOP Presidential Campaign. In *Piety, Politics, and Pluralism: Religion and the Courts in the 2000 Election*, ed. Mary Segers. Lanham, Md.: Rowman & Littlefield.

Rozell, Mark J., and Clyde Wilcox. 1996. *Second Coming: The New Christian Right in Virginia Politics*. Baltimore: Johns Hopkins University Press.

Ruane, Michael. 1999. A Church with Four Faces. *Washington Post*, February 21.

Salladay, Robert. 1999. Mormons Now Target California: After Defeating Gay Marriage in Hawaii, Alaska, Church Asks Members to Back State Ballot Initiative. *San Francisco Examiner*, July 4.

Salt Lake Tribune. 1998. Transcript of Interview Conducted April 23, 1998, with Marlin Jensen of the 1st Quorum of the Seventy of the Church of Jesus Christ of Latter-Day Saints. www.sltrib.com.

Sanchez, George. 1993. *Becoming Mexican American: Ethnicity, Culture and Identity in Chicano Los Angeles, 1900–1945*. Oxford: Oxford University Press.

Segers, Mary C. 2003. Catholics and the 2000 Presidential Election: Bob Jones University and the Catholic Vote. In *Piety, Politics, and Pluralism: Religion, the Courts, and the 2000 Election*, ed. Mary C. Segers. Lanham, Md.: Rowman & Littlefield.

Selznick, Gertrude J., and Stephen Steinberg. 1969. *The Tenacity of Prejudice*. New York: Harper & Row.

Shaw, Daron, Rodolfo O. de la Garza, and Jongho Lee. 2000. Examining Latino Turnout in 1996: A Three-States, Validated-Survey Approach. *American Journal of Political Science* 44:338–46.

Shingles, Richard. 1981. Black Consciousness and Political Participation: The Missing Link. *The American Political Science Review* 75:76–91.

Sigelman, Lee. 1991. If You Prick Us, Do We Not Bleed? If You Tickle Us, Do We Not Laugh? *Journal of Politics* 53:977–92.

Singer, Eleanor. 2000. Comment [On Bolce and De Maio]. *Public Opinion Quarterly* 64:106–7.

Sklare, Marshall. 1964. Intermarriage and the Jewish Future. *Commentary* 37:46–52.

Smidt, Corwin E. 1987. Evangelicals and the 1984 Election: Continuity or Change? *American Politics Quarterly* 15:419–44.

———. 1993. Evangelical Voting Patterns: 1976–1988. In *No Longer Exiles: The Religious New Right in American Politics.*, ed. Michael Cromartie. Washington, D.C.: Ethics and Public Policy Center.

Smidt, Corwin E., Lyman A. Kellstedt, John C. Green, and James L. Guth. 2003. Religion and Politics in the United States. In *The Sacred and the*

Secular: Nation, Religion, and Politics, ed. William Safran. London: Frank Cass.

Smith, Christian. 1996. *Resisting Reagan: The U.S. Central America Peace Movement*. Chicago: University of Chicago Press.

———, ed. 2003. *The Secular Revolution: Power, Interests, and Conflict in the Secularization of American Public Life*. Berkeley: University of California Press.

Smith, Jane L. 1999. *Islam in America*. New York: Columbia University Press.

Smith, R. Drew, and Tamelyn Tucker-Worgs. 2000. Megachurches: African-American Churches in Social and Political Context. In *The State of Black America 2000*, ed. Lee Daniels. New York: National Urban League.

Smith, Tom W. 2001. *Estimating the Muslim Population in the United States*. New York: American Jewish Committee.

Spencer, Jon Michael. 1990. *Protest and Praise: Sacred Music of Black Religion*. Minneapolis: Fortress Press.

Stanley, Harold W., and Richard G. Niemi. 2004. Partisanship, Party Coalitions, and Group Support, 1952–2000. In *Models of Voting in Presidential Elections: The 2000 U.S. Election*, ed. Herbert F. Weisberg and Clyde Wilcox. Stanford, Calif.: Stanford University Press.

Stark, Rodney, Bruce D. Foster, Charles Y. Glock, and Harold E. Quinley. 1971. *Wayward Shepherds: Prejudice and the Protestant Clergy*. New York: Harper & Row.

Steensland, Brian, Jerry Z. Park, Mark D. Regnerus, Lynn D. Robinson, W. Bradford Wilcox, and Robert D. Woodberry. 2000. The Measure of American Religion: Toward Improving the State of the Art. *Social Forces* 79:291–318.

Steinfels, Peter. 2006. Voters' Guides Define Moral Compromises to Take to Polls. *New York Times*, October 14.

Stimson, James A. 1985. Regression in Time and Space: A Statistical Essay. *American Journal of Political Science* 29:914–47.

———. 1991. *Public Opinion in America: Moods, Cycles, Swings*. Boulder, Colo.: Westview Press.

Stouffer, Samuel A. 1955. *Communism, Conformity, and Civil Liberties*. New York: Doubleday.

Suro, Roberto, Richard Fry, and Jeffrey Passel. 2005. *Hispanics and the 2004 Election: Population, Electorate, and Voters*. Washington, D.C.: Pew Hispanic Center.

Svonkin, Stuart. 1997. *Jews against Prejudice: American Jews and the Fight for Civil Liberties*. New York: Columbia University Press.

Sweet, Leonard. 1989. The Modernization of Protestant Religion in America. In *Altered Landscapes: Christianity in America, 1935–1985*, ed. David Lotz. Grand Rapids: William B. Eerdmans.

Tate, Katherine. 1994. *From Protest to Politics: The New Black Voters in American Elections*. New York: Russell Sage Foundation.

Taylor, Andrew J. 1996. The Ideological Development of the Parties in Washington, 1947–1994. *Polity* 29:273–92.

Thomas, Cal, and Ed Dobson. 1999. *Blinded by Might: Can the Religious Right Save America?* Grand Rapids: Zondervan.

Thuesen, Peter. 2002. The Logic of Mainline Churchliness: Historical Background since the Reformation. In *The Quiet Hand of God: Faith-Based Activism and the Public Role of Mainline Protestantism*, ed. Robert Wuthnow and John Evans. Berkeley: University of California Press.

Tomás Rivera Policy Institute. 2000. *Religion in Latino Public Life: Findings from the HCAPL National Survey*. Claremont, Calif.: Tomás Rivera Policy Institute.

Torpy, Bill, and Rhonda Cook. 2002. Primary 2002: The Day After; McKinney in Defeat: "There Is Still Work to Be Done." *Atlanta Journal and Constitution*, August 22.

Torres, Maria de los Angeles. 2003. *The Lost Apple: Operation Pedro Pan, Cuban Children in the U.S., and the Promise of a Better Future*. Boston: Beacon Press.

U.S. Conference of Catholic Bishops. 1986. *Economic Justice for All: Pastoral Letter on Catholic Social Teaching and the U.S. Economy*. Washington, D.C.: United States Catholic Conference.

Verba, Sidney, and Norman H. Nie. 1972. *Participation in America: Political Democracy and Social Equality*. Chicago: University of Chicago Press.

Verba, Sidney, Kay Lehman Schlozman, and Henry E. Brady. 1995. *Voice and Equality: Civic Voluntarism in American Society*. Cambridge, Mass.: Harvard University Press.

Wald, Kenneth D. 2003. *Religion and Politics in the United States*, 4th ed. Lanham, Md.: Rowman & Littlefield.

Wald, Kenneth D., Dennis E. Owen, and Samuel S. Hill Jr. 1988. Churches as Political Communities. *American Political Science Review* 82:531–48.

———. 1990. Political Cohesion in Churches. *Journal of Politics* 52:197–215.

Wald, Kenneth D., and Clyde Wilcox. 2006. Getting Religion: Has Political Science Rediscovered the Faith Factor? Working paper, Department of Political Science, University of Florida and Georgetown University.

Wallis, Jim. 2005. *God's Politics: Why the Right Gets It Wrong and the Left Doesn't Get It*. San Francisco: HarperCollins.

Warren, Mark R. 2001. *Dry Bones Rattling: Community Building to Revitalize American Democracy*. Princeton, N.J.: Princeton University Press.

Washington, Joseph R. 1964. *Black Religion: The Negro and Christianity in the United States*. Boston: Beacon Press.

Waxman, Chaim I. 1999. Center and Periphery: Israel in American Jewish Life. In *Jews in America: A Contemporary Reader*, ed. Roberta Rosenberg Farber and Chaim I. Waxman. Hanover, N.H.: Brandeis University Press.

Weems, Renita. 1988. *Just a Sister Away: A Womanist Vision of Women's Relationships in the Bible*. San Diego: LuraMedia.

Weisberg, Herbert F., and David C. Kimball. 1995. Attitudinal Correlates of the 1992 Presidential Vote: Party Identification and Beyond. In *Democracy's Feast: Elections in America*, ed. Herbert F. Weisberg. Chatham, N.J.: Chatham House.

Weisberg, Herbert F., and Stephen T. Mockabee. 1999. Attitudinal Correlates of the 1996 Presidential Vote: The People Reelect a President. In *Reelection 1996: How Americans Voted*, ed. Herbert F. Weisberg and Janet M. Box-Steffensmeier. New York: Chatham House.

Weisskopf, Michael. 1993. Energized by Pulpit or Passion, the Public Is Calling: "Gospel Grapevine" Displays Strength in Controversy over Military Gay Ban. *Washington Post*, February 1.

West, Cornel. 1979. Black Theology and Marxist Thought. In *Black Theology: A Documentary History 1966–1979*, ed. Gayraud Wilmore and James Cone. Maryknoll, N.Y.: Orbis.

Wilcox, Clyde. 1992. *God's Warriors: The Christian Right in Twentieth-Century America*. Baltimore: Johns Hopkins University Press.

———. 2000. *Onward Christian Soldiers?: The Religious Right in American Politics*, 2nd ed. Boulder, Colo.: Westview Press.

———. 2003. The Christian Right in the GOP: Infiltration, Invasion, or Assimilation? Paper presented at meeting of European Consortium for Political Research, Marburg, Germany.

Wilcox, Clyde, and Sue Thomas. 1992. Religion and Feminist Attitudes among African American Women: A View from the Nation's Capital. *Women & Politics* 12:19–40.

Wilcox, Clyde, Linda Merolla, and David Beer. 2007. The Gay Marriage Issue and Christian Right Mobilization. In *The Values Campaign?: The Christian Right in the 2004 Elections*, ed. John C. Green, Mark J. Rozell, and Clyde Wilcox. Washington, D.C.: Georgetown University Press.

Wilgoren, Jody. 2004. The 2004 Campaign: The Vermont Governor, Dean Narrowing His Separation of Church and Stump. *New York Times*, January 4.

Williams, Delores. 1993. *Sisters in the Wilderness: The Challenge of Womanist God-Talk*. Maryknoll, N.Y.: Orbis.

Wilson, J. Matthew. 1999. Blessed Are the Poor: American Protestantism and Attitudes toward Poverty and Welfare. *Southeastern Political Review* 27:421–37.

————. 2004. American Catholic Attitudes on Poverty and Welfare: Distinctiveness or Convergence?" Paper presented at meeting of Midwest Political Science Association, Chicago.

————. 2007. From JFK to JFK: The Changing Catholic Voter in America. In *A Matter of Faith?: Religion in the 2004 Presidential Election*, ed. David E. Campbell. Washington, D.C.: Brookings Institution Press.

Wolfinger, Raymond E., and Steven J. Rosenstone. 1980. *Who Votes?* New Haven, Conn.: Yale University Press.

Wood, Richard L. 2002. *Faith in Action: Religion, Race, and Democratic Organizing in America*. Chicago: University of Chicago Press.

Wuthnow, Robert. 1988. *The Restructuring of American Religion: Society and Faith since World War II*. Princeton, N.J.: Princeton University Press.

————. 1994. *God and Mammon in America*. New York: Free Press.

————. 1999. Mobilizing Civic Engagement: The Changing Impact of Religious Involvement. In *Civic Engagement in American Democracy*, ed. Theda Skocpol and Morris P. Fiorina. Washington, D.C.: Brookings Institution Press.

————. 2000. The Moral Minority: Liberal Protestant Denominations Are Still a Force for Social Justice. *American Prospect* 11:31–33.

Wuthnow, Robert, and John H. Evans, eds. 2002. *The Quiet Hand of God: Faith-Based Activism and the Public Role of Mainline Protestantism*. Berkeley: University of California Press.

Young, Josiah U. 1986. *Black and African Theologies*. Maryknoll, N.Y.: Orbis.

Contributors

Louis Bolce is associate professor of political science at Baruch College of the City University of New York. He received his Ph.D. from the University of Cincinnati in 1976. His research, dealing primarily with issues of race and politics and religion and politics, has been published in such scholarly journals as *The American Political Science Review*, *Public Opinion Quarterly*, and *Polity*. In addition, his political insights and commentary have appeared in a variety of more popular outlets, including *The Public Interest*, *Policy Review*, *First Things*, and various major newspapers. He is currently, with Gerald De Maio, at work on a book chronicling the rise of secularist influence in the Democratic Party and the growing prominence of Christian fundamentalism as a negative political referent in American politics.

David E. Campbell is associate professor of political science at the University of Notre Dame. He received his Ph.D. from Harvard University in 2002. His interests center chiefly on questions of social capital, education policy, and religion and politics. He is the author of *Why We Vote: How Schools and Communities Shape Our Civic Life* (Princeton University Press, 2006), editor of *A Matter of Faith? Religion and the 2004 Presidential Election* (Brookings Institution Press, 2007), and coauthor of *Democracy at Risk: How Political Choices Have Undermined Citizenship and What We Can Do about It* (Brookings Institution Press, 2005). His work has been published in *The Journal of Politics, Public Opinion Quarterly, Political Behavior*, and a variety of edited books. He is a two-time recipient of the award for the best paper in religion and politics presented at the American Political Science Association's annual meeting.

Gerald De Maio is associate professor of political science at Baruch College of the City University of New York. He received his Ph.D. from New York University in 1976. His research is focused primarily on religion and politics, electoral systems, and political methodology. He is the coauthor of a statistics textbook, and his work has been published in a variety of scholarly journals, including *The Journal of Politics*, *Western Political Quarterly*, and *Social Science Quarterly*. He is currently, with Louis Bolce, at work on a book chronicling the rise of secularist influence in the Democratic Party and the growing prominence of Christian fundamentalism as a negative political referent in American politics.

Louis DeSipio is associate professor of political science and chair of the Department of Chicano/Latino Studies at the University of California, Irvine. He received his Ph.D. from the University of Texas in 1993. He is a leading scholar in the areas of Latino politics and immigrant incorporation, and is the author, coauthor, or coeditor of nine volumes in those fields, most notably his book *Counting on the Latino Vote: Latinos as a New Electorate* (University of Virginia Press, 1996). In addition, he has published numerous book chapters and articles in professional journals, such as *International Migration Review* and *Latin American Research Review*.

Paul A. Djupe is associate professor of political science at Denison University. He received his Ph.D. from Washington University in 1997. His research is wide ranging within the field of religion and politics, including some of the only extant empirical work on the contemporary politics of American Jews. He is the coauthor of two books, most recently *The Prophetic Pulpit: Clergy, Churches, and Communities in American Politics* (Rowman & Littlefield, 2003), and with Laura R. Olson is coeditor of *The Encyclopedia of American Religion and Politics* (Facts on File, 2003). In addition, his work has been published in a variety of scholarly journals, including *The American Journal of Political Science*, *The Journal of Politics*, and *Political Research Quarterly*. He has served as chair for two terms of the American Political Science Association's Religion and Politics Section.

John C. Green is a senior fellow with the Pew Forum on Religion and Public Life as well as Distinguished Professor of Political Science and director of the Ray C. Bliss Institute at the University of Akron. He received his Ph.D. from Cornell University in 1983. He has done extensive research on religion and American politics. He is a coauthor of *Religion and the Culture Wars: Dispatches from the Front* (Rowman & Littlefield, 1996), *The Bully Pulpit: The Politics of Protestant Clergy* (University Press of Kansas, 1997), *The Diminishing Divide: Religion's Changing Role in American Politics* (Brookings Institution Press, 2000), and coeditor of numerous collections of essays, most recently *The Values Campaign? The Christian Right and the 2004 Elections* (Georgetown University Press, 2006).

Melissa Harris-Lacewell is associate professor of politics and African American studies at Princeton University. She received her Ph.D. from Duke University in 1999. Her research explores a variety of topics in African American politics, including issues of gender and religion. She is the author of *Barbershops, Bibles, and B.E.T.: Everyday Talk and Black Political Thought* (Princeton University Press, 2004). Her articles have been published in *Women and Politics* and *The Journal of Black Studies*.

Stephen T. Mockabee is assistant professor of political science at the University of Cincinnati. He received his Ph.D. from Ohio State University in 2001. His research centers on public opinion, political methodology, and religion and politics. His work has been published in a variety of professional journals, including *Political Analysis*, *American Politics Research*, and *The Journal for the Scientific Study of Religion*. In addition, he currently serves on the Executive Council of the American Political Science Association's Religion and Politics Section.

J. Quin Monson is assistant professor of political science and assistant director of the Center for the Study of Elections and Democracy at Brigham Young University. He received his Ph.D. from Ohio State University in 2004. His work focuses primarily on campaigns and elections, public opinion, and religion and politics. He is coeditor of *Dancing without Partners: How Candidates, Parties, and Interest Groups Interact in the Presidential Campaign* (Rowman & Littlefield, 2007) and *Electing Congress: New Rules for an Old Game* (Prentice Hall, 2007). He has also published a variety of articles in journals such as *Political Research Quarterly*, *Political Analysis*, and *The Journal for the Scientific Study of Religion*.

Laura R. Olson is professor of political science at Clemson University. She received her Ph.D. from the University of Wisconsin in 1996. She is a leading figure in the field of religion and politics, having authored, coauthored, or coedited eight volumes, including (with Sue E. S. Crawford and Melissa M. Deckman) *Women with a Mission: Religion, Gender, and the Politics of Women Clergy* (University of Alabama Press, 2005) and (with Paul A. Djupe) *The Encyclopedia of American Religion and Politics* (Facts on File, 2003). In addition, her articles have been published in a variety of journals, including *Social Science Quarterly* and *The Journal for the Scientific Study of Religion*. From 1999 to 2000, she was a visiting fellow at Princeton University's Center for the Study of Religion.

Carin Robinson is a doctoral student in government at Georgetown University. She received her M.A. in media and public affairs from George Washington University in 2003. Her research focuses on religion and politics, with a specific interest in evangelical political behavior. She has contributed to numerous edited volumes on religion and politics and is the coauthor of the third edition of *Onward Christian Soldiers? The Religious Right in American Politics* (Westview Press, 2006).

Corwin E. Smidt is professor of political science and holds the Paul B. Henry Chair in Christianity and Politics at Calvin College. He received his Ph.D. from the University of Iowa in 1975. He was a pioneer empirical researcher in the field of religion and politics. He has authored, coauthored, edited, or coedited ten books, most recently *Religion as Social Capital: Producing the Common Good* (Baylor University Press, 2003). In addition, he has published dozens of articles, including in *The American Journal of Political Science*, *Western Political Quarterly*, and *Legislative Studies Quarterly*. He previously served as chair of the American Political Science Association's Religion and Politics Section and as president of Christians in Political Science.

Clyde Wilcox is professor of political science at Georgetown University. He received his Ph.D. from Ohio State University in 1984. He is a leading scholar not only in the field of religion and politics but also of American political behavior in general. He is the author or coauthor of eight books, including *The Financiers of Congressional Elections:*

Investors, Ideologues, and Intimates (Columbia University Press, 2001), and the editor or coeditor of eighteen more. His dozens of journal articles, spread across the fields of political science, sociology, history, and literature, include essays in *The Journal of Politics*, *Political Research Quarterly*, and *Comparative Political Studies*. He serves on the editorial boards of several major journals, and he previously served as chair of the American Political Science Association's Religion and Politics Section.

J. Matthew Wilson is associate professor of political science at Southern Methodist University. He received his Ph.D. from Duke University in 1999. His work focuses on public opinion, political participation, and religion and politics, and it has been published in a variety of scholarly journals, including *The American Journal of Political Science*, *The Journal of Politics*, and *Political Research Quarterly*. He is currently at work on two book projects, one on political sophistication and causal attribution in the American electorate, and the other on the political behavior of American Catholics. He currently serves on the Executive Council of the American Political Science Association's Section on Elections, Public Opinion, and Voting Behavior.

Index

abortion, 5, 10, 53, 273, 278–82, 284; and black clergy, 16, 280; Catholics and, 3, 81, 86–87, 92–93, 96, 99–101, 282; and fundamentalists, 272; Jews and, 190–91; John Kerry and, 2; Latinos and, 176–78; and mobilization, 22; Mormons and, 112; Muslims and, 225, 240–42; Republican Party and, 24; secularists and, 267–70; Southern Baptists and, 112–13

abstinence education, 1

ACLU, 4

affirmative action, 57; Jews and, 188, 199; Muslims and, 224, 239

Afghanistan, 213, 225, 285

African American church, 1, 10, 11, 26, 131–60, 222, 283; assimilation model of, 132; compensatory model of, 132; conceptions of Christ in, 131–32; and Democratic Party, 158, 280; as inspiration for political action, 132–33; interpretation of the Bible, 8–9; isolation model of, 132; mobilization over civil rights, 11, 132; origins of, 134; and political action, 8, 12, 154–56, 279; and Republican Party, 159. *See also* Black Liberation Theology; black protestants; prosperity gospel

Alinsky, Saul, 168

Almanac of American Politics 2002 (Barone), 274

American Civil Liberties Union, 191

American Jewish Committee, 186, 191, 199

American Jewish Congress, 191

American Muslim Council, 214

American Muslim Taskforce on Civil Rights and Elections (AMT), 230

American National Election Studies (ANES), 6–7, 82–101, 108–11, 123, 252, 258–59, 271, 274–75

American Religious Identification Survey (2001), 215

Annual Survey of American Jewish Opinion, 186

Anti-Defamation League, 191, 199

antifundamentalists, 13, 251–76; and anti-Religious Right animus, 266–70; Democratic Party and, 256; history of, 253–54; and John Kerry, 274; partisan implications of antifundamentalism, 254, 264–65; Republican party and, 251; voting patterns, 64–65, 267–70. *See also* secularists

Anti-Semitism Study of October 1964, 50n9

apartheid, 59

Ashcroft, John, 212
Assemblies of God, 18–19

Baptists, black, 151–52. *See also*
    African American church
Barone, Michael, 274
Barth, Karl, 279
Benson, Ezra Taft, 110, 121
black Christ, 137–38, 143, 146–47,
    150–57. *See also* Black
    Liberation Theology
black church. *See* African American
    church
Black Contract with America on
    Moral Values, 159
Black Liberation Theology, 10, 26,
    131, 133–58; and Black
    Nationalism, 155; image of
    Christ in, 137–39, 150; influence
    on black churches, 140; political
    implications of, 146–47, 154–56;
    second generation of, 147
The Black Messiah (Cleage), 135,
    137
Black Nationalism, 155, 217
Black Political Theology (Roberts),
    135
Black Power movement, 131, 135,
    137–38, 146
black protestants, 35–46. *See also*
    African American church
Black Theology and Black Power
    (Cone), 135
"Black Theology and Black
    Women" (Grant), 137
"Black Theology and Marxist
    Thought" (West), 137
Black theology movement. *See* Black
    Liberation Theology
Blinded by Might (Thomas and
    Dobson), 281
Bob Jones University, 81
Boggs, Lilburn W., 110

Bolce, Louis, 28, 251–76, 277, 309
Boykin, William, 23–24
Bradley, Bill, 71
Bread for the World, 58
Brigham Young University, 121
Brown, Hugh B., 110
Bryant, Anita, 255
Buchanan, Pat, 15, 182
Bush, George Herbert Walker, 14,
    15, 85, 90, 188
Bush, George W., 1–2, 13, 14, 15,
    99, 195, 211, 285; and 2004
    election, 53; abortion, stance on,
    81; and African American
    church, 158; appeal to Catholics,
    81; and black vote, 159; and
    Catholic vote, 96, 98; and
    fundamentalist support, 251; and
    Islam, 24; Israel, support for, 27;
    and Latino vote, 181–83; and
    Mormon support, 107; and
    Muslim support, 214, 228, 232–
    33, 242, 246; and Protestant
    support, 47, 71, 86; and
    secularists, 265, 274–75

Call to Renewal, 58
Campbell, David E., 26, 105–29,
    280–81, 309
Camp David Accords, 194
Campolo, Tony, 60
capital punishment. *See* death
    penalty
Carter, Jimmy, 15, 85, 197
Catholic Church, 2, 81–104, 275,
    280–81, 283; and abortion, 2, 6,
    99, 281; and contraception, 6;
    and culture war, 3; and death
    penalty, 25, 99; and Democratic
    Party, 6; growth of in 1990s, 19;
    and health care, 4; and
    homosexuality, 6; and Iraq War,
    99; and Latinos, 161–75; and

scandals, 20, 103, 169; secularist antipathy toward, 259–61, 274. *See also* Catholics; Vatican II

Catholics, 81–104, 242, 252, 254, 256, 285; and abortion, 96, 99–101, 112–13; changes in political behavior of, 89–94; church attendance among, 116; contrasted with Protestants, 35–46; and death penalty, 99–101; and Democratic Party, 81–90, 94, 96–98, 185, 195; and gender roles, 111–12; generations of (pre-and post-Vatican II), 95–98; and Iraq War, 99–101; and mobilization, 89, 126; and partisanship, 26, 82–94, 96, 99–103; perceptions of party differences by, 89–92; and religious giving, 116–17; and Republican Party, 24–25, 83–91, 93, 98, 108; and same-sex marriage, 99–101; and socioeconomic status, 86–88, 92–93, 205; and voting behavior, 283–84; as voting bloc, 82; and worship style, 11. See *also* Catholic Church; Latino Catholics; Vatican II

Census of Religious Congregations and Membership (2000), 214

Cheney, Dick, 7

Chicano Movement, 168

Christian Coalition, 8, 13–17, 19, 24, 49, 102, 258; mobilization efforts, 126; secularist antipathy toward, 259, 261. *See also* Reed, Ralph

Christian left, 25. *See also* religious left

Christian Right, 12–15, 17–18, 25, 27, 48–49, 53; mobilization efforts, 126; and Mormons, 106; and secularists, 255, 261, 264, 270, 273. *See also* Religious Right

Christian Voice, 17

Church of the Brethren, 60

Church of Jesus Christ of Latter-Day Saints, 105; and abortion, 113; and Equal Rights Amendment, 123; and gambling, 124–25; and partisanship, 122–24; and political involvement, 122–24; and political mobilization, 106–7, 120, 126–27; and political neutrality, 123; and same-sex marriage, 125–26; structure of, 121–22. *See also* Mormons

Citizen Participation Study, 171

civil rights, 56, 57; Jewish support for, 188, 196, 201, 211

civil rights movement, 132, 199, 280

civil unions, 13

Civil War, 4

Cleage, Albert, 135–38, 147

Clinton, Bill, 1, 16, 71, 85, 90, 188, 197, 267; health care plan, 6

Clinton, Hillary, 21, 275

cloning, 23; Muslims and, 225

Cochran, Clarke, 24

Cold War, 96, 193

Community Services Organization, 167

Concerned Women for America, 17

Cone, James, 135–36, 138

Convention Delegate Study (CDS), 257

Copeland, Kenneth, 141

Cortes, Ernesto, 168

Cuban Americans: and Catholicism, 162–64, 167; and Republican Party, 179. *See also* Latinos

Cuban Revolution, 167

cultural modernists, 256
"culture wars," 2, 23; and Catholics, 101; and Jews, 211–12; and Mormons, 111, 252, 255, 257, 259, 277

Daley, Richard J., 256
Danforth, John, 252
Darrow, Clarence, 274
Darwin, Charles, 55
Dean, Howard, 2, 275
death penalty, 284; and Catholic Church, 25, 99; and Catholics, 99–101; and Jews, 190–91; and Latinos, 176–78; and Muslims, 224, 239
Delaney, James, 256
Delay, Tom, 212
De Maio, Gerald, 28, 251–76, 277, 309–10
Democratic Party: and African American church, 158, 280; and Catholics, 6, 26, 82–89; factionalizing of, 256–57; and Jews, 185, 188, 195, 198–200, 212; and Latinos, 179, 181–83; and Mormons, 111; and Muslims, 227–28; and secularists, 256, 270, 275
DeSipio, Louis, 26, 161–84, 310
Dionne, E. J., 102
Direct Action Research and Training, 59
Djupe, Paul A., 27, 185–212, 213–50, 280, 282, 310
Dobson, Ed, 281
Dole, Bob, 182
Dollar, Creflo, 141, 158
Drinan, Robert, SJ, 17

ecumenism, 64–65, 77
Egypt, Jewish opinions of, 193–94

Eisenhower, Dwight, 95, 110
election of 2000, 47, 81
election, 2004, 2, 53; Democratic nomination contest, 2; evangelical Protestants and, 47
Emerge (magazine), 139
Engel v. Vitale, 255
Episcopalians, 214
Equal Rights Amendment, 255; and Mormons, 106, 123
euthanasia, 282
evangelical Protestants, 1, 25, 29–51, 185, 253, 255–56, 281, 283–85; activism of clergy and congregation, attitudes toward, 73–77; African American, 3–4, 8; age distribution of, 39–40; attitudes toward Catholics, 49; consensus among, 41–44; courted by Reagan, 188; differences from mainline Protestants, 33–34; distribution of over time, 37–39; educational attainment of, 39–41; exclusivism, 35–36; history of, 32–33; ideological orientation of, 43–44; and Latinos, 169; literal interpretation of the Bible, 8, 35; mobilization of, 126; opposition to environmental programs, 9; partisanship of, 45–47; political influence of, 73–74; political resources of, 39; politicization of, 44–45, 70–71, 279; as Republican delegates, 257; and Republican Party, 201, 281; and same-sex marriage, 4; secularist antipathy toward, 259–61, 274; theological characteristics of, 36–37. *See also* fundamentalists; Latino Protestants; mainline Protestants
Evangelicals for Social Action, 58

Evangelical Environmental
  Network, 9

Falwell, Jerry, 4
Federal Council of Churches, 34
federal grants for faith-based
  institutions, 1
Filipinos, 167
Focus on the Family, 280
Foley, Mark, 280
fundamentalists, Christian, 71, 251–
  54, 275; Democratic delegates'
  opinions of, 258; as "menace,"
  274; opposition to abortion, 272;
  opposition to gay rights, 272;
  and Religious Right, 261; as
  Republican delegates, 257;
  secularist antipathy toward, 259–
  61, 270–71; secularist
  conceptions of, 264. *See also*
  evangelical Protestants

Gaines, Kevin, 142
Gamaliel Foundation, 59
gay marriage. *See* same-sex
  marriage
gay rights, 24, 57, 86, 255, 272–73,
  282; fundamentalists and, 272;
  Jews and, 190–91; Latinos and,
  176–78; secularists and, 259. *See
  also* same-sex marriage
gender roles: religious attitudes
  about by race, 9
General Social Survey (GSS), 186,
  191, 193, 194, 201, 215
Gingrich, Newt, 182
Gonzalez, Alberto, 158–59
Gore, Al, 71, 81, 85, 197–98, 265;
  and Muslim support, 232
Grant, Jacquelyn, 137–38
*The Great Investment: Balancing
  Faith, Family, and Finance to*

Build a Rich Spiritual Life
  (Jakes), 143
Great Society, 78
Green, John C., 27, 213–50, 282,
  310

Hagin, Kenneth, 141
Harris-Lacewell, Melissa, 10, 26,
  131–60, 311
Helms, Jesse, 15
High Impact Leadership Coalition,
  159
Himmelfarb, Milton, 195
Hinckley, Gordon B., 122
Hispanic Churches in American
  Public Life (HCAPL), 168–69,
  174
Hutchinson, Kay Bailey, 15

illegal immigration; Catholic views
  on, 98
India, 227
Industrial Areas Foundation (IAF),
  24, 59, 79, 168
Inherit the Wind (Lawrence and
  Lee), 253
Interfaith Alliance, 15, 58
Iraq war, 5, 22, 27, 267; African
  American church and, 158;
  Catholics' position on, 98;
  Muslims and, 213, 225
Islam, 23–24, 213, 233, 242, 244;
  and African Americans, 137. *See
  also* Muslims
Islamic Society of North America,
  24
Israel, 4, 27, 189, 194, 196, 199,
  225; and Six-Day War, 193

Jackson, Jesse, 280
Jakes, T. D., 143–45, 149, 158
Jensen, Marlin K., 111

Jews, 4, 10, 27, 35–46, 185–213,
242, 280, 282–83; and abortion,
190–91; civil liberties positions
of, 191–93; and Democratic
Party, 185, 188, 195, 198–200,
212; domestic policy opinions of,
189–90; foreign affairs opinions
of, 193–95; and gay rights, 190–
91; geographic dispersion of,
202–4; and gun control, 190–91;
and moral issues, 190–91;
partisanship among, 195–98,
200–204, 209, 211–12; political
fragmentation among, 198–201;
and political ideology, 187, 200–
202, 206–8; and pluralism, 185,
209–11; religious intermarriage
among, 205, 212; religious
observance of, 201–2; social class
of, 205; and Republican Party,
195, 212; and *tzedakeh*, 201
John XXIII (Pope), 95
John Paul II (Pope), 22

Kanawha County, West Virginia
school wars, 255
Kashmir, 227
Kennedy, John F., 2, 81, 83, 85–86,
198
Kerry, John, 85, 265; and abortion,
2, 81–82; and
antifundamentalists, 274; and
Catholicism, 2, 81–82; and
Catholic vote, 96, 98–99, 103n2;
and Muslim support, 214, 233,
246
King, Martin Luther, Jr., 11, 149
King, Rodney, 189
Kristol, Irving, 187

Land, Richard, 24
Latino Catholics, 161–81

Latino National Political Survey,
172
Latino Protestants, 162–65, 175–78,
181; evangelical, 162, 168, 172,
176; mainline, 162, 168, 174,
176
Latinos, 3, 13, 26–27, 161–84, 283;
and Catholicism, 161–73;
electoral participation, 171–74;
issue preferences, 176; new
immigrants, 169–70; partisanship
among, 179–83; political
attitudes, influence of religion on,
174–76; and Protestantism, 168–
69, 172, 174; and religious
preference, 161–64, 170. *See also*
Latino Catholics; Latino
Protestants
Lawrence, Jerome, 253
Lee, Robert E. (writer), 253
Let Freedom Ring, 14
Lewis, Sinclair, 253
Lieberman, Joseph, 197–98
Lincoln, Abraham, 4, 252
López-Tijerina, Reies, 168
Lutherans, 214

mainline Protestants: 4, 25, 29–51,
56, 252; activism of clergy and
congregation, attitudes toward,
73–77; age distribution of, 39–
40; consensus among, 41–44;
and homosexuality, 20; declining
numbers of, 18, 37–38;
differences from evangelical
Protestants, 33–34; distribution
of over time, 37–38; educational
attainment of, 39–41, 69–70; and
environment, 10; ideological
orientation of, 43–44;
partisanship of, 45–47; political
influence of, 73–74; political

interest of, 69; political resources of, 39–40; politicization of, 44–45, 70–71; as Republican delegates, 257; theological characteristics of, 36–37. *See also* evangelical Protestants; Latino Protestants
Malcolm X, 137
Massachusetts Supreme Court, 12, 23, 267
Maurice, F. D., 283
McCain, John, 251
McKinney, Cynthia, 196
Meany, George, 256
megachurches, 7, 19; African American, 139–40, 148; political mobilization, in African American, 148
Mencken, H. L., 253, 274
Mennonites, 60
Mexican Americans: and Catholicism, 162, 165–67; and partisanship, 179; and Protestantism, 165. *See also* Latinos
Mockabee, Stephen T., 26, 81–104, 311
Monson, J. Quin, 26, 105–29, 280–81, 311
Moral Majority, 15, 48–49
Moral Majority, Ohio, 8
Mormons, 6, 18, 25, 105–29, 285; and abortion, 112–14; birthrate among, 114; and civic involvement, 118; church attendance among, 116; and Democratic Party, 111; distribution of, 105; and Equal Rights Amendment, 106, 123; expectations of members, 114–16; and gender roles, 111, 114; growth of Mormon Church, 19,

105; and partisanship, 107–8, 280; and political involvement, 118–20, 281; and political mobilization, 107, 120; and polygamy, 107; religious giving among, 117; and Republican Party, 107–14; and same-sex marriage, 6, 106, 281; as voting bloc, 109–11; voting patterns of, 107–11. *See also* Church of Jesus Christ of Latter-Day Saints
Muslims, 10, 23–24, 27, 50n6, 213–50, 282–83, 285; and abortion, 225, 240–42; and affirmative action, 224, 239; African American, 217–44; and aid to the poor, 240–42, 282; Arab, 217–44; and civic engagement, 228; and death penalty, 224, 239; debt relief for poor nations, opinions on, 240–42; and dissatisfaction with American society, 234–37; Democratic Party and, 227–28; demographics of, 217–21; and discrimination, reported, 233–37; and euthanasia, 239; foreign policy views, 225–27; geographic concentration of, 215, 218; and ideology, 228, 239, 242; issue positions of, 222, 237–42; numbers of, 214–15; partisanship, 213, 227–28, 239, 242, 246; and political participation, 233, 237, 244–46; and religion in politics, role of, 228; religiosity, effect on issue positions of, 237–42; 240; religious commitment of, 221, 239; and same-sex marriage, 225, 239; and school vouchers, 224–25, 239; Shiite, 221; South

Muslims (*continued*)
Asian, 217–44; and stem cell research, 225, 239; Sunni, 221; vote, determinants of, 242–45; voting patterns of, 232–33, 237. *See also* Islam

Nader, Ralph: and Muslim support, 232–33
National Association of Evangelicals, 9, 34; and Creation Care, 9
National Black Politics Study (1994), 134, 150–57
National Committee of Black Churchmen, 141
National Committee of Negro Churchmen, 135
National Council of Churches, 34
National Council of Churches of Christ in the USA (NCC), 58
National Election Poll (2004), 181
National Interfaith Committee for Worker Justice, 58
National Jewish Population Study, 186
National Religious Partnership for the Environment, 58
National Republican Senatorial Committee, 15
National Right to Life Committee, 15
National Survey of Religion and Politics (2004), 215
Nation of Islam, 217, 221
Nauvoo, Illinois, 110
New Deal, 48, 78, 94, 185, 195, 201, 252, 256, 279
Nicene Creed, 139
Nixon, Richard, 85

Obama, Barack, 275
Olson, Laura R., 25, 53–79, 280–81, 312
Operation Pedro Pan, 167

Pacific Institute for Community Organizing, 59
Pakistan, 227
Palestine, 193, 196, 199, 225, 227
Parks, Rosa, 149
People for the American Way, 4
People's Party, 110
Percy, William Alexander, 253
Perot, Ross, 90
Pew Research Center surveys, 215
Podhoretz, Norman, 187
political mobilization into religion, 3, 13–17; concerns about, 16; congregations as locus of, 7–8; denominations as locus of, 5–6; doctrine as locus of, 8–9
Powell, Colin, 227
Praise the Lord (television program), 141
Price, Fred, 159
Prohibition, 252
Project Muslims in the American Public Square (MAPS), 215–22, 232, 234, 246
Progressive Religious Partnership, 58
pro-life movement, 12, 21. *See also* abortion
Proposition 22, 124–26;
prosperity gospel, 10, 26, 131, 134, 140–56; image of Christ in, 143–45, 148–50; influence on political action, 158; political implications of, 146–49, 154–58
Puerto Ricans: and Catholicism, 162–65; and partisanship, 179; and Protestantism, 165. *See also* Latinos

Quakers (Friends), 60

Reagan, Ronald, 13, 56, 85, 90, 96, 194; Jewish support for, 188–89, 197, 208

Reed, Ralph, 15
Reid, Harry, 106
Religion and Politics 2000 Survey, 34–52
religiopolitical progressivism, 55–79; as agenda, 58; history of, 55–56; socialization toward, 69. *See also* Christian left, religious left
religiosity and mobilization, 10–13
Religious Coalition for Reproductive Choice, 58
religious left, 16, 53–79, 282–83; and abolition of slavery, 282; activism of clergy and congregation, attitudes toward, 73–77; decline in size of liberal traditions, 72; demographic characteristics of, 63–64; political attitudes of, 66–69; political influence of, 73–74; political interest of, 69; political participation of, 70–72; religious attitudes of, 63–65; religious behavior of, 65–66; by religious tradition, 61–63; satisfaction with status quo, 77–78; and "scriptural relativism," 78; self-identification of members, 60–61
Religious Right, 53, 54, 56, 78; and antifundamentalists, 267–73; and fundamentalists, 261; secularist antipathy toward, 259–61. *See also* Christian Right
religious mobilization into politics, 3–12, 15
religious tradition: as analytical framework, 30–31; vs. traditionalism, 30
Republican Party: and Catholics, 85–89; and fundamentalists, 263–64; and Jews, 195, 212; and Latinos, 179, 183; and

Mormons, 107–8; as party of cultural conservatism, 110; and pro-life activity, 14; strategies to appeal to religious constituencies, 1–2; as "white Christian party," 275
Roberts, J. Deotis, 136
Roberts, Oral, 141
Robertson, Pat, 15, 258
Robinson, Carin, 1–28, 280, 312
Roe v. Wade, 12, 113, 255
Romney, Mitt, 106
Rooney, John, 256
Roosevelt, Franklin Delano, 95, 198
Rove, Karl, 2, 23
Russia, 193–94

Salt Lake Tribune, 111
same-sex marriage, 1–2, 4, 12–13, 23, 99, 159, 267, 280–81, 284; Catholics and, 99–101; evangelical Protestants and, 4; Mormons and, 6; Muslims and, 225, 239
Schiavo, Terri, 251
School District of Abington Township v. Schempp, 255
Scopes trial, 253, 271
secularists, 27–28, 35–46, 251–76; and abortion, 267–70; antagonism toward religion, 259–61; and Democratic Party, 256, 270, 275; fundamentalists, conceptions of, 261–63; and gay rights, 259; and ideology, 259–60; and partisanship, 264–65; and relativistic morality, 259, 272; and Republican Party, 270; voting patterns, 264–65. *See also* antifundamentalists
secularization, 20
segregation, 11, 17, 22; Massive Resistance, 17

September 11, 2001, 4, 23, 57; American Muslims and, 215, 225, 228, 232–34, 246

Sharpton, Al, 280

Shays, Christopher, 251

Six-Day War, 193

slavery, 4, 11, 107, 136

Smidt, Corwin E., 25, 29–51, 312

Smith, Joseph, 110

Smith, Tom, 214

Social Capital Community Benchmark Survey (SCCBS) (2000), 116–19

social construction of doctrine, 8–10

Social Gospel, 34, 55–57, 159

Southern Baptist Convention, 5, 22–24

Southern Baptists, 108; and abortion, 112–13; church attendance among, 116; and gender roles, 111–12; and religious giving, 117. *See also* Southern Baptist Convention

Southern Christian Leadership Conference, 11–12

Soviet Union, 193–94

stem cell research, 22–23, 282; Muslims and, 225

Syeed, Sayyid M., 24

tax exemption for religious groups, 16

Third National Survey of Religion and Politics (2000), 107

Thomas, Cal, 281

Tilton, Robert, 141

Truman, Harry S., 95, 193

Unitarian Universalist Association (UUA), 60

United Church of Christ (UCC), 60

United Farmworkers, 167

United Nations, 81; Jewish opinions on, 194

Vatican, 81

Vatican II, 31, 95

Vietnam War, 12, 22, 53, 59

Vines, Jerry, 23

Virgin of Guadalupe, 167–68

voodoo, 144

voodun, 144

Wallis, Jim, 60

Walnut Grove United Methodist Church, 9

Washington, Joseph, 134–35

welfare, 87, 92, 282, 284; Jewish support for, 188–89, 196; reform, 16, 57

West, Cornel, 137

Whitman, Christine Todd, 252

Wilcox, Clyde, 1–28, 280, 312–13

Wilson, J. Matthew, 28, 277–85, 313

Wilson, Pete, 182

World Changers' Church International, 141

World War I, 217

Wuthnow's Religion and Politics Survey (2000), 209

Zogby postelection survey (2004), 215